Protecting Apartments, Condominiums, and Gated Communities

A Guide to Security for Homeowner's Associations and Property Managers

Protecting Apartments, Condominiums, and Gated Communities

A Guide to Security for Homeowner's Associations and Property Managers

First Edition

Michael A. Silva, CPP, CSC

2021

Some content contained within this book may have originally appeared in Security Tips published by the author on the Silva Consultants website (www.silvaconsultants.com).

First Printing: 2021 01

Silva Consultants
PO Box 8799
Covington, Washington 98042
www.silvaconsultants.com
Telephone: +1 (888) 645-2299
Email: publisher@silvaconsultants.com

ISBN: 978-1-7378587-1-3

Table of Contents

About the Author i

Foreword iii

Terminology Used in this Book v

Compliance with Local Codes and Regulations v

Part I – Planning a Security Program 1

Chapter 1: Providing Security at Multifamily Properties 3

Chapter 2: Understanding Your Security Risks 7

Chapter 3: Basic Concepts for Good Security 17

Chapter 4: Security Planning 27

Part II – Physical and Electronic Security Systems 31

Chapter 5: Site Security Barriers 33

Chapter 6: Security Lighting 51

Chapter 7: Doors 65

Chapter 8: Locks and Door Hardware 77

Chapter 9: Windows 113

Chapter 10: Security Signage 123

Chapter 11: Access Control Systems 127

Chapter 12: Security Intercom Systems 145

Chapter 13: Alarm Systems 153

Chapter 14: Video Surveillance Systems 165

Part III – Security Strategies 187

Chapter 15: Securing the Perimeter of the Site 189

Chapter 16: Securing Outdoor Areas 195

Chapter 17: Securing the Perimeter of the Building 207

Chapter 18: Securing the Interior of the Building 215

Chapter 19: Securing Parking Garages 229

Chapter 20: Securing Residential Units 235

Chapter 21: Securing Gated Communities 241

Chapter 22: Securing Mixed-Use Properties 251

Part IV – Security Operations 257

Chapter 23: Security Management and Operation 259

Chapter 24: Security Policies and Procedures 265

Chapter 25: Security Awareness Training 289

Chapter 26: Security Staffing 295

Chapter 27: Reducing Security Officer Turnover 315
Chapter 28: Buying Security Products and Services 319
Chapter 29: Using an Independent Security Consultant 333
Chapter 30: Solving Specific Types of Security Problems 339
Part V - Appendices 343
Appendix A: Best Practices for Securing Doors 345
Appendix B: Security Survey Checklist 351
Appendix C: Security Manual Outline 361
Appendix D: Example of Resident's Security Guide 363
Index 375

About the Author

Michael A. Silva is the Principal of Silva Consultants, an independent security consulting firm that is based in Seattle. The firm specializes in security assessment, planning, and design. Michael has over 45 years of security industry experience including over 35 years of experience as an independent consultant. Michael provides both security management consulting and technical security consulting.

Michael has extensive experience in providing security consulting services for multifamily housing complexes including apartment buildings, condominiums, and gated and planned communities. His experience includes conducting security assessments for more than 1,000 individual multifamily housing complexes throughout the United States.

In addition, Michael has served clients in a wide variety of other industries including healthcare, medical research, software development, manufacturing, warehousing, and distribution. Michael's experience includes working as both a self-employed consultant as well as a manager for Kroll, one of the world's largest security consulting firms.

Michael is board-certified as a Certified Protection Professional (CPP) and is a member of the International Association of Professional Security Consultants (IAPSC), an organization made up exclusively of independent, non-product affiliated security consultants. Michael has earned the Certified Security Consultant (CSC) credential issued by IAPSC that indicates specific proficiency in practicing as an independent security consultant.

Michael is the author of the book *Becoming an Independent Security Consultant – A Practical Guide to Starting and Running a Successful Security Consulting Practice*, as well as a contributor to many other books and articles on the topic of physical and electronic security.

Foreword

Crime is an unfortunate fact of life in nearly every residential community, regardless of where it is located. While crime rates vary from community to community, nearly every homeowner's association and property manager will have to deal with issues related to crime at one time or another. At some properties, the level of criminal activity has risen to the point where it is the number one concern expressed by residents, making solving crime problems a top priority for the owners and managers of these properties.

Most homeowner's association board members and property managers have had little training on security matters. This requires them to look to outside sources for guidance on how to solve their security problems. While local law enforcement agencies can provide some simple crime prevention advice, most do not have the ability to develop a comprehensive security plan for a multifamily property. In addition, most law enforcement agencies lack expertise in physical security design and aren't up to date on the latest in security technology.

One source of information that is often relied upon is the advice given by sellers and installers of various security products and services. While well-intentioned and probably knowledgeable of their own particular discipline, most "consultants" of this type do not possess the wide range of technical skills necessary to be a true security consultant. Further, the solutions offered by this type of "consultant" generally involve the use of the specific type of products that he or she sells; for example, the person selling camera systems will recommend the installation of cameras, the person selling guard services will recommend the use of guards, etc. This does not imply dishonesty on the part of the person offering the advice—but is only a reflection of this person's limited scope of knowledge and the natural tendency to want to sell his or her own product.

The purpose of this book is to provide a source of unbiased technical advice to people who have responsibility for managing security at a multifamily property. This includes private owners, homeowner's association (HOA) board members, property managers, community association managers, and others who have an interest in providing improved security at their residential property. While this book is not directed towards individual homeowners or renters, learning the information presented here can be helpful in understanding the types of security measures commonly used in multifamily properties and in communicating your security concerns to the people who manage your property.

This book is intended to be used at multifamily properties both large and small. Understandably, some security measures are more appropriately used at larger properties than smaller properties, but most principles mentioned within this book can be applied to properties of all sizes.

Terminology Used in this Book

This book is intended to apply to multifamily properties of all types, including apartment buildings, condominiums, cooperative housing (co-ops) and planned and gated communities. Within this book, I will use the term "multifamily property" to refer to all of these property types, pointing out any specific differences between property types when appropriate.

Multifamily properties can be made up of individual homes, apartments, or co-op or condominium units. Within this book, I will use the term "residential unit" to describe any of these dwelling types.

Multifamily properties can be managed in a number of different ways: by individual owners, partnerships, corporations, community associations, or by professional property or community managers. Within this book, I will use the term "property manager" to describe any person or group that has responsibility for managing a multifamily property. When property management responsibilities are divided between multiple people, the term "property manager" refers to the person assigned responsibility for the task being described.

This book is written using terminology and practices that are common in the United States. While terms and practices may vary in other parts of the world, most of the concepts presented here should be capable of being adapted for use at multifamily properties located anywhere.

Compliance with Local Codes and Regulations

The advice provided in this book is based on security best practices commonly used at multifamily properties nationwide. However, building codes vary throughout the country and some of these codes may restrict the types of security measures that can be used or impose requirements that are different from those recommended in this book. The property manager should always check local codes and regulations before making any changes. When code requirements are unclear, a licensed architect or engineer familiar with the applicable codes should be hired to provide assistance.

State and local laws may also regulate the use of security personnel, specify certain minimum security standards that must be complied with, or restrict or prohibit certain types of security measures. When planning the security program, the property manager should determine what, if any, laws may apply in the jurisdiction where the property is located. If there are doubts, an attorney that is well-versed in security law should be consulted.

Part I – Planning a Security Program

Chapter 1: Providing Security at Multifamily Properties

Security Challenges at Multifamily Properties

Multifamily properties face many security challenges that do not exist at single family homes. When a home is occupied by a single family, the actions or inactions taken by family members generally only impact that family. For example, if a family member leaves an exterior gate unlocked, only that family's home is placed at risk. However, if an exterior gate at a multifamily complex is left unlocked, all families that live in that complex are placed at risk.

Occupants of single-family homes also know who should be on their property at any given time and have the ability to quickly spot unusual or suspicious conditions. For example, if a resident sees someone in their driveway that is not a family member or other known person, this would be cause for immediate concern. However, if a resident of a multifamily property sees an unknown person on the property, it is not immediately obvious if this is a problem or not. Is this person an intruder – or another resident who they have not met yet, the visitor of another resident, or a contractor who has been hired to do work on the property? If the actions of the unknown person are not clearly suspicious, the resident may choose to ignore the situation rather than take the time to investigate further.

Owners of single-family homes have a vested interest in protecting their investment and in keeping their home safe. Condominium owners have a similar interest in protecting the units that they own, but concern about commonly owned areas can vary depending on the individual owner and the location of their unit. For example, owners of units on the ground floor may have a greater interest in protecting the outdoor grounds surrounding the buildings than owners who occupy units on the upper floors. Similarly, owners who make frequent use of the fitness center may have a greater interest in keeping it safe than owners who never use the facility.

At multifamily properties that are occupied by renters, the sense of "ownership" of the property can vary greatly from renter to renter. Some renters are every bit as diligent as owners and will make every effort to keep the property safe and secure. At the other end of the spectrum are renters who could care less about the property and seem to deliberately take actions that place other residents at risk. In between these two extremes are renters who are ambivalent about security – they will follow established rules but won't go out of their way to protect the property.

Responsibility for Security

Owners and managers of multifamily properties are usually responsible for managing all aspects of the property, including security. While some very large properties may have a professional security manager on staff, the responsibility for managing security generally falls on the people who manage and maintain the property.

At rental properties such as apartment complexes, decisions about what types of security measures are ultimately made by the property owner, whether it be a single individual, or ownership group such as a real estate investment trust (REIT). When making decisions, owners usually rely heavily on recommendations made by the local property manager but may override these recommendations if they feel they are too costly or inappropriate.

At condominiums, co-ops, and gated communities, decisions regarding security are usually made by an elected leadership group, such as a homeowner's association (HOA) Board of Directors. At larger properties, the Board may appoint a special committee to research security issues and provide direction to the Board. While the Board alone can make some decisions, most decisions involving large capital investments usually require a vote and approval by a majority of homeowners. HOA Boards often hire a property management company to handle the day-to-day operations of the property. If a property management company is hired, any security decisions made by the Board are usually delegated to the property manager to carry out.

Legal Requirements to Provide Adequate Security

The legal requirements to provide adequate security vary depending on property type and location. At condominiums and gated communities, the homeowner usually has primary responsibility for providing security in the unit that they occupy, while the HOA has responsibility for security in common areas. At rental properties, the property owner may have responsibility for security of all areas. Owners and managers of multifamily properties should consult with their attorney to determine the scope of their security responsibilities for the properties that they own and manage.

The property owner or HOA has a responsibility to know the risks of crime at their property, and to take reasonable steps to mitigate any risks that are foreseeable. While few jurisdictions specifically prescribe the exact types of security measures that must be used, these measures must be appropriate and reasonable given the level of security risk that the property faces.

There have been numerous lawsuits filed against property owners, property managers and HOAs alleging "negligent security". The basis of these lawsuits is often the failure to notify residents of known security risks, failure to implement adequate security measures, failure to maintain equipment, failing to address resident complaints about security, not having adequate procedures, or failing to follow procedures that already exist. Many of these lawsuits have resulted in multi-million-dollar awards or settlements.

News about big negligent security case awards or settlements has motivated many multifamily property owners who previously ignored the topic of security to now take it seriously. Unfortunately, some owners only learn about the importance of having adequate security after having been sued themselves.

Some property owners attempt to minimize the risks of legal liability by inserting disclaimers within their rental agreements and contracts or by posting signs stating that they have no responsibility for providing security for residents or visitors. These measures are often challenged by the attorneys representing the parties filing negligent security lawsuits and are usually ineffective.

Other Reasons to Provide Adequate Security

In addition to any legal requirements that may exist, there are other benefits to providing an adequate level of security at a multifamily property. These include:

<u>Better Quality of Life</u>

No one wants to live in a place where they don't feel safe or secure. Perception is just as important as reality. Even minor crimes, such as vandalism and car break-ins, can make residents feel uneasy and erode their sense of well-being. Taking adequate security precautions can make residents feel better about where they live, as well as reduce their actual risks of becoming a victim of crime.

Decreased Losses

The theft or destruction of property results in both direct and indirect costs. Direct costs include the costs of repairing or replacing the property stolen or destroyed. Indirect costs include the time spent investigating and reporting the incident, as well as time spent making arrangements for repairs or replacement. There can also be indirect costs incurred when a specific item is not available when needed. For example, there can be lost productivity when a maintenance worker goes in search of a needed tool only to find that it has been stolen. Even when the replacement of property is covered by insurance, there is usually no reimbursement for any indirect costs that were incurred.

Having an adequate security program in place can provide better protection of the assets owned by individual residents, as well as assets belonging to the HOA or building owner. Providing better protection can result in reduced losses.

Reduced Insurance Premiums

Properties that have a history of significant security problems often have difficulty in obtaining insurance. If insurance is available, it is often expensive and has very high deductibles.

Some insurance companies will offer discounts to multifamily properties and to individual owners and renters if it can be demonstrated that certain types of security measures are in place. Your insurance broker should be consulted to determine what, if any, types of discounts may be available.

Improved Reputation of Property

Individual multifamily properties can develop a reputation within the community as being safe or unsafe. Rightly or wrongly, a property can be tagged as a high-crime location and a place to avoid. Sharing information about properties has never been easier due to the widespread use of social media and rating sites. At rental properties, negative reviews can make properties much more difficult to rent or lease and drive away the most desirable tenants. At condominiums and gated communities, negative reviews can make properties more challenging to sell and can affect resale values.

Having an effective security program in place at a multifamily property can not only decrease the risk of crime but can create a positive perception of the property in the community. Just as a property can develop a reputation for being unsafe, it can develop a reputation for being a very safe and desirable place to live.

Chapter 2: Understanding Your Security Risks

The Need to Understand Security Risks

To properly manage security risks at your multifamily property you need to know what they are. Fully understanding security risks is the first step in developing an effective security program for your property. Just as a doctor would not prescribe medications without first having diagnosed his patient's medical condition, it is foolish to start making security improvements at your property until you have a good understanding of the specific security problems that you are trying to solve.

Determining the Risks of Local Crime

It is amazing just how many property managers are totally ignorant of the types of crimes occurring in their community or even within their own property. Properties who are sued by a resident or visitor for "negligent security" often find out too late just how important having knowledge of local crime conditions is. Often the first thing the plaintiff's attorney does is to obtain local crime data for the site where the alleged incident occurred in order to determine if the crime was "foreseeable", and if so, was "reasonable care" taken on the part of the property owner to prevent the crime from occurring.

It looks very bad to the jury when the property owner's representative on the witness stand is asked: "How many crimes of a similar type were committed in your neighborhood over the last three years?" or "What did you do to determine the degree of potential crime at your property?" and the witness cannot properly answer. If you don't know the type and degree of crime at your site, how could you have possibly designed an effective security program to prevent it?

Aside from legal liability considerations, there are many practical reasons for accurately knowing local crime conditions. Most security budgets are tight, and it makes sense to direct the money being spent to areas where it matters most. For example, if the risk of residential burglary is high at your property, money should probably be spent on burglary prevention before making security investments elsewhere.

There are many sources of data that can help property managers to determine the risks of local crime. Most of these data sources are publicly available at little or no charge; a few require the payment of a fee. Because no source of data is perfect, it is necessary to gather information from multiple sources in order to gather a complete picture of the crime risks at your location.

There are six primary sources of local crime data: internal incident reports, crime data provided by neighboring facilities, police crime statistic reports, police calls-for-service reports, commercial crime forecast reports, and custom crime analyses prepared by security consultants.

Internal Incident Reports

One important source of information is the actual track record of security incidents that have occurred at your property. Some multifamily properties have an internal security incident reporting system that gathers data about crimes and other security incidents that have occurred at their property. Residents report crimes and security incidents to a central source such as the property manager, and this data is compiled on a periodic basis to produce reports that summarize the rate of reported crime at the facility. If well managed, an internal incident reporting system can produce a highly accurate picture of the rate of crime at any given property.

If your property has not been keeping good track of security incidents, you can attempt to reconstruct this information by conducting interviews with residents and property management staff. Because this information relies on the memory of people, it is less than perfect, but does provide a good starting point.

During the interview, each person should be asked the following questions:

- "How long have you been associated with this property?"
- "What types of crimes and security incidents have occurred at the property during the time that you have been here?". As the person gives answers, try to get as many details as possible, such as exactly where and when the incident occurred, how the intruder gained access, what was taken or damaged, and who was suspected to have committed the crime.
- After you have let the person describe the security incidents that they can recall, go back, and ask them about specific types of security incidents that may have occurred (assaults, bicycle thefts, burglaries of residential units, burglaries of storage rooms, car prowls, graffiti, package theft, robberies, trespassers, vandalism). Often prompting them about specific types of crimes will allow them to recall additional incidents.

The more people that you interview, the better. If you interview lots of people, you may start hearing about the same incident multiple times, but you will usually also get some information on things that you have not previously heard about.

A common mistake is for property managers to think that they already know everything that has happened at the property. This is rarely the case. Conducting interviews with a larger group of residents and staff members can often be eye-opening and reveal security problems that owners and property managers have never previously heard about.

Crime Data Provided by Neighboring Properties

The type and frequency of crimes occurring at neighboring properties are very significant when attempting to determine the risk of crime at your property. While some of this type of information may be obtainable through public sources such as police reports, it is best to get it directly from your neighbors when possible. This can be a delicate situation, as people often don't want to share information about security problems with outsiders. These objections can usually be overcome when a mutually beneficial relationship with the neighbor has been established in advance.

People who are responsible for security at a property should reach out to their counterparts at neighboring facilities. For example, if you are a property manager at a downtown condominium, you should contact your counterpart at every other similar property within your immediate neighborhood. Introduce yourself and explain that you want to establish an informal network for sharing information about security problems occurring within the neighborhood. Some businesses actually form a "crime watch" group and have regular meetings; others just get together for coffee occasionally to discuss areas of mutual concern.

Once your information sharing "network" has been established, you should proactively reach out to neighbors to get periodic updates on what types of security problems that they have been experiencing. You should consider this information to be an important indicator of the types of crimes that could occur at your facility.

Police Crime Statistics Reports

Police departments and other local law enforcement agencies maintain some type of crime reporting system and typically provide crime statistics reports on at least an annual basis. Although agencies are encouraged to use the Uniform Crime Reporting (UCR) Program and National Incident-Based Reporting System (NIBRS) established by the FBI, participation is voluntary. As a result, there is vast inconsistency in the type and quality of police crime statistics available as you go from city to city throughout the United States.

In general, each city or county will be divided up into multiple geographical areas, which may be called "zones", "sectors", or "precincts". Each of these areas may be further sub-divided into "beats" or "districts". These areas sometimes correspond with US Census Bureau Census Tracts. Crimes are usually categorized by type and whether they are "violent" or "non-violent". Some police agencies provide detailed breakdowns of each type of crime, others summarize crimes in a more general way.

Periodically, the police agency may produce an updated Crime Statistics Report. This is usually done at least annually, but some better agencies also produce reports on a quarterly or even monthly basis. An example of a typical Crime Statistics Report is shown below.

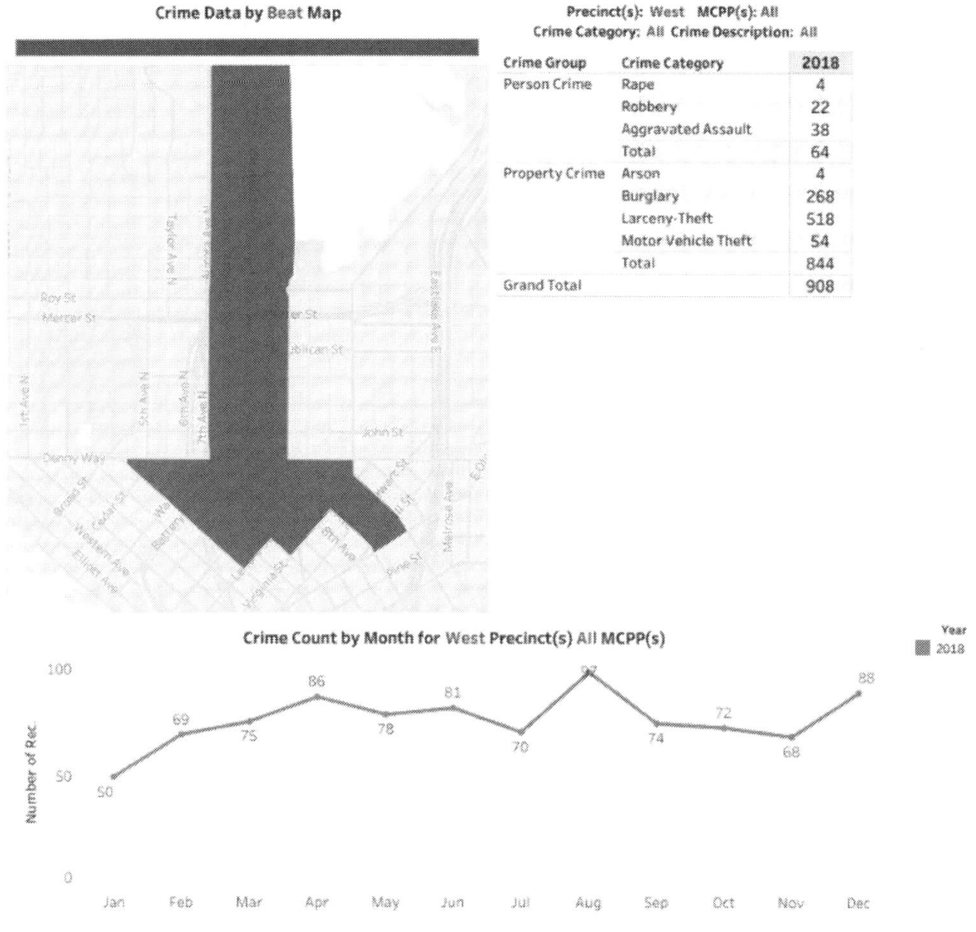

Precinct(s): West MCPP(s): All
Crime Category: All Crime Description: All

Crime Group	Crime Category	2018
Person Crime	Rape	4
	Robbery	22
	Aggravated Assault	38
	Total	64
Property Crime	Arson	4
	Burglary	268
	Larceny-Theft	518
	Motor Vehicle Theft	54
	Total	844
Grand Total		908

Figure 2-1 - Example of Police Crime Statistics Report

Police crime statistics can be a useful tool in determining the level of security risk at your site, but are not perfect. Often, the geographical areas used in police crime statistics reports may be too large to accurately indicate crime conditions at your specific site. For example, if the "beat" in which your facility is located is five square miles in size, it is unlikely that crime is evenly distributed throughout this geographic area. There may be one or more "hotspots" within this area that are responsible for generating a large percentage of the reported crime.

Police crime statistics are best used to provide a general awareness about crime occurring in your city and neighborhood and to establish whether crime has increased or decreased within recent years. By obtaining several years' worth of reports, and comparing them year to year, it may be possible to establish a trend as to which types of crimes are on their way up and which types are on their way down.

Police Calls-for-Service Reports

Almost every local law enforcement agency today uses some form of computerized dispatch system. These systems keep track of every call made to 911, and log the time the call was received, the location, the nature of the incident, the officers who were sent to the call, and the final disposition of the call. Using the computerized dispatch system, it is possible to create a report of every call made to the police concerning any given address in the city. These reports are known as "Calls-for-Service" reports.

Calls-for-Service reports often can be obtained from the law enforcement agency for free or for a small charge. In some jurisdictions, a report can be created using an online tool provided by the law enforcement agency. In other jurisdictions, reports can be requested by telephone or email. In a few jurisdictions, the agency is reluctant to share data and a formal request must be filed using Freedom of Information Act procedures.

Reports are requested by providing the address of the facility and the time period for which the information is needed. For example, one might request all calls-for-service information for the address 101 Main Street for the years 2018, 2019 and 2020. In some cases, requests can be made for a range of street addresses (100 block of Main Street through 1200 block of Main Street) rather than just for a single address.

Once obtained, the Calls-for-Service report will provide a listing of incidents at the location by date, including type of incident (theft, vandalism, etc.) and disposition (arrest made, report taken, false alarm, etc.) An example of a Calls-for-Service report is shown below.

SEATTLE POLICE DEPARTMENT

Calls for Service at 1191 2nd Avenue

TOTAL: 158

SIN / RIN	DATE	EVENT LOCATION	LOCATION DESCRIPTION	TYPE	PRI	MIR	DISP
S060023080	01/17/06	1191 2 AV	SECOND & SENECA BLDG	THRET	3	245	Q
S060034413	01/25/06	1191 2 AV	SECOND & SENECA BLDG	ALARC	2	207	M
S060053067	02/07/06	1191 2 AV	SECOND & SENECA BLDG	DISTO	3	CAN	
S060068303	02/17/06	1191 2 AV		BURGT	3	052	C
S060082927	02/27/06	1191 2 AV #____	SECOND & SENECA BLDG	AUTO	3	071	C
S060100000	03/11/06	1191 2 AV	near SENECA ST <100>	ALARC	3	212	M
S060106129	03/15/06	1191 2 AV	near SENECA ST <100>	UNKA	1	282	U
S060113268	03/20/06	1191 2 AV	near SENECA ST <100>	UNKA	1	391	M
S060113651	03/20/06	1191 2 AV #____	SECOND & SENECA BLDG	THRET	3	041	C
S060128047	03/30/06	1191 2 AV #____	SECOND & SENECA BLDG	THEFT	3	065	C
S060139433	04/07/06	1191 2 AV	near SENECA ST <100>	UNKA	1	391	U
S060152726	04/17/06	1191 2 AV	near SENECA ST <100>	UNKA	1	391	U
S060155778	04/19/06	1191 2 AV	near SENECA ST <100>	UNKA	1	280	V
S060187657	05/10/06	1191 2 AV #____	near SENECA ST <100>	UNKA	1	CAN	
S060194607	05/15/06	1191 2 AV	near SENECA ST <100>	DETOX	3	177	V
S060211955	05/26/06	1191 2 AV	near SENECA ST <100>	DETOX	3	177	U
S060244218	06/16/06	1191 2 AV #____		THEFTT	3	065	C
S060250869	06/20/06	1191 2 AV #____		FU	8	065	H
S060251012	06/20/06	1191 2 AV	SECOND & SENECA BLDG	THEFT	3	063	C
S060251277	06/20/06	1191 2 AV	near SENECA ST <100>	PEACE	3	063	H
S060260220	06/26/06	1191 2 AV	SECOND & SENECA BLDG	ALARC	2	207	U
S060265354	06/29/06	1191 2 AV #____	near SENECA ST <100>	SHOP	2	065	U
S060266911	06/30/06	1191 2 AV	near SENECA ST <100>	HARAS	3	081	C
S060278176	07/06/06	1191 2 AV	near SENECA ST <100>	ALARC	2	207	M
S060301723	07/21/06	1191 2 AV #____	near SENECA ST <100>	SHOP	2	065	A
S060322361	08/02/06	1191 2 AV #____	near SENECA ST <100>	THEFT	3	062	Q
S060345033	08/16/06	1191 2 AV	SECOND & SENECA BLDG	FOUND	3	390	U

Figure 2-2 - Example of Police Calls-for-Service Report

It is important to note that most Calls-for-Service reports are not written to be used by the average consumer. They are cryptic in nature and provide raw data that may include numerous codes and abbreviations. You will need to get explanations of each type of code in order for the data to be meaningful and will need patience in attempting to make sense of the report. Also, there are usually no summaries or recaps provided in the report, you will need to do this yourself to get statistics that can be properly analyzed.

While Calls-for-Service reports can be difficult to obtain and hard to use, they are one of the best sources of crime data available as they provide actual information about reported crime at any given location.

Commercial Crime Forecast Reports

There are commercial service providers who sell crime forecast reports that specifically rate the risk of crime at any given address. These reports are created using a computer model that evaluates police crime statistics as well as many other factors that may include population data, economic data, housing data, and other socioeconomic conditions. Two popular providers of crime forecast reports are CAP Index, which provides CRIMECAST® Reports, and Location, Inc, which provides SecurityGauge® Reports.

Commercial crime forecast reports can be purchased online. To obtain a report, you simply type in the address of the facility and within minutes a customized report is available for download. This report provides numeric scores for each type of crime including homicide, rape, robbery, assault, burglary, larceny, and car theft. Separate scores are provided that compare crimes on a county, state, and national level. Scores for previous years as well as projected scores for future years are provided that allow you to establish whether crime is on the upswing or downswing. A map is provided with the report that shows crime scores at the site as well as in the surrounding neighborhoods.

The advantage of commercial crime forecast reports is that they are quick and easy to obtain, and that they allow rapid apples-to-apples comparison of crime rates between sites. For example, if you operate 30 different multifamily apartment complexes in different cities, you can obtain commercial crime forecast reports for each one, allowing you to quickly identify locations that have higher than average crime scores. Trying to do this through other means (such as by using police crime statistics reports) is extremely difficult because of the inconsistency in the ways in which different police departments provide crime data. Because of this, commercial crime forecast reports are widely used by organizations who operate facilities in multiple locations throughout the country.

Despite the popularity of commercial crime forecast reports, some security professionals are skeptical of their accuracy. These professionals claim that the computer algorithms and methodology used to create the crime forecast scores are proprietary and have not been subject to any type of peer review. Further, many security professionals are opposed to the use of any type of socioeconomic data in crime forecasting as they feel that it is inaccurate and possibly discriminatory.

Custom Crime Analyses

Because of the complexities of determining the risks of local crime, some property owners choose to hire a security professional to conduct a custom crime analysis for their facility. This can be done as a part of a complete security assessment for the facility by an independent security consultant, or can be done as a separate engagement by a consultant who specializes in crime analysis.

The consultant will gather data from sources such as incident reports, crime statistics, and calls-for-service reports and compile it into a usable format. The data can then be analyzed and presented to the property owner in a meaningful way. Most consultants who specialize in this work have spreadsheets or computer programs that simplify the data gathering and analysis process.

While probably the most expensive method of obtaining crime data, custom crime analyses are the most accurate. They should be used when contemplating major investments in security improvements or when litigation is a possibility.

Other Sources of Crime Data

There are several other sources of crime data that may be available at your location:

- Many police departments now provide online crime maps that provide real-time information on reported crimes occurring within their jurisdiction. Be careful; there are some commercial providers that offer crime maps that are inaccurate or provide incomplete information.
- Some police departments now offer real-time Twitter feeds that provide notification when certain types of crimes are reported in the community. If your police department doesn't offer this service, consider using Google Alerts to create your own notifications when local crimes occur in your community.
- Many communities have online neighborhood forums and blogs where information about crimes occurring locally is shared. The people who participate in these forums are usually quick to report thefts and other security problems, making them an excellent source of current information about what's going on in your community.

Conducting a Security Risk Assessment

After you have obtained information about the types of crimes that could occur at your multifamily property, it's time to conduct a security risk assessment. This assessment can be conducted using the following steps:

Step #1 - Identify Assets

Identify and list all types of assets that exist at the property. Major categories of assets include people, property, and information. This list should include assets that are personally-owned by residents, as well as assets that are owned by the HOA or property owner.

Step #2 - Identify Possible Loss Events

A "loss event" is an incident that could jeopardize or put any of the assets identified in Step #1 at risk. Loss events include things such as thefts, burglaries, vandalism, armed robberies, physical assaults, the theft of personal data, and other types of crimes.

Step #3 - Predict Likelihood of Loss Events

Predict the likelihood that each type of loss event identified in Step #2 will occur. Rank the likelihood of each type of loss event using the following criteria:

VL	Very Likely to Occur:	Greater than 90% chance of occurrence.
L	Likely to Occur:	Between 50% and 90% chance of occurrence.
ML	Moderately Likely to Occur:	Between 10% and 50% chance of occurrence.
U	Unlikely to Occur:	Between 3% and 10% chance of occurrence.
VU	Very Unlikely to Occur:	Less than 3% chance of occurrence.

Figure 2-3 - Ranking Likelihood

Determining likelihood involves consideration of numerous factors, including:

- History of events that have occurred at this property or other properties in the immediate area.
- Crime rate at this location as determined by local police crime statistics or crime forecast reports.
- History of events that have occurred at similar properties not in the immediate area but elsewhere in the region.
- Complaints about crime conditions from residents, employees, and visitors.
- Information from local, state, or national law enforcement agencies about potential threats.
- Nearby presence of "crime magnets" – adjacent or nearby facilities that may attract crime or disorderly conduct. (For example, nearby parks or businesses known to have a history of criminal activities.)

Determining likelihood is far from an exact science and requires some educated guesswork on the part of the person doing the assessment. Even seasoned security professionals struggle with this part of the risk assessment process. While it is impossible to accurately predict what might happen in the future, carefully considering all of the factors listed above will produce a result that is accurate enough for security planning purposes.

Step #4 - Identify Consequences of Loss Events

Predict the impacts or consequences that would be experienced if each type of loss event were to occur. Impacts include financial costs, personal injury and death, loss of use of facilities due to downtime, effects on reputation, and potential legal liabilities. Rank the consequences of each type of loss event using the following criteria:

NS	Not Serious	No injuries, $0 to $500 financial loss.
NTS	Not Too Serious	Minor injuries possible, $500 to $5,000 financial loss.
S	Serious	Serious injuries possible, $5,000 to $50,000 financial loss, risk of legal liabilities.
VS	Very Serious	Loss of life or severe injuries possible, $50,000 to $500,000 financial loss, risk of legal liabilities.
ES	Extremely Serious	Loss of multiple lives or multiple severe injuries possible, greater than $500,000 financial loss, risk of legal liabilities.

Figure 2-4- Ranking Consequences

Step #5- Determine Priority of Loss Events

Each possible loss event should be ranked as "Low Risk", "Medium Risk", or "High Risk" based on the combination of likelihood and consequences. The matrix shown in Figure 2-5 can be used to determine the level of security risk for each loss event.

	Ranking	CONSEQUENCES				
		Extremely Serious	Very Serious	Serious	Not Too Serious	Not Serious
LIKELIHOOD	Very Likely	High Risk	High Risk	High Risk	Moderate Risk	Moderate Risk
	Likely	High Risk	High Risk	Moderate Risk	Moderate Risk	Low Risk
	Moderately Likely	High Risk	Moderate Risk	Moderate Risk	Moderate Risk	Low Risk
	Unlikely	Moderate Risk	Moderate Risk	Moderate Risk	Low Risk	Low Risk
	Very Unlikely	Moderate Risk	Low Risk	Low Risk	Low Risk	Low Risk

Figure 2-5 - Risk Ranking Matrix

A summary of the risk assessment should be prepared using a simple spreadsheet that lists the possible types of loss events, the likelihood and consequences of each loss event, and the corresponding risk ranking for each loss event. An example of this type of summary is shown in Figure 2-6 below.

"High Risk" loss events are those that would pose the greatest risk to the multifamily property. The top priority of the security program should be to prevent High Risk loss events from occurring, with ample resources dedicated to this effort.

"Moderate Risk" loss events pose a significant security risk to the multifamily property, but not as great as High Risk loss events. Adequate resources should be devoted to preventing Moderate Risk events from occurring, but ownership may choose to make certain compromises between the costs of security measures and risk so long as the personal safety of residents and visitors is not jeopardized.

"Low Risk" loss events are those that pose a risk to the multifamily property, but whose occurrence is not likely or the resulting damages from the event occurring is not great. The security program should attempt to discourage Low Risk loss events from happening, but ownership may not wish to devote significant resources to prevent them. This may result in having to accept some losses from Low Risk loss events as a normal cost of doing business.

Acme Condominium
Risk Assessment Summary

Possible Loss Event	Likelihood	Consequences	Rank
Arson	VU	ES	M
Assault	VU	VS	L
Auto Theft	VL	S	H
Bicycle Theft	VL	NTS	M
Burglary of Residential Apartment	L	S	M
Burglary of Common Area Room	VL	NTS	M
Car Prowl	VL	NTS	M
Disturbances/Disorderly Conduct	L	S	M
Domestic Violence	U	S	M
Graffiti	VL	NS	M
External Theft of Property	L	NTS	M
Internal Theft of Property	U	NTS	L
Robbery	U	VS	M
Trespassers	VL	NS	M
Vandalism	VL	NS	M

Figure 2-6 - Example of Risk Assessment Summary

Chapter 3: Basic Concepts for Good Security

While security is not an exact science, there are certain fundamental principles that are the foundation of any effective security program. Having a good understanding of these principals will help you to clarify your security goals and allow you to develop your security program in an organized rather than haphazard manner. Within this chapter, we describe five basic concepts that are the foundation of a successful security program.

These concepts are Basic Crime Theory, The 3 D's of Security, The Balanced Approach to Security, Concentric Circles of Protection, and Crime Prevention through Environmental Design.

Basic Crime Theory

Basic crime theory states that three elements must exist for a crime to occur:

- The criminal's desire to commit a crime.
- The criminal's ability to commit a crime.
- The criminal's opportunity to commit a crime.

These three elements are often displayed using a "crime triangle", shown in the figure below.

Figure 3-1 - Crime Triangle

Basic crime theory suggests that the elimination of any one of these three elements will prevent crime from occurring. Effective crime prevention strategies focus on finding ways to minimize the criminal's desire to commit a crime, ability to commit a crime, and opportunity to commit a crime.

For example, having visible deterrents can reduce the criminal's ***desire*** to commit a crime because they send the message that the crime will be difficult to carry out and the chances of getting caught are high. Installing effective doors and locks can limit the ***ability*** of the average criminal to gain entry to the property, preventing a crime from occurring. Keeping desirable property properly secured and out of the view of would-be thieves can reduce the ***opportunity*** for a crime to be committed.

The 3 Ds of Security

The security program at a multifamily property should be designed to meet three primary objectives: to ***Deter*** the potential criminal from committing crimes on the property, to ***Detect*** the criminal's presence on the property, and to ***Delay*** the criminal's ability to commit crimes on the property. These are known as the "Three Ds of Security" [1].

Methods of deterring, detecting, and delaying the criminal are discussed in detail in other chapters of this book.

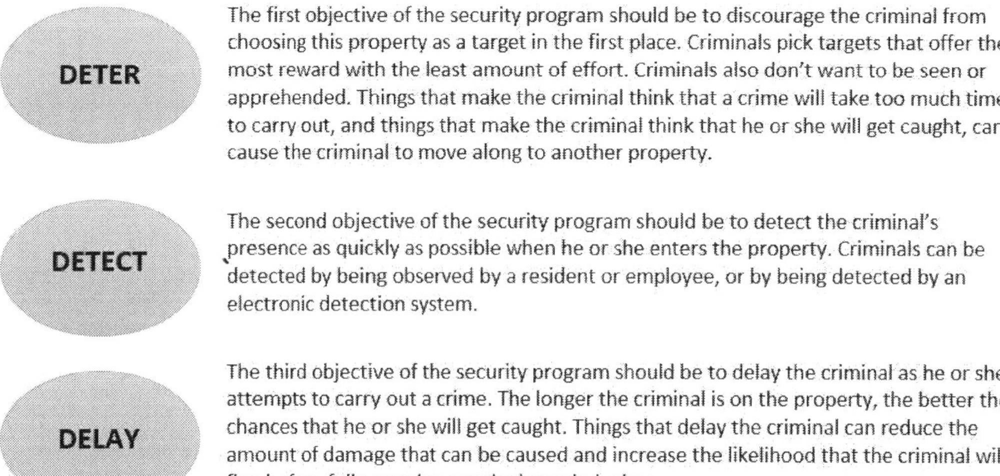

Figure 3-2 - 3 Ds of Security

Balanced Approach to Security

The security program at a multifamily property should use a combination of different types of preventive measures. These can include operational security measures, site and building features, and electronic security systems. All of these measures must work together to provide effective protection of the property's assets.

---

[1] Some security practitioners use additional "Ds" that can include other factors such as "deny" and "defend".

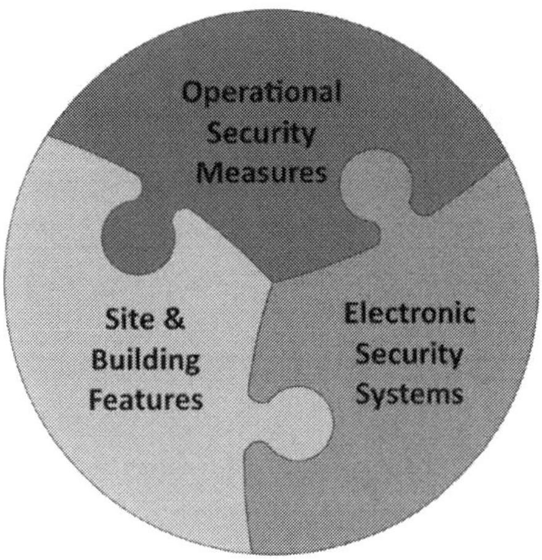

Figure 3-3 - Balanced Approach to Security

A balanced security program should include the following:

Operational Security Measures

Operational measures can include resident security awareness training, security policies and procedures, security incident reporting procedures, security program management, and security officer staffing.

Electronic Security Systems

Electronic security systems can include access control systems, alarm monitoring systems, video surveillance systems, security intercom systems, and other electronic security devices.

Site & Building Features

Site features can include fencing, gates, perimeter barriers, landscaping, signage, and security lighting. Building features can include doors, locks, security glazing, and other physical security devices.

All of these types of security measures are discussed in detail in other chapters of this book. It is important to understand that no single type of security measure can provide effective security by itself – all measures must work together in order for the security program to be successful.

Concentric Circles of Protection

An important concept for providing good security at multifamily properties is known as "Concentric Circles of Protection". This concept involves the use of multiple "layers" of security. The first layer is located at the site perimeter, and additional layers are provided as you move inward through the property. This concept is illustrated in Figure 3-4 below, and is sometimes compared to the layers of an onion.

When the concentric circles of protection concept is used to protect a property, the criminal must penetrate a series of layers to reach his or her intended target. While breeching a single layer may be possible, having to breech additional layers makes gaining entry exponentially more difficult. The more layers that exist, the more difficult it is for the criminal to gain entry.

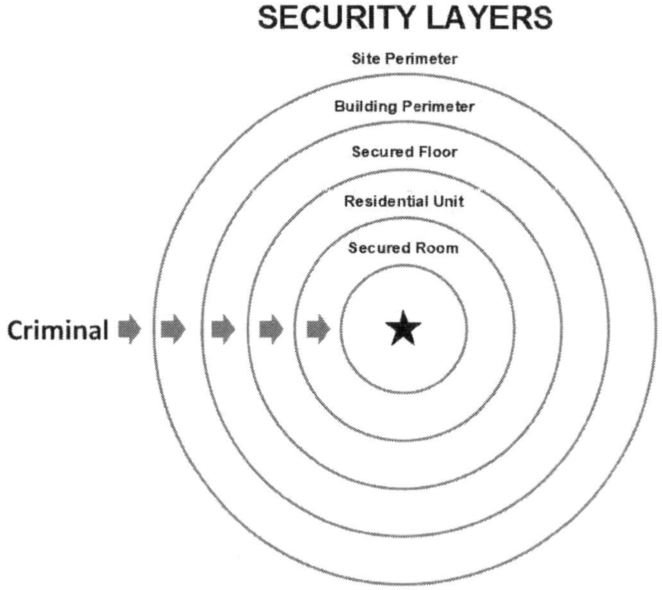

Figure -3-4 - Concentric Circles of Protection

An example would be a multi-story building that was located on a controlled-access site and where access to each of the residential floors was separately controlled. The first layer of security would be the fence at the perimeter of the site. The second layer of security would be at the perimeter of the building. The third layer of security would be at the elevators and stairways that controlled access to the floors. The fourth layer of security would be at the doors to the residential units.

A criminal who wanted to burglarize a residential unit would have to bypass the perimeter fence (Layer 1), make entry into the building (Layer 2), gain access to a residential floor (Layer 3), and make entry into the residential unit (Layer 4). The resident could provide additional security by creating a secured room within the residential unit (Layer 5), and installing a safe within that room (Layer 6) to store high-value assets.

The following are some basic principles of the concentric circles of protection concept:

- Providing multiple layers of security increases the difficulty of gaining entry to the property and decreases the criminal's chances of success.
- The more layers that you have, and the more effective that each layer is, the better that your security will be.
- Relying on only a single layer of security requires that this layer be perfect – something that is almost never possible to achieve.
- Simple things, such as the locking of interior doors and cabinets, can provide additional security layers at no additional cost.

Ways to create security layers within a multifamily property are discussed in detail in other chapters of this book.

Crime Prevention Through Environmental Design

Crime Prevention Through Environmental Design (CPTED) is a strategy based on the principle that many types of criminal behavior can be influenced by the physical environment. CPTED revolves around four [2] basic principles: Natural Surveillance, Natural Access Control, Territorial Reinforcement, and Maintenance. The following is a summary of each of these CPTED principles:

Natural Surveillance

Criminals do not like to be seen as they carry out their crimes, and like places where they can hide and not be noticed. Therefore, anything that can be done to allow criminals to be more easily spotted and to eliminate places where they can hide helps to reduce crime. This technique is known as "natural surveillance".

Natural surveillance is achieved through effective design of both the site and the interior and exterior of the buildings. The design and maintenance of landscaping is particularly important as it has a major impact on how well natural surveillance can be accomplished in outdoor areas.

In many cases, landscaping is arranged in such a way that it obstructs the view of buildings, pathways, and parking areas. This may have been done intentionally to provide privacy, or landscaping may have simply been neglected and allowed to become overgrown. An example of this type of landscaping is shown in Figure 3-5 below.

To allow natural surveillance to be accomplished, landscaping should be designed and maintained so that residents can view activity occurring outside of their residential units, and to allow activity to be observed by neighbors and by people passing by on the surrounding streets. An example of this type of landscaping is shown in Figure 3-6 below.

Natural surveillance can be achieved by trimming shrubbery so that it is no more than three feet high, and pruning trees so that the bottom of tree canopies are at least six feet off the ground. This creates an "area of visibility" that allows activity to be observed. Recommended guidelines for maintaining landscaping are shown in Figure 3-7 below.

Good lighting of outdoor areas is also necessary to allow natural surveillance to occur at night.

Figure 3-5 - Landscaping That Obstructs Visibility

[2] Some CPTED practitioners may use additional principles that further expand upon these four basic ones.

Figure 3-6 - Landscaping Properly Trimmed to Allow Visibility

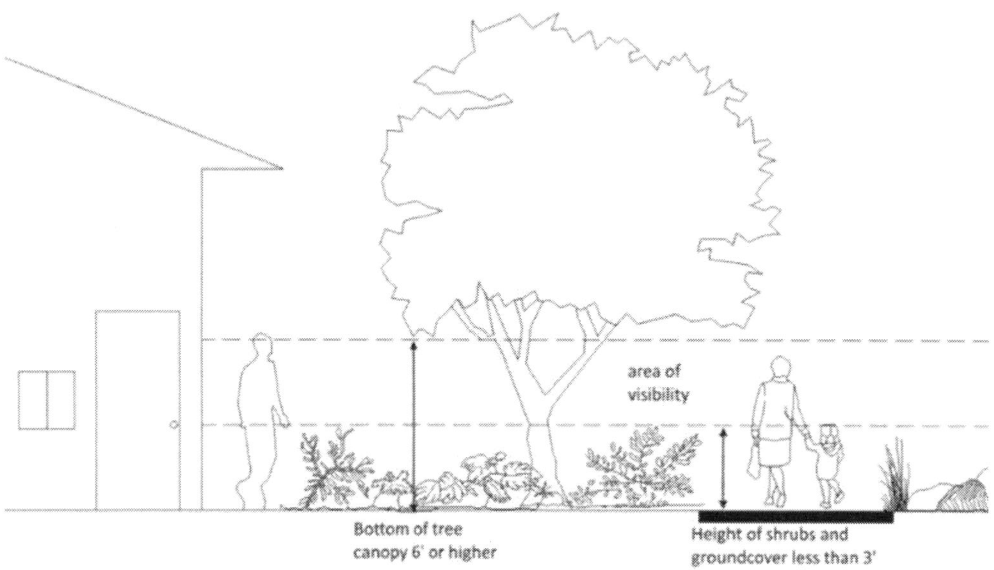

Figure 3-7 - Guidelines for Maintaining Landscaping

Natural Access Control

Criminals like to freely come and go and don't like their movements to be restricted. A property that has many points of access is preferred by criminals as it allows them to choose an entry point where they are less likely to be observed, and it gives them multiple options for escape if they are detected.

On the other hand, criminals dislike properties that have only a single point of access as it gives them limited options to enter the property unobserved, and limited options for escape if they have been detected.

An example of a property that has multiple points of access is shown in Figure 3-8 below. In this example, there are four locations where a criminal can freely enter the property. The criminal is most likely to choose the point of entry where he or she cannot be easily observed by residents. If the criminal is detected, escape can be made using any of the four exits.

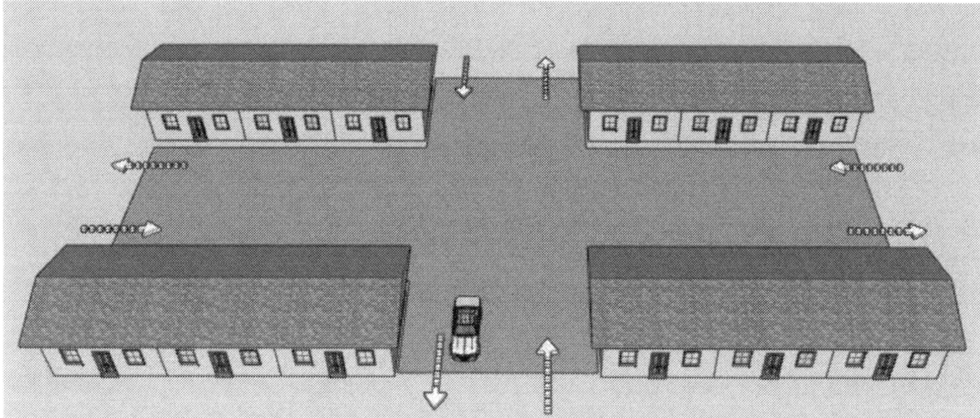

Figure 3-8 - Site with Multiple Points of Access

An example of a property that has only a single point of access is shown in Figure 3-9 below. In this example, there is only one location where a criminal can freely enter the property. All other potential entry points have been blocked off, requiring that the criminal take an overt action (such as climbing a wall or fence) in order to enter the property. If the criminal is detected, he or she has limited ways to escape, most often requiring that the criminal exit the same way that he or she entered.

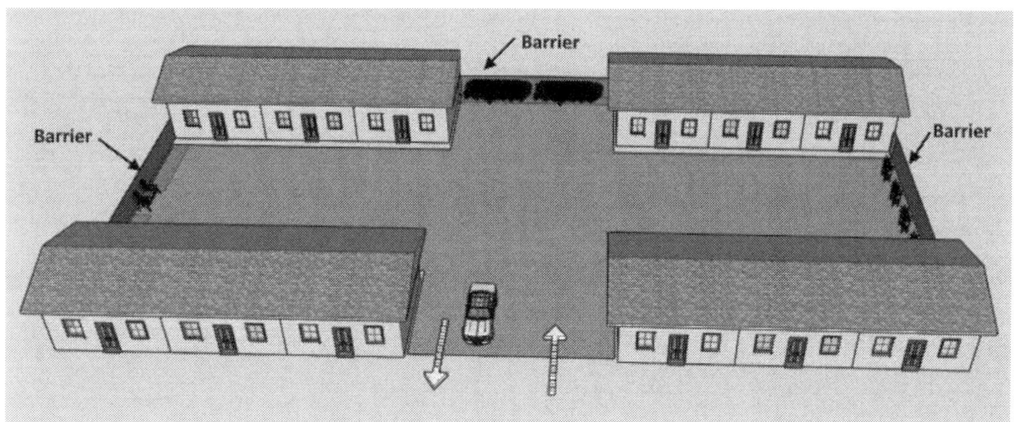

Figure 3-9 - Site with a Single Point of Access

Natural access control can be achieved by using landscaping, fencing and other architectural features to define the boundaries of the property and to create well-defined access points. When possible, these access points should be located in visible spots that can be easily observed by residents. The number of access points should be kept to an absolute minimum.

Natural access control techniques can also be used to direct the flow of both vehicle and pedestrian traffic. This can be accomplished by fencing, landscaping, or a combination of both. This allows visitors to be funneled to the proper building entrances and allows people who wander off designated paths to be more easily detected.

Territorial Reinforcement

Criminals like places where they can blend in with others and not appear to be out of place. They are most comfortable in places where no one seems to be in charge of the property, and where no one seems to care about what is going on. This allows the criminal to operate freely with little chance of them being caught or apprehended.

Anything that can be done to communicate to the criminal that a property is under the control of people who will quickly detect their presence and possibly take action will deter crime. This technique is known as "territorial reinforcement". The goal of territorial reinforcement is to create an atmosphere where legitimate users feel welcome, but intruders feel unwelcome and out of place.

Territorial reinforcement can be accomplished by establishing a line between public and private property to definitively establish ownership [3] of the space, and by creating separate spaces within the property that appear to be under the control of individual occupants. Territorial reinforcement works hand in hand with the natural access control techniques described above, as things done to provide access control also tend to support territorial reinforcement.

Figure 3-10 below provides an example of a multifamily property site with no defined boundaries. This site provides no territorial reinforcement and establishes little ownership of the yards in front of the individual residential units. As presently designed, this site does little to discourage a criminal from entering, and if confronted, the criminal can simply claim that he or she didn't know that this was private property.

Figure 3-10 - Site with No Defined Property Boundaries

Figure 3-11 below provides an example of a multifamily property site with defined site boundaries. This site uses fencing to clearly establish the boundaries between the public sidewalk and private property. Fencing is also used to separate the front yards of each unit, giving each resident a sense of ownership of their yard. Residents have also added lawn furniture and other items to personalize their space, further contributing to the sense of ownership.

This site sends a message that it is private property and that unauthorized people entering the space are likely to be quickly noticed. Because of this, most criminals are less likely to want to enter this site than a site with no defined property boundaries.

---

[3] The term "ownership" as used in this chapter refers to the right to use the property by legitimate parties including property owners, renters, or authorized visitors.

Figure 3-11 - Site with Defined Property Boundaries

It should be noted that fencing is not the only way to define property boundaries – this can be done using walls, landscaping, and other site features such as pools and rockeries. Security signage can also be used to define the boundaries between public and private property.

Maintenance

A widely-known crime prevention theory is known as the "broken windows theory" [4]. This theory states that visible signs of crime and anti-social behavior creates an environment that encourages further crime and disorder.

Multifamily properties that have graffiti painted on the walls, damaged fencing, burned-out lights, and trash scattered within the parking lots can attract crime, while properties that are well-maintained can discourage crime.

Having a well-maintained property sends a message that people notice and care about what goes on, establishing a strong sense of guardianship for the property. Having a poorly maintained property sends the opposite message – that no one knows or cares about what goes on and that anyone can do anything.

Properly maintaining the property should include making regular inspections to spot items that require attention. promptly repairing or replacing damaged items, removing graffiti quickly, and keeping the property clear of trash and debris.

Figure 3-12 - Example of Lack of Maintenance

[4] The broken windows theory was presented in 1982 by social scientists James Wilson and George Kelling.

Chapter 4: Security Planning

Using a Planned Approach to Security

Many property managers give very little thought to security until something bad happens: an apartment is broken into, a car is stolen, or a resident is assaulted on the property. Then they take action, putting new security measures in place quickly and sometimes without thinking how effective these measures may be long-term. Within a few weeks or months, memories of the incident begin to fade, and the reasons behind why these security measures were put into place begin to be forgotten. This process can repeat itself every time a new security incident occurs.

As they carry out their duties, property managers usually focus on solving the specific problem at hand, and may never stop to take a big picture look at their property's security needs. While this reactive approach to security is all too common, it is not an effective way to protect multifamily properties. Making security improvements on a piecemeal basis in response to specific security incidents is often a waste of money and can convey a false sense of security to residents and employees. Always solving yesterday's security problems can prevent you from seeing even bigger problems that could occur in the future.

To provide effective protection of a multifamily property, a proactive approach to security must be taken. This requires the creation of a comprehensive security plan that is based upon the proven security concepts described in Chapter 3.

Creating a Security Plan

All multifamily properties should have a written security plan. While the security plan for a high-rise residential tower with hundreds of apartments will be more complicated than the plan for a fourplex, the underlying concepts are the same regardless of the size of the property.

The security plan can be created by the property manager, the HOA Board, or by a specially appointed committee. An independent security consultant can also be hired to create the plan.

The following steps should be used to create the security plan:

Step #1 - Identify Security Risks

The first step in the planning process is to identify the specific security risks faced by the property. This can be accomplished by conducting the security risk assessment as described in Chapter 2.

Step #2 - Identify Goals of Security Program

The second step in the planning process is to identify the goals of the security program at the property. The primary goal will usually always be to mitigate or protect against the security risks identified in Step #1, but there may be other goals as well. These goals could be to make residents feel safer and more secure, to improve the reputation of the property, or to comply with requirements imposed by insurance companies or regulatory agencies.

Step #3 - Conduct Security Assessment

The third step in the planning process is to conduct a security assessment. The purpose of the security assessment is to determine how well the existing security program at the property is meeting the goals identified in Step #2. The assessment should include examination of all aspects of physical security, including:

- Operational Security: security policies and procedures, contractor and visitor control procedures, security training for residents and staff, use of guard and patrol services and other aspects related to the daily operation of the security program.
- Site and Building Features: fencing, gates, perimeter barriers, landscaping, signage, security lighting, doors, locks, security glazing, and other physical security devices.
- Electronic Security Systems: access control systems, alarm monitoring systems, video surveillance systems, security intercom systems, and other electronic security systems.

The security assessment should include a review of existing security policies and procedures, interviews with property management staff and other stakeholders, and a physical survey of the property. It can be helpful to use a checklist as you conduct the survey. A sample security assessment survey checklist is provided in Appendix B. As you conduct the security survey, identify all security vulnerabilities and deficiencies that you discover. At the conclusion of the security survey, make a written list of all vulnerabilities and deficiencies.

Step #4 - Develop Recommendations for Security Improvements

The fourth step in the planning process is to develop specific recommendations for security improvements at your property. In general, each recommendation will be in response to a specific security vulnerability or deficiency identified during the security assessment. For example, if the security assessment revealed that there was a hole in the perimeter fence, the recommendation might be to repair or replace the fence. Similarly, if the assessment revealed that residents were careless about security and frequently left exterior doors unlocked, the recommendation might be to provide security awareness training to residents.

In some cases, there may be a security vulnerability where the solution to solve the problem is not obvious. In these cases, it may be necessary to consult with a security professional to determine possible ways in which the problem can be solved. In these situations, the recommendation would be to identify a security professional to assist in solving the problem.

Step #5 - Determine Costs and Prioritize Recommendations

After recommendations have been developed, the approximate cost of implementing each recommendation should be determined. While some costs may already be known, it may be necessary to obtain bids or quotes from contractors and service providers to determine actual costs.

Once costs are known, recommendations should be prioritized using a ranking system that includes at least three categories:

Priority 1: Recommendations that address significant security vulnerabilities that put the property at great risk. Priority 1 recommendations are urgent and should be implemented as soon as possible.

Priority 2: Recommendations that would greatly improve security at the property but are not urgent. Implementing Priority 2 recommendations would make the security program more responsive to the risks identified in the risk assessment, and bring the property in line with "best practices" for security employed at similar properties. Priority 2 recommendations may be implemented in phases over several years if this is necessary.

Priority 3: Recommendations that provide an enhanced level of security and can be implemented as desired after all Priority 1 and Priority 2 recommendations have been implemented.

When prioritizing recommendations, always keep the security risks identified in Step #1 and the security goals identified in Step #2 in mind. Recommendations that address the property's greatest security risks should be the highest priority, while recommendations that address lesser security risks should be a lower priority.

Step #6 - Develop Implementation Strategy

The final step is to develop a specific strategy for implementation of the recommendations. This plan should identify sources of funding, assign responsibility to specific individuals for implementation, and establish a timeline for completion.

Bringing Your Security Plan Together

When finalizing your security plan, the following questions should be asked:

- Am I taking a "big picture" look at security, or am I only focusing on my most recent security problems?
- Am I adequately addressing all of the security risks identified in the risk assessment?
- What specific steps am I taking to help Deter, Detect or Delay a criminal?
- Am I taking a balanced approach to security, or placing too much reliance on a single type of security measure?
- Do I understand the Concentric Circles of Protection concept, and have I created enough security layers?
- Are there opportunities to create additional layers of security or to improve the effectiveness of my existing layers?
- Have I adequately incorporated CPTED principals into my security plan?
- Am I doing things that really improve security long-term, or just implementing things that will make residents *think* that something is being done about security?
- Am I thinking that technology such as video surveillance systems are a "magic bullet" that will solve all of my security problems?

Keeping Your Security Plan Current

Security plans should be regularly reviewed to make sure that they continue to meet the needs of your property. As security risks increase or decrease, the types of security measures used should be adjusted accordingly. An increase in security risk may require the use of additional security measures or an increase in security staffing, while a decrease in security risk may allow the relaxing of certain measures or a reduction in staffing.

Making changes that reduce the level of security at a property should be carefully considered from a liability perspective. As a general rule, eliminating or reducing established security measures should only be done if there is a documented reduction in the security risks faced by the property, or if alternative security measures that provide an equal or better amount of protection are implemented.

Reducing or eliminating security measures for purely budgetary reasons should be done with great caution. Saying that "we did it to save money" may not be an excuse that is well received by a judge or jury if the property were ever sued for negligent security. If contemplating the reduction or elimination of security measures just to reduce costs, it is recommended that the matter be reviewed with your attorney before making any changes.

Part II – Physical and Electronic Security Systems

Chapter 5: Site Security Barriers

Fencing

Fencing is the most popular type of site security barrier used at multifamily properties. When used correctly, fencing can be an effective deterrent to unauthorized entry to the site and establish a well-defined boundary between public and private property.

There are four types of fencing that are most commonly used at multifamily properties:

Chain-link Fencing

Chain-link fencing is a component based fencing system that is constructed on site. Chain-link fencing is considered to be the most cost effective type of fencing and is therefore the most widely used.

The chain-link fencing system includes two primary components, the fence framework, and the fence fabric. The fence framework is the "skeleton" that holds the fence together and includes the fence posts that run vertically, and the top and bottom rails that run horizontally. The fence posts are normally spaced about ten feet apart. The fence fabric is the material that makes up the majority of the fence and is installed between the fence posts.

Chain-link framework components are available in a variety of grades, ranging from economy grade components that are available from do-it-yourself outlets to commercial grade components used by professional fence installers. The primary differences between these components are the diameter and thickness of the metal used for the fence posts and rails. For fencing used at multifamily properties, a minimum fence post diameter of 2" is recommended, with a minimum pipe wall dimension of .090 inches.

Figure 5-1 -Chain-link Fencing

Chain-link fence fabric is also available in a variety of grades, based on the diameter of the wire used to manufacture the fabric. Wire thickness is specified in gauges, with a lower number representing a larger diameter wire. Economy grade fence fabric available from do-it-yourself outlets can be as thin as 12 gauge, while industrial grade fence fabric used by professional installers can be as thick as 6 gauge. For fencing used at multifamily properties, a fence fabric with a minimum thickness of 9 gauge is recommended.

Chain-link fence fabric is created by weaving the wire into a pattern that has diamond shaped openings. The width of these openings is known as the mesh size. Although a mesh size of 2" is most traditional, fence fabric is available with mesh sizes ranging from 3/8" to 2-3/8".

Fence fabric with mesh sizes below 1" is often referred to as "mini-mesh" fencing. Although more expensive than traditional fence fabric, mini-mesh fencing is more difficult to climb or cut and is often a good choice for multifamily properties that face increased security risks.

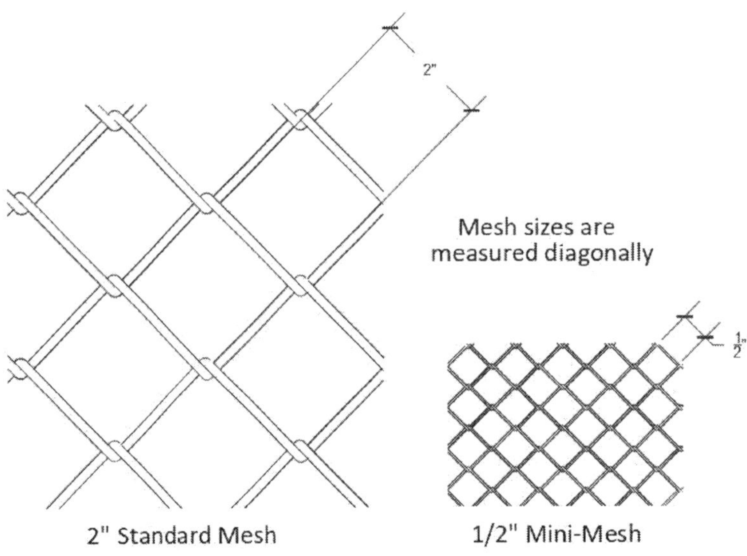

Figure 5-2 - Measuring Mesh Size

The most commonly used type of fence fabric material is carbon steel wire that is galvanized with a zinc coating. If desired, this fabric can be painted to improve its appearance and to provide increased protection against rusting.

Fence fabric is also available in an aluminized version, where an aluminum coating is applied over the steel wire, or in an all-aluminum version where the wire itself is constructed of aluminum. Aluminized fence fabrics or all-aluminum fence fabrics offer increased resistance to corrosion and are often the best choice for use in corrosive environments such as near seashores.

Vinyl coated fence fabric is also available. This fabric is constructed by applying a coating of PVC vinyl over the galvanized steel wire. This provides additional protection of the wire as well as creates a fence fabric that is better looking and doesn't require painting. Vinyl coated fence fabric is available in many common colors and is often a good choice for use at properties where appearance is important.

The top and bottom of the fence fabric can be formed in one of two ways. The first way is to use a knuckled end, where the wire is folded back upon itself. The other way is to use a barbed end, sometimes called a twisted end, where the wire is twisted together to form a two-pronged spike. A knuckled end is typically used at the top and bottom of fences that are below

6' high. On higher fences, a knuckled end is typically used at the bottom of the fence, but a barbed end may be provided at the top of the fence to discourage climbing.

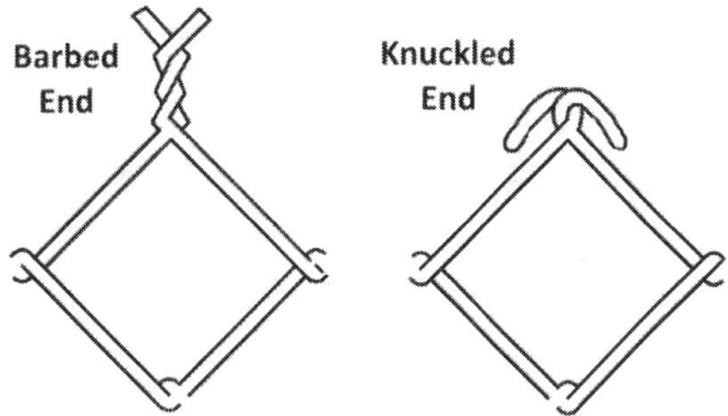

Figure 5-3 - Types of Ends on Chain-link Fence Fabric

Chain-link fences may be installed with or without a top rail. When a top rail is not provided, a tension wire is installed along the top of the fence. Although this is often done as a cost saving measure, it also increases security as the absence of a top rail makes the fence more difficult to climb.

Fence toppings can be installed along the top of the fence to provide increased resistance to climbing. Fence topping materials include barbed wire, concertina wire, and anti-climb strips.

The most common type of fence topping is barbed wire. This is installed by placing metal arms, known as outriggers, on the top of the fence posts. These outriggers point outward at a 45 degree angle. Three strands of barbed wire are then installed along the top of the fence between the outriggers. The strands of barbed wire are placed approximately 4 inches apart.

Figure 5-4 - Barbed Wire on Top of Fence

For higher-security applications, concertina wire can be installed at the top of the fence. In these applications, a Y-shaped outrigger with arms that point both inward and outward can be installed on the top of the fence posts. A coil of concertina wire is then installed along the top of the fence and placed within the arms of the outrigger. Concertina wire can simply be a coil of barbed wire, but is most often constructed using a metal strip which has very sharp pointed spikes on it. These coiled metal strips are sometimes called razor wire or razor ribbon.

Concertina wire is commonly used in conjunction with regular barbed wire. Strands of barbed wire are installed between the outriggers in the usual manner, and then a coil of concertina wire is installed between the arms of the outriggers.

Anti-climb strips are another type of climbing prevention device. Anti-climb strips are metal or plastic strips that have spikes. These strips are installed along the entire length of the top rail of the fence. Though less effective than barbed wire or concertina wire, these strips cost less and have less of a visual impact.

The decision to use barbed wire, concertina wire, or other type of anti-climb device at a multifamily property requires careful consideration. These can give a property a harsh industrial or militaristic look that is off putting to residents, visitors, and members of the general public. Using these devices can also create a safety hazard (particularly in locations with children), and may be restricted by local code or ordinance.

Figure 5-5 - Concertina Wire on Fence

Figure 5-6 - Anti-Climb Strips on Fence

While much emphasis is placed on preventing climbing over the fence, keep in mind that intruders can also compromise the fence by climbing under it. This can be a particular problem when fencing is installed along a sloping surface such as a hillside, where the soil can erode or be washed away beneath the fence. This can create an opening large enough for an intruder to crawl under. The simplest way to solve this problem is to drive metal rods (such as steel rebar) into the ground beneath the fence. These rods should be spaced 6" to 8" apart beneath the fence for the entire distance where entry under the fence is possible. The rods should extend about 6" above the ground to provide a space where the fence fabric or bottom rail can be tied to the rod.

One advantage of chain-link fencing is that it provides the ability to see through the fence to permit natural surveillance of the site. However, there may be some situations where privacy is desired. This can be accomplished by installing vertical plastic slats within the chain-link fabric openings. These slats can be ordered in a variety of colors. In addition to providing privacy and improving appearance, slats can also make the fence more difficult for an intruder to climb.

Ornamental Iron Fencing

Ornamental iron fencing is custom made for each specific project rather than constructed of premanufactured components. Despite its name, ornamental iron is actually constructed using steel. Ornamental iron fencing is sometimes confused with wrought iron fencing, which is very similar, but is produced using pure iron rather than steel. Manufacturing true wrought iron fencing requires lots of hand labor, which makes it cost prohibitive for most commercial and residential applications. However, wrought iron components are often used for the decorative elements (picket caps and scrolls) on ornamental iron fences.

Because most ornamental iron fencing is custom designed, the number and types of design options are nearly limitless. Many properties stick with a more traditional design that consists of vertical pickets and horizontal top and bottom rails, while others may choose a more exotic design that incorporates a particular theme or logo.

Ornamental iron fencing is inherently much more secure than chain-link fencing in that it is much more difficult to cut through steel bars than it is to cut through chain-link fence fabric. Also, if designed correctly, ornamental iron fences can be more difficult to climb.

When using a non-traditional fence design, care should be taken so that the fence not only looks good but still provides an effective security barrier. A common mistake is to custom design an ornamental iron fence that contains openings or horizontal bars that allow the fence to be used as a ladder.

Ornamental iron fencing is available in two common grades, a residential grade, and a commercial grade. The primary difference between these two grades is the thickness of the steel used to construct the fence. For example, a residential grade fence may use pickets made of 1/2" steel, while a commercial grade fence may use pickets constructed of 3/4" steel. Similarly, a residential grade fence may use 1" rails, while a commercial grade fence may use 1-1/2" rails. For multifamily properties, the use of commercial grade materials is recommended.

Overall, ornamental iron fencing can cost three to four times as much as chain-link fencing. Many property owners consider the additional cost to be a wise investment because of the improved appearance of the ornamental iron fencing and the increased security that it provides.

Figure 5-7 - Ornamental Iron Fencing

Manufactured Metal Fencing

Manufactured metal fencing is similar in appearance to ornamental iron fencing except uses premanufactured rather than custom-built components. The primary component of this fence system is a premanufactured fence panel of a predetermined height and width. These panels are connected together to create the fence.

The specific components needed for the project are ordered and then assembled on-site. Most manufactured fencing uses components made of steel, although manufactured fencing made of aluminum is also available.

Manufactured metal fencing is available in a variety of heights and styles and in both residential and commercial grade. Most products have been mass produced over a period of time, allowing the manufacturer to make continuous improvements based on feedback from its customers.

As with ornamental iron fencing, manufactured metal fencing is inherently much more secure than chain-link fencing in that it is much more difficult to cut through steel bars than it is to cut through chain-link fence fabric. Most manufactured metal fencing is also designed to resist climbing.

Manufactured metal fencing is a popular choice of industrial and governmental users who have a need for greater than average security. The producers of manufactured metal fencing have developed several high-security fence products specifically to meet this need. These include fences that have spiked and outwardly curved pickets at the top of the fence that make climbing even more difficult.

Manufactured metal fencing is the most expensive type of fencing available, with standard fencing costing about three to four times the cost of chain-link fencing, while high security fencing can cost as much as eight times the cost of chain-link fencing.

As a result of its cost, manufactured metal fencing is used primarily at higher-end multifamily properties, and at properties where the risks require the use of a higher security product.

Figure 5-8 - Manufactured Metal Fencing

Wood Fencing

Wood fences are constructed on site using wood building materials. There are literally thousands of different styles and types of wood fences available. The two most common types of wood fences used at multifamily properties are the wood panel fence and wood picket fence.

The wood panel fence uses wood fence posts spaced approximately ten feet apart. A top and bottom rail is then installed horizontally between the fence posts. In some cases, one or more additional horizontal rails may be installed. Wood boards, usually about 3" or 4" wide are then attached vertically to the rails. The boards are placed side by side to form a continuous panel. This panel is solid and prevents seeing through the fence.

The picket fence uses wood fence posts spaced approximately ten feet apart. A top and bottom rail is then installed between the fence posts. Wood pickets, approximately 2" to 4" wide are then attached vertically to the top and bottom rail. A gap of approximately 2" to 3" is left between the pickets, allowing you to see through the fence. The pickets typically extend a short distance above the top rail to further enhance the open appearance of the fence.

Wood fences can be constructed using many different species of wood, including cedar, oak, pine, and redwood. The wood should be pressure treated to provide protection against insects and moisture. Wood fencing should also be stained or painted to provide protection against the elements and to improve its appearance.

Wood fencing requires regular maintenance throughout its life. This maintenance can include cleaning and repainting or resealing every three to five years. The fence posts are often the weak link in a wood fence and sometimes begin to rot in ten years or less. This problem can be minimized by properly treating the wood and installing the posts in a manner that keeps moisture out.

The cost to install wood fencing is usually one to three times the cost of chain-link fencing depending on style of fence and materials used. However, when the cost of maintenance is factored in, the lifetime costs of wood fencing can be greater than other fencing options. Nonetheless, wood fences can provide an effective security barrier and are often a good choice for use at multifamily properties where appearance is important.

Figure 5-9 - Wood Panel Fencing

Exterior Walls

Exterior walls can be used to create a physical barrier around all or a portion of the perimeter of a site. Walls are most commonly constructed of brick, stone, masonry block, or concrete. Walls can be completely solid, or can include decorative openings. Walls can be used alone, or in conjunction with some type of fencing. For example, one common technique is to use a short (3' to 4') wall with ornamental iron fencing installed on top of it to create a perimeter barrier. Another technique is to install a short wall with pillars that have ornamental iron fencing between them.

When designing a wall that contains decorative openings or ornamental iron components, care should be taken so that these elements cannot be used to make it easier to climb the wall. For example, metal bars placed horizontally within a wall opening can serve as a "ladder" that makes it easy to climb up and over the wall.

Walls can provide a formidable security barrier, providing protection not only against climbing, but against physical penetration attempts. A well-constructed wall can last a lifetime and requires far less maintenance than most other types of perimeter barriers. Walls also provide privacy and can serve as an impediment to the transmission of sounds from nearby roadways.

On the negative side, walls can prevent natural surveillance of a property, allowing criminals to work undetected once behind the wall. Walls can also be an attractive target for graffiti artists, although this can be mitigated by the use of anti-graffiti wall surfaces and protective wall coatings.

Figure 5-10 - Exterior Wall Used as Security Barrier

Heights of Fences and Walls

The effectiveness of a fence or wall as a security barrier is largely determined by its height. Fences and walls less than five-feet in height can be climbed over easily and serve more as a method of defining the boundaries of the site than they do as a security barrier. Fences and walls that are six-feet or higher in height can serve as an effective perimeter barrier, with greater heights providing a correspondingly higher amount of security. A fence or wall height of seven or eight feet is commonly used as it is considered to provide a reasonable tradeoff between physical appearance and security. Higher fence or wall heights are used at higher-risk facilities where security is more important than appearance.

Local building codes and other regulatory requirements should always be reviewed prior to designing a perimeter fence or wall. Many local codes and ordinances may restrict the height of the fence or wall and specify minimum setback distances between the fence or wall and any public right-of way. Codes or restrictive covenants may also limit the types of materials and colors that can be used in the construction of the fence or wall.

Pedestrian Gates

Pedestrian gates provide a means for residents and visitors on foot to enter and exit through a fence or security barrier wall.

The height of a pedestrian gate would normally match the height of the fence or wall that surrounds it; for example, if you had a 6' high fence, the pedestrian gate would also be 6' high. When a very high fence or wall is used, the height of the gate should be 7', and a section of fencing should be installed above the gate to make up the difference in height. For example, if you had a 10' high fence, you would provide a 7' high gate with a 3' section of fencing above it. The width of a pedestrian gate should be 32" to 48" to comply with the Americans with Disabilities Act (ADA). Gate widths of 36" or 48" are most commonly used.

A pedestrian gate installed within a fence would normally be constructed using the same material used for the fence itself. For example, a gate constructed of chain-link material would be used in conjunction with a chain-link fence. When a gate is installed within a wall, an ornamental iron gate is most commonly used.

It is important that pedestrian gates be carefully designed with security in mind. Many fencing contractors take shortcuts when constructing pedestrian gates in an attempt to minimize costs. The result is gates that fail to close and lock reliably, or gates that can easily be compromised by an intruder.

The following guidelines should be used when constructing a pedestrian gate:

- The gate should be rigidly constructed so that there is minimum horizontal and vertical deflection when the gate is twisted.
- Heavy-duty gate hinges for the gate should be provided. Any exposed fasteners on the hinges should be tack-welded or peened to prevent entry through the gate by removing the hinges.
- Heavy-duty lock hardware should be provided for the gate. If the gate is an emergency exit required by code, a rim exit device should be used. Otherwise, a heavy-duty mortise lockset with lever handle should be used. All lock hardware should be rated for outdoor use.
- If the gate will be used with a security intercom system or access control system, an electric strike should be provided. Alternatively, the exit device or mortise lockset can be equipped with an electric unlocking feature.
- Weld-in boxes should be provided for the lock hardware and electric strike. The boxes should be specifically designed for the models of hardware being used. The boxes should be welded into the gate and frame.
- Care should be taken so that the deadlatch on the rim exit device or mortise lockset properly rests upon the strike plate. This will allow the lock's dead-latching feature to work correctly, preventing the latch from being pushed back from the outside.
- A protective metal plate should be installed on the latch side of the gate. This plate should fully extend from the top to the bottom of the gate and completely cover the gap between the gate and gate frame. The purpose of this plate is to protect against the manipulation of the latch and to make it more difficult to pry open the gate.
- A hydraulic gate closer should be provided for the gate. The closer should be of a type designed specifically for use on outdoor gates. Spring type hinges should not be used as they slam the gate closed, causing excessive wear on the lock hardware.
- Protective measures should be installed on the gate and surrounding fence to prevent the gate from being opened by an intruder from the outside. These measures should include lever guards to protect the lever handle of mortise locksets, protective boxes to protect the push bar on rim exit devices, and metal screening on the gate and adjacent fencing to prevent people from reaching through.

Figure 5-11 - Pedestrian Gate

Vehicle Gates

Vehicle gates are used to allow vehicles belonging to residents and visitors to enter and exit the site. Vehicle gates are also used to allow access by delivery vehicles, service vehicles, and emergency responders.

Vehicle gates can be operated either manually or automatically. While manually operated gates are used occasionally, most vehicle gates used at multifamily properties are automatic gates.

Automatic gates consist of two basic components:

1. Gate: The gate is the physical object that is moved to block the gate opening. Most gates used at multifamily properties are made of either ornamental iron or chain-link material and are usually designed to match the fencing adjacent to where the gate is installed.
2. Gate Operator: The gate operator is the machinery that moves the gate in and out of the gate opening. Gate operators are electrically-powered and may be chain-driven, gear-driven, or hydraulic depending on the type of operator.

There are four types of automatic gates commonly used at multifamily properties. These include the slide gate, cantilever gate, swing gate and barrier arm gate. The following is a brief description of each type of gate:

<u>Slide Gate</u>

The slide gate is mounted parallel to the inside of the fence and slides horizontally back and forth across the gate opening. The slide gate uses rollers on the bottom of the gate to support it. These rollers ride along a metal track that has been installed along the ground across the gate opening. Slide gates are sometimes also called "rolling gates" or "V-track gates".

Because this type of gate uses rollers that must run along the ground, there can be problems with the rollers getting blocked by snow, ice, or debris. The rollers can also be a source of friction, making the gate operator have to work harder to open and close the gate.

Figure 5-12 - Slide Gate

Cantilever Gate

The cantilever gate is similar to the slide gate, but does not use rollers that slide along the ground to support it. Instead, the cantilever gate is supported from rails that run along the inside of the fence structure. This gate gets its name from the fact that the gate "cantilevers" (hangs over) the gate opening. Cantilever gates need to be much wider than slide gates in order to provide a section along the fence structure where the gate is supported. This section is called a "counterbalance" and is usually at least 1/2 the width of the gate opening itself

Cantilever gates are suspended across the gate opening from the counterbalance, with no rollers running along the ground to provide friction or to become obstructed. Because of this, cantilever gates are considered to be much more reliable than slide gates, and are commonly used for heavy-duty and industrial gate applications.

One downside to using cantilever gates is the additional width required to accommodate the counterbalance. This can prevent the use of these gates at sites that have limited space available beside the gate.

Figure 5-13 - Cantilever Gate

Swing Gates

Swing gates are hinged on one side and swing open and closed like a door. Swing gates travel a 90 degree arc between their open and closed positions. Swing gates can consist of a single-leaf or double-leaves and can be in-swinging or out-swinging.

Swing gates are commonly used in multifamily housing applications because of their low cost and ease of installation. Because swing gates travel over a large arc, space must be available to allow vehicles approaching the gate to remain clear while the gate opens or closes. The swinging arc of the gate also requires additional safety considerations to prevent people or vehicles from being hit or trapped by the moving gate.

When double-leaf swing gates are used, it is often possible to pull the gate apart at the center of the opening where the leaves meet. Sometimes, the leaves can be pulled apart far enough to permit a person to squeeze through. To prevent this, electromagnetic locks are often installed at the edges of the gates to hold the gate leaves together. This can increase the complexity of the gate installation and can sometimes create service headaches as the gate ages.

Figure 5-14 - Double-Leaf Swing Gates

Barrier Arm Gates

Barrier arm gates consist of a vertical barrier arm that is rotated in and out of the gate opening. Barrier arm gates are used to control vehicle traffic, but can be easily bypassed by a pedestrian. Because of this, barrier arm gates are considered to be traffic control devices rather than security devices.

Barrier arm gates are most commonly used to control access in and out of parking facilities, and at entrances to gated communities. Barrier arm gates may also be used in conjunction with other types of gates or overhead doors to reduce tailgating.

Figure 5-15 - Barrier Arm Gate

Automatic Gate Accessories

There are many accessories that may be used in conjunction with automatic gates. Some of these include:

- Access control systems: Automatic gates can be operated by a variety of access control devices, including card readers, RFID tag readers, digital keypads, license plate recognition (LPR) systems, and portable wireless transmitters.
- Intercom systems: Intercom stations are often provided at automatic gates to give visitors and delivery drivers a means to contact residents. Most of these systems will allow the gate to be remotely opened by the resident once the visitor's identity has been verified.
- Free exit devices: In many cases, it is desirable to have the gate open automatically when a vehicle exits the property. Devices that can be used to provide free exit include loop detectors, photoelectric beams, and motion detectors.
- Postal service and utility company access: The postal service and many utility companies may require a means to enter through the gate. This usually requires the use of one or more key-operated switches that are keyed to the postal service's or utility company's standard key.
- Emergency access: Most fire departments and many law enforcement agencies require a means to gain access to your property through your gate at all times. Devices used to provide access can include fire department key switches, strobe or siren activated sensors, and radio receivers that can be activated by the emergency vehicle's two-way radio.

Gate Safety Devices

Automatic gates can weigh as much as 20,000 pounds or more and can travel at speeds as high as 36 inches per second or faster. As a result, gates have the potential to cause serious property damage, injury, or death. Therefore, it is extremely important that safety considerations be included when planning any type of automatic gate installation.

The primary guideline for automatic gate safety is Underwriters Laboratories (UL) Standard 325. This standard defines classes of automatic gate operators and the various techniques that should be used to prevent entrapment and reduce the potential for injury. Gate safety measures can include warning signage, audible warning devices, photoelectric sensors, contact (pressure) sensors, screening, safety cages, and other devices.

Because some of the requirements of UL 325 are difficult and costly to implement, many gate installers have chosen to downplay or ignore these requirements. It is often easy to get away with this because there is little enforcement of these standards in many parts of the country. However, the property owner who installs an automatic gate that is in violation of recognized standards does so at his or her own peril and may be held liable if someone is injured by the gate.

Considerations When Choosing an Automatic Gate

The following are some basic things that must be considered when choosing an automatic gate:

- Opening size: The overall size of the opening will be a major determining factor in deciding what type of automatic gate to use. In general, the wider the gate opening, the more expensive it will be to install a gate. While gate widths of over 80' are possible, gate widths over 40' tend to be more expensive and more problematic.
- Availability of Space: the amount of space available on all sides surrounding the gate can limit the type of automatic gate that can be used. If the gate is located on a large rural site that has plenty of space, probably just about any type of automatic gate can be used. Facilities located in crowded urban or downtown areas where space is at a premium may be limited to only one or two options for automatic gates.
- Weight of gate: The overall weight of the gate determines the type and grade of gate operator required. In general, the wider and taller the gate, the more it will weigh. Gates of the same size will weigh differently depending on whether they are constructed of steel, aluminum, or wood. Allowance must also be made for any increase in weight that may be caused by accumulations of rain, snow, or ice on the gate surfaces.
- Opening and Closing Speed: Different applications require different opening and closing speeds. Opening speeds that are too slow can cause traffic backups and user frustration. Closing speeds that are too slow can encourage "tailgating" and other security violations.
- Duty Cycle: The number of times the gate will be opened and closed each day must be considered when selecting an automatic gate operator. Certain types of gate operators designed for residential use may only be intended to be cycled a dozen times per day or less. These types of gate operators will fail quickly at a busy multifamily housing facility where the gate is cycled hundreds of times per day.
- Grade: Most gate operators are designed to operate gates that are on a level, flat grade. Gates that must open or close going up or down an incline can cause excessive wear on the gate operator and lead to premature failure.
- Gate Construction: Simply adding a gate operator to a gate that was originally designed for manual operation can be a real mistake. Gates need to be specifically designed for automatic operation. Special types of rollers, bearings and other hardware are often needed to make a gate work reliably with an automatic gate operator. These items add relatively little cost to the overall installation, but make a big difference in gate performance and reliability.
- Weather Conditions: Special precautions must be taken when installing gates in regions where there are extreme hot or cold temperatures, high winds, or heavy snow or ice.

Landscaping

Landscaping elements such as trees, plants, and shrubs can be used as security barriers. These elements can be used alone, or in conjunction with other measures such as fences or walls.

One particularly useful landscaping element is the hedge, which can serve as an attractive yet extremely effective security barrier. Hedges should be dense enough to prevent penetration, and high enough to serve as an obstacle to intruders. Like with walls, hedges five feet high or less serve primarily to identify the boundaries of the site, while hedges six feet high and taller can provide an effective perimeter barrier.

There are numerous species of plants that can be used to create hedges. For security purposes, thorny plants such as Holly and Pyracantha work best. The specific species of plant to be used should be determined based on local growing conditions and the desired height and characteristics of the hedge. A qualified plant expert familiar with local conditions should be used to assist with the selection of the appropriate plant.

One drawback of hedges is the time that it takes for newly planted plants to grow and be trimmed and shaped into an effective hedge. This can take four years or more. To overcome this limitation, there are suppliers of pre-finished hedges, sometimes called "instant hedges". These can be used to provide an effective hedge on the day that it is installed.

Hedges offer a level of privacy similar to that provided by a wall, but also similarly prevent the natural surveillance of the property. Hedges require ongoing maintenance that may include watering, fertilizing, and frequent trimming. Plants may also perish due to improper maintenance, insects, or disease, requiring the periodic replacement of some plants in order to maintain an effective hedge.

Figure 5-16 - Hedge Used as Security Barrier

Site Features

Site features include things such as flowerbeds, planters, rockeries, berms, pools, and fountains. These features can be used in conjunction with walls and fences to create a security barrier that is both effective and aesthetically pleasing.

When incorporating site features into your overall site design, care should be taken so that they enhance rather than compromise security. For example, terraced flower beds placed directly adjacent to a security wall can act as a stairway that allows an intruder to easily climb over the wall. Similarly, landscaping trellises placed next to a fence can be used as a ladder to allow the fence to be easily climbed over.

Chapter 6: Security Lighting

Importance of Security Lighting

Security lighting is lighting that is intended to deter criminal activity. At multifamily properties, security lighting is used outdoors to illuminate parking areas, walkways, building entrances, and amenity areas such as swimming pools. Indoors, security lighting is used to illuminate building lobbies, hallways and corridors, stairways, and parking garages.

It is generally believed that having good security lighting reduces crime, but surprisingly, there are few scientific studies that support this. The studies that do exist are not recent and offer conflicting conclusions; with some studies suggesting that good lighting reduces crime, and others suggesting that it has little effect.

Despite the lack of hard data to support it, most security professionals believe that having good security lighting reduces crime and should be used as part of the overall CPTED strategy for a multifamily property. Good lighting allows residents and staff to better identify people on the property to determine if they are friend or foe, and to spot suspicious activity more quickly. Good lighting also allows residents to avoid safety hazards and prevents slips and falls that can occur when lighting is poor. Good lighting also improves the performance of any video surveillance cameras that may be in use on the property.

In addition to the practical benefits of having good security lighting, there is the issue of the perception of lighting conditions by users of the property. Most residents and visitors feel safer when good security lighting is provided at a property, and feel less safe when lighting at the property is poor. In many cases, the desire to make tenants feel safe is one of the driving factors in making a decision to provide improved security lighting at a multifamily property.

Basics of Lighting Design

The design of lighting systems is a highly technical science that can take years of training to learn. While it is unlikely that most property managers will ever become lighting experts, there are a few fundamentals of lighting design that are important for every property manager to know.

The following is an explanation of some basic lighting principles. While a lighting expert may take issue with some of these simplified descriptions, they are accurate enough for the purposes of this book.

There are five basic considerations when evaluating a lighting system:

- Intensity of the lighting: how bright is the light?
- Uniformity of lighting: how consistent is the light level from place to place throughout the lighted area?
- Color of lighting: how accurately does the lighting render colors?
- Efficiency of lighting: how much light per watt of electricity does the lighting system deliver?
- Life of illuminating source: How long do the lamps or light emitting diodes (LEDs) last before they must be replaced?

Intensity of Lighting

The intensity of any given light source can be measured at the point where the source emits the light: at the luminaire [5]. The intensity can also be measured at the surface on which the light falls: the object or area that is intended to be illuminated by the light. When measuring the intensity of light at the source, a unit of measure known as the Lumen is used. When measuring the intensity of light at the surface on which the light falls, a unit of measure known as the Lux is used. [6]

The Lumen measurement is used when specifying lighting luminaires. For example, a catalog sheet for a luminaire may indicate that a specific luminaire gives off 3,500 Lumens of light. The Lux measurement is normally used when specifying the amount of light needed to cover any specific area of a property. For example, a property manager may tell her lighting contractor that she wants there to be at least 60 Lux of lighting throughout a parking garage area. The contractor would then determine the number and type of luminaires needed to achieve this goal.

Lighting designers often use special software to calculate the number and type of luminaires needed to achieve a specific Lux level within a given area. This program takes into account the number of luminaires that will be used, the Lumens that each luminaire emits, the dispersion pattern of each luminaire, the distance between the luminaire and the area that is to be illuminated, and other factors.

Uniformity of Lighting

Uniformity refers to how consistent the light level is from place to place throughout the lighted area. The contrast between well-lit areas and poorly lit areas can create shadows that can make it difficult to properly observe activity. Having areas of darkness can also create places for intruders to hide.

Lighting uniformity is specified using a ratio known as the uniformity ratio. This ratio is most commonly calculated by comparing the average lighting intensity in an area with the minimum lighting intensity in an area. For example, if the average light level in a lobby is 30 Lux, and the minimum light level in the lobby is 10 Lux, the uniformity ratio would be 3:1. For most security lighting applications, the uniformity ratio should never exceed 4:1.

Color of Lighting

Light sources each emit different colors of light. The color of light emitted has a direct impact on what the user sees when looking at the illuminated area. Sunlight is considered to be a perfect source of light as it accurately renders all colors. A metric known as the Color Rendering Index (CRI) is used to specify how closely a light source renders colors compared to sunlight. The index uses ratings from 1 to 100, with 100 indicating that colors under the light source appear identical to how they would appear under sunlight. Luminaires commonly used at multifamily properties have CRIs ranging from a low of about 17 to a high of nearly 100.

Having a high CRI is especially important in security lighting applications so that the colors of clothing and vehicles can be accurately identified. Using luminaires with a low CRI can distort the perception of colors and cause people to misidentify the color of objects.

---

[5] Luminaires are commonly called "light fixtures".

[6] Lumen and Lux are Metric measurements and will be used throughout this book. The Imperial equivalent of the Lumen is the Candela, and the Imperial equivalent of the Lux is the Foot-Candle. For conversion, 1 foot-candle = 10.764 lux.

Efficiency of Lighting

The efficiency of a light source is determined by how much light is delivered per watt of electricity used. Lighting efficiency is specified in Lumens per Watt (LM/W). The Watt is a unit of electrical power and is used as the basis for what the property pays for electricity. The greater the number of Watts used over a period of time, the more the property pays for electricity.

Lumens per Watt is calculated by dividing the total Lumens emitted by the light source by the total number of Watts required to operate it. Luminaires commonly used at multifamily properties have Lumens per Watt ratings ranging from a low of 13 to a high of 200.

Life of Lighting

All light sources eventually wear out and have to be replaced. Different types of light sources have different lifespans, ranging from a low of about 1,000 hours, to a high of 25,000 hours or more. Light sources that have shorter lifespans have to be replaced more often, increasing maintenance costs.

Types of Light Sources

There are seven types of light sources commonly used at multifamily properties:

Incandescent

Incandescent lamps are the oldest type of light source, and up until recently, were among the most commonly used. Incandescent lamps consist of a wire filament enclosed within a glass bulb. Incandescent lamps are very inefficient, converting less than 10% of the energy that they use in light, with the remaining energy dissipated as heat. Incandescent lamps provide almost perfect color rendering, but have the shortest life of any type of life source. Incandescent lamps are currently being phased out in the United States because of their energy inefficiency.

Fluorescent

Fluorescent lamps are gas-discharge lamps that use fluorescence to create light. The lamp consists of a glass tube with mercury vapor gas inside of it. Electrodes are provided at each end of the tube. When an electric current is applied, the gas excites the mercury vapor, creating ultraviolet light. This ultraviolet light causes a phosphor coating on the inside of the glass tube to glow, creating visible light. Fluorescent lamps have a poor to fair ability to accurately render colors.

Fluorescent lamps are more efficient than incandescent lamps, but less efficient than most other types of lamps. Fluorescent lamps have a lifespan that is as much as 20 times longer than that of an incandescent lamp. Fluorescent lamps contain mercury, causing them to be classified as hazardous waste. In many parts of the country, this requires that special disposal procedures be used when the lamps are discarded.

Metal Halide

Metal halide lamps are a high-intensity gas discharge lamp that produce light by passing an electrical arc through a gas mixture. Metal halide lamps offer excellent color rendition, giving off a nearly white light. Metal halide lamps are three to 5 times more efficient than an incandescent lamp. The lifespan of metal halide lamps is longer than that of incandescent lamps, but shorter than that of other types of light sources. One major drawback of metal halide lamps is the amount of time that they take to warm up. It can take them 15 to 20 minutes to become fully operational when they are turned on. This makes them unsuitable for use as motion-activated lights.

Prior to the introduction of LED lighting, metal halide lamps were often considered the best choice for outdoor security lighting because of their excellent color rendering abilities.

High Pressure Sodium

High pressure sodium lamps are a high-intensity gas discharge lamp that produce light by passing an electrical arc through a gas mixture. Standard high pressure sodium lamps give off a golden-pink color and provide very poor rendering of colors. There are special versions of high pressure sodium lamps that provide a whiter light, but the color rendering ability of even these is only fair when compared to other light sources. High pressure sodium lamps take about four minutes to warm up once they are turned on.

High pressure sodium lamps are relatively energy efficient and relatively long lasting. Prior to the introduction of LED lighting, high pressure sodium lamps were often considered by lighting designers to be the most cost effective option for outdoor lighting, despite these lamp's relatively poor ability to render colors.

Low Pressure Sodium

Low pressure sodium lamps share many characteristics of high pressure sodium lamps, but are longer lasting and even more energy efficient. However, these lamps give off an orange-yellow colored light that gives them the worst color rendering abilities of any light source.

Although once widely used in street lighting applications, the use of low pressure sodium lamps is gradually being phased out in favor of better lighting options.

Mercury Vapor

Mercury vapor lamps are a high-intensity gas discharge lamp that produce light by passing an electrical arc through a gas mixture. Mercury vapor lamps are long lasting and relatively energy efficient. Mercury vapor lamps provide somewhat better color rendering than that provided by high pressure sodium lamps, but the blue-green light emitted by these lamps still makes them less than optimum for security purposes.

Mercury vapor lighting is gradually being phased out in the United States for both environmental and energy savings reasons.

Light Emitting Diode (LED)

Light emitting diodes (LEDs) create light by passing electric current through a semi-conductive material such as silicon or selenium. When current passes through the material, it creates visible light. Each LED is relatively small in size, requiring that multiple LEDs be used to provide a useful amount of light. These LEDs are formed in horizontal, vertical, or circular arrays depending on the style of the luminaire.

LED luminaires are extremely energy efficient and extremely long-lasting. LEDs can be selected that provide different colors of light. When the correct color is selected, a LED luminaire can provide a nearly white light that has excellent color rendering abilities. LEDs come on almost instantly when powered, making them ideal for use with motion-activated lighting controls.

LED luminaires are the newest type of lighting technology and quickly becoming the most popular due to the many benefits that they provide.

The table below provides a comparison of the seven types of light sources most commonly used at multifamily properties.

Type of Light Source	*Color Rendering Index (CRI)*	*Lumens per Watt (LM/W)*	*Lifespan (Average Life in Hours)*
Incandescent	95-100	13-18	1,000
Fluorescent	50-75	45-75	20,000
Metal Halide	85	75-100	6,000-15,000
High Pressure Sodium	20-60	85-150	12,000
Low Pressure Sodium	0	100-200	18,000
Mercury Vapor	15-50	35-65	24,000-50,000
Light Emitting Diode (LED)	99	80-100	50,000-100,000

Figure 6-1 - Comparison of Various Types of Light Sources

Types of Luminaires

Luminaires are used to contain the light source and to project the lighting in the desired direction. There are hundreds of varieties and styles of luminaires. Some light sources, such as LEDs, are available in nearly every style of indoor and outdoor luminaire, while other light sources, such as metal halide and high pressure sodium, are available in only a limited number of types of luminaires. The following are some of the types of luminaires commonly used at multifamily properties.

Indoor Luminaires

- Pendant lights – hung from ceiling, provide 150° beam of light beneath luminaire.
- Recessed can lights – flush mounted in ceiling, provide 90° beam of light beneath luminaire.
- Recessed troffer lights – flush mounted in ceiling, usually within a ceiling grid, provide 150° beam of light beneath luminaire.
- Sconce lights – wall mounted, provide beams of light either up, down, or both, commonly used in hallways, at doorway entrances, and to illuminate specific architectural features. Provide 90° to 120° beam of light.
- Surface ceiling lights – mounted to ceiling or suspended below, provide 60° or wider beam of light beneath luminaire.

Outdoor Luminaires

- Barn lights – wall mounted luminaire with gooseneck arm holding shade, provide 40° beam of light beneath luminaire.
- Bollard lights – Free-standing bollard, 3’ to 4’ high, with top mounted luminaire, provide 360° beam of light around bollard.
- Drop lens canopy lights – surface mounted to underside of canopy or soffit, provide 150° beam of light beneath luminaire.

- Flood lights – wall or pole mounted, provide directional beam of light with beams ranging from 10° to 130° or wider.
- Pole arm mounted lights – mounted on arm that extends perpendicular to light pole, square or cobra head shaped luminaire, provide beam of light beneath luminaire ranging from 15° to 360°.
- Pole top mounted lights – luminaire sits directly on top of pole, can be luminaire suspended above pole that directs light downward, or acorn or lantern type luminaire that radiates light omnidirectionally.
- Cylinder lights – wall mounted, provide beams of light either up, down, or both. Provide 90° to 120° beam of light.
- Wall pack lights – Wall mounted luminaire, provide 80° beam of light beneath luminaire.

The beam angles stated above can vary by manufacturer and style of light. Some luminaires are available in different models that offer different beam angles.

It is important that the design of any luminaire focus the light source towards its intended area of coverage. Any light focused in other directions is wasted and creates light pollution. In a multifamily housing setting, it is especially important that outdoor lighting luminaires don't project unwanted light into the residential units or neighboring homes. Many local communities have regulations concerning "light trespass" (the projection of light into unwanted areas) and require the use of shielded luminaires to control the direction that the light is focused.

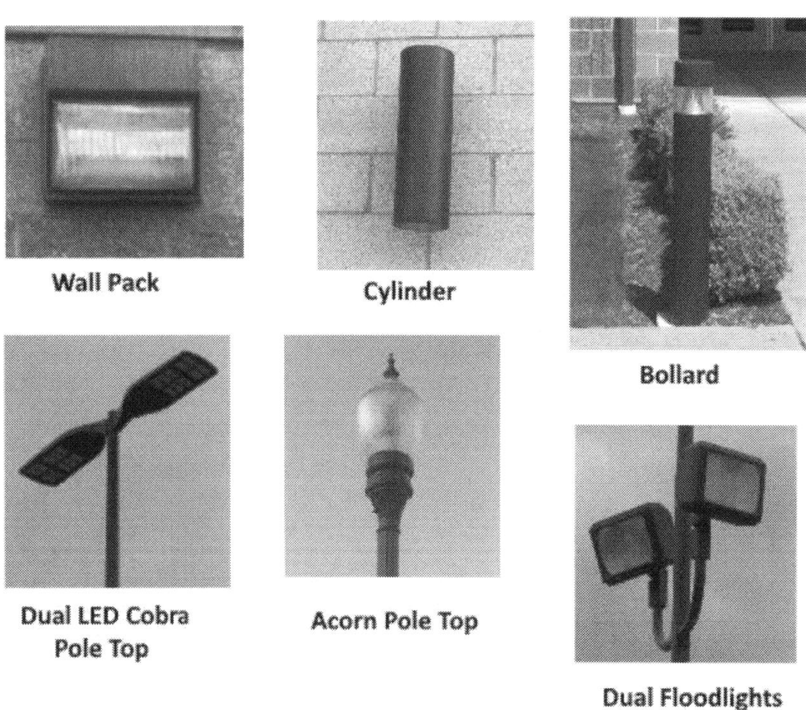

Figure 6-2 - Examples of Outdoor Luminaires

How Much Light is Needed?

The exact amount of light needed in any area of a multifamily property is a hotly debated topic among security and building design professionals and one on which there is no general consensus.

One widely referenced guideline is *IES G-1-16 Guide for Security Lighting for People, Property, and Critical Infrastructure*, published in 2016 by the Illuminating Engineering Society (IES). IES G-1-16 provides guidelines for lighting in many types of facilities, including multifamily residences, dormitories, and senior living facilities. The lighting recommendations in IES G-1-16 generally go above and beyond what is commonly seen in real-world lighting designs and are considered excessive by some industry professionals. To temper these concerns, IES G-1-16 prefaces most of its lighting recommendations with the phrase "when security is an issue", and leaves it to the reader to determine if security is an issue or not. This leaves much ambiguity when trying to determine exactly how much lighting should be provided in any given area of a facility.

Other lighting guidelines have been developed by local governments and professional organizations and by IES itself. These guidelines are often in conflict with IES G-1-16 and seem to focus on minimum safety requirements (is there enough light so you don't trip?) rather than security requirements. There is also a significant movement towards obtaining LEED (Leadership in Energy and Environmental Design) certification for buildings that places an emphasis on energy savings, often achieved by providing an absolute minimum amount of lighting. Some local building codes may also place a restriction on how much energy per square foot of building space can be used. The result is much confusion about what is an acceptable level of security lighting at any given location in a property, leaving property managers scratching their heads.

Figure 6-3 below provides the author's general suggestions for security illumination levels at multifamily properties. These suggestions have been compiled from a variety of sources and can be used as a starting point in planning or evaluating lighting at your property.

Check the local building codes at your property to determine if there are any specific requirements or restrictions concerning the use of lighting. If your building is LEED certified, you should also make sure that any lighting changes that you make don't jeopardize your LEED status.

Location	*Minimum Illumination in Lux*
Building Entrances	30 to 50 Lux
Building Lobbies	10 to 35 Lux
Elevator Lobbies	10 to 35 Lux
Entrances to Residential Units	10 to 20 Lux
Garage Entrances	30 to 50 Lux
Hallways and Corridors	10 to 35 Lux
Indoor Parking Garages	20 to 70 Lux
Mailboxes and Package Rooms	50 to 100 Lux
Outdoor Areas, General	10 to 20 Lux
Outdoor Amenity Areas	15 to 20 Lux
Outdoor Parking Lots	10 to 40 Lux
Outdoor Play Areas	10 to 40 Lux
Parking Lot Pathways	10 to 20 Lux
Sidewalk and Exterior Walkways	10 to 40 Lux
Site Entrances	30 to 50 Lux
Stairways	30 to 50 Lux
Trash/Recycle Areas	10 to 40 Lux
Uniformity level of lighting should not exceed a maximum of 4:1 in all locations	

Figure 6-3 - Minimum Recommended Illumination Levels

As a person ages, there are changes in their eye that requires more light for them to see the same things that they did when they were younger. As a result, multifamily properties that are occupied primarily by seniors may need to provide lighting that exceeds the minimum recommendations stated above [7].

Lighting Controls

For security lighting to be effective, it must be turned on when it is needed. It is recommended that lighting be turned on 30 minutes before sunset, and turned off 30 minutes after sunrise.

While security lighting can be turned on and off manually, in most cases this is done automatically by some type of control system. The three types of control systems most commonly used are:

Timer Controls

Timer controls turn the lights on and off based on a preprogrammed time schedule. There are numerous types of timer controls available, ranging from simple 24-hour mechanical timer controls to sophisticated 365 day timer controls.

Simple timer controls require frequent reprogramming to accommodate seasonal changes (lights should stay on longer in the winter than in the summer) and daylight savings times. More sophisticated timer controls allow the schedule for an entire year to be programmed, minimizing the need to make programming changes.

[7] One guideline for lighting in senior living facilities is IES RP-28-16 Lighting and the Visual Environment for Seniors and the Low Vision Population.

Timer controls work best when all security lighting is connected to the same electrical circuit. In reality, this is rarely the case at many multifamily properties, requiring the recircuiting of luminaires and/or the installation of multiple timer controls.

Photocontrols

Photocontrols use a photoelectric cell that automatically turns the lights on when it gets dark and back off again when it gets light. Photocontrols can be installed to control individual luminaires, or a centrally placed photocontrol can be used to control a lighting circuit that powers multiple luminaires.

Unlike timer controls, photocontrols require no reprogramming to accommodate seasonal changes. When individual photocontrols are used at each luminaire, there can be some variation in the times when lights turn on and off due to variations in photo electric cell placement and sensitivity.

Motion-Activated

Motion-activated lights turn the lights on and off based on the detection of motion. Passive infrared (PIR) motion detectors are commonly used. These detectors sense the movement of objects within their viewing area and turn on the lights for a period of time when movement is detected. This period of time is adjustable, but is usually set for one to three minutes.

Motion detectors can be installed to control individual luminaires, or a centrally placed motion detector can be used to control multiple luminaires. While motion detectors can be used with many types of light sources, they are unsuitable for light sources such as metal halide which require a significant amount of time to warm up.

Motion-activated lights are great for energy savings as they only turn on the lights when they are needed. In an application such as a parking garage, which can be unoccupied much of the day, the savings can be tremendous. However, from a security standpoint, leaving all of the lights off poses a risk. A criminal can enter the garage, find a corner to lurk in, and then wait until the motion activated lights turn off. When the resident walks to his or her car in the garage, the lights are activated, allowing the resident to see the criminal – but by then it may be too late.

If motion detectors are used to control security lighting, they should only control a portion of the luminaires in any given area. Some luminaires should be left on to provide a minimum level of illumination, and then when motion is detected, the additional luminaires can be turned on.

Common Problems in Security Lighting Design at Multifamily Properties

The unfortunate reality is that most multifamily properties were designed with little, or no thought given to security. This is particularly true when it comes to security lighting, where shortcuts are often taken in an attempt to reduce construction costs. Also, many designers are not knowledgeable about security and design things that may look good, but are less than optimum from a security standpoint.

Here are some common problems found in security lighting at multifamily properties:

Luminaires Spaced Too Far Apart

Too few luminaires, spaced too far apart are used. This most frequently occurs in parking lots, where light poles may be placed as much as 100' or more apart. This results in very high illumination levels (1,000 Lux or more) directly beneath the luminaire at the pole, with very poor illumination levels (as little as 1 Lux) at the midpoint between the poles. This creates an unacceptably high uniformity ratio that results in many dark areas and blind spots within the coverage area.

While this problem can be helped somewhat by adding floodlights to the poles to better illuminate the spaces between the poles, this creates glare and provides an uneven level of lighting throughout the coverage area. The best long-term solution is to provide additional poles with additional luminaires spaced between the existing poles.

Luminaires Obscured by Landscaping

There is frequently no coordination between the lighting design and the landscaping design. The lighting design is based on an unobscured path between the luminaires and the intended coverage area, and when trees and shrubbery mature to full height, much of the lighting is blocked.

This problem can be solved by trimming the trees and shrubbery, but in some cases, the amount of trimming required to achieve good lighting compromises the appearance of the landscaping and is unacceptable to the property owners. Local regulations may also limit the extent to which trees may be trimmed.

Decorative Rather Than Functional Luminaires Used

Many lighting luminaires are chosen strictly for their architectural appearance and provide very little illumination that is useful for security purposes. Some of these luminaires cast light for only a few feet. Pole top mounted dome lights and many lantern style luminaires fall into this category.

This problem can be solved by leaving the existing luminaires in place and adding supplemental luminaires to provide security lighting, or by replacing the luminaires with a type more suitable for security purposes.

Pathway Lighting Used in Place of Security Lighting

There are a number of different types of luminaires used outdoors to illuminate pathways and exterior garden areas. These include bollard style luminaires, pathway luminaires, garden luminaires, and stair luminaires. These luminaires are designed to illuminate the area near the ground and rarely project light above a height of about three feet. This makes them unsuitable for use as security lights, where the ability to see a man-sized object (5' to 6' high) is desirable.

Pathway lighting should always be used in addition to, not in place of security lighting. Where only pathway lighting is installed, additional luminaires should be added to provide security lighting.

Figure 6-4 - Example of Poor Security Lighting Provided by Pathway Luminaires

Using Only Building Mounted Luminaires

In an attempt to avoid the cost of installing light poles in parking lots and other outdoor areas, designers sometimes attempt to provide outdoor lighting by mounting luminaires only on the buildings. Flood lights are installed and expected to provide coverage of areas located hundreds of feet away. This creates glare and provides uneven lighting that rarely provides the desired illumination levels throughout the coverage area.

The best long-term solution to this problem is to install pole mounted luminaires where they are needed within the outdoor area itself. Poles should be spaced to provide lighting with an acceptable uniformity ratio throughout the intended coverage area.

No Regularly Scheduled Maintenance

Many multifamily properties have no scheduled lighting maintenance program and only replace lights when one or more are reported to be burnt out.

Lighting requires regular maintenance in order to continue to be effective. Maintenance should include regular cleaning of the inside and outside of the luminaires, as well as a periodic replacement of the lamps. Many lamps provide degraded performance towards the end of their life and should be replaced even if they have not completely burnt out. Lenses on luminaires can become weathered over time and should be replaced when they get cloudy or discolored. LED luminaires don't require scheduled lamp replacement but still require regular cleaning and inspection.

Conducting a Lighting Survey

The best way to evaluate the security lighting at your multifamily property is to conduct a lighting survey. This is often done by independent security consultants as a part of an overall physical security assessment, or can be done by hiring a lighting engineer or contractor.

To avoid the expense of hiring a professional, the property manager can conduct his or her own lighting survey. While this will not be as accurate or detailed as a survey conducted by a professional, it will provide sufficient information to allow you to determine if the lighting at your property is adequate and help to identify areas where lighting improvements may be needed.

The following are the steps to conduct your own lighting survey:

1. Purchase a light meter. Once very expensive, light meters are now available from online sellers for less than $200. Be sure that the meter that you buy is capable of providing readings at least between 1 Lux and 4,000 Lux. Some meters intended for photographic use don't provide accurate readings at lower Lux levels. If you intend to use the meter with LED lighting, be sure that the meter specifically states that it can be used with LED lights.

Figure 6-5 - Light Meter

2. Obtain accurate drawings of the areas that you intend to survey. For indoor areas such as parking garages, try to obtain architectural floor plans of the building. For outdoor areas, try to obtain site plan drawings. If site plans are not available, you can sometimes use aerial photos from mapping services found online. If all else fails, draw simple sketches of the areas that you are surveying.
3. When surveying outdoor areas, wait until it gets fully dark. This is usually at least one hour after sunset.
4. With your drawings and light meter in hand, begin your survey. Start at one end of the area and take readings approximately every five or ten feet. Write the readings down at the location on the drawings where the readings were taken. When surveying parking lots or garages, it can be helpful to use the painted parking stalls as reference points. When surveying hallways, it can be helpful to use room or apartment numbers as reference points.
5. When taking readings, hold the meter horizontally at about four feet above the ground with the sensor pointed up. Take care to make sure that your body is not blocking the light. When taking readings, it is not uncommon for the number displayed to bounce around (8.1 Lux, then 9.3 Lux, then 7.2 Lux, etc.) This is normal. Pick a reading that is somewhere in the middle, write it down, and then move along to the next location. Remember that this is not a scientific study and that only approximate light level readings are required.
6. Areas that should be included in any outdoor survey include the entrances to the site, the parking areas, the sidewalks and walking paths, and the entrances to the buildings. When surveying interior areas, be sure to include the parking garages, entry lobbies, elevator lobbies, hallways, and stairways.
7. Make note of any luminaires that are burned out or blocked by landscaping.
8. When your survey is complete, review all drawings to see if you have missed any areas. If so, go back and take readings in the missing areas.

The following are some additional tips when conducting lighting surveys:

- While lighting surveys can be conducted alone, it is helpful to have two people – one to take the readings and call them out, the other to write the readings down on the drawings.
- Most light meters have a fitting that allows them to be used with a standard photographic tripod. Using a tripod makes it easier to take the readings, especially when working alone.
- It is helpful to have a hard backed surface to enable writing on the drawings. For smaller drawings, a clipboard can be used. For larger drawings, a piece of wood or plastic can be used as a backing board.

Evaluating Your Results and Making Improvements

Once the results of the lighting survey are in, compare the light levels recorded at various areas in your property with the recommended illumination levels stated in Figure 6-3 above. If the readings are at or above the recommended levels, no action is required. If the readings are only slightly below recommended levels, it may be possible to solve the problem by simply repairing luminaires and making some minor changes.

If the readings are significantly below recommended levels, then a lighting improvement project will likely have to be undertaken. For smaller projects, one or more qualified lighting contractors should be invited to review the results of your survey and asked to submit a proposal for lighting improvements. For larger or more complicated projects, an independent lighting engineer or designer should be hired to conduct a professional photometric lighting study and make recommendations.

Chapter 7: Doors

Pedestrian Doors

Pedestrian doors are the most widely used type of door at multifamily properties. Pedestrian doors are used at the exterior and interior of the common areas of the building, and on the exterior and interior of the residential units.

Pedestrian doors consist of two parts, the door leaf, and the door frame. The door "leaf "is the door itself, while the door frame is what is attached to the walls. Pedestrian doors are available as single doors, which have only one door leaf, and double doors which have two door leaves. Double doors are also sometimes called "pairs of doors".

Doors are available in various heights and widths. The most common height of single doors is 7', and the most common width of a single door is 36". Double doors most commonly have two 36" door leaves, for a combined width of 72". Doors are available in both in-swinging and out-swinging versions. In-swinging doors swing into the room that they provide access to, while out-swinging doors swing out from the room that they provide access to.

Double doors are available in versions where only one door leaf opens, or in a version where both door leaves open. When only one door leaf opens, this leaf is known as the "active leaf", while the leaf that doesn't open is known as the "inactive" leaf.

Pedestrian doors are available in different types of materials and in different styles. The following are the types of pedestrian doors most commonly used at multifamily properties:

Wood Doors

Wood doors are a popular choice for use as exterior and interior doors at smaller buildings and for use as entrance doors to residential units. There are three types of wood doors: solid wood doors, hollow-core doors, and solid-core doors.

Solid wood doors are constructed of all wood materials. Despite their name, most solid wood doors are actually constructed using frames and panels rather than from a single slab of wood. Solid wood doors are the most expensive type of wood door and are typically only used for exterior doors. Solid wood doors are very strong and offer good security when used with the right door frame and lock hardware.

Hollow-core doors are constructed using a honeycomb core of cardboard or plastic over which a thin layer of wood is applied. The result is a light, inexpensive door. Hollow-core doors are most commonly used as interior doors at buildings when keeping construction costs down is important. Hollow-core doors provide little physical strength and are a poor choice for use as exterior doors or doors that provide access to areas of security concern.

Solid-core doors are constructed using a solid core of composite or engineered material over which a high-quality wood veneer has been applied. Solid-core doors in some cases are actually stronger than solid wood doors and provide most of the same benefits at a lower cost. Like solid wood doors, solid-core doors offer good security when used with the right door frame and lock hardware.

The door frames used with wood doors are also constructed of wood, although some wood doors are used with hollow-metal door frames. When wood doors and frames are used, the door frame is usually the weak link when the door is attacked. Often the frame is constructed of thin wood (1" thick or less) that readily gives way when the door is kicked. Wood doors and frames can be strengthened using door and frame reinforcement kits.

Wood doors are often preferred by architects and designers because of their aesthetic qualities and the wide variety of design options available in these doors.

Figure 7-1 - Wood Door

Hollow-Metal Doors

Hollow-metal doors are the door of choice at commercial buildings and are widely used at larger multifamily properties. Hollow-metal doors consist of a steel frame within which a core is placed. This core can be honeycomb cardboard, polystyrene or polyurethane foam, or mineral board. Outer sheets of metal are then applied to make up the exterior of the door.

Hollow-metal doors are used with hollow-metal door frames. Hollow-metal doors and frames are rugged and long lasting and provide excellent security when used with the right lock hardware.

Because of their commercial appearance, some architects and designers avoid using hollow-metal doors in areas where appearance is important.

Figure 7-2 - Hollow-metal Door

Aluminum Storefront Doors

Aluminum storefront doors are used as a part of an aluminum storefront system. These systems are widely used at commercial and retail buildings, but also used at the primary entrances of many larger multifamily buildings.

Aluminum storefront systems are constructed using a frame made up of vertical and horizontal aluminum channels, most commonly 2" wide by 4" deep. Glass windows are then installed between the channels to make up a wall that is mostly glass.

Aluminum storefront doors are specifically designed to fit within the aluminum storefront system and are constructed of the same materials. Both single and double doors are available. Doors are available in narrow stile (2-1/4" wide), medium stile (3-1/2" wide), and wide style (5" wide) versions. The physical strength of the door is directly proportional to the width of the stile, so wide stile width doors are preferred from a security standpoint.

Figure 7-3 - Aluminum Storefront Door

All-Glass Doors

All-glass doors, also called frameless doors, are constructed entirely of tempered glass. This glass ranges from 1/4" to 1" in thickness and is tempered to provide strength. Architects and designers consider all-glass doors to be the ultimate in elegance and often specify these at the lobby entrances at high-end multifamily buildings.

All-glass doors are very strong, but not unbreakable. When broken, these doors shatter into thousands of small pieces. The options for lock hardware on these doors are limited when compared with other types of doors. This sometimes makes it difficult to provide the electric lock hardware necessary to use these doors with a security intercom system or access control system. Also, all openings for hardware must be cut into the glass before it is tempered, making after-the-fact modifications to the door almost impossible.

Figure 7-4 - All-Glass Door

Fire-Rated Doors

Fire-rated doors are doors used within a building to prevent the spread of fire and smoke. Fire-rated doors are commonly used along hallways, at stairway entrances, and at places that separate different parts of the building. The exact locations where fire-rated doors are required are specified by local fire and building codes.

All components of a fire-rated door must be tested by an approved testing agency such as Underwriters Laboratories (UL). This includes the door leaf, door frame, and lock hardware. Doors are rated based on the amount of time that they are expected to provide protection against fire. These ratings range from 20 to 240 minutes depending on where the door is being used. When a door passes these tests, a label can be attached to the door that specifies its fire rating. These doors are then known as "fire-rated doors" or "labeled doors"

Both wood and hollow-metal doors can be used as fire-rated doors, but fire ratings greater than 90 minutes usually require the use of a hollow-metal door.

Once installed, fire-rated doors should not be modified except by skilled craftsmen familiar with the applicable code requirements. Once a fire-rated door has been modified, it is usually necessary to have it recertified on-site and a new fire-rating label applied. This requirement is often overlooked when installing electric lock hardware for an access control system or when installing accessories that require modification of the door.

Figure 7-5 - Example of Fire Rating Label

Emergency Egress Doors

Emergency egress doors are doors that are along the required path of egress from a building. These doors are typically exterior doors at street level and doors that provide access to stairways. Because these doors can be used as exits in case of fire, people sometimes mistakenly call them "fire doors" and think that they have to be fire-rated and have a fire-rating label. This is not always true.

Emergency egress doors must allow free exit at all times. Depending on code requirements, emergency egress doors may need to be equipped with certain types of lock hardware, such as an exit device, but do not necessarily have to be fire-rated. An example would be an aluminum storefront door at a building entrance, which would be an emergency egress door but not a fire-rated door.

However, some doors are both emergency egress doors and fire-rated doors. An example would be a door to a stairway off of a hallway. This door would be along the path of exit so would be considered an emergency egress door, but would also need to be fire-rated because it provides fire separation between the hallway and stairway.

Automatic Sliding Doors

Automatic sliding doors are sometimes used at the lobby entrances of larger multifamily buildings. These doors open automatically when a person approaches, making them very convenient to use, particularly at busy entrances.

Automatic sliding doors are usually installed in conjunction with an aluminum storefront system. The doors are constructed similar to an aluminum storefront door, but slide from side to side rather than swing in and out. An electrically operated door opening mechanism is used to move the doors from side to side. This mechanism is usually operated by motion detectors installed on both sides of the door. These motion detectors activate the door opening mechanism when a person approaches the door, causing the door to open.

At times when it is necessary to lock a sliding door, the power to the door opening mechanism is turned off, and the sliding door is locked into place with a manual lock. To comply with emergency egress requirements, sliding doors are often designed with "breakaway" door leaves. These door leaves can swing outward, even when the doors are locked, allowing people to exit in an emergency.

Because anyone can enter through an automatic sliding door, they are most commonly used at entrances that are attended by a concierge or security officer. Automatic sliding doors are not a good choice for use at unattended entrances because of the difficulties associated with electrically locking and unlocking them. This is necessary when using them in conjunction with a security intercom system or access control system.

The traditional way to electrically control an automatic sliding door is by turning on and off the power to the opening mechanism. When controlled in this manner, the door leaves are prevented from moving only by the resistance of the door opening mechanism itself. It is often possible to open the door by simply applying force to the door leaves to spread the door apart. To address this concern, some manufacturers offer a positive locking feature, where an electric bolt is used to lock the doors. This feature is available when a new door is purchased, but may be difficult or impossible to add to an existing door.

Figure 7-6 - Automatic Sliding Door

Revolving Doors

Revolving doors are sometimes used at the lobby entrances of larger multifamily buildings. Revolving doors consists of three or four door leaves that are mounted to a central shaft. The door leaves rotate counter-clockwise around the shaft within a circular glass enclosure.

The primary reason for installing revolving doors is energy efficiency. Revolving doors provide an airlock that prevents drafts and keeps hot air out in the summer and cool air out in the winter. Revolving doors are also used at the entrances to high-rise buildings to minimize the "stack effect", a phenomenon that causes air movement within a building because of differences of temperature.

There are three types of revolving doors. The first type is the mechanical revolving door. This door operates completely manually, requiring users to push on the door leaves as they enter or exit.

The second type of revolving door is the automatic revolving door. This door operates similar to the mechanical revolving door, but provides an electric motor that assists in moving the door leaves, requiring less effort on the part of the user.

The third type of revolving door is the security revolving door. This door is similar to the automatic revolving door, but contains special features that allow it to be used in conjunction with an access control system. Security revolving doors are designed to allow only one person to enter when an access card is used, preventing unauthorized people from following in behind them.

Both automatic revolving doors and security revolving doors contain sensors that detect obstructions and prevent people from being trapped in the door. Security revolving doors contain additional sensors that detect improper use of the door, such as people attempting to enter in the wrong direction, or more than one person attempting to enter at the same time.

Mechanical and automatic revolving doors are most commonly used at entrances that are attended by a concierge or security officer. While the door is attended, it is kept unlocked, but when it is unattended, it is kept locked. When a manual revolving door must be locked, this is done by using a manual lock at the top or bottom of one of the door leaves. When an automatic revolving door is locked, this is done by turning off the power to the door and manually locking one of the door leaves.

Security revolving doors can be kept locked at all times, always requiring the use of an access card to enter, or can be kept unlocked during the hours when the entrance is attended.

Most revolving doors are equipped with a "breakaway" feature that allows the door leaves to be folded outward to allow egress in an emergency. However, even with this feature, many building code officials don't consider revolving doors to be an approved means of emergency egress. This often requires that a separate set of swinging doors be provided next to the revolving door to serve as the approved emergency egress door.

Security revolving doors are excellent for security purposes but are very expensive, making them suitable for use only at high-end multifamily properties.

Figure 7-7 - Revolving Door

Overhead Doors

Overhead doors are used at the entrances to parking garages and loading docks and to control access to service areas such as trash and recycle rooms. Two types of overhead doors are commonly used at multifamily properties: the sectional overhead door, and the rolling overhead door.

Sectional overhead doors consist of horizontal wood or metal panels that are hinged together. There are tracks on both sides of the door opening that extend along the wall and then curve above the door.

Wheels installed at the edge of each door panel ride within these tracks. When the door is opened, the panels rise and then bend over the curved portion of the track, resting perpendicular above the door opening when the door is fully open. Sectional overhead doors usually cost less than rolling overhead doors when installed, but can cost more to maintain.

Figure 7-8 - Sectional Overhead Door

Rolling overhead doors, also called coiling overhead doors, consist of slats of metal that are interlocked together to form a flexible door panel. This panel is connected to a horizontal drum at the top of the door. When the door is opened, the panel coils around the drum, leaving a clear door opening. Rolling overhead doors usually cost more to install than sectional overhead doors, but can cost less to maintain because the door contains fewer moving parts. Rolling overhead doors can also be the preferred choice when space above the door is limited.

Figure 7-9 - Rolling Overhead Door

While both sectional overhead doors and rolling overhead doors can be operated manually, in most cases overhead doors at multifamily properties are controlled by an automatic door operator. These operators are available in a variety of grades, ranging from light-duty residential grade to heavy-duty industrial grade. The door operator chosen should be able to accommodate the weight of the door and the number of open/close cycles expected at the location where the door is used. Sometimes buying a more expensive door operator initially can actually save you money in the long run.

Door operators can be activated using a variety of methods, including manual pushbuttons, key-operated switches, wireless radio controls, and access control devices.

Overhead doors with automatic operators are equipped with safety devices to prevent the door from closing on people and vehicles. Safety devices can include photoelectric beams that stop the door from closing when the beam is blocked, and safe edges which are attached to the bottom of the door and reverse the door when an object is contacted.

The opening and closing speed of overhead doors varies depending on the size of the door and type of door operator used. Typical speeds range from 20 seconds to 60 seconds or more for a complete open/close cycle.

The types of materials used to construct overhead doors can sometimes create security vulnerabilities. For example, the panels used with sectional overhead doors are sometimes constructed of expanded metal mesh. This mesh allows natural ventilation and provides the ability to see through the door. However, mesh of this type can often easily be cut-through with wire cutters or nippers. Along the same lines, some rolling overhead doors are constructed of horizontal rods made of aluminum alloy. These rods can often be easily cut-through using bolt cutters. Some overhead doors are constructed using panels made of very thin wood that can be easily kicked-through.

When choosing an overhead door to provide security, its ability to be compromised by an intruder should be considered. Doors with solid panels rather than open panels are usually a better choice for security. The materials used to construct the panels should make it difficult for an intruder to break through them.

If you have an existing sectional overhead door that is vulnerable, it is often possible to strengthen it by adding metal bars or perforated metal sheeting across the panel opening. This makes it more difficult for an intruder to enter, even if the panel itself is cut.

Figure 7-10 - Metal Bars Added to Strengthen Overhead Door

High-Performance Overhead Doors

When a resident activates an overhead door, it takes time for the door to fully open. The door then remains open for a preset period of time, and then closes. Depending on the type of door and door operator used, it typically takes between 20 and 60 seconds to complete this open/close cycle. While the time period that the door stays open once fully raised is adjustable, the actual time that it takes to raise and lower the door is limited by the mechanical characteristics of the door and door operator.

These periods of time when the door is open provide opportunities for an intruder to sneak into the building. This is known as "tailgating" and is the overhead door's biggest weakness from a security standpoint. While this problem can be reduced somewhat by asking residents to wait for the overhead door to fully close before driving off, this doesn't always happen, leaving plenty of opportunities for intruders to enter.

To help reduce the potential for tailgating, special high-performance overhead doors have been developed. These doors are specifically designed to open and close very fast, with open/close cycles as quick as six seconds. This greatly reduces the potential for tailgating, as the door closes behind a vehicle very quickly as it enters or exits, leaving little time for an intruder to enter.

High-performance doors are expensive, but are often the only real solution to the tailgating problem at parking garage entrances.

When purchasing a high-performance overhead door, be sure that the door is designed for security use and that the door itself is constructed of metal panels. Some versions of these doors are constructed with cloth or plastic panels and are primarily intended for weather and insect control. These doors can be cut-through with a knife or razor blade and are not suitable for security use.

Chapter 8: Locks and Door Hardware

Types of Locks

There are dozens of different types and styles of locks used on doors. Here are some of the most often used types of locks at multifamily properties:

Cylindrical Locksets

Cylindrical locksets are commonly used in single family homes, multifamily residential housing, and light commercial construction. Cylindrical locksets consist of a cylindrical lock body that is installed within a hole drilled in the door. There are knobs or lever handles on both sides of the door that connect to the lock body. There is a hole drilled in the edge of the door where the door latch is connected to the lock body. A strike plate is installed on the door frame to accept the door latch.

Cylindrical locksets can be installed in either wood or hollow-metal doors. When installed in wood doors, the drilling can be done at the project site when the door is installed, or the doors can be ordered from the factory with the holes pre-drilled. When a cylindrical lockset is installed in a hollow-metal door, it is most common to order the door with the holes pre-drilled.

Cylindrical locksets are available with either knobs or lever handles. To comply with Americans with Disabilities Act (ADA) requirements, most locksets used today are provided with lever handles. The lock cylinder where the key is inserted is installed within the knob or lever on the outside of the door.

Cylindrical locksets provide a moderate level of security, but offer less resistance to physical attack than other types of locks. A common technique used by burglars is to take a pipe wrench to the lockset on the outside of the door. This wrench is then used to twist the entire lockset to gain entry.

Figure 8-1- Cylindrical Lockset

Mortise Locksets

Mortise locksets are commonly used at commercial and industrial facilities and at higher-end homes and multifamily properties. Mortise locksets consist of a rectangular lock body that is installed within a cavity in the edge of the door. This cavity is cut into, or "mortised" within the door, giving this lock its name. Holes are drilled on both sides of the door to accommodate the knobs or lever handles. A hole for the lock cylinder is also drilled on the outside of the door.

A strike plate is installed on the door frame to accept the door latch. Many mortise locksets provide both a latch and bolt. In these cases, the strike plate has holes to accommodate both.

Mortise locksets can be installed in either wood or hollow-metal doors. Due to the extent of door preparation required to install a mortise lockset, it is most common to order the doors from the factory with the mortise cavity and holes already cut.

Mortise locksets are available with either knobs or lever handles, but lever handles are most commonly used today. Many mortise locksets are available with vandal-resistant levers that make it more difficult to damage the lock by twisting the lever.

Mortise locksets cost more than cylindrical locksets but offer increase protection against physical attack, making them a better choice for use on doors where security is of a concern.

Figure 8-2 - Mortise Lockset

<u>Deadbolt Locks</u>

Deadbolt locks are most often used as a secondary lock on a door and would typically be installed in addition to, not in place of, a cylindrical lockset or mortise lockset. Deadbolt locks consist of a lock body installed within the door and a movable bolt that projects into the door frame. The bolt is manually extended to lock the door, and manually retracted to unlock the door.

The bolt that extends from the deadbolt lock into the door frame comes in several different lengths. A bolt that is at least one inch long should be used for best security.

Either a lock cylinder or thumb-turn can be used to extend and retract the bolt. The most common arrangement is to use a lock cylinder on the outside of the door and a thumb-turn on the inside of the door. This is known as a single cylinder deadbolt. Deadbolt locks are also available with lock cylinders on both sides of the door. This is known as a double cylinder deadbolt. Care should be taken when using double cylinder deadbolts as they can prevent occupants from exiting the building in an emergency. Local building codes should be consulted to determine where the use of double cylinder deadbolts is permitted.

Most deadbolt locks have a cylindrical lock body and install just like a cylindrical lock; however, mortise style deadbolt locks are also available.

In multifamily properties, deadbolt locks are recommended for use on the doors of individual residential units and on the doors to rooms such as offices. Deadbolt locks typically can't be used on the common entrance doors of multifamily buildings because of building code restrictions [8].

Even where permitted by code, deadbolt locks typically don't work well on doors to common areas as it is unlikely that residents will take the time to manually relock the deadbolt every time that they pass through the door.

Figure 8-3 - Deadbolt Lock

Exit Devices

Building codes require that a means for people to quickly exit from the building in an emergency be provided. When buildings contain large numbers of people, codes often require that a special type of lock hardware be used on the doors along the path of egress. This hardware is called panic hardware, and the devices used are called "exit devices". Some people also call these types of devices "crash bars".

Exit devices are installed horizontally on the door, usually at a height between 34" and 48". The exit device contains an actuating mechanism, such as a cross bar or push pad. This actuating mechanism extends at least half the width of the door, and when pressed, unlocks the door.

There are three commonly used styles of exit devices. The first style of exit device is the rim exit device, which latches to the door frame at the side of the door. The second style of exit device is the mortise exit device, which uses a mortise lock on the edge of the door that is operated by the exit device's actuating mechanism. The third style of exit device is the vertical rod exit device which uses vertical rods to latch at the top and bottom of the door. These rods can be installed on the surface of the door (exposed vertical rods), or recessed within the inside of the door (concealed vertical rods).

Rim or mortise exit devices are most commonly used on single doors, while vertical rod exit devices are most commonly used on double doors. Combinations of different devices may also be used on double doors to meet special requirements.

Exit devices always allow free egress from the inside by pressing the cross bar or push pad. If access from the outside is required, a piece of hardware known as "trim" is provided on the

---

[8] Most building codes state that "the unlatching of any door or leaf shall not require more than one operation." When a deadbolt lock is used, two operations are typically required; one to unlock the deadbolt, and another to operate the latch on the door. There are some locks known as "interconnected locks" that release both the latch and the deadbolt simultaneously when the lever is turned.

outside of the door. Trim is available with knobs, lever handles and thumb pieces, and can be provided with or without a lock cylinder. The most popular type of trim used at building entrances at multifamily properties is lever handle trim with a keyed lock cylinder. To enter, the resident uses a key in the lock cylinder and then turns the lever to unlock the door.

It is sometimes desirable to leave a door with an exit device unlocked during certain hours of the day. This can be accomplished using a feature known as "dogging". This feature allows the cross bar or push pad to be pressed and locked into place, allowing free passage through the door. A key or special tool is usually required to lock the cross bar or push pad in place.

Exit devices can be installed on either wood or hollow-metal doors. Rim exit devices and exit devices with exposed vertical rods are typically installed at the site, while mortise exit devices and exit devices with concealed vertical rods often require that the door be ordered with the necessary openings to accommodate the hardware.

Exit devices provide excellent protection against physical attack. In some cases, it can be desirable to install exit devices on doors for their security benefits, even if not required by building codes.

The primary method that intruders use to defeat exit devices is to insert a tool through the door on the outside and use it to operate the cross bar or push pad on the inside. This is normally only a problem on double doors where there is a significant gap between the door leaves. This can be prevented by installing an astragal to cover the gap.

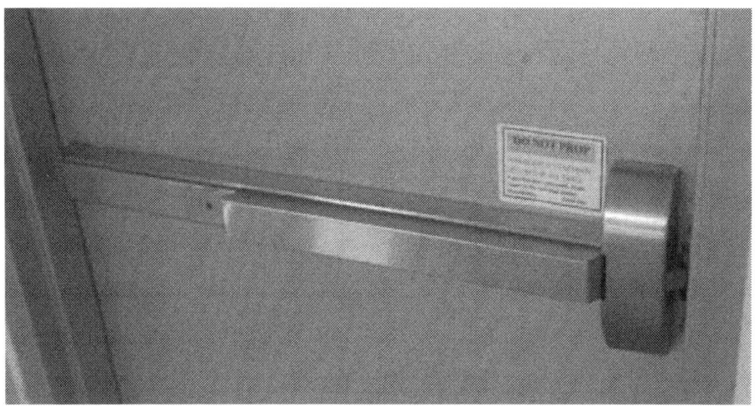

Figure 8-4 - Rim Exit Device

Figure 8-5 - Lever Handle Trim with Keyed Lock Cylinder Used with Exit Device

Aluminum Storefront Door Locks

Because aluminum storefront doors are constructed very differently than either wood or hollow-metal doors, a different type of lock is required to secure them. These locks are specially designed to fit in the limited space available in the aluminum door. Three types of locks are commonly used: the deadlock, the deadlatch, and the exit device.

The deadlock consists of a lock body that recesses into the edge of the door. This lock body has a large steel bolt that swings out and recesses within a strike plate on the door frame. In some cases, the bolt is hook shaped so that it better grasps the strike plate. The bolt is extended and retracted from the outside using a keyed lock cylinder. The bolt is extended and retracted from the inside using either a thumb-turn or keyed lock cylinder. Because the latch must be extended and retracted manually, deadlocks are best suited for use on doors that are left open for an extended period of time, such as a door to a public lobby that is left open during daytime hours.

The deadlatch is similar to the deadlock, except uses a latch rather than a bolt. This allows the latch to be retracted to unlock the door, but once the door is closed again, it automatically relocks. This makes the deadlatch better suited for use on building entrance doors, where the ability for the door to automatically relock is desired. The latch is momentarily retracted from the outside using a keyed lock cylinder. A thumb-turn or push paddle is provided to retract the latch from the inside of the door.

Exit devices are often used on aluminum storefront doors that are considered by code to be emergency exits. These exit devices are nearly identical to those used on wood or hollow-metal doors, except use thinner bodies that allow them to be mounted on the narrow aluminum frame. There are also special exit devices made specifically for aluminum storefront doors, as well as aluminum storefront doors that have exit devices built within the door itself.

Figure 8-6 - Deadlock on Aluminum Storefront Door

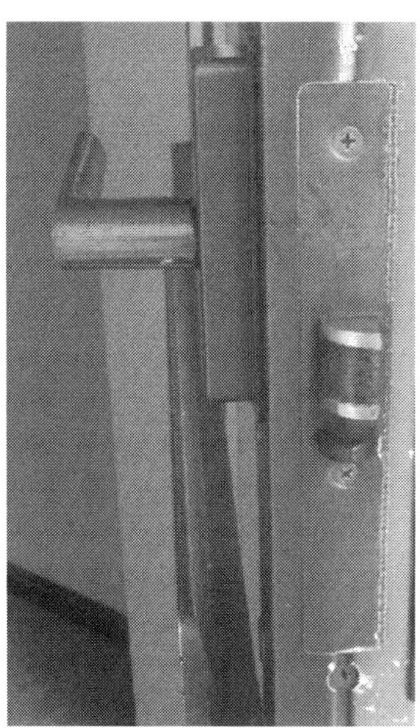

Figure 8-7 - Deadlatch Used on Aluminum Storefront Door

Fire-Rated Lock Hardware

All lock hardware used on fire-rated doors must also be appropriately fire-rated. Some functionality found in regular lock hardware may not be available in fire-rated hardware. For example, the dogging feature is not available in fire-rated exit devices because fire rated doors must always remain closed and latched. Dogging the door open would leave it unlatched, something that is never permissible for a fire-rated door.

When adding lock hardware to a fire-rated door, be sure that it has a fire rating that is equal to or better than that provided by the door itself.

Lock Functions

Cylindrical locksets and mortise locksets are available in many different configurations, each which provide different capabilities. The capabilities of a lock are known as its "function". While locks may look identical in appearance, their function determines how they operate.

While there are fifty or more different lock functions, the following five are most commonly used at multifamily properties:

Entrance Function

Entrance function locksets have a lever with a keyed lock cylinder on the outside, and a lever with a pushbutton on the inside. The outside lever is normally locked, requiring the use of a key to enter. The inside lever is always unlocked, allowing free egress. The pushbutton on the inside lever can be pressed to unlock the outside lever, allowing free passage in either direction.

In multifamily buildings, entrance function locksets are typically used at the entrances to the individual residential units. Entrance function locksets should not be used at building entrances or on doors to common areas at multifamily properties because they have the potential to be left in the unlocked position by anyone who has access to the inside of the door.

Storeroom Function

Storeroom function locksets have a lever with a keyed lock cylinder on the outside, and a plain lever inside. The outside lever is always locked, requiring the use of a key to enter. The inside lever is always unlocked, allowing free egress.

Storeroom function locksets should be used at building entrances and on doors to common areas at multifamily properties. Storeroom function locksets should also be used on doors that provide access to stairways when the ability to control access to individual floors is desired. When used on stairway doors, storeroom function locks allow free egress to the stairways from the floor, but require the use of a key to reenter the floor from the stairway.

Classroom Function

Classroom function locksets have a lever with a keyed lock cylinder on the outside, and a plain lever inside. The outside lever is locked, requiring the use of a key to enter. The inside lever is always unlocked, allowing free egress. In this way, classroom function locks are identical to storeroom function locks, except that the classroom function lock also has the capability to be left in an unlocked condition at times when this is desired.

To allow the outside lever to be left in the unlocked position, a key is inserted in the lock cylinder and turned 360 degrees. The outside lever can be relocked again by turning the key 360 degrees in the opposite direction.

The ability to leave the outside lever unlocked is similar to that provided by the entrance function lockset, except with a classroom function lockset, the lever can only be left unlocked by an authorized person with a key.

At multifamily properties, classroom function locksets can be useful to control access to areas that must be left open at certain times, such as a party room that must be left unlocked when an event is taking place.

Privacy Function

Privacy function locksets have levers on the inside and outside that allow free passage in either direction. There is a button on the inside lever that allows the outside lever to be locked, preventing entry when a person is on the inside. In case of emergency, privacy locksets can be opened from the outside using a tool.

At multifamily properties, privacy function locksets are used primarily on the doors to restrooms and changing rooms.

Passage Function

Passage function locksets have levers on the inside and outside that allow free passage in either direction at all times. Passage function locksets are used to keep a door latched, but provide no security.

At multifamily properties, passage function locksets are most commonly used on doors to rooms where there is no need to control access, and on stair doors where there is no desire to control access to the individual floors.

Lock Grades

Lock hardware is available in many different grades, ranging from light residential grade products to heavy-duty commercial products. While residential grade hardware may be suitable for use on individual residential units, commercial grade hardware is the best choice for use on common area doors at multifamily properties.

A grading system for commercial lock hardware has been developed collaboratively by the American National Standards Institute (ANSI) and the Builders Hardware Manufacturers Association (BHMA). This system establishes three grades of lock hardware:

ANSI/BHMA Grade 1

Grade 1 products represent the best quality products available in their class and are suitable for use in all industrial, commercial, and residential applications.

ANSI/BHMA Grade 2

Grade 2 products are considered to be very good, but not as good as Grade 1 products. Grade 2 products are suitable for use in light commercial and residential applications.

ANSI/BHMA Grade 3

Grade 3 products are good, but less durable than Grade 1 and Grade 2 products. Grade 3 products are designed to be used with less frequency and in less abusive environments than products in the other grades. Grade 3 products are suitable for use in residential applications.

The primary difference between grades depends on the number of operating cycles that a product can endure before it fails. This varies by product type. Separate categories have been established for cylindrical locks, mortise locks, exit devices, and other types of hardware products. As an example of the difference between grades, Grade 1 cylindrical locks can withstand five times the number of operating cycles that Grade 3 cylindrical locks can.

The locks used on the common area doors of larger multifamily properties are usually subject to the same conditions found at a commercial property. Consequently, it is recommended that a minimum of Grade 2 be specified for use at multifamily properties, with Grade 1 products being preferable. This is one of those cases where you literally get what you pay for, and specifying lower grade products can actually cost you more in the long run.

Lock Cylinders and Keys

Most types of locks consist of two separate parts, the lock body, which contains the lock mechanism itself, and the lock cylinder, which is the part in which you insert the key. Lock cylinders each use a specific keyway, which in most cases corresponds with the brand of lock being used. For example, if a Schlage brand cylindrical lock was purchased, it would most often come with a Schlage keyway and use a Schlage key.

Some types of locks, such as mortise locks and exit devices, use what are known as "mortise lock cylinders". These cylinders are generally interchangeable, allowing any brand cylinder to be used with any lock that accepts a mortise cylinder.

While numerous types of lock technologies are available, the one most commonly used today is the pin tumbler lock cylinder. This technology was developed more than 150 years ago and is widely used throughout the world. Despite their widespread use, pin tumbler lock cylinders and keys have many weaknesses that make them less than ideal from a security standpoint. These weaknesses include:

- Pin tumbler lock cylinders can be "picked" or "bumped" open. Lock picking involves the use of tools known as lock picks which are inserted in the keyway to manipulate the lock pins. Lock bumping is accomplished by inserting a special bump key into the keyway and hitting it with a hammer or other object. Both lock picks and bump keys can be readily purchased online. Instructional videos on how to pick and bump locks are widely available on the internet. Lock picking has become a recreational activity known as "locksport" and has many enthusiastic followers. While the majority of people engaged in locksport are honest, some criminals have also learned these techniques and use them to carry out crimes.
- Many pin tumbler lock cylinders are constructed of soft metals and can be easily defeated by drilling into the face of the cylinder.
- The keys used with pin tumbler lock cylinders can be easily duplicated by anyone at a locksmith shop, hardware store, or home improvement store. It is also possible to duplicate keys at self-service kiosks located in retail stores and shopping centers. Simply stamping "*Do Not Duplicate*" on a key does little to prevent it from being copied. Once a key has been issued to a resident or contractor, there is no telling how many unauthorized copies of the key may have been made.

Special high-security lock systems have been developed to overcome the weaknesses of standard pin tumbler lock cylinders and keys. These systems use advanced lock technologies that make the lock cylinders much more resistant to "picking" or "bumping". In addition, these lock cylinders have components that make them more difficult to drill or force open. The combination of these features creates a lock cylinder that is extremely difficult for the average intruder to compromise.

High-security lock cylinders use patented keyways, and the distribution of keys and key blanks is strictly controlled. Additional keys can only be ordered through authorized channels, and only by authorized people. When a high-security key is issued and returned, the property manager can have a high degree of confidence that an unauthorized copy has not been made.

Figure 8-8- High-Security Keys

High-security lock manufacturers offer cylinders that fit many popular brands of locks, allowing a high-security lock cylinder to be installed in an existing lock. This eliminates the need to replace the entire lock – just the cylinder can be replaced.

High-security lock cylinders and keys are considerably more expensive than standard versions of these products, with high-security keys costing as much as ten times or more of the cost of standard keys. However, the security benefits that they provide makes the additional cost a wise investment in most cases.

High-security lock cylinders and keys are highly recommended at multifamily properties. If budget does not permit the installation of high-security lock cylinders on all doors, then at a minimum they should be used on all building entrance doors and on doors to common area rooms. Standard locks can continue to be used on other doors. This will in most cases require that residents carry at least two keys, one for the high-security locks, and another for the standard locks. [9]

It should be noted that high-security lock cylinders are not "unpickable". There are a number of highly-skilled individuals in the country who can defeat them using specialized knowledge and the right tools. However, overcoming these locks usually requires capabilities that go far beyond those possessed by the average street criminal.

Keying of Locks

Once the types of lock cylinders and keys that will be used at the property have been determined, the next step is to determine how the lock system will be "keyed". On new construction projects, this process is normally facilitated by a hardware consultant. For existing properties, this process is normally handled by a locksmith working in consultation with property management and maintenance staff. The process involves creating a matrix that shows all doors in the buildings, and establishing which categories of people need access through each of the specific doors.

Once this process is completed, the hardware consultant or locksmith will design the keying system and create a keying chart. This chart may be simple or complicated depending on the type of facility and total number of doors to be controlled. An example of a simple keying chart is shown below.

---

[9] Some manufacturers may offer keys that are capable of working in both their high-security locks and their regular locks, eliminating the need for residents to carry two keys.

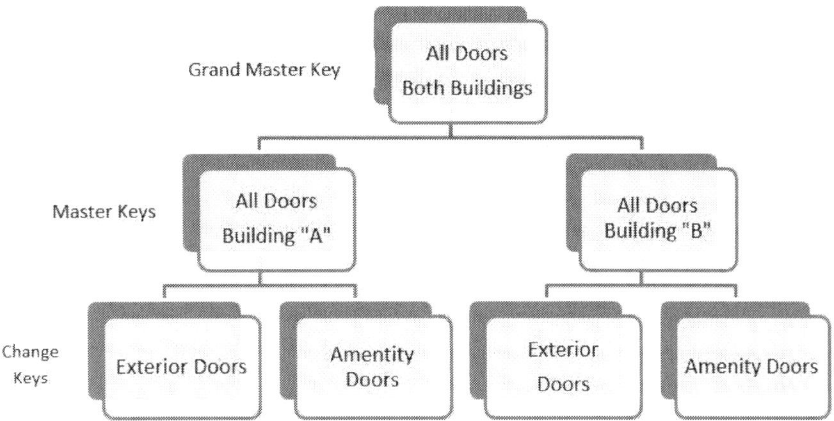

Figure 8-9 - Keying Chart

The chart above shows three levels of keying for a condominium that consists of two buildings . The keys at the lowest level are known as "change keys". These keys operate a single door or group of doors that are alike. In the example above, there are two change keys for each building: one that operates the exterior doors, and one that operates the doors to amenity areas. The change key that operates the exterior doors at Building "A" would not operate the exterior doors at Building "B" or vice versa. Similarly, the key that operates the amenity doors at Building "A" would not operate the amenity doors at Building "B" or vice versa.

The keys at the next level are known as "master keys". These keys allow access to all of the areas shown below them on the keying chart. For example, in the chart above, the Building "A" master key would operate both the exterior doors and amenity doors at Building "A". Similarly, the master key for Building "B" would operate both the exterior doors and amenity doors at Building "B". However, the master key for Building "A" would not operate the doors at Building "B" or vice versa.

The key at the top of the chart is known as the "grand master key". This key would allow access to all doors at both Building "A" and Building "B".

The design of a keying system can be a very complex subject and this book just touches on some of the basics. However, when designing a keying system, the following should be considered:

- There is always a trade-off between security and convenience. While it is very convenient for a manager to have a grand master key that opens every door on the property, consider the damage that would be caused if this key fell into the wrong hands. Also, having such a key lost or stolen would require rekeying the entire property. If the property had lots of locks, this would be very costly.
- When using standard security lock cylinders, master keying makes the lock more susceptible to both "picking" and "bumping".
- The master-keying of residential units creates great security risks and is not recommended at most multifamily properties. Residential units should be keyed to individual change keys. If there is a need to store keys for residential units in a central location, it should be done using good key control procedures (See page 270.)
- There is sometimes a need to key locks so that they are not part of the master key system. This is called keying "off-master" and is used when access to an area must be tightly controlled. For example, there may be a room that contains sensitive personal and financial information about

residents and only one or two people are authorized to have access to it. However, keying locks off-master should be done sparingly, otherwise you may end up with a complicated and unwieldy key system.

- The keying system should be designed to accommodate future growth. For example, if you are constructing one building on a property that is expected to eventually have three buildings, the keying system should be designed with this in mind.

When an access control system is used, the card reader controlled doors often have lock cylinders on them to allow the door to also be opened with a key. These lock cylinders should not be keyed to any key that is routinely carried by residents or employees. Having the ability to open an access-controlled door with both a key and a card defeat many of the benefits provided by the access control system. For example, the access control system can't provide a record of entry if a person uses a key rather than a card to enter. Also, revoking the access privileges of a card does no good if the person with the card still has a key that opens the door.

To provide a backup means of access in case of extended system failure, the lock cylinders on access-controlled doors can be keyed to a special "emergency key". Copies of these keys would be kept in a secure location and handed out only in the event that the access control system was to be out of service for an extended period of time. The keys would be retrieved when operation of the access control system was restored.

Rekeying Locks

Most lock cylinders are capable of being rekeyed to allow them to be used with a different key. For example, most multifamily properties routinely rekey the lock cylinders on residential units when one resident moves out and another moves in. This typically requires that the cylinder be removed and disassembled so that new pins corresponding to a new key can be installed. The lock cylinder is then reinstalled, and the new key is given to the new resident. This process requires the services of a locksmith [10] and there is a cost involved anytime a lock is rekeyed. There can also be a delay between when the locksmith is called and when he or she can respond to rekey the lock.

There are two types of lock cylinders designed to make the rekeying process quicker and more convenient:

<u>Interchangeable Core Lock Cylinders</u>

Interchangeable core (IC) lock cylinders consist of two parts, a housing that goes into the lock, and a core that slides into the housing. The core is the part that the key is inserted in and contains the pins. The core can be removed using a special key known as a "control key".

To rekey a lock, the user uses the control key to remove the existing core, and then inserts a new core that is keyed to a different key. This process can be done in seconds, allowing locks to be quickly rekeyed.

Most multifamily properties who use IC lock systems keep a supply of spare cores and keys on hand so that locks can be changed immediately on residential units when a tenant moves out. IC lock systems can also allow all common area doors to rekeyed quickly if a common area key has been lost or stolen.

---

[10] Some larger properties may have in-house maintenance staff that is capable of rekeying locks and making new keys.

IC lock cylinders are more expensive than standard lock cylinders, but the additional cost is often offset over time through reduction in the costs of rekeying. There are also some limitations on the types of locks available with IC lock cylinders.

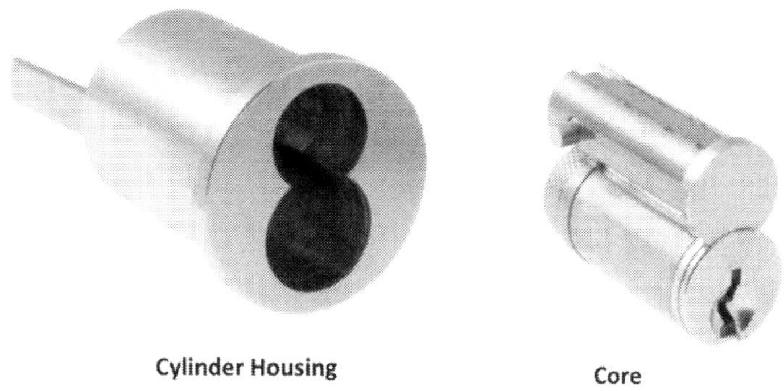

Figure 8-10 - Interchangeable Core Lock Cylinder

"Quick-Change" Lock Cylinders

Some manufacturers produce what are called "quick-change" locks. These locks allow the cylinder to be reset to a new key without disassembling the lock or replacing the pins. This is typically done by inserting the existing key, turning it to a special position, and then using a tool to activate the change feature. Without turning the key, the existing key is then removed, and the new key is inserted. The new key is then turned, causing the lock to be reset to the new key.

The use of quick-change locks is particularly popular at rental properties that have frequent turnover. However, properties who use these locks should be aware of their potential limitations. Some early models of these locks were notoriously easy for a criminal to defeat using tools and techniques widely available on the internet. Later models offered better protection but could still be defeated by a skilled attacker.

It is recommended that you conduct research to determine any vulnerabilities associated with the quick-change locks that you are using or contemplating buying.

Specialty Locks

There are a number of types of specialty locks that may be used at multifamily properties:

Padlocks

Padlocks are widely used at multifamily properties to secure outdoor gates, storage lockers, and various types of equipment. Padlocks range widely in shape, size, and quality. Padlocks can cost as little as three dollars or less, or as much as several hundred dollars or more.

Most inexpensive padlocks can be quickly compromised by a criminal, using techniques such as cutting or breaking the shackle, using a shim to release the shackle, or drilling or picking the lock cylinder. There are also various methods that allow the code of combination type padlocks to be determined within minutes.

More expensive padlocks have features that make them more difficult to compromise. These features include the use of high-security lock cylinders, hardened metals, enclosure of the shackle, and other devices that make the lock more difficult to pick or drill.

The important thing is to match the type of padlock used with the value of the asset being protected. It would be unwise to use a three-dollar padlock to secure a storage locker that contained tens of thousands of dollars' worth of equipment. It would be equally unwise to spend $300 for a padlock that is used to lock a trash container.

Most manufacturers of high-security lock cylinders also offer high-security padlocks. When purchasing a padlock that will be used for securing higher-value assets, look for the following features:

- Lock shackle diameter at least 12 mm.
- Hardened alloy steel shackle.
- Double ball bearing shackle locking mechanism that is shim resistant.
- Hardened anti-drill plates on lock body.
- Protective shroud around shackle.
- High-security lock cylinder to resist picking.

Because of the ease in which most combination padlocks can be compromised, they should never be used for securing anything other than low value assets. If a padlock with a standard pin tumbler lock cylinder is used rather than a high-security lock cylinder, choose a five or six pin cylinder over a four pin cylinder. (more pins equal increased resistance to picking).

The type of hasp used should match the quality of the padlock. When a higher security padlock is used, the hasp should be constructed of hardened steel. The hinge pins used should be constructed of hardened steel and be protected against attack. The fasteners used to secure the hasp should be fully concealed and protected when the hasp is locked.

Cabinet and Cam Locks

Cabinet locks are small locks used to secure cabinets and access doors to things such as payment drop boxes. Cam locks are small locks used to secure electrical enclosures and various types of equipment. While some cabinet and cam locks use pin tumbler lock cylinders, many use wafer lock cylinders.

Most standard cabinet locks and cam locks can be "picked" open in seconds and should not be relied upon for security. Most manufacturers of high-security lock cylinders also offer high-security versions of cabinet and cam locks, and these should be used when higher value assets are being protected.

Surface and Flush Bolts

Surface bolts are a simple type of lock hardware used to secure doors. The most common use of surface bolts is to secure the inactive leaf of a double door. When used for this purpose, surface bolts are installed inside of the door at the top and bottom edge of the inactive leaf. Strike plates are installed at the door frame at the top and on the floor at the bottom. To lock the door leaf in place, the surface bolts are manually slid into the strike plates. To open the door leaf, the bolts are slid out of the strike plates, allowing the door leaf to be opened.

Surface bolts are also sometimes used as a supplementary lock on a door, or as the only lock on a door when it is opened exclusively from the inside. Surface bolts are never used on doors that must be opened from the outside as there is no means to retract the bolt from this side.

Flush bolts are similar to surface bolts, but are installed concealed within the edge of the door leaf rather than on the surface of the door. There are recessed levers on the side of the door that are used to manually extend and retract the bolts. There are also automatic flush bolts. These automatically lock the inactive leaf when the active leaf is closed, and automatically unlock the inactive leaf when the active leaf is opened.

Figure 8-11 - Types of Surface and Flush Bolts

Surface and flush bolts are used at double doors where only one leaf of the door is normally needed for entry and exit, but there is occasionally a need to open both leaves. An example would be a door to a storage room, where tenants normally use only one door leaf to get in and out, but occasionally open the second leaf to load and unload larger objects.

There are specific code restrictions on using surface and flush bolts on emergency egress doors and fire-rated doors. The use of these devices may be prohibited entirely, or there may be special requirements for the type of hardware used and the way that it is installed.

Flush bolts can be problematic from a security standpoint as these bolts often extend only a short distance into the door frame. This can be a particular problem on older and poorly fitting doors, where the bolt can often protrude into the frame a quarter-inch or less. Often the hole in the floor for the bottom strike becomes clogged with debris, preventing the bolt from extending fully into the strike.

The amount of security provided by surface bolts varies greatly by their design. Some bolts are designed primarily for their architectural appearance and are constructed of very weak metals that provide very little strength. Other surface bolts are constructed of rugged materials and are very strong.

For best security, surface bolts rather than flush bolts should be used. The surface bolts should be the heavy-duty type. The strike plates for the surface bolts should be securely fastened into the door frame. When mounting to wood frames, the mounting screws for the strike plates should extend through the wood frame and into the header above.

For doors with existing flush-bolts, it is usually possible to add surface bolts to the door by disabling the flush-bolt rods and leaving the rest of the flush bolt mechanism in place.

Hinges and Pivots

Hinges are used on wood and hollow-metal doors to connect the door to the door frame.

Hinges are available in a wide variety of different types, styles, and finishes. The most common type of hinge is the butt hinge. Like locksets, hinges are available in several ANSI/BHMA grades. Grade 1 hinges are considered heavy duty hinges, Grade 2 hinges are considered standard-duty hinges, and Grade 3 hinges are considered light-duty hinges. Fire-rated hinges are available for use on fire-rated doors.

While little thought is usually given to hinges, they can be one of the first points of failure on a heavily-used door. The result is a door that sags and fails to close and lock properly. The hinges used on all exterior doors at multifamily properties should be heavy-duty Grade 1 hinges with ball bearings.

Hinges are normally installed at the top, middle and bottom of each door. Some taller or wider doors may have additional hinges. The largest percentage of the weight of the door is carried by the top hinge, so this is usually the one that is first to fail. For doors that are very heavily used or subject to abuse, the use of continuous hinges should be considered. Continuous hinges extend from the top to the bottom of the entire door, providing better distribution of the door's weight across the entire hinge.

In-swinging doors have their hinges on the inside, while out-swinging doors have their hinges on the outside. Many hinges have removable hinge pins that allow the two halves of the hinge to be separated. This can be useful when it is necessary to temporarily remove a door for maintenance purposes, but can also pose a security vulnerability on out-swinging doors – an intruder can simply remove the hinge pins to gain entry.

To solve this problem, hinges with non-removable hinge pins can be used, or security studs can be provided that prevent the removal of the door even if the hinge pins are removed. Some hinges have security studs built-in. Security studs can also be easily and inexpensively added to existing hinges and doors.

Pivots are similar to hinges, except are attached at the top and bottom of the door rather than to the side of the door frame. Pivots are most commonly used on aluminum storefront doors and all glass doors.

Door Closers

Door closers are used to automatically close a door after it is used. Door closers are used on doors where it is intended that the door be closed at all times. Door closers are almost always used on security doors because it is important that these doors automatically close and lock. It does no good to have a lock on a door if the door is left open. For similar reasons, door closers are important for use on fire-rated doors as it is essential that these doors remain closed and latched in order to prevent the spread of fire and smoke.

There are different types of door closers and different methods of mounting them depending on the conditions at the door. Door closers can be installed on either the door or frame, or on the inside or outside of the door. There are also concealed door closers that can be installed at the head of the door or in the floor.

While at first door closers may be thought of as simple devices, they actually are complex mechanisms, controlling both the speed and force of the door throughout the opening and closing cycle.

Like other types of hardware, door closers are available in several different ANSI/BHMA grades. Grade 1 closers are considered heavy-duty, Grade 2 closers are considered standard-duty, and Grade

3 closers are considered light-duty. The door closers used on all exterior doors at multifamily properties should be heavy-duty Grade 1 closers.

Door closers are available that have a built-in hold open mechanism. This can be useful when it is necessary to hold a door open for loading and unloading, but can create a security vulnerability in that the door can be deliberately or accidently left open by a resident. Property managers should weigh the benefits of having the hold open feature against the drawbacks of having it and make a decision erring on the side of good security.

Building codes require that fire-doors be kept closed at all times, however some codes allow a fire-door to be held open provided that a means to automatically close it when the fire alarm is activated be provided. Door closers used on fire-rated doors are available with a hold open feature that is electrically controlled. This provides the ability for the door closer to be connected to the building's fire alarm system. This allows the door to be held open when needed, but to automatically close when the fire alarm is activated. This functionality can also be provided by using a standard door opener with an external device known as an electromagnetic door holder. This device mounts to the wall or floor and holds the door open until the fire alarm is activated.

ADA Door Openers

ADA door openers are designed to automatically open doors for people with disabilities as required under the Americans With Disabilities Act (ADA). Although this law was originally intended to apply to commercial and institutional facilities rather than multifamily properties, some state and local laws may require ADA door openers at multifamily buildings. Multifamily projects that are government financed or subsidized may also need to meet ADA requirements. Even if not required by law, many property managers may choose to voluntarily install ADA door openers to make their buildings more accessible and more appealing to residents.

ADA door openers are installed in place of a regular door closer and are used to both open and close the door. ADA door openers can be activated using a variety of methods, including manual push buttons, motion detectors, and card readers. ADA door openers are programmed to keep the door open for a period of time after the door is opened to allow people to get through.

Figure 8-12 - Door with ADA Door Opener

To minimize the security vulnerabilities caused by ADA door openers, the following is recommended:

- Keep the time that the door is held open to a minimum to reduce opportunities for unauthorized people to enter the building.
- Use manual pushbuttons rather than motion detectors to activate the doors when possible.
- If motion detectors are used, adjust them so that they only detect motion near the door and are not activated by people passing by.
- Discourage use of the door opener by able-bodied people who don't need to use it.

Door Coordinators

Door coordinators are used on double doors to control the sequence in which the door leaves close. This is necessary when using certain types of door accessories such as astragals. If the leaves close in the wrong order, the door doesn't close properly. The door coordinator prevents the active leaf of the door from closing until the inactive leaf has fully closed.

There are two types of door coordinators available. The first type is known as a bar coordinator, which is installed along the top of the door frame on the inside of the door. The second type is known as a gravity coordinator, which is installed at the top of the door on the outside. The use of the bar coordinator is recommended at multifamily properties because it is less prone to vandalism.

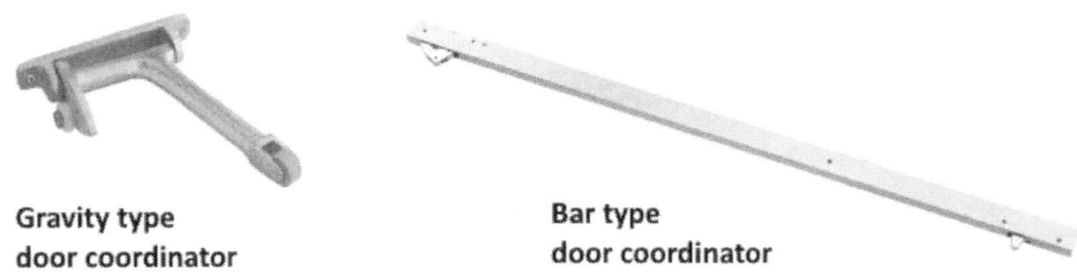

Figure 8-13 - Door Coordinators

Protective Devices

Criminals have devised numerous ways to compromise doors and lock hardware in order to gain entry into a building or secured area. There have been a number of products designed specifically to slow down criminals and make forced entry more difficult. Some of these products commonly used in multifamily properties include:

<u>Latch Guards</u>

On out-swinging doors, criminals often use a screwdriver or prybar to force a door open where the door latch meets the frame. On in-swinging doors, criminals often use a knife blade or thin piece of plastic to force back the door latch. To prevent these types of attacks, devices known as latch guards have been developed. Different types of latch guards are used on in-swinging and out-swinging doors.

Latch guards for out-swinging doors are rectangular metal plates that are installed on the outside edge of the door. This plate covers the area of the door and frame where the door latch is located to protect against attacks by tools.

Latch guards for in-swinging doors consist of two metal channels, one of which is installed on the door, the other which is installed on the door frame. When the door is closed, these channels interlock, preventing a tool from being used to manipulate the latch.

Out-Swinging Door

In-Swinging Door

Figure 8-14 - Latch Guards

Astragals

Astragals are similar to the latch guards used on out-swinging doors, but extend fully from the bottom to the top of the door. This provides complete protection of the gap between the door and door frame, protecting the latch and reducing the chances that the door can be forced open. Astragals cost more than latch guards but provide a greater level of protection.

Astragals can also be installed on double doors to prevent the use of what is known as a "double-door tool". Intruders can insert this tool in the gap between the door leaves and use it to activate the exit device push bar to unlock the door. Double-door tools are available for sale online and homemade versions of this tool can also be made.

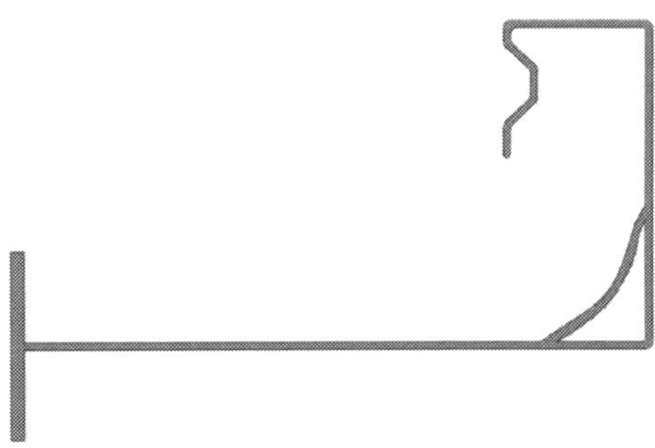

Figure 8-15 - Double-Door Tool

There are three types of commonly used astragals: the flat bar astragal, the interlocking astragal, and the automatic astragal. The flat bar astragal is simply a flat piece of metal that is attached to the door to cover the gap between the door and the frame. The interlocking astragal consists of two pieces, one installed on the door, and the other installed on the door frame. When the door is closed, the two pieces interlock. The automatic astragal is used on double doors when both door leaves are active. The automatic astragal stays out of place until both door leaves are closed, then snaps into place to cover the gap when the door is fully shut.

Figure 8-16 - Interlocking Astragal on Double Doors

Cylinder Protection

Mortise lock cylinders are used on wood and hollow-metal doors that have mortise locks or exit devices. Mortise lock cylinders are also used on aluminum storefront doors. Criminals commonly make forced entry through a door by using a wrench to twist the mortise lock cylinder from the outside, causing the door to unlock.

Several different types of devices have been designed to protect against this type of attack. The simplest of these is the cylinder guard ring. These devices have spinning collars that make it difficult for a wrench to turn the cylinder.

There are other devices that either partially or fully enclose the lock cylinder, leaving nowhere for a wrench to grip. The devices that fully enclose the cylinder also protect the cylinder from being drilled, another method of attack used by criminals. Some devices combine a cylinder guard with a latch guard, allowing a single device to serve both purposes.

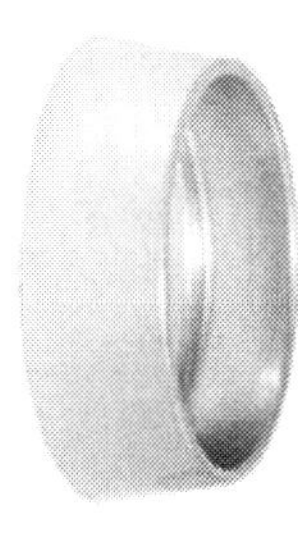

Figure 8-17 - Cylinder Protection Devices

Knob or Lever Protection

Cylindrical locks can be defeated by using a wrench to twist the entire lock body, causing the door to unlock. These locks can also be defeated by using a hammer to smash the lock. To protect against these types of attacks, there are devices known as knob guards or lever guards that can be attached to the outside of the door to fully enclose the exposed portion of the lock.

Knob guards and lever guards allow a key to be inserted to unlock the door and provide a handle that allows the door to be opened and closed.

Figure 8-18 - Lever Guard

Door Bottoms and Thresholds

When locksets with lever handles are used on doors, it is often possible to open them from the outside using a device known as an "under-door tool". This device is inserted in the gap underneath of the door and used to grab the inside handle of the lock, allowing entry. This instantly defeats any security that may be provided by the card reader or key-operated lock installed on the door.

Under-door tools can easily be purchased online. There are also instructions on the internet for making a homemade version of this tool. Under-door tools are often used by more sophisticated criminals and can allow entry to be made without leaving any signs of forced entry.

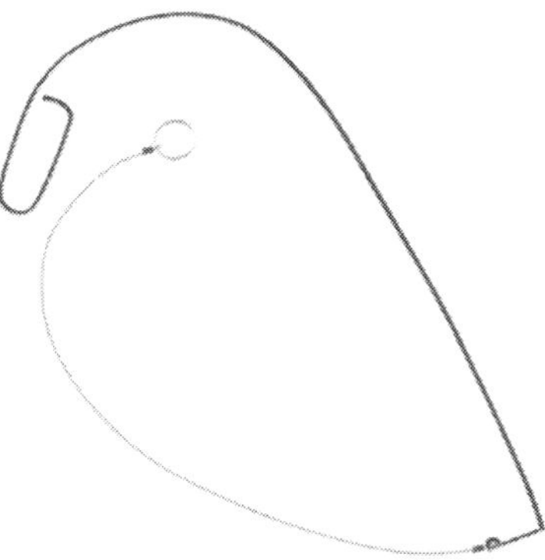

Figure 8-19 - Under-Door Tool

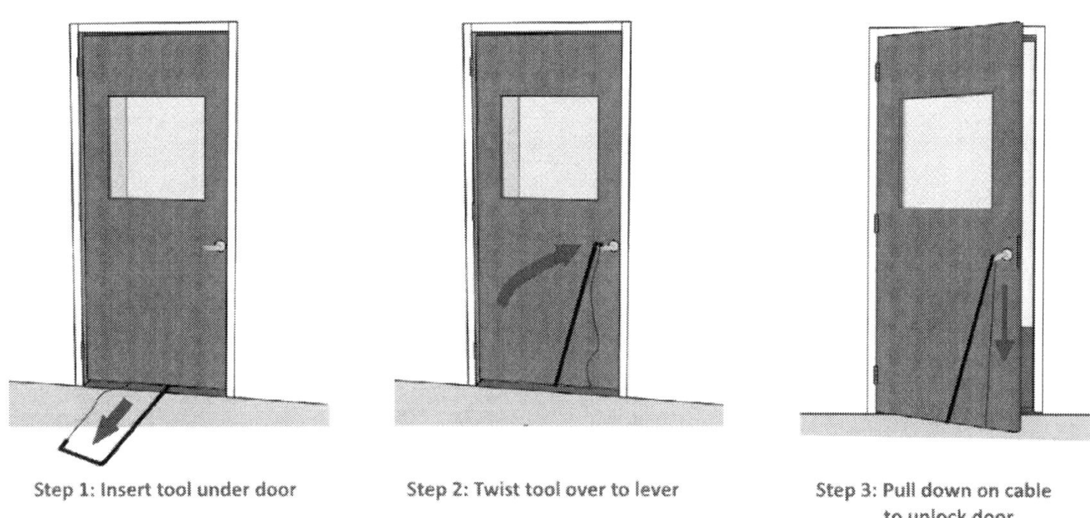

Figure 8-20 - Use of Under-Door Tool to Open Door (View from Inside)

This vulnerability can be reduced by using a combination of a threshold and door bottom on the door. The threshold is a strip of wood or metal installed on the floor directly underneath of the door. The door bottom, sometimes called a door sweep, is installed at the bottom of the door, and provides a seal that rests on top of the threshold. Most door bottoms provide a passive seal that is always in place. There are also automatic door bottoms that lower the seal when the door is closed. Automatic door bottoms provide a tighter seal because the seal is only deployed when the door is closed – there is no concern about the seal dragging on the floor as the door is opened.

The usual purpose of the threshold and door bottom is to provide protection against drafts and insects, but they also provide protection against the use of under-door tools. For even more protection, there are special automatic door bottoms made specifically for security. These have a retractable seal that rests against a protective stop bar installed on top of the threshold when the door is closed. This creates a rigid barrier that prevents an under-door tool from being inserted under the door.

Figure 8-21 - Door Bottom

Figure 8-22 - Threshold

Hinge Protection

Out-swinging doors have their hinges on the outside of the door. If the door has removable hinge pins, criminals can remove the pins and force the door open from the hinge side. To solve this problem, the existing hinges can be replaced with hinges that have non-removable hinge pins, or security studs can be added that prevent the removal of the door even if the hinge pins are removed.

There are several varieties of security studs available. One of the most popular types is installed by removing one of the existing hinge screws on one side of the hinge and replacing it with the security stud. The corresponding screw on the opposite side of the hinge is then removed and the hole drilled out to receive the security stud.

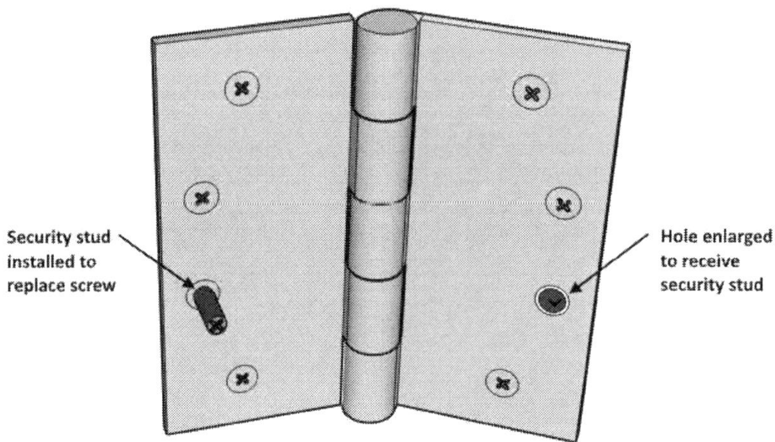

Figure 8-23 - Security Stud Installed on Hinge

Door and Frame Reinforcement

Wood doors and frames are inherently less secure than hollow-metal doors and frames. The weak point is at the door frame, where a thin piece of wood is typically the only thing that secures the strike plate for the door latch. In-swinging doors are particularly vulnerable because when the door is kicked, the full force of energy of the kick is transferred to the portion of the frame where the strike plate is attached. It is usually possible to break through the door with only one or two kicks.

One device used to increase the strength of wood door frames is the extended height strike plate. These can range in height from 8” to 18” and are used in place of the usual 2-1/2” high strike plate that comes with the lock. These extended height strike plates transfer the energy caused by a kick to be applied to a greater surface area of the frame. This reduces the amount of energy applied to any one area of the frame, decreasing the likelihood that the frame will break. The effectiveness of the extended height strike plate can be further improved by mounting it with long screws that extend through the wood frame and attach to the wood or metal studs behind.

Some manufacturers produce what is known as a “door and frame reinforcement kit”. These kits provide parts to reinforce the door, door frame, and hinge. These parts can be installed on an existing door and replace the existing strike plates used with the lock and deadbolt. When installed correctly, these kits can greatly increase the strength of a wood door and frame.

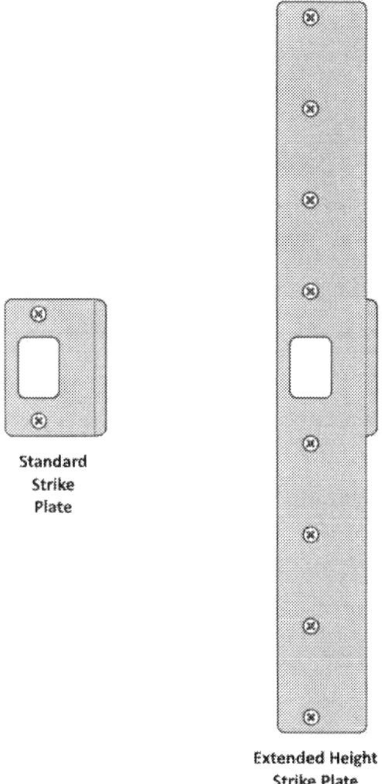

Figure 8-24 - Standard & Extended Height Strike Plates

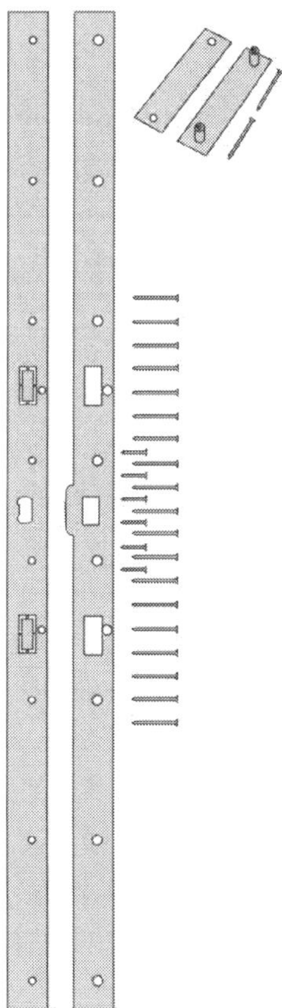

Figure 8-25 - Door and Frame Reinforcement Kit

Electric Locking Hardware

Electric locking hardware allows doors to be unlocked electrically in addition to being unlocked manually by a key. Electric locking hardware is necessary when a door is to be controlled by an access control system or security intercom system. Electric locking hardware is also used when it is necessary to unlock a door upon activation of a fire alarm system.

Here are the types of electric locking hardware commonly used at multifamily properties:

Electric Strikes

Electric strikes are used with cylindrical locksets, mortise locksets, and rim exit devices. Electric strikes may also be used with deadlatch locks on aluminum storefront doors. Electric strikes are installed on the door frame in place of the regular strike plate.

The electric strike consists of two primary parts, the strike body, and the keeper. When the door is closed, the door latch extends into the strike body and rests against the keeper. The keeper is held rigidly in place by an electrical mechanism in the strike body. The door is secure because the latch is held by the keeper, preventing the door from being opened. When the electric strike is activated, the electrical mechanism releases, allowing the keeper to be moved. This allows the door latch to come out of the strike body when pressure is applied to the door, allowing the door to be opened.

Electric strikes are less expensive than other types of electric lock hardware and are commonly used in conjunction with telephone entry systems and access control systems at multifamily properties. Electric strikes are also used with ADA door openers as they release the latch allowing the opener to open the door.

Electric strikes are not suitable for use on fire-rated doors that must automatically unlock when the fire alarm is activated. This is because the codes that require that fire-rated doors unlock on fire alarm state that the door must unlock, but not unlatch, when activated by the fire alarm. Electric strikes by their very nature are devices that unlatch a door, making them unsuitable for use in this application.

Electric strikes provide less security than other types of lock hardware because they introduce an additional point of weakness in the door, making it less resistant to physical attack. There can also be problems with the alignment of the door latch in relation to the electric strike that can allow the latch to be manipulated by an intruder. For these reasons, a latch guard or astragal should always be used on doors with electric strikes.

Figure 8-26 - Electric Strike

Electric Locks

Both cylindrical locksets and mortise locksets are available in electrically locking versions. These are often called "electric locks". Electric locks operate identically to storeroom function locksets, except that an electrical mechanism has been added to lock and unlock the outside lever handle. Under normal conditions, the outside lever remains rigid, preventing entry without using a key. When the electrical mechanism is activated, the outside lever is released, allowing it to be turned to gain entry through the door.

Because electric locks are mounted on the door, some method of getting the electrical wiring to the lock must be provided. This can be accomplished by using a door loop, which is a surface mounted armored cable between the door and the door frame, or by using an electric hinge, which is a special hinge that has wires within it.

Electric locks are excellent for use on fire doors that must unlock when the fire alarm is activated. This is because electric locks unlock, but do not unlatch, when the fire alarm is activated. Electric locks cannot be used on doors with ADA openers as they do not unlatch the door.

Exit Devices with Electrified Trim

Electrified trim can be used in conjunction with rim exit devices, mortise exit devices, and vertical rod exit devices. Electrified trim works identically to an electric lock. Like an electric lock, electrified trim is a good choice for use on fire-rated doors that must unlock when the fire alarm is activated. Electrified trim is unsuitable for use on doors with ADA door openers because it does not unlatch the door.

A door loop or electric hinge must be used with electrified trim to provide a means of getting wiring between the door and door frame.

Exit Devices with Latch Retraction

Latch retraction is a feature available with most rim exit devices and vertical rod exit devices. Latch retraction is accomplished by using a solenoid or small electric motor within the exit device to physically retract the latch or rods. Exit devices with the latch retraction feature are often called "latch retraction exit devices".

Latch retraction exit devices are used when it is necessary to physically unlatch a door, such as when a door is used with an ADA door opener. Latch retraction exit devices are not suitable for use on fire-rated doors that must unlock when the fire alarm is activated.

Latch retraction exit devices often require considerably more power to operate than other types of electric lock hardware. This can require that special power supplies be installed near the door and that heavier gauge wiring be used.

A door loop or electric hinge must be used with latch retraction exit devices. There are also devices known as electric power transfers that are specifically designed to transfer the wiring between the door and the door frame when latch retraction exit devices are used.

Electromagnetic Locks

Electromagnetic locks consist of two parts, a lock body, and an armature plate. The lock body is typically mounted to the top of the door frame, and the armature is installed on the door itself. When the door is closed, the armature plate rests against the lock body. The lock body contains an electromagnet. When power is applied to the electromagnet, a magnetic force firmly grips the armature plate. This holds the door in place with as much as 1,600 pounds or more of holding force.

Unlike other types of electric locking hardware, electromagnetic locks provide no mechanical means of unlocking them. The only way to release the electromagnet is by turning off the power to it. Common methods used to release power to an electromagnetic lock include push buttons, motion detectors, or special exit device bars with release switches. Electromagnetic locks can also be released by an access control system or security intercom system.

Because electromagnetic locks can be only released electrically and not mechanically, there are specific code requirements that restrict where they may be used and how they must be installed. In general, at least two methods of releasing the lock must be provided, and the lock must be connected to the fire alarm system so that it unlocks when the alarm is activated.

Most electromagnetic locks are mounted at the top of the door and only secure the door from the top edge. This can be a problem on certain types of doors because it is often possible to flex the bottom of the door a considerable distance when a person pulls on the door when it is locked. This can eventually cause warping of the door.

Electromagnetic locks require power to stay locked. While back-up batteries can keep the locks powered for a short period of time, buildings without an emergency generator may end up with unlocked doors if there is a power failure for an extended duration.

Because of the complexities and difficulties associated with electromagnetic locks, it is recommended that they not be used when the use of any other type of electric lock hardware is possible. Some installers who are not knowledgeable of lock hardware use electromagnetic locks as a one-size-fits-all solution and inappropriately install electromagnetic locks on doors where an electric lock or electric strike would have been a better choice.

A particularly problematic type of electromagnetic lock is the electromagnetic shear lock. These are often a popular choice of architects because the lock body can be completely concealed within the door frame. Unfortunately, experience with these types of locks at multifamily buildings has been almost entirely negative.

First of all, the door must align perfectly in order for these locks to work. If the door doesn't fully close and seat properly in the opening, the lock will not bond properly. It's tough to get a door to align perfectly when its new, and nearly impossible to keep it aligned properly as the door ages.

Second, most electromagnetic shear locks are very noisy. When the door closes, the electromagnet in the door frame pulls the armature mounted at the top of the door against the lock. This metal-on-metal contact can make a loud "clunking" sound that many users find annoying. This noise can be particularly pronounced in places that have hard acoustical surfaces such as building lobbies.

Figure 8-27 - Surface Mounted Electromagnetic Locks

Fail-Safe versus Fail-Secure Lock Hardware

Most electric lock hardware [11] is available in both a "fail-safe" and "fail-secure" version. Fail-safe hardware requires power to stay locked. When power is removed, the lock unlocks. Fail-safe hardware requires power to unlock. When power is removed, the lock stays locked.

Using fail-safe lock hardware on doors requires that power be continually available to keep the door locked. Batteries can be used to provide power for short periods, but during extended power failures, the doors will become unlocked unless a long-term source of emergency power (such as a generator) is available.

Fail-safe hardware is normally required on fire-rated doors that must automatically unlock when the fire alarm system is activated. An example would be stairway doors that are locked between the stairway and the floor. Many building codes require that these doors automatically unlock (but remain latched) to allow reentry from the stair to the floor when the fire alarm is triggered.

Unless specified otherwise by local codes, the hardware used on most doors should be fail-secure rather than fail-safe . Many people mistakenly specify fail-safe hardware on all doors because they want the building to be "safe" and think that using fail-safe hardware is necessary to comply with code. This is typically not the case, because when the right type of hardware is used, free egress is always possible by simply turning a lever or pushing a push pad, regardless of whether the hardware is fail-safe or fail-secure.

Delayed-Egress Locking Systems

Delayed-egress locking systems are a special system designed for use on emergency egress doors that pose a security risk. An example would be an emergency egress door out of a parking garage that

---

[11] Electromagnetic locks are only available in fail-safe versions.

provided access to a secured residential corridor in a multifamily building. Anyone who managed to sneak into the parking garage could use this door to gain access to the residential areas.

Exit alarms [12] do a good job of discouraging misuse of the emergency egress doors, but don't always stop a more aggressive intruder. This is because the intruder knows that it will take time for a resident or staff member to respond to the door when the alarm sounds. This gives the intruder ample time to pass through the door and be well within the building before anyone has a chance to respond.

In recognition of this problem, many building codes have been modified to allow the use of "delayed-egress locking systems" on emergency egress doors. The delayed egress locking system typically consists of an exit push bar, an auxiliary locking device, an audible alarm, and a special electronic control package. The delayed-egress locking system operates as follows:

1. When a person approaches the door to exit, they press on the exit push bar. This causes the audible alarm to immediately sound, but does not unlock the door.
2. The alarm continues to sound for a preset period (usually 15 seconds).
3. At the end of the preset period, the door unlocks, allowing free exit.

The advantage of the delayed-egress locking system is that it provides a delay between the time that a person activates the alarm and when the door actually unlocks. This delay gives additional time for a resident or staff member to respond to the door once the alarm has been activated. The delayed-egress locking system serves as a deterrent to the criminal who doesn't want to wait 15 seconds or more to pass through the door.

There are three basic types of delayed-egress locking systems.

The first type of delayed-egress system uses an electromagnetic lock in conjunction with either a standard mechanical push bar or an electronic "touch sense" bar. These types of systems usually require an external control panel.

The second type of delayed-egress system uses an electromagnetic lock that contains a built-in control system and a built-in "exit sensor". The exit sensor detects when the door is pushed open and eliminates the need for any special type of exit push bar. This makes it ideal for retrofit installations on existing exit doors.

The third type of delayed-egress system uses a special type of mechanical exit device. All components of this system are contained within the exit device itself. This type of system minimizes the number of components required at the door.

There are detailed building code requirements related to the installation of delayed-egress systems. These codes typically specify connection to the building's fire alarm system, the ability for the door to automatically unlock on power failure, emergency lighting at the door, and special signage.

Approval from local building code officials should always be obtained before installing a delayed-egress system. The use of these systems may be restricted or prohibited entirely in some jurisdictions.

[12] For more on exit alarms, see Chapter 13.

Figure 8-28 Delayed-Egress Device with Electromagnetic Lock

Door Viewers

Door viewers are installed on doors and provide the ability to see who is standing outside of the door before opening it. Door viewers are sometimes called "peephole viewers" or "peepholes". Door viewers are most commonly used at the entrance doors to residential units, but can also be used at other doors, such as the entry door to an office.

Standard door viewers provide a viewing angle of about 160 degrees. Some newer door viewers offer viewing angles as wide as 290 degrees, allowing the entire area outside of the door to be clearly seen.

The lenses used on door viewers make it easy to see from the inside to the outside of the door, but difficult to see from the outside to the inside. However, there are devices manufactured that are specifically designed to allow people to see through door viewers from the outside. While the risk of someone using this type of device is probably very small, users who have privacy concerns should install a privacy cover on the inside lens. This cover can be moved to the side to allow looking out, but left in place at other times to provide privacy. Privacy covers are built-in to some door viewers, or can be purchased as a separate add-on.

Door viewers should be securely fastened to the door so that they cannot be loosened from the outside.

Key Boxes

Key boxes are used on the exterior of multifamily properties to allow access to the site and buildings by authorized parties. Key boxes typically contain keys or access cards that allow entry through exterior doors and gates.

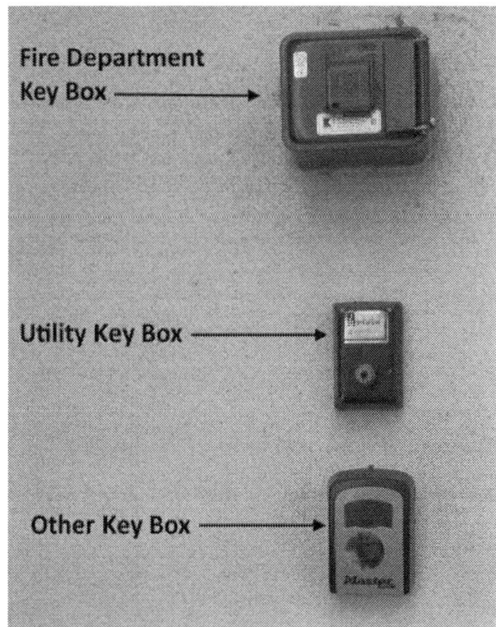

Figure 8-29 - Examples of Types of Key Boxes

The following types of key boxes are commonly used:

<u>Fire Department Key Boxes</u>

Many governmental agencies require that multifamily properties install key boxes on the exterior of their buildings to allow fire department access. These boxes are usually installed at primary building entrances and contain things such as master keys, access cards, and building floor plans. One major manufacturer of fire department key boxes is the Knox Company, so these key boxes are often called "Knox ® Boxes ".

Fire department key boxes are purchased and installed by the building owner. The boxes come without an exterior lock. After the box has been installed, the owner arranges an appointment with the fire department, who comes out to the site and installs the exterior lock. At this time, the owner places building master keys, access cards, and floor plans into the box, and it is locked by the fire department. Once the box has been locked, the owner no longer has access, and it can only be accessed by the fire department.

<u>Utility Company Key Boxes</u>

Many utility companies request that property owners allow them to install key boxes that provide access to the building. This can include cable companies, telephone companies and utility companies that provide power, water, and sewer.

Utility company key boxes typically contain an exterior door key to allow building access, and interior door keys that open the specific rooms where the utility company requires access.

<u>Real Estate Key Boxes</u>

At condominiums, co-ops, and gated communities, real estate agencies may request to install key boxes that contain the keys for properties that are up for sale. These keys would be used by real estate agents to show the properties. In addition to the keys to the residential units, these boxes often contain keys to the exterior of the building and to common areas such as fitness centers and party rooms.

Real estate key boxes are typically provided by the Multiple Listing Service (MLS) that is responsible for the geographical area where the property is located. All agents that belong to that MLS normally have access to the key box. Many of the lock boxes used by MLSs are very well constructed and have electronic tracking systems that provide accountability for who opened each box and when. Some MLSs may still be using older key boxes that are not as well constructed and provide no accountability.

Figure 8-30 - Real Estate Key Box

<u>Other Key Boxes</u>

Property managers may install other types of key boxes at the property for use by contractors or other service providers. Residents may install their own key boxes to allow access by housecleaners, dog walkers, short-term renters, and family members.

Key boxes can be a weak spot in the property's overall security program because anyone who has access to the key box has access to the building. An intruder who compromises a key box that contains a master key literally has the "keys to the castle" and can go almost anywhere that he or she wants.

The level of security provided by key boxes varies greatly. Most fire department key boxes and real estate key boxes are well-constructed and designed to resist attack. Other types of key boxes are often so poorly built that they can be compromised by an intruder in minutes. There are numerous online videos that show techniques for defeating many popular brands of key boxes. Most key boxes that use a mechanical combination type lock are particularly easy to open.

Intruders who compromise a key box and use a key to gain entry can often do so without leaving any signs of forced entry. Intruders who learn how to compromise a key box can make repeated entries into the building over a long period of time without being detected.

Here are some tips to minimize the risk of key boxes:

- Determine if there is really a need to have the key box on the property at all. A key box may not be needed if there is an alternative means for authorized people to gain access. This could be accomplished by using a telephone entry system to call an authorized person to gain entry, or by being let in by on-site property management staff or a security officer.
- The property manager should approve the use of all key boxes that contain exterior door keys and common area door keys. Residents should not be allowed to install key boxes without permission.

- The keys in key boxes should only provide access to the specific areas needed, not the entire building. For example, if the utility company needs to enter an electrical room to read meters, the key in the key box should only provide access to the exterior door closest to the electrical room and the electrical room itself.
- If the property has an access control system on the exterior doors, an access card should be placed in the key box rather than an exterior door key.
- Key boxes should be installed in a well-lit location that is visible from the street. Avoid having the key boxes installed in hidden or out-of-the way places.
- It is preferable to use wall-mounted key boxes rather than key boxes that are hasp-mounted to a doorknob or railing.
- Recess-mounted fire department key boxes are considerably more attack-resistant than surface mounted key boxes and should be used whenever possible. If you don't currently have a good place to install a recess-mounted box, consider constructing a concrete or masonry pillar next to the entrance just to hold the key box. An existing wall can also be faced with masonry veneer to provide a place where a recess-mounted box can be installed.
- If a key box will be surface mounted, make sure that it is rigidly attached to a structural support member and not fastened to just the wallboard or siding.
- Avoid mounting key boxes on the surface of doors. If a key box must be attached to a door, use bolts that extend fully through the door. Provide a backing plate or washers in conjunction with a nut on the inside of the door. Key boxes fastened using wood or sheet metal screws attached only to the exterior skin of the door can usually be easily removed.
- Rather than allowing real estate key boxes to be mounted anywhere, the property manager should establish a central location on the property where these key boxes are to be installed. The real estate key boxes should be securely fastened to a suitable mounting surface such as a pipe or railing. This mounting surface should make it difficult for the key boxes to be removed.
- If your building has an access control system or intrusion alarm system, consider equipping your fire department key box with tamper switches connected to one of these systems. This will allow property management or security staff to be notified whenever the box is opened or removed from the wall.

Key-Operated Switches

Key operated switches, commonly called "key switches", provide a means to use a key to operate an electrical circuit. Key-operated switches are used to control automatic gates, overhead doors, elevators, and other electrically-operated equipment.

Key-operated switches are commonly used at smaller properties that don't have an access control system to operate things such as elevators. In facilities that have automatic gates, local regulations often require that a fire department key switch be installed to give emergency responders a way to gain access through the gate in an emergency. Some utilities, such as gas or electric companies, may also require that a key switch be provided to give their crews access to the site.

Figure 8-31 - Key-Operated Switches

There are two types of key switches: switch locks, and mortise key switches.

Switch locks are self-contained devices that consist of a lock mechanism and a built-in electrical switch. Switch locks are compact units that can usually be mounted in a 3/4" hole. The limitation of switch locks is that they are available in only a limited number of keyways. This means that in most cases, they cannot be keyed to the building's regular key system, requiring that separate keys for the switch lock be issued to users.

Mortise key switches consist of two parts, a key switch mechanism, and a mortise lock cylinder. The advantage of mortise key switches is that they can be used with virtually any type of lock cylinder. This allows them to be keyed to the building's regular key system, letting users operate the key switch using the same key that they use at other doors.

The disadvantage of mortise key switches is that they are relatively large, requiring that they be flush-mounted in the wall or installed in a surface mounted box. Many mortise key switches use a standard single-gang or double-gang faceplate, allowing them to be mounted to standard electrical boxes.

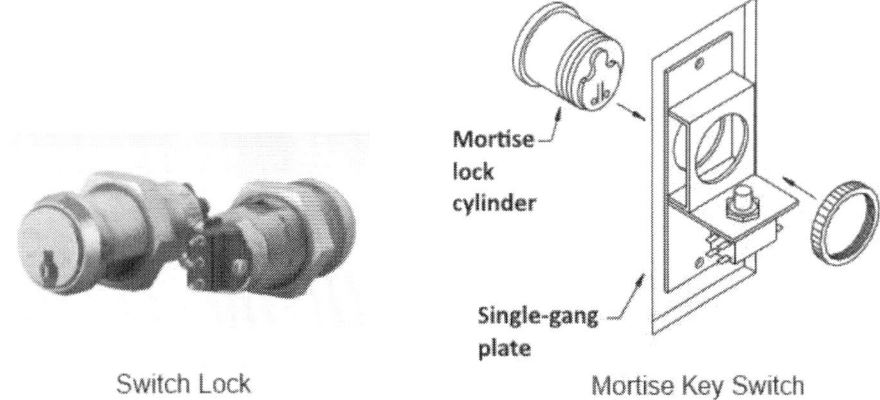

Figure 8-32 - Types of Key-Operated Switches

Chapter 9: Windows

Vulnerabilities of Glass

Glass windows are a vulnerable point of entry on the exterior of a building. Criminals are quick to exploit this vulnerability, making entry through a broken window a popular technique used by burglars.

From a pure security standpoint, a building would be designed with no glass on the exterior. However, this would be impractical in most cases and would create a building that no one would want to live or work in. Many building codes also have requirements for windows and constructing a building without windows would probably never be allowed.

While windows cannot be eliminated entirely, their vulnerability should be recognized, and every effort taken to make them as secure as possible.

Types of Glass

Window glass is available in a variety of different types and thicknesses. The following are some common types of glass used at multifamily properties:

The first type of glass is annealed glass. This type of glass can be easily broken, and when shattered, breaks into large shards. Annealed glass is the least expensive type of glass and the type that has been the most extensively used in construction projects over the last fifty years.

The second type of glass is heat-strengthened glass, which is annealed glass that has been heated and cooled to improve its strength. Heat strengthened glass is about twice as strong as annealed glass.

The third type of glass is tempered glass, which is annealed glass that has also been heated, but subjected to a quicker cooling process. This creates a product that is four to five times stronger than annealed glass, making it more difficult to break. When tempered glass does break, it shatters into many small pieces rather than large shards. Despite its increased strength, tempered glass can actually be easier for an intruder to penetrate because once the window is shattered, there are no obstacles to entry.

The fourth type of glass is laminated glass, which is created by laminating two sheets of glass together with a sheet of polyvinyl butyral (PVB) film. When impact is applied to laminated glass, the glass breaks, but the broken glass shards are held together by the PVB film. This makes it more difficult to penetrate a laminated glass window than either an annealed glass window or tempered glass window. The strength of laminated glass is directly proportional to the thickness of the PVB film. Laminated glass that uses a thicker film is sometimes called "impact resistant glass" and is used in areas where tornados and hurricanes are prevalent. Laminated glass, and particularly impact resistant glass, provide greater protection against forced entry than other types of glass.

The fifth type of glass is insulated glass, which is created by combining two or more sheets of glass into what are known as insulated glass units (IGUs). The glass panes are separated by a vacuum or space filled with gas. Either heat strengthened glass, tempered glass, or laminated glass can be used to create IGUs. Windows constructed using IGUs are sometimes called "double-pane windows" or "triple-pane" windows. These windows are more difficult for an intruder to penetrate as there are multiple layers of glass to go through. Double or triple pane windows that use laminated glass can provide a reasonable level of protection against forced entry.

There is a concern that people will get injured by glass shards when a window is broken. This could occur when a person accidently falls through a window or breaks the glass in a door as they are passing through it. To address this concern, building codes require that approved "safety glass" be used in locations where people are likely to become injured by broken glass. Safety glass is commonly used as the glass in doors, as shower doors, and to construct partition walls such as found around a swimming pool.

To be approved as safety glass, the glass must not create dangerous glass shards when shattered. Both tempered glass and laminated glass can meet this requirement, as tempered glass breaks into small pieces that are less hazardous, and laminated glass holds the glass shards in place when a window is broken.

Types of Windows

There are numerous types and styles of windows used at multifamily properties. The following are some of the most commonly used types:

Fixed Windows

Fixed windows, sometimes called inoperable windows, are a window that is fixed in place and does not open. Larger fixed windows are often called picture windows.

Awning and Hopper Windows

Awning windows are hinged at the top and swing out from the bottom. Awning windows are usually operated with a crank. A close relative of the awning window is the hopper window, which is identical, except is hinged at the bottom and swings out from the top.

Figure 9-1 - Awning Window

Casement Windows

Casement windows are similar to awning windows but are hinged at the side rather than at the top. Casement windows swing open like a door and are typically operated with a crank.

Figure 9-2 - Casement Window

Sliding Windows and Doors

Sliding windows slide along a track and open from side to side. Sliding doors, also called patio doors, are simply large sliding windows that extend fully to the ground, allowing them to be used to enter or exit the building.

Figure 9-3 - Sliding Window

Double-Hung and Single-Hung Windows

Double-hung windows consist of two stacked window sections called sashes. Both sashes can be slid up or down, allowing either the top or the bottom of the window to be left open. Most modern double-hung windows also allow both the top and bottom sash to be tilted inward for cleaning. A single-hung window is identical to a double-hung window except that the top sash is fixed and cannot be opened.

Figure 9-4 - Double-Hung Window

Windows in Doors

Both wood doors and hollow-metal doors are available with windows built into them. When windows are installed within a door, they are often referred to as a "light". Small rectangular glass panes at the edge of the door are called "narrow lights" , while large full-panes on doors are known as "full lights". Most aluminum storefront doors have large glass panes, and of course, all-glass doors are made up entirely of glass.

Windows in doors must use safety glass. Windows in fire-rated doors often use wired glass, which consists of glass with thin wires embedded within it.

Locking Hardware on Windows

Intruders may choose to force open an operable window rather than to break the glass. If they do break the glass, they may reach inside to open the window rather than to crawl through the opening with broken glass. The type of locking hardware used on the window largely determines how easy it is to force the window open.

Up until about fifteen years ago, little thought was given to security when windows were designed. As a result, the locking hardware used on most older windows is very poor and can be easily defeated by an intruder.

The locking hardware used on newer windows has greatly improved. Most newer windows have excellent locking hardware that is considerably more difficult for an intruder to defeat. These include multipoint locks that secure the window in multiple locations rather than a single location. Newer windows usually have tighter seals to make them more energy efficient and this also improves the security of the windows. As a result, most newer windows are difficult to force open, requiring that an intruder enter through the glass in order to get through the window.

To make older windows more secure requires that supplemental locking devices be added to the window. These devices would be in addition to the factory supplied locks that came with the windows. Commonly used types of supplementary locking devices include:

- Retractable metal bars or wood dowel rods placed in the tracks of sliding windows and doors.
- Clamp-on type sliding window locks that can be attached to the window track.
- Sliding door lock that consists of a floor-mounted baseplate and removable arm that blocks movement of the door.
- Key-operated sash locks for double-hung and single-hung windows.
- Window opening control devices that limit the distance that a window can be opened.
- Double-bolt locks that can be installed at the edge of sliding patio doors.
- Twist or key-operated pin locks that are installed on window or frame that prevent movement when the pin is engaged.

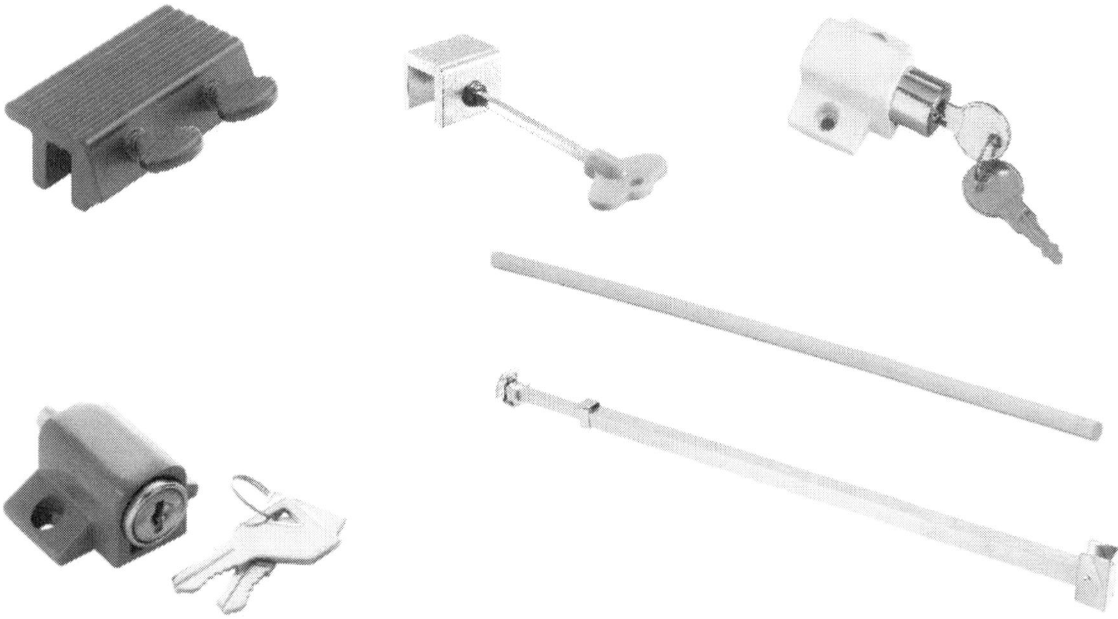

Figure 9-5 - Examples of Supplementary Locking Devices

Window locks can be used to lock the window in place when it is fully closed. Window locks can also be used to lock the window in place when it is partially open. This allows the window to be opened wide enough to provide ventilation, but not wide enough to allow an intruder to enter.

Options to Make Windows More Secure

Because of the inherent vulnerability of windows, there are a number of options available to make them more secure. Some of these options include:

<u>Security Window Film</u>

Security window film can be used to strengthen the glass in windows. While an intruder can shatter the glass, the film keeps the glass shards together, making entry through the window opening much more difficult. The film is nearly invisible and doesn't significantly alter the appearance of the glass.

Security window film consists of one or more layers of polyester film, laminated together with special adhesives. Security window film typically ranges in thickness from 4 mils (100 micron) to 14 mils (350 micron). In general, the thicker the film is, the stronger it is. As the thickness of the film increases, the degree of break strength, tear strength, and puncture strength also increases.

Security window film is installed on the inside of existing windows. The installation is done at the job site, and involves the cutting and applying of the film to the surface of the glass of each window. The film is attached using a special adhesive and must be carefully installed to eliminate creases and air bubbles. Correctly installing security window film requires a high degree of skill and is done by professional installers.

Security window film can be used alone, but works best when used with an attachment system. These systems are mounted to the window frame and used to mechanically attach the film to the sides, top and bottom of the frame and greatly increase the protection provided by the window film.

Security window film works well on most types of glass. The exception is tempered glass, where security window film only works when used with an attachment system, and even then, provides a reduced level of protection. Security window film does not work with all glass frameless tempered doors because, when broken, the glass would crumble into small bits and there would be nothing to prevent the glass and window film from simply falling to the ground.

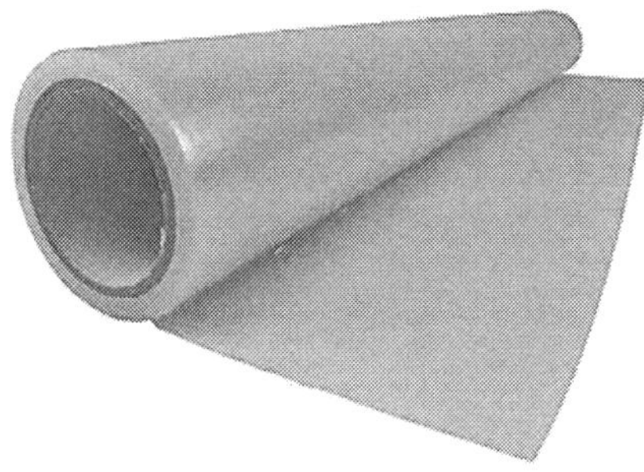

Figure 9-6 - Security Window Film

Polycarbonate Glazing

Polycarbonate glazing can be used to replace the glass in windows. Polycarbonate glazing is available in thicknesses ranging from 1/4" thick to 1-1/4" thick. In most cases, polycarbonate glazing can be installed in existing window frames.

Polycarbonate glazing greatly increases the strength of the windows and makes forced entry extremely difficult. Polycarbonate glazing costs more than security window film, but provides considerably better protection. Polycarbonate glazing on exterior windows should be considered for use at higher-risk properties.

Figure 9-7 - Polycarbonate Glazing

Bullet-Resistant Glazing

Bullet-resistant glazing can be used when there is a need to provide protection against bullets being fired through a window. Bullet-resistant glazing is sometimes incorrectly called "bulletproof" glass. Bullet-resistant glazing is in fact not bulletproof, but will only provide protection against certain types of firearms for a certain period of time.

Firearms are available in a wide variety of calibers, each which have a different ability to penetrate a bullet-resistant material. Even within cartridges of the same caliber, there are different bullet weights and types and different powder loadings. Rifle cartridges generally have much more power than handgun cartridges, and shotguns may pose a different type of threat than either handguns or rifles. Repeated gunfire against the same surface also has a different effect than a single bullet does.

To help sort through all of these variables, Underwriters Laboratories (UL) has developed a written standard, UL 752, that establishes ratings for bullet-resistant materials. UL 752 specifies eight levels of bullet-resistant ability, ranging from Level 1 to Level 8.:

- Level 1 - Provides protection against 9 mm and less powerful handgun cartridges.
- Level 2 - Provides protection against .357 magnum and less powerful handgun cartridges.
- Level 3 - Provides protection against .44 magnum and less powerful handgun cartridges.
- Level 4, 5, 7, and 8 are needed to provide protection against common rifle cartridge calibers. UL 752 also has supplementary ratings for threats from a shotgun.

In general, the higher the rating level, the better the protection, but the greater the cost. Higher rated materials are also usually thicker and weigh more, and there may be a limited availability of materials and accessories at the higher rating levels.

A comprehensive approach must be taken when installing bullet-resistant glazing. The wall, glazing, and any accessories used must all be rated to provide the same level of protection. For example, it doesn't make sense to provide a bullet-resistant window when the wall surrounding the window is unprotected. Also consider the possibility of ricochet and the potential for a bullet to penetrate the adjacent walls, ceilings, and floors.

Most multifamily properties will have no need for bullet-resistant glazing, however some properties in very high-risk environments may find the use of this product beneficial. For example, at some rental properties located in high-risk areas, bullet-resistant glazing can be used on the windows of the leasing office to provide increased protection for the staff working there. In areas where drive-by shootings are common, bullet-resistant glazing can be used on the exterior of the buildings where shootings are most likely to occur.

If there is a need for bullet-resistant glazing, a qualified installer of bullet-resistant products should be contacted to discuss the options available and to determine the level of protection required.

Security Window Screens

Security window screens can be added to windows to provide increased protection. Security window screens are most commonly installed on the outside of the windows, but can be installed inside when needed, such as when used with awning or casement windows. One benefit of security window screens is that they provide protection both when the window is open and closed.

Security window screens are somewhat similar to the traditional screens used to provide insect protection but are specifically constructed for security purposes. Security window screens are made using marine grade high-tensile strength wire mesh that resists cutting and physical impact. A heavy-duty screen frame is used, and this screen is firmly attached to the window frame or wall using tamper-resistant fasteners.

When security screens are used on bedroom windows and windows used as fire escapes, they must be equipped with an emergency release mechanism that allows them to be opened from the inside.

Figure 9-8 - Security Window Screen

Window Bars

Window bars can be added to the interior or exterior of windows to provide additional security. Some people have a negative impression of window bars because they are thought to have a harsh industrial appearance, but they can be a very cost effective option for window protection.

Window bars are now available in many styles, colors, and architectural designs. Some window bars are so attractive that they are actually used for decorative purposes as much as they are for security.

Window bars are available as premanufactured off-the-shelve products, or can be custom-manufactured. Window bars are most commonly made of ornamental iron or steel, but can also be made of aluminum.

Like security screens, window bars must be equipped with an emergency release mechanism that allows them to be opened from the inside when used on bedroom windows and windows used as fire escapes.

Figure 9-9 - Window Bars

Chapter 10: Security Signage

Importance of Security Signage

Security signage is an important part of the overall security program at a multifamily property. While security signage cannot physically stop a person from entering, it can create an atmosphere that may cause an intruder to pass up your property and move along to the next one that does not appear to have as much security.

Security signage includes "No Trespassing" signs and signs indicating that the property is protected by security officers, video surveillance systems, intrusion alarm systems, or by some combination of all of these.

Security signage can also be used to direct visitors, delivery drivers, and emergency responders to the correct location on the property, avoiding confusion and reducing delays.

No Trespassing Signs

No Trespassing signs are particularly important as they can serve as a deterrent and deny the intruder the right to claim that *"I didn't know that this was private property"*. Many state and local laws also require the posting of No Trespassing signs in order to allow intruders to be arrested and prosecuted for trespassing.

At a minimum, No Trespassing signs should state that the facility is private property, and that trespassing is not allowed. The applicable state or local law or ordinance that prohibits trespassing should also be indicated on the sign. An example of a No Trespassing sign is shown in the figure below.

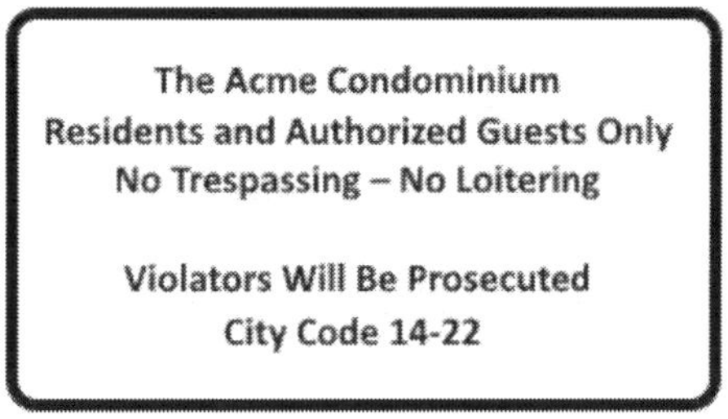

The Acme Condominium
Residents and Authorized Guests Only
No Trespassing – No Loitering

Violators Will Be Prosecuted
City Code 14-22

Figure 10-1 - No Trespassing Sign

No Trespassing signs should be posted at the following locations:

- At all vehicle and pedestrian entrances to the site.
- At all entrance doors to the buildings
- Along the fences or walls at the perimeter of the site. Signs along walls and fences should be placed approximately 50' to 100' apart around the entire site perimeter.
- Within outdoor parking lots. Signs should be placed at all parking lot entrances and at 50' intervals within the parking lot itself.
- At the entry points to any outdoor areas such as swimming pools, tennis courts, cabanas, and other amenity areas.

Signs that indicate that the property is patrolled by security officers, is under video surveillance, or is protected by electronic security systems can also be installed as an additional deterrent. In some cases, property owners may place such signs even though the claimed security measure may not actually exist. While this may be thought to have value as a deterrent, it can create false expectations on the part of residents and visitors. The use of signs that make false claims is strongly discouraged.

Directional Signs

Directional signs are used to direct visitors, delivery drivers, and emergency responders to the correct location. The following types of directional signs are commonly used at multifamily properties:

Site Entrance Signs

Site entrance signs are used to identify the entrances to the site. These signs should be clearly visible from the street both during the day and at night. If your site has dedicated entrances that are to be used for special purposes (such as a service entrance), these should be clearly marked. Minimum size of letters used on site entrance signs should be 12-inches.

Signs with maps should also be provided at the site entrances. These maps should show the location of all buildings in relationship to where the viewer is standing.

Building Identification Signs

A system of signage should be provided so that all buildings on the property can be located quickly. This allows visitors to easily navigate the property and are invaluable to emergency responders who may not be familiar with the site.

All buildings should be identified with signs that show both street address and building letter or number, if used. Signs should be visible from all directions from which the building can be approached. Minimum size of letters used on building identification signs should be 8-inches.

Entrance Identification Signs

Signs that show the locations of the entrances to the buildings should be provided. If some doors are to be used by residents only, the signs on these doors should indicate this and provide directions to the proper visitor or delivery entrance. Minimum size of letters used on entrance identification signs should be 8-inches.

Residential Unit Signs

Signs should be provided that indicate the unit number or address of each of the individual residential units. Minimum size of letters used on signs on units within multifamily buildings should be 3-inches. Minimum size of letters used on signs at standalone homes should be 3-inches if located 30’ or less from the roadway, and 8-inches if located farther away.

Security Awareness Signs

Security awareness signs are used to remind residents of the procedures that should be followed to effectively protect the property and themselves.

Examples of security awareness signs include:

- "Wait for Door to Fully Close Before Driving Off".
- "Don't Leave Doors Propped Open".
- "Don't Leave Valuables in Car".
- "Remember to Lock Your Bicycle".
- "Don't Let People That You Do Not Know Into the Building".
- "Use The "Buddy System" When Walking to and From Your Car at Night".
- "Security Escorts Are Available – Call 999-333-1133".

For Security Reasons, Residents Are
Not Allowed to Let People That
They Do Not Know Into The Building

Please Don't Be Offended
When Our Residents
Comply With This Policy

Figure 10-2 - Examples of Security Awareness Signs

Chapter 11: Access Control Systems

What is an Access Control System?

An access control system is any type of system that is used to control access into an area. The traditional lock and key systems that have been used for centuries are one simple form of access control system.

Today, the term "access control system" is most often used to describe an electronic system used to control access through a door, gate, or elevator. Access control systems most commonly use an access card or combination rather than a metal key.

When used at multifamily properties, access control systems can provide some or all of the following benefits:

- Provide ability to issue each user a unique access card or code. The access privileges of each card or code can be uniquely defined, allowing users to have access to only the specific areas that they need.
- Provide ability to control the specific times and days of week when the access card or code may be used.
- Provide ability to cancel one user's access card or code without affecting other users. This eliminates the need to rekey locks and reissue keys when a key is lost or stolen or when the user no longer requires access.
- Provide ability to track the use of the access card or code, allowing reports to be created showing where each user entered and when.

Access control systems vary widely in type and complexity, ranging from systems that control just a single door, to systems that control thousands of doors. Access control systems can consist of a standalone device that is installed at a single door, or a networked system that interconnects many doors within a multifamily housing complex.

Mechanical Pushbutton Locks

Mechanical pushbutton locks are the simplest form of access control device. Mechanical pushbutton locks are used to replace the standard cylindrical or mortise lockset installed on a door. Mechanical pushbutton locks have a series of numeric pushbuttons on the face of the lock. When these pushbuttons are pressed in the correct order, the lock unlocks. Mechanical pushbutton locks use a single code that is shared by all users. This code is between three and five digits and is programmed manually at the lock.

Mechanical pushbutton locks are entirely mechanical and require no type of batteries or electrical power. Mechanical pushbutton locks provide no ability to control when a code is used, no record of who entered or when, and no ability to issue unique codes to users. When a code is compromised, the lock must be reprogrammed, and a new code issued to all users.

Criminals have developed techniques to defeat most popular brands of mechanical pushbutton locks. These techniques are posted in online forums and shown in online videos. Because of their vulnerabilities, mechanical keypad locks should only be used where a minimal level of security is required, such as on the doors to restrooms. Mechanical keypad locks should never be used on building entrances or on doors to rooms that contain high-value assets.

Figure 11-1 - Mechanical Keypad Lock

Electronic Keypad Locks

Electronic keypad locks are used to replace the standard cylindrical or mortise lockset installed on a door. Electronic keypad locks have a numeric keypad on the face of them. When the correct numeric code is entered, the lock unlocks. The numeric codes are usually between three and six digits.

The capabilities of electronic keypad locks vary greatly. Some very simple types provide only a limited number of user codes and no ability to track when a code was used. Other types provide full access control capabilities including the ability to issue thousands of user codes, control the specific times that a code may be used, and provide a record of who used each code and when.

Simple electronic keypad locks are programmed at the door itself using the keypad on the lock or a handheld programming device. More sophisticated electronic keypad locks can be programmed wirelessly from a central location. Some electronic keypad locks can be connected to home automation systems, or be programmed and controlled using a smartphone app.

Some electronic keypad locks allow the use of a proximity access card to gain access in place of or in addition to the numeric code. Electronic keypad locks are available in different qualities ranging from inexpensive grade residential locks to commercial grade ANSI/BHMA Grade 1 locks.

Simple residential grade electronic keypad locks can be used on the doors to individual residential units, while more sophisticated commercial electronic keypad locks are a better choice for use on building entrances and common area doors.

Electronic keypad locks can be an effective solution at smaller multifamily properties that have the need for only a small number of access controlled doors. Electronic keypad lock systems can become unwieldly when large numbers of doors are being controlled. Having to regularly change batteries on a large number of locks can be costly, particularly when the cost of labor is factored in. Locks that require that programming changes be made at the door can also require an excessive amount of time to manage.

Figure 11-2 - Electronic Keypad Lock

Server-Based Access Control Systems

Server-based access control systems are the preferred choice at larger multifamily properties where there are many doors to be controlled, and when there is a need for advanced features such as the ability to control gates and elevators.

Unlike electronic keypad locks which consist of a single component, server-based access control systems consist of multiple components connected together to form a unified system. The components of a basic server-based access control system include the following:

Door Devices

Door devices are the pieces of equipment installed at each door controlled by the access control system. At a minimum, door devices would include a card reader or keypad, and some type of electric lock hardware.

Additional devices at the door could include a magnetic contact switch to tell the system whether the door is open or closed, and a request-to-exit motion detector to tell the system that someone is exiting through the doors. These devices are used to monitor the door to determine if it has been forced-open or propped-open.

Intelligent Control Panels

Intelligent control panels are electronic processors that are wired to the card readers, electric lock hardware, and other devices at each access controlled door. When an access card is presented to a card reader, a signal is sent to the intelligent control panel. The intelligent control panel decides if this particular card is authorized at this particular door at this particular time. If so, the intelligent control panel sends a signal to the electric lock hardware at the door, causing the door to unlock. The intelligent control panel then records the card number, door number and date and time the card was used.

Intelligent control panels are available in different configurations depending on the manufacturer. Most panels today actually consist of multiple modules that can be combined together as needed to support the number of doors that the panel controls. Some panels include a built-in power supply, while others require that separate power supplies be provided to power the panels, card readers, and lock hardware.

Intelligent control panels are typically installed in an electrical or mechanical room nearest to the doors that they control. A small building might have only one intelligent control panel that serves the whole building, while a large high-rise building may have dozens of intelligent control panels distributed throughout the building. A multi-building housing campus would likely have at least one intelligent control panel in each building.

Access Control Server Computer

The access control server computer is a centrally located computer that runs the access control system. This computer is usually a dedicated computer that has special access control system software installed on it. In some cases, an "access control appliance" is used instead of an access control server computer. The access control appliance provides the same functions as the server computer, but comes as a prepackaged unit that is easier to install.

The access control server computer communicates with all of the intelligent control panels within the building or campus. In most cases, this communication occurs over the building or campus data network, or over an internet connection. An access control server computer can be used to control only a single building, or to control multiple buildings or campuses.

At smaller properties, programming of the access control system is typically done at the access control server computer itself. At larger properties, access control client software can be installed on multiple computers throughout the property. This client software connects to the access control server computer, allowing programming to be accomplished remotely.

For example, at a larger property, it would be common to have computers with client software installed at the building office, maintenance office, and at each of the concierge desks. The client software can coexist with other software, allowing the computer to continue to be used for other purposes. Some access control systems allow programming of the system over the network using a standard web browser. This eliminates the need for client software and allows the system to be programmed by anyone with an authorized username and password.

The per door cost of server-based access control systems is usually more than the per door cost of electronic keypad locks. This is primarily due to the cost of installing cabling between the door devices and the intelligent control panels and the cost of the control panels themselves.

However, using a server-based access control system eliminates the need to change batteries at each door, and allows all programming changes to be made from a central location. Server-based systems can also be connected to more types of electric lock hardware and can be used to control overhead doors, gates, and elevators. The software used with server-based systems provides more flexibility and better reporting capabilities. These benefits can reduce operating costs, making the use of a server-based system actually more economical than the use of electronic keypad locks over the long-run.

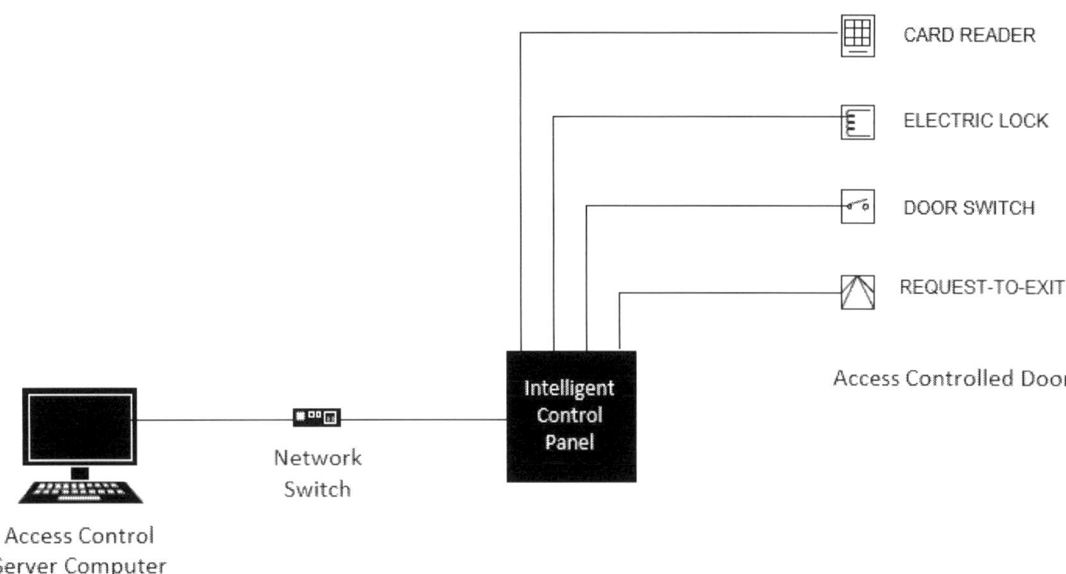

Figure 11-3 - Block Diagram of Simple Server-Based Access Control System

Cloud-Based Access Control Systems

Cloud-based access control systems are identical to server-based access control systems, except that there is no access control server computer installed at the property. Instead, the intelligent control panels at the property communicate over the network to a server installed at an outside service provider's facility. A monthly subscription fee is paid to the service provider for this service.

Using a cloud-based system eliminates the need to purchase and maintain an access control server at the property. The service provider also performs automatic data backups and periodically installs updates to the access control software, eliminating the need for the property management team to do this.

Most providers offer two levels of cloud-based services: unmanaged and managed.

When using an unmanaged service, the system operates identically to a server-based system. The property management team uses a web browser to connect with the access control system server computer and is responsible for making all programming changes. For example, if a leasing agent needed to program an access card for a new resident, he or she would use a web browser to sign on to the system and then enter the new resident's card number and other information into the software.

When using a managed service, the service provider, not the property management team, is responsible for doing the actual programming. For example, if a leasing agent needed to program an access card for a new resident, he or she would call or email the service provider and tell them that a new access card had been issued. An employee of the service provider would then enter the new resident's card number and other information into the software.

Managed services cost considerably more than unmanaged services, but are often a good choice for properties that don't have an on-site staff. Some properties also use a managed service to eliminate the need to train staff on how to program the access control system.

Hybrid Access Control Systems

There are advantages and disadvantages of both server-based access control systems and electronic keypad locks. To get the best of both worlds, some manufacturers allow electronic keypad locks to be connected to a server-based access control system. These systems are known as "hybrid" systems.

Most hybrid systems use traditional card readers and electric lock hardware on exterior doors, but use electronic keypad locks on interior doors. For example, at a multifamily building, regular card readers would be used at the building entrances, and electronic keypad locks would be installed on the doors to amenity areas such as fitness centers and party rooms. At some higher-end properties, electronic keypad locks may also be used on the doors to the individual residential units. When an electronic keypad lock is used with a hybrid system, it most often includes a built-in proximity card reader. This allows the same access card to be used at both exterior and interior doors.

When using electronic keypad locks in conjunction with a server-based system, some method of communication between the lock and the server is needed. This is accomplished in different ways by different manufacturers. The most common method is to use a wireless radio system to communicate between the lock and the server. Some systems allow the use of the property's existing Wi-Fi network, while others require the use of the manufacturer's own special wireless radio system.

The per door cost of a hybrid access control system can be less than that of a server-based access control system, particularly if the electronic keypad locks use Wi-Fi and the property already has excellent Wi-Fi coverage. However, the cost advantage of a hybrid system can be greatly diminished if it is necessary to install a completely new wireless network to communicate with the electronic keypad locks.

The use of a hybrid system does not eliminate the need to change batteries at the electronic keypad locks. In fact, battery life can actually be shorter because of the additional power needed to transmit the wireless signal. This can result in the need for more frequent battery replacement.

There is a special type of hybrid system that does not require the use of wireless radio communications. This system uses a combination of hardwired card readers and wireless card reader locks. The hardwired card readers are installed at the doors that residents use most, such as the building entrances. The wireless card reader locks are typically installed at doors inside of the building, such as at party rooms, fitness centers, and other amenity areas. In some cases, these locks may also be used at the doors to the individual residential units in place of regular locks.

There are no radio communications to the wireless card reader locks, instead programming changes are carried on the access card itself. When a resident uses a card at a hardwired card reader, programming change information (card additions and deletions) is downloaded to the access card. When the resident uses his or her card at a wireless lock, the programming information is uploaded to the lock.

The drawback of this system is that there can be a delay between when a programming change is made and when the change is uploaded to the wireless locks. This could allow a lost or stolen card to continue to work at a door until such time as another resident used his or her card at the door. These systems also do not allow the wireless locks to send real-time notifications of events such as a door being held open or being propped open. Despite these limitations, this type of system can be a cost-effective solution when you have many interior doors that you wish to control with a card reader.

Access Cards and Card Readers

Access cards are the most commonly used method to unlock an access controlled door. At a multifamily property, access cards would be issued to all residents and employees and to authorized vendors and contractors. Card readers are the devices at the door used to read the access cards. To gain entry through a door, the user holds the access card next to the card reader, and if the user is authorized, the door unlocks.

There are numerous types of cards and card reading technologies available. Common card types include bar code cards, magnetic stripe cards, proximity cards, contact smartcards, and contactless smartcards. As a general rule, the type of card reader used must match the card. For example, if a proximity access card were used, a proximity card reader would also need to be used. Some card readers can read only a single type of card, while others are capable of reading multiple card types.

Most server-based access control systems will work with all types of access cards or card readers. When card readers are embedded in electronic keypad locks, the choice of cards and card readers is much more limited, with some models allowing the use of only a single type of card, usually a proximity card.

The two most popular types of access cards used at multifamily properties are:

<u>Proximity Access Cards</u>

Proximity access cards get their name because the card can be held close to (in the proximity of) the card reader to open the door. This is different than other types of card reading technologies, such as magnetic stripe, where the card must be inserted into some type of a slot.

Proximity access cards are credit card sized and contain an antenna and embedded memory chip. Each proximity card has a unique identification number assigned to it and this number is programmed into the memory chip. Most proximity access cards operate at a radio frequency of 125 Kilohertz (KHz), and because of this, are called "125 KHz proximity cards".

The proximity card reader is continuously transmitting a low-powered radio signal. When the proximity card is held close to the proximity card reader, the radio signal is picked up by the antenna in the proximity card. This causes the identification number in the card's memory chip to be transmitted back to the card reader. The typical distance that a proximity card can be read by the card reader is between 2" and 6".

Proximity access "fobs" are devices that work similarly to a proximity access card and can be used with the same card readers. Proximity access fobs consist of plastic disks, about 1-1/4" in diameter, in which an antenna and memory chip have been embedded. The disk has a tab connected to it that allows it to be attached to a key chain. Proximity access fobs are especially popular at multifamily properties because most residents find them more convenient to use than a proximity access card. The typical distance that a proximity access fob can be read by the card reader is between 1" and 3".

Because access fobs are so commonly used at multifamily properties, many users may refer to the access control system that uses these fobs as a "fob reader system" and the card readers as "fob readers" [13].

---

[13] Within this book, the term "card reader" rather than "fob reader" will be used, and both cards and fobs will be referred to as "access cards".

125 KHz proximity access cards have been widely used with all brands of access control systems for over 25 years. Unfortunately, in recent years, hackers have developed methods to easily copy 125 KHz proximity cards and fobs. There is equipment sold on the internet for as little as $30 that allows a proximity card or fob to be copied. Copies of proximity cards and fobs can also be ordered at self-service key-copying kiosks and from online "key-cloning" sites.

Because of their vulnerabilities, 125 KHz proximity access cards or fobs should not be used for new access control system installations. Properties that are already using 125 KHz proximity access cards or fobs should be aware of their vulnerabilities and begin to make plans for their eventual replacement with a higher-security type of access card or fob.

Contactless Smartcards

Contactless smartcards work similarly to 125 KHz proximity access cards except operate at the higher frequency of 13.56 Megahertz (MHz). Contactless smartcards are also different in that it is possible to transmit information both to and from the memory chip on the card. This is different from the proximity card, where information can only be transmitted from the card. The capacity of the memory chip on the card is much greater, allowing more information to be stored on the card and providing some processing capabilities.

Contactless smart cards and card readers use an encrypted method of transmitting information to and from the card. This makes it extremely difficult to copy the card or compromise the card reader using external devices, providing much better security. The typical distance that a contactless smart card can be read by the card reader is between 1" and 3".

Some manufacturers of contactless smartcards also offer a "smart fob" version of their product. The distance that a smart fob can be read by the card reader is very short, usually 1" or less.

There are several different formats of contactless smartcards available. Some use industry standards that are available from multiple manufacturers, while others use proprietary formats that are available only from a single manufacturer. When choosing a contactless smartcard, be sure that the card will continue to be widely available in the years to come.

The use of contactless smartcards is recommended for all new access control systems and when upgrading older systems that currently use proximity access cards.

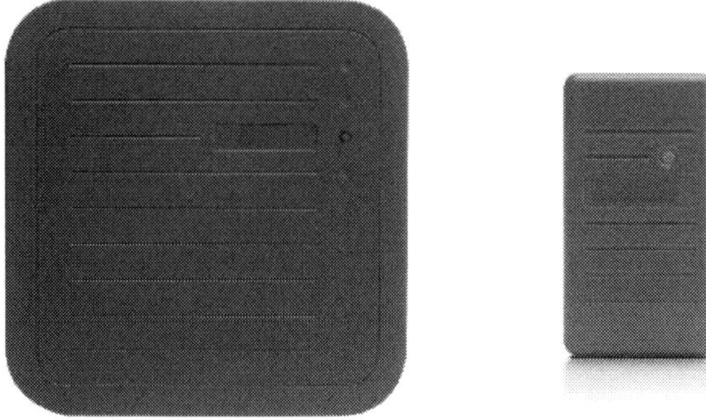

Figure 11-4 - Proximity Card Readers

Figure 11-5 - Proximity Card and Proximity Fob

Mobile Device Access

Many modern access control systems allow mobile devices such as smartphones to be used in place of access cards. In order to do this, special "mobile-enabled" smartcard readers must be used. These readers work with most popular types of mobile device operating systems and communicate with the mobile device wirelessly. These readers continue to be capable of reading contactless smartcards, giving residents the option of using either their phone or a smartcard to gain access.

The use of the mobile device must be authorized by the person managing the access control system. To start the process, this person signs on to a website and uses a menu to send an email invitation to the mobile device user. The mobile device user then clicks on a link in the email to download an app to the mobile device. Once this app is installed, the device can be used at a card reader just like a regular access card.

The mobile device user has options to set the device so that it can be used only when the device is unlocked, or at any time when the device is turned on. An option can also be set so that the user has to twist the device in a specific way at the card reader in order to unlock the door. This feature is used to prevent accidental activations of card readers as users walk by.

The access privileges of mobile devices can be deleted when a mobile device is lost or stolen or when the user no longer requires access.

There is a licensing fee that must be paid for each mobile device registered. This fee is roughly comparable to the cost of purchasing a contactless smartcard.

Keypads

Numeric keypads can be used to control access at doors and gates. These keypads allow entry if the correct code is entered on the keypad. This code is known as a Personal Identification Code or "PIN" code.

Numeric keypads are similar to keypad locks except require the use of external electric locking hardware, such as an electric strike. Keypads are available that are self-contained units that function alone, or keypads can be connected to a server-based access control system. There are also card readers available that have numeric keypads built-into them.

When a card reader with a keypad is used, the access control software can be programmed so that either a PIN code or a valid access card can be used. The software can also be programmed so that both the PIN code and a valid access card must be used. This is known as "PIN + Card" mode. Pin + Card mode offers a higher level of security because the user must both possess a valid access card and know the correct code in order to gain entry.

Figure 11-6 - Access Control Keypad

Using numeric PIN codes is convenient and avoids the expense of having to issue access cards. Numeric codes can also be given out by phone or in a text or email, eliminating the need to deliver an access card to a user. However, because of the ease in which PIN codes can be given out or compromised, the use of PIN codes alone provides less than optimum security. (See page 271).

Biometric Devices

Biometric devices are devices that use a human characteristic rather than an access card or PIN code in order to gain entry. Common types of biometric devices include fingerprint readers, hand geometry readers, and retinal scan readers. Other biometric devices include facial recognition systems, and voice recognition systems.

Most biometric devices are capable of being connected to a server-based access control system and are commonly used in conjunction with a card reader or numeric keypad at the door.

In the past, the accuracy of many types of biometric devices was questionable, resulting in authorized people being denied access, or worse yet, allowing unauthorized people to gain access. Also, many early biometric devices were slow, often taking ten seconds or more to recognize a user and grant access. Some users also had safety, privacy, and hygiene concerns when it came to using a biometric device, and were reluctant to place their finger on a fingerprint reader or to place their head up to a device to look into a retinal scan reader.

Although the speed and accuracy of many types of biometric devices has improved greatly, they are still rarely used at multifamily properties. This may change as technology advances in the future and the use of biometric devices becomes more widely accepted.

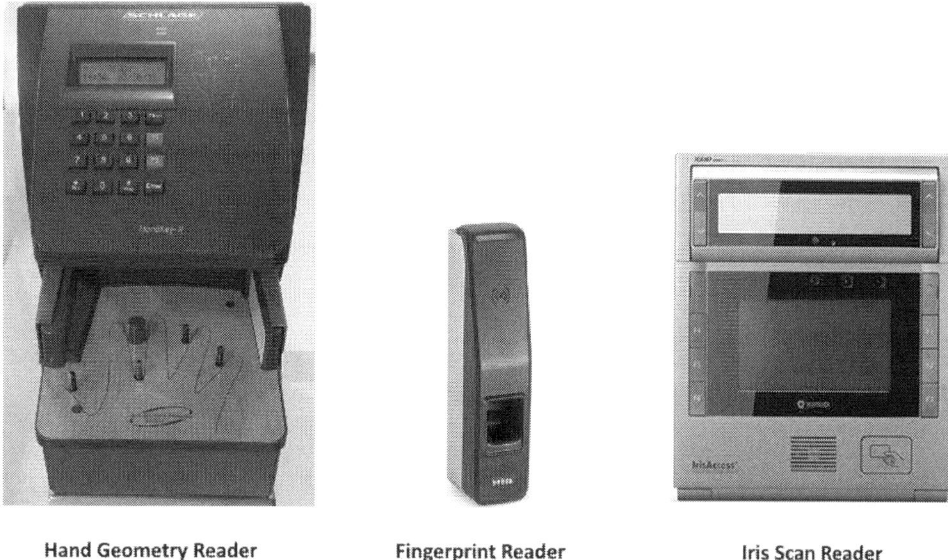

Hand Geometry Reader Fingerprint Reader Iris Scan Reader

Figure 11-7 - Examples of Biometric Devices

Long-Range RFID Readers and Tags

Long-range RFID (Radio Frequency Identification) readers are frequently used at the entrances to parking garages and gated communities. Long-range RFID readers work similarly to proximity card readers, except have a much greater range.

Long-range RFID readers work in conjunction with RFID tags. These RFID tags work similarly to proximity access cards except are designed to be mounted on the inside of the vehicle's windshield or attached to the license plate frame. There are also RFID tag stickers that can be attached to a vehicle's headlight.

The use of long-range RFID readers and tags eliminates the need for a driver to stop and roll down their window to use a regular access card. As the vehicle approaches the overhead door or gate, the RFID reader automatically reads the RFID tag, and if authorized, the overhead door or gate automatically opens.

Long-range RFID readers connect to server-based access control systems, allowing RFID tags to be programmed just like regular access cards. In most cases, a resident would be issued both an access card and an RFID tag, and both would be programmed into the system at the same time.

The use of long-range RFID readers and tags is more expensive than other methods of controlling vehicle access, but offers the most convenience for residents.

Figure 11-8 - Long-Range RFID Reader at Gate

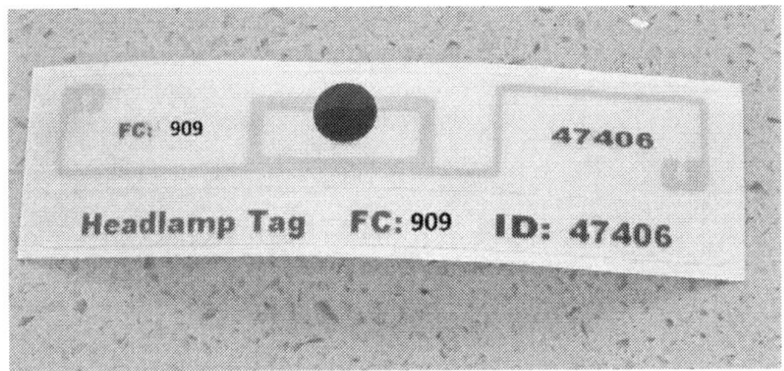

Figure 11-9 - RFID Sticker Tag for Headlight

Wireless Radio Controls

Wireless radio controls are often used at the entrances to parking garages and gated communities. Wireless radio controls consist of two components: wireless transmitters, and wireless receivers.

Wireless transmitters are small battery-powered devices that are issued to residents. These devices have a button on them, that when pressed, open the overhead door or gate. Some wireless transmitters have multiple buttons on them, allowing them to control several different overhead doors and gates. For example, this would be useful when a multifamily housing complex has a gate at the entrance to the community, and an overhead door at the garage entrance to each building.

Wireless receivers are devices that are installed at the overhead door or gate. When a button is pressed on a wireless transmitter, it sends a low-powered radio signal to the wireless receiver. The wireless receiver receives this signal, and then activates the overhead door or gate.

Figure 11-10 - Wireless Transmitters

There are three types of wireless radio control systems commonly used at multifamily properties:

Fixed-Code Radio Controls

Fixed-code radio controls are the oldest and least expensive type of radio control system. Each wireless transmitter is programmed with a fixed-code. This code is typically set using small switches within the transmitter itself. A matching code is set within the wireless receiver. If the codes on the transmitter and receiver match, the overhead door or gate will open when the button on the transmitter is pressed.

All wireless transmitters used with an overhead door or gate must be set to the same code. If a wireless transmitter is lost or stolen, the code on the receiver should be changed to prevent the transmitter from being used by an unauthorized person. This requires that the codes of all other transmitters also be changed. While this is not a problem at a smaller property, it can be a major undertaking at a larger property that has hundreds of residents.

Fixed-code radio controls use a limited number of different code combinations, often 256 codes or less. An intruder with a compatible transmitter can manually try various code combinations until they find one that works. There are also homemade devices that can rapidly scan through all code combinations quickly, allowing the overhead door or gate to be opened in a manner of minutes.

Rolling Code Radio Controls

Rolling-code radio controls are an improved system designed to overcome many of the vulnerabilities associated with fixed-code radio controls. These systems use a "rolling code" technology that selects a new code from billions of possible combinations each time that a transmitter is used. This makes it nearly impossible for an intruder to ever match or compromise the code.

Rolling-code radio controls also use unique codes for each transmitter, allowing the transmitters used by each resident to be separately programmed into the receiver. This allows a lost or stolen transmitter to be deleted from the system without requiring that all other transmitters be reprogrammed. Programming of the transmitters must be performed at the wireless receiver. If there are multiple overhead doors or gates, each receiver must be programmed separately.

The benefits of rolling code radio controls make them the preferred choice for use at multifamily housing complexes. Properties that are currently using fixed-code radio controls are encouraged to upgrade them to rolling-code radio controls as soon as possible.

System-Connected Radio Controls

System-connected radio controls are similar to rolling-code radio controls, except that special wireless receivers are used and are connected to the property's access control system. When connected in this manner, the wireless receiver acts like a "card reader", and each wireless transmitter acts as an "access card". The access control system, not the wireless receiver, makes the decision as to whether or not to grant access when a wireless transmitter is used.

System-connected radio controls offer the following benefits:

- All programming can be done through the access control system. There is no need to go to each overhead door or gate to add or delete transmitters.
- The access control system can allow more precise control of where and when a wireless transmitter can be used. For example, a transmitter assigned to a contractor can be programmed to only work on the specific days and at the specific times that the contractor is scheduled to be on the property.
- The access control system provides an accurate record of when and where each wireless transmitter was used.

When system-connect radio controls are used, wireless transmitters are programmed just like regular access cards. In most cases, a resident would be issued both an access card and a wireless transmitter, and both would be programmed into the system at the same time.

HomeLink Systems

Many modern vehicles are equipped with systems that can be used to replicate the function of a wireless transmitter. One widely used system of this type is the HomeLink® system.

HomeLink systems can be used to operate overhead doors and gates by pressing a button inside of the vehicle. HomeLink systems are programmed by holding a wireless transmitter next to the button inside of the vehicle and pressing both the button on the transmitter and the button on the vehicle at the same time. This causes the information in the transmitter to be duplicated in the HomeLink system in the vehicle. Once this process is completed, there is no longer a need to use the transmitter, as the overhead door or gate can be opened using the button in the vehicle.

Many residents like the convenience of using the HomeLink system as it eliminates the need to carry a separate wireless transmitter. However, using a HomeLink system can create security vulnerabilities. Because a wireless transmitter can be programmed into more than one vehicle, some residents give access to all of their friends, family members, and contractors. The property manager loses control of who has access to the property. Also, when vehicles are sold, the HomeLink button will continue to have the ability to gain access to the property unless deliberate steps are taken to delete the wireless code.

Rolling-code radio controls and system-connected radio controls are available from some manufacturers in two versions, one version that is compatible with the HomeLink system, and another version that is not. Property managers need to make a decision as to whether the convenience of allowing the use of a HomeLink system outweighs the security risks when deciding which version to use.

Elevator Access Control

Access control systems can be used to control elevators in multi-story buildings. There are two ways that elevators can be controlled.

The first way is to install a card reader at the call button on the outside of the elevator on each floor. This is known as "call button control" and requires that a valid access card be used in order to call the elevator to the floor. Once the elevator has responded to the floor, a person may enter and travel to any floor served by the elevator.

The second way is to install a card reader in the elevator car itself. This card reader controls the buttons in the elevator that allow the selection of each floor. This is known as "floor button control" and requires that a valid access card be used in order to select the floor that will be travelled to.

My

Figure 11-11 - Card Reader in Elevator for Floor Button Control

Floor button control can be configured so that using any valid access card allows access to all floors, or so that each access card only allows access to a specific floor or group of floors. For example, in a high-rise apartment building, it is sometimes a policy that residents are allowed access only to the floor on which they live plus any floors that contain shared amenity areas.

Elevator access control can be expensive to implement, particularly when installed at buildings with older elevators. Floor-by-floor control of elevators can be particularly expensive, especially when there are many floors and multiple elevator cars. The costs are high because work must be done by both the elevator contractor and the contractor installing the access control system.

Once elevators are connected to the access control system, access privileges can be assigned within the access control system software. This allows the access cards for each resident to be programmed to allow access to the specific floor or group of floors required.

There are several security vulnerabilities that exist when using elevator access control. Some of the ways that an intruder can compromise elevator security include:

Join the Group

People without a valid access card can enter the elevator car and ride to secured floors along with other passengers. Stepping on and off of elevators with other people is completely natural, and it is rare that anyone will stop and challenge a person getting off of an elevator on a secured floor. The busier the elevators, the bigger this problem becomes.

Wait for a Ride

A person can call an elevator to an unsecured floor such as a lobby or parking garage, step into the elevator, and wait for the elevator to be called to a secured floor. In a busy building, this can usually be accomplished by waiting in the elevator for only a few minutes.

Share a Card Swipe

Most interfaces between access control systems and elevator control systems are one-way only and don't provide feedback to the access control system when a floor selection button is pressed. When a user who has multi-floor access privileges uses his or her card, the selection buttons for all authorized floors become activated and remain activated for several seconds after his or her card is used. This allows a second person to "piggyback" on the access privileges of the first person by selecting a secured floor immediately after the first person has used his or her card.

Use Fire Service Override

Elevator security controls are completely over-ridden when the elevator is placed in "Fire Service Mode". This mode of operation is required by building codes to permit use of the elevators by firefighters during emergencies. The elevator is placed into Fire Service Mode using key-operated switches in the lobby and in the elevator car.

Unfortunately, the keys used with these switches are often standardized between all elevators of the same brand, and in some cases, all elevators within a specific geographical area are all keyed alike. This allows anyone who has a fire service key to any elevator to have a key that operates all elevators. Most fire service keys are also available for purchase online from a variety of sources. Anyone who has a fire service key has access to any floor without needing to have an access card.

The following are some tips for successfully using elevator access control at your multifamily property:

- Recognize that access controlled elevators provide only a moderate level of security and can be compromised in many ways.
- If at all possible, provide barrier walls with card reader controlled doors between unsecured floors and elevator lobbies. For example, because of the ease in which intruders can sneak into parking garages, the elevators on parking garage floors should be located within a locked elevator lobby, not freely accessible from the garage.

- Consider using card readers at both the call buttons on the floors and in the elevator cars to provide an additional layer of security. This would require users to first use their access card to call the elevator, and then use it a second time in the elevator car to select their floor.
- If your access control system supports it, consider connecting outputs from the elevator floor select buttons as inputs to the access control system. This can be used to immediately reset the card reader output when a user presses a floor select button, preventing a second user from piggybacking on the first user's card swipe. This also permits the access control system to know which floor select button was pressed when a card was used, allowing more accurate activity reporting.
- Elevators that open directly into residential units pose a particular security risk. For best security, walls with lockable doors should be provided between the elevator and the unit. If this is not possible, ask your elevator company if they can provide a dry-contact output from the elevator control system that closes anytime that the elevator is placed into Fire Service Mode.

  This output should be connected as an input to your access control or intrusion alarm system so that security or property management staff are immediately notified when any elevator is switched to Fire Service Mode. The residential unit should also be equipped with an intrusion alarm system that includes a motion detector to detect anyone stepping off of the elevator when the home is unoccupied.

License Plate Recognition Systems

License plate recognition (LPR) systems are sometimes used to control access to gated communities and parking garages. These systems use LPR cameras in conjunction with special software in order to read license plates. These systems can be connected to a server-based access control systems or can operate as a standalone system.

The license plate numbers of residents and authorized visitors is entered into a database. When a vehicle approaches the gate or overhead door, the camera reads the license plate. If the license plate number matches one that is in the database, the system sends a signal to open the door or gate.

The use of an LPR system requires precise placement of the LPR camera in order to capture license plate images accurately. There can also be issues with glare from headlights and weather that can adversely impact the ability of the LPR camera to reliably read license plates.

Remote Access Systems

One of the leading online retailers, Amazon, offers a remote access system that allows delivery drivers to gain access through a door or gate. This system is called Amazon Key and requires the installation of a small cellular device near the door or gate that is to be controlled. This device is often installed in or near the telephone entry system.

Delivery drivers use a mobile device with a special app to gain access. The driver presses a button on the device to open the door or gate. Access is allowed only if the driver is carrying a package that is addressed to that specific property. Once the package has been delivered, the driver no longer has access. The system tracks the date and time that the device was used.

It is expected that other carriers (UPS, FedEx, etc.) will soon adopt similar systems to allow access for their drivers.

Chapter 12: Security Intercom Systems

What is a Security Intercom System?

A security intercom system is a two-way voice communications system that is used for security purposes. Some security intercom systems also allow one-way or two-way video observation, allowing users to both see and talk with people at the other end of the intercom.

Security intercom systems are widely used at multifamily properties of all sizes.

Telephone Entry Systems

Telephone entry systems are commonly used at the lobby entrances of multifamily buildings and at the unattended entrances at gated communities. The primary purpose of a telephone entry system is to provide a means to let authorized visitors into the property.

The typical telephone entry system is a rectangular box that has a speaker, microphone, numeric keypad, and visual display on it. Depending on the model of system, the visual display may serve as a resident directory, or a separate printed directory may be provided next to the telephone entry system.

When used at building entrances, the telephone entry system is connected to electric lock hardware that can unlock the door when activated. When used at gate entrances, the telephone entry system is connected to activate the gate.

When a visitor arrives, they look up the resident that they wish to visit on the directory, and then select the resident's name on the visual display or enter a series of numbers on the numeric keypad. The intercom then dials a preprogrammed telephone number, typically the resident's house phone or cell phone. The visitor and resident then communicate, and if the resident wishes to let the visitor in, he or she presses a button on their telephone, allowing entry through the door or gate.

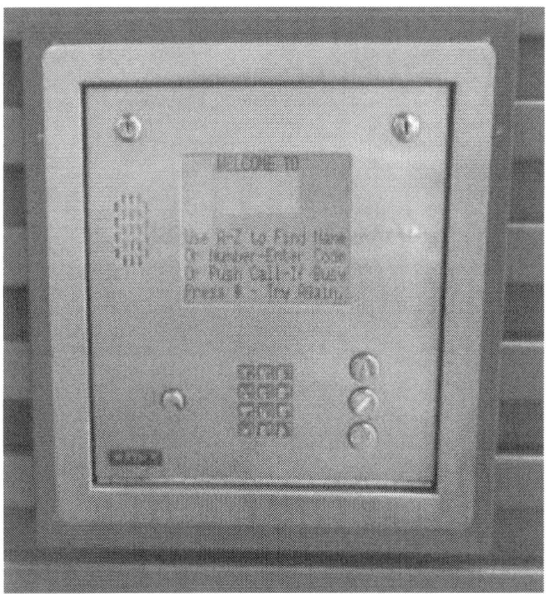

Figure 12-1 - Telephone Entry System

Telephone entry systems traditionally used POTS [14] telephone lines to communicate, but now many telephone entry systems are capable of communicating over an internet or cellular phone connection.

Many telephone entry systems include a "postal lock" feature. This allows a special lock provided by the United States Postal Service to be installed in the face of the entry system. Postal delivery people can use a special key in this lock to unlock the door or gate in order to deliver mail and packages.

Most telephone entry systems can also serve as simple access control systems on the door or gate that they are installed at. Residents can gain access by entering a PIN code on the telephone entry systems keypad. A card reader can also be directly connected to the telephone entry system, allowing entry when an access card is used.

Some telephone entry systems can be expanded to provide access control capabilities at doors beyond the one that they are installed at. This can allow card readers to be installed to control other doors in the building, without requiring that a separate access control system be used. This can be useful at smaller properties that have simple access control needs. However, larger properties with many access controlled doors are generally better served by installing a separate access control system. This is because most telephone entry systems don't have the advanced capabilities needed to efficiently manage large numbers of doors and users.

Some telephone entry systems can also be used to allow the card reader control of elevators. Card readers are installed in the elevator cars, allowing residents to travel to the floors to which they are authorized. When visitors are let into the building by the telephone entry system, the elevator floor of the resident that they are visiting can also be automatically activated, eliminating the need for the resident to come to the lobby to greet the visitor.

The latest type of telephone entry system is the "app-based" telephone entry system. These systems work in conjunction with an app that is installed on each resident's smartphone. App-based systems are similar to the traditional telephone entry system but typically include a larger visual display and a camera.

Upon arrival, visitors select the name of the resident that they wish to visit on the visual display. The system then connects to the app on the resident's smartphone. The resident can then both see and communicate with the visitor. If the resident wishes to let the visitor in, he or she presses a button on the smartphone, allowing entry.

Most app-based telephone entry systems are also capable of dialing a regular POTS telephone number in the rare cases where the resident doesn't have a smartphone or has chosen not to install the smartphone app.

Some older telephone entry systems require programming at the entry system itself. Most newer systems allow remote programming using either the manufacturer's programming software or through the manufacturer's online web portal. The software or web portal allows residents to be added and deleted from the system using a smartphone or computer.

There are ongoing costs associated with the use of telephone entry systems. These include the costs of telephone service, cellular service, or internet service. Some manufacturers may also charge a subscription fee to use their web portal for programming.

---

[14] Plain Old Telephone Service (POTS) refers to a legacy hardwired telephone lines that were widely used for more than 100 years. POTS telephone lines are now being displaced by Voice Over Internet Protocol (VOIP) phones and other technologies and are gradually becoming obsolete.

Hardwired Entry Systems

Hardwired entry systems are similar to telephone entry systems, except use hardwired connections rather than telephone lines or the internet to communicate with the residential units. Hardwired entry systems pre-date telephone entry systems and have been in use for decades.

Hardwired entry systems consist of two primary components, an intercom entry panel, and tenant intercom stations.

The intercom entry panel is used at the lobby entrances of multifamily buildings and at the unattended entrances to gated communities. The intercom entry panel has a speaker and microphone, as well as individual call buttons for each of the residential units. There is usually a name tag next to each of the call buttons that has the resident's name and/or unit number printed on it.

Figure 12-2- Intercom Entry Panel

Tenant intercom stations are small boxes that are installed in each of the residential units. Each intercom station includes a speaker, and a talk, listen, and door release button. The tenant intercom stations are connected to the intercom entry panel with "hardwired "cabling, giving these systems their name.

When a visitor arrives, he or she looks for the resident's name on the intercom entry panel, and then presses the call button next to the name. This causes the tenant intercom station in the residential unit to sound an alert. The resident can then speak to the visitor by using the listen and talk buttons on the intercom station. If the resident wishes to allow access, he or she presses the door release button.

There are many variations in hardwired entry systems depending on the manufacturer and model chosen. Some options include:

- Video camera at the entry panel and small video monitors in each of the tenant intercom stations, allowing residents to see who is at the door.
- Handset at the tenant intercom station to allow two-way communications without requiring the use of talk and listen buttons.

- Electronic directory at entry panel to eliminate the need for individual call buttons for each resident.

The disadvantage of hardwired entry systems is that they require that a tenant intercom station be installed in each residential unit. Depending on the size of the property, this can greatly increase the cost of a hardwired entry system over the cost of a telephone entry system.

The advantage of a hardwired entry system is that there are no ongoing costs for telephone or internet service and that the system requires no programming after it is installed. A hardwired system is also more reliable because it consists of fewer components and is not reliant on telephone or internet connections.

Traditional hardwired entry systems are not capable of dialing a resident's cell phone [15]. While this may be considered a disadvantage, many property managers consider it to be an advantage because only residents who are actually in their residential units can unlock doors for visitors. This prevents residents who are away from the building from opening the door for people. This can increase security and prevent violation of house rules.

Point-to-Point Intercom Systems

Point-to-point intercom systems are used to communicate between two or more designated locations in a building. For example, in a high-rise condominium, there may be a need to communicate between a loading dock door and a concierge desk so that delivery drivers can be let into the building when they arrive.

A simple point-to-point intercom system consists of one "master station" and one "sub-station". The master station is located at the point inside the building where communications is to be received. The sub-station is located at the point where the communication is to be originated. Using the example above, the intercom master station would be installed at the concierge's desk, and the sub-station would be installed on the wall outside of the loading dock door.

The master station provides control of the intercom system and typically includes a station selector switch, talk button, speaker, amplifier, and volume control. The sub-station typically includes just a speaker and call button. When the delivery driver arrives, he or she presses the call button on the sub-station. This causes the master station to ring.

To accept the call, the concierge presses the station selector switch. When this button is pressed, the concierge can instantly listen to sounds at the sub-station. To talk to the delivery driver, the concierge presses the talk button. When finished speaking, the concierge releases the talk button to listen to the reply from the driver. This goes back and forth for as long as the conversation continues, with the concierge pressing the talk button when he or she wishes to speak, and releasing the talk button when he or she wishes to listen.

At the conclusion of the conversation, the concierge presses the station selector switch again to terminate the connection.

---

[15] Some newer hardwired entry systems are available with an option that allows them to dial outside telephone numbers.

Figure 12-3 - Intercom Master Station

Intercom master stations are available in versions that can support one, five, or ten or more sub-stations. Some master stations include door release buttons that can be used to unlock the doors or gates where the sub-stations are located. Some point-to-point intercom systems have video cameras in each of the sub-stations and a small video monitor in the intercom master station, allowing the person at the sub-station to be seen as well as heard.

Auto-Dialing Telephones

Autodialing telephones are self-contained units that typically contain a call button, speaker, and microphone. Most autodialing telephones are packaged in a rugged enclosure and are weather-resistant, allowing them to be used both indoors and outdoors. Autodialing telephones are available in versions that allow communications over both regular POTS telephone lines and VOIP (Voice Over Internet Protocol) lines.

Autodialing telephones are programmed to dial a preset telephone number. When the call button is pressed, this number is automatically dialed. When the person receiving the call answers, two-way communications is established, allowing both parties to both talk and listen.

Figure 12-4 - Autodialing Telephone Used as Emergency Phone

Autodialing telephones can be used in a variety of applications at multifamily properties. Some of these applications include:

- Used as point-to-point intercom systems at loading dock doors, service gates, and other locations where delivery or service people may require access.
- Used as emergency telephones at swimming pools, spas, and other recreational facilities. The phones would be used to call 911 in the event of an emergency. These phones are sometimes required by local regulations.
- Used as emergency "call boxes" in parking garages and in surface parking lots. These phones can be programmed to call 911 or on-site security officers when help is needed. Phones used for this purpose are often used in conjunction with flashing lights and emergency signage.

There are usually ongoing costs for the telephone lines used by autodialing telephones unless they are connected to an internal telephone system. These costs can add up over a period of years. When an autodialing telephone is used for communications between two points within a building, it is sometimes more cost-effective to use a point-to-point intercom system, eliminating the need to pay for a telephone line.

Video Doorbells

Video doorbells are devices intended to replace a regular doorbell button at the entrance door to a residential unit. Video doorbells have a speaker, microphone, and video camera. Video doorbells are typically powered by the existing doorbell wiring, although there are also versions available that can be powered by batteries. Video doorbells communicate using a Wi-Fi connection.

Video doorbells work in conjunction with a smartphone app that is installed on the resident's phone. When a person arrives at the door, they press the call button on the video doorbell. This causes an alert to sound on the resident's phone. The resident can then see and communicate with the person at the door.

Figure 12-5 - Video Doorbell

Most video doorbells provide a motion detection feature that can notify the resident when there is motion detected at the door. This can provide an early alert of people approaching the door even before they have had a chance to press the call button.

A strong Wi-Fi signal at the video doorbell is required for it to operate reliably. In some cases, a Wi-Fi signal that works well within a residential unit can't reach the video doorbell. This may require relocation of the router or the installation of a Wi-Fi extender.

Most manufacturers of video doorbells offer a service that allows the recording of the images produced by the video camera. This feature allows the video doorbell to serve as a simple video surveillance system. There is usually a small monthly charge for this service.

Chapter 13: Alarm Systems

What is an Alarm System?

An alarm system is an electronic system that is intended to provide a warning of an abnormal or hazardous condition. Common types of alarm systems include fire alarm systems, burglar alarm systems, and panic alarm systems. Alarm systems can sound an audible warning to notify occupants on the premises, send a signal to notify responsible parties at locations off-premises, or both.

The goals of an alarm system can include providing safety for occupants by allowing them to escape hazardous conditions, summoning necessary help in an emergency, and encouraging people intent on doing harm to flee.

Intrusion Alarm Systems

Intrusion alarm systems, also called burglar alarm systems, are used to detect forced entry into a building. An intrusion alarm system is turned on when the occupants are away, and turned off when the occupants return. Intrusion alarm systems used in homes may also allow a portion of the system to be turned on when the occupants are at home.

Intrusion alarm systems are made up of the following components:

Detection Devices

Detection devices are used to detect conditions that indicate that an intruder has entered the premises. Common types of detection devices include:

- Magnetic contact switches: these are installed on doors and windows to detect when the door or window has been opened. Magnetic contact switches consist of two parts, a magnet that is installed on the door or window, and a magnetic switch installed on the door or window frame.
- Motion detectors: these are installed to detect the presence of motion in a room or other area. Motion detectors are mounted on the wall or ceiling and pointed in the direction where detection is wanted. The most popular type of motion detector is the passive infrared (PIR) motion detector, which detects body heat.
- Glass breakage detectors: these are installed on the wall or ceiling near the windows on the inside of the building. These detectors have microphones that listen for the sounds of breaking glass.
- Photoelectric beams: these consist of two units, a photoelectric transmitter, and a photoelectric receiver. These two units are pointed at each other, and an invisible beam of infrared light is transmitted between the two. If this beam is broken, the alarm is activated.

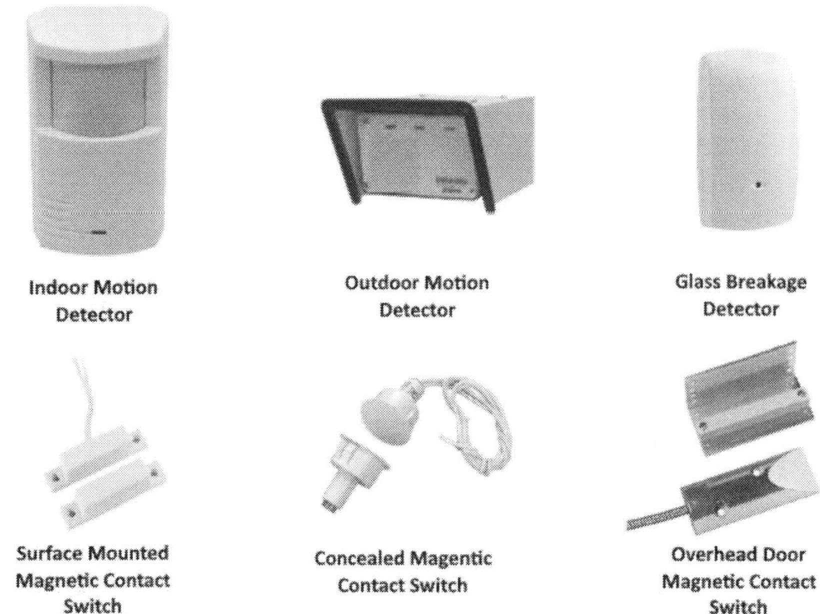

Figure 13-1 - Examples of Alarm Detection Devices

Most detection devices are available in both wireless and wired versions. Wireless devices are easier and less expensive to install because there is no need to install wiring. However, wireless devices can be more prone to failure and require periodic battery replacement. Wired devices cost more to install but are more reliable and don't require battery replacement.

<u>Signaling Devices</u>

Signaling devices are used to notify building occupants and others that the intrusion alarm system has detected an intruder. Common types of signaling devices include:

- Electronic sirens: These can be installed inside or outside of the building and produce a loud sound when the intrusion alarm system has detected an intruder. Several types of sounds can be produced by these sirens, the most common sounding like the siren used on an emergency vehicle.
- Digital voice announcers: These can be installed inside or outside of the building and broadcast a prerecorded message in a human voice when the intrusion alarm system has detected an intruder. This message is intended to warn the intruder that his or her presence has been detected, hopefully causing them to flee.
- Strobe lights: These can be installed inside or outside of the building and provide a visual warning when the intrusion alarm system has detected an intruder. Strobe lights create pulsing flashes of high intensity light that allow them to be easily noticed. Strobe lights are often used in addition to electronic sirens or digital voice announcers.

Figure 13-2 - Examples of Alarm Signaling Devices

Arming Stations

Arming stations are the devices used by occupants to arm (turn-on) and disarm (turn-off) the intrusion alarm system.

The first type of arming station is the keypad arming station. Keypad arming stations have a numeric keypad, visual display, and indicator lights. Each user of the system is issued a numeric code. This code allows the user to arm and disarm the system as well as to control other functions. The visual display and indicator lights tell the user whether the system is armed or disarmed and shows if there are any problems with the system.

Keypad arming stations are typically installed inside of the building near the main entrance. To allow users to exit the building after the system has been armed, the system provides a short delay between when the arming command is entered and when the system actually arms. This is known as the "exit delay" period. To allow users to enter the building without setting off the alarm, the system provides a short delay between when the entrance door is opened and when the alarm is actually set off. This is known as the "entry delay" period, and gives users time to get inside the building to disarm the alarm when they enter.

Figure 13-3 - Keypad Arming Station

Keypad arming stations contain a sounder that provides audible feedback to the users. This includes sounding a warning during the exit and entry delay periods, as well as sounding a loud alarm when the system has detected an intrusion.

The second type of arming station is the key-switch arming station. This is a simple device that contains a key-operated switch and one or more indicator lights. Each user of the system is issued a key that can be used to arm and disarm the system. Key-switch arming stations are much simpler to use than keypad arming stations but provide far fewer capabilities.

The third type of arming station is not a separate physical device, but rather an app that is installed on the user's smartphone. This app allows authorized users to arm and disarm the intrusion alarm system remotely. The use of this type of app may not be supported by all control panels and may require that a separate subscription fee be paid to the company that installed or monitors the system.

Control Panel

The control panel is the heart of the intrusion alarm system. All detection devices, signaling devices, and arming stations are connected to the control panel. Modern control panels contain a microprocessor and programmable memory which allow them to be specifically programmed to meet the needs of the facility in which they are installed.

Most control panels also contain a built-in digital communicator that allows them to send signals to an off-site alarm monitoring center. Communications options include telephone line connections, internet connections, cellular telephone connections, and long-range radio connections. Some of these options are provided directly by the control panel, while others may require the addition of an external accessory.

Most control panels support the use of wireless detection devices, either directly, or through connection to an external wireless receiver.

In most cases, the control panel does its work behind the scenes and the user has no need to interact with it. Because of this, control panels are usually installed in a telephone room, electrical room, or other secure location inside of the building.

Here are some ways that intrusion alarm systems can be used at multifamily properties:

Residential Units

Intrusion alarm systems can be installed within the individual residential units. When units are individually owned, this is typically done at the discretion and expense of the individual homeowner, although some developers may install an intrusion alarm system in all units as a part of the original construction process.

At rental units, intrusion alarm systems can be installed at the renter's option, but the types of systems that can be used and how they are installed should be specified by the property manager. At higher-end rental units, intrusion alarm systems can be installed by the building owner and offered as an amenity to residents.

Intrusion alarm systems in residential units typically consist of magnetic contact switches on exterior doors, motion detectors in hallways, an inside electronic siren, a keypad arming station, and a control panel.

Offices and Shops

At larger multifamily properties, intrusion alarm systems can be installed to protect building offices, maintenance shops, and other rooms that have high-value assets. These systems would be armed at times when property management staff was not on the premises.

Intrusion alarm systems in offices and shops typically consist of magnetic contact switches on the interior and exterior doors that lead into the room, motion detectors in the room itself, an inside electronic siren, a keypad arming station, and a control panel. Glass breakage detectors may also be used if the room has windows that are vulnerable.

Resident Storage Rooms

At multifamily properties where there is a high risk of burglaries at resident storage lockers, intrusion alarm systems can be installed on the storage rooms. These systems would be turned on and off by residents using a keypad arming station or key-switch arming station. The systems can also be automatically disarmed for a predetermined time period when a resident uses an access card to enter the room.

Intrusion alarm systems used in storage rooms typically consist of magnetic contact switches on the storage room doors, motion detectors in the storage room, an inside electronic siren, a keypad or key-operated switch arming station, and a control panel.

Object Protection

Intrusion alarm systems can be used to protect specific objects located in common areas of a multifamily property. These objects could include television sets, computers, artwork, furniture, and other high-value items.

The intrusion alarm systems used to protect objects are typically left armed at all times and only disarmed when the item needs to be moved or serviced by a member of the property management team. For example, an intrusion alarm could be used to protect a piece of artwork in a building lobby. Residents could come and go freely through the lobby without setting off the alarm. However, if someone attempted to remove the artwork, it would sound an alarm.

Intrusion alarm systems used for object protection typically consist of a magnetic switch installed on the object, a keypad arming station, and a control panel. Often, a little creativity is needed so that the magnetic switch is hidden and is not activated when the object is used normally, but provides a positive activation when the object is removed.

In many cases, the magnetic contact switch installed on the object can be connected to another intrusion alarm control panel, such as the one used in the building office. This eliminates the need to install a keypad arming station and control panel just for object protection.

Outdoor Protection

Intrusion alarm systems can be used to detect intrusions into outdoor areas of a multifamily property. Examples of locations where intrusion alarm systems can be used outdoors include:

- Outdoor swimming pools, to detect entry into the pool area during the times that it is closed.
- Rooftops, to detect intruders who may attempt to gain access to the property by climbing over from the roof of a neighboring property.
- Fences and walls, to detect intruders climbing over.
- Outdoor utility areas, to detect intruders entering in an attempt to steal or vandalize equipment.

Intrusion alarm systems used outdoors must be carefully designed for the specific conditions that exist at the location where they will be installed. In many cases, outdoor photoelectric beams or outdoor motion detectors can be used. In other cases, fence detection systems or other special outdoor detection systems must be used.

Because most outdoor intrusion alarm systems are intended to scare away intruders, they usually include outdoor electronic sirens or digital voice announcers as well as strobe lights. They may also be connected so that they automatically turn on flood lights to illuminate the area when an intrusion is detected.

Outdoor intrusion detection systems include a keypad arming station and control panel installed inside the building. Some outdoor intrusion detection systems are left armed at all times except when authorized staff is working in the area. An example would be an intrusion alarm system on a rooftop, which would only need to be disarmed when someone was working on the roof.

Other outdoor intrusion alarm systems are only armed when the area being protected is unoccupied. An example would be an outdoor swimming pool area, which would be armed only after the pool had closed for the day. These systems can be armed and disarmed manually by property management staff, or can be programmed to automatically arm and disarm according to a predetermined time schedule.

Panic Alarm Systems

Panic alarm systems are used to summon help quickly and silently when needed. At multifamily properties, panic buttons are commonly installed at locations where property management staff most frequently interacts with the general public. These locations can include building offices, concierge desks, and gatehouses. Panic buttons can also be used at locations on the property where residents may feel isolated and need a means to call for help. These locations can include fitness centers, locker rooms, laundry rooms and other such areas.

There are two types of panic buttons available: wired panic buttons, and wireless panic buttons.

Wired panic buttons are small devices that are mounted on a wall or on the underside of a desk or countertop. The panic button has an actuator button that activates when pressed. Most panic buttons have a protective shroud surrounding the actuator button to prevent it from being pushed accidentally. Some panic buttons have two actuator buttons, both which must be pressed simultaneously in order to activate the alarm. This is to provide further protection against false activations.

Figure 13-4 - Wired Panic Button

Wireless panic buttons are portable devices that are actually small radio transmitters. Wireless panic buttons have one or more actuator buttons on them, that when pressed, send out a radio signal that activates the alarm. Wireless panic buttons are designed to be worn or to be carried on a person, but can also be mounted to a wall or the underside of a desk or counter.

Wireless panic buttons must be used in conjunction with at least one wireless receiver. This receiver is installed in the general area where the wireless panic buttons will be used. Depending on the type of wireless system used and the total area where coverage is required, several wireless receivers may be needed.

Figure 13-5 - Wireless Panic Button

Wired panic buttons and wireless panic receivers must be connected to an alarm control panel. At properties that already have an intrusion alarm system, the same control panel can be used for both the panic buttons and the intrusion alarm. At properties without an intrusion alarm, it is necessary to install a separate control panel just for the panic buttons.

Panic buttons are almost always programmed as a "silent" alarm that send a signal to an off-site alarm monitoring center. While it is possible to program panic buttons so that they also activate an electronic siren, this is rarely recommended because of the potential for an agitated person to become even more dangerous when they know that a panic button has been pressed.

Portable Panic Alarm Devices

Portable panic alarm devices allow panic alarms to be sent from almost anywhere, not just inside of a building. Portable panic alarm devices can be carried and used by people on the move, and as long as there is cell phone coverage, the device is operational.

Portable panic alarm devices are ideal for employees who travel throughout a property, such as leasing agents, on-site managers, and maintenance and housekeeping employees. Portable panic alarm devices can also be used by individual residents who wish to have a panic button that can be activated when travelling outside of their homes.

There are two categories of portable panic alarm devices, those that are cell phone based, and those that are standalone. Cell phone based systems require that the user has a functioning cell phone with them. On some systems, the panic alarm system is activated using an app on the cell phone itself. Some of these systems also allow the use of a portable panic button that is connected to the cell phone via Bluetooth. This allows the panic alarm to be activated remotely without having to use the screen on the cell phone, but the cell phone is what is actually used to send the alarm.

Standalone systems operate completely independently and do not require a cell phone. Some standalone systems come in the form of an ID badge that is worn around the neck with a lanyard or clipped on to clothing. Other standalone systems come in the form of a portable device that is similar to a wireless panic button.

When the button on a portable panic alarm device is pressed, it can send a silent alarm signal to an off-site monitoring center, or can directly notify friends or coworkers. All portable panic alarm devices use a GPS signal to identify the place where the user is located.

Most portable panic alarm devices require the initial purchase of a device or app, and then subscription to a monitoring service that has an annual fee. Some cell-phone based systems use apps that are available for free and can send notifications to friends and coworkers without requiring a subscription.

Environmental Alarm Systems

Although not directly related to security, alarms can be provided at multifamily properties to alert management of adverse environmental conditions. Two popular types of environmental alarms are:

<u>Water Leak Detectors</u>

Water leak detectors detect the presence of water on a floor. The detectors can be used in laundry rooms, mechanical rooms, and other areas prone to flooding to provide an early warning of water leaks.

<u>Temperature Detectors</u>

Temperature detectors detect high and low temperature conditions. These detectors allow the setting of both a minimum and maximum temperature. When the temperature goes above or below the established settings, the detector is activated. Temperature detectors can be used in mechanical rooms, pump rooms, walk-in coolers and freezers, community wine cellars, and other areas where high or low temperatures would have an adverse effect.

At properties that already have an intrusion alarm system, the existing control panel can be used for both the intrusion alarm and the water leak or temperature detectors . At properties without an intrusion alarm, it will be necessary to install a separate control panel just for the water leak or temperature detectors.

Exit Alarms

Exit alarms are used on emergency egress doors at buildings where the use of such doors would compromise security. An example would be an emergency egress door out of a parking garage that provided access to a secured residential corridor in a multifamily building. Anyone who managed to sneak into the parking garage could use this door to gain access to the residential areas.

Exit alarms consist of an audible sounder and some type of actuating device. This device can be a magnetic contact switch mounted to the door, or an electrical switch built into a mechanical exit device. Exit alarms can be mounted on the door itself, or mounted on the wall next to the door. Some exit alarms are used in conjunction with the existing lock hardware on the door, while others also serve as the mechanism that locks the door. When the door is opened, the alarm sounds.

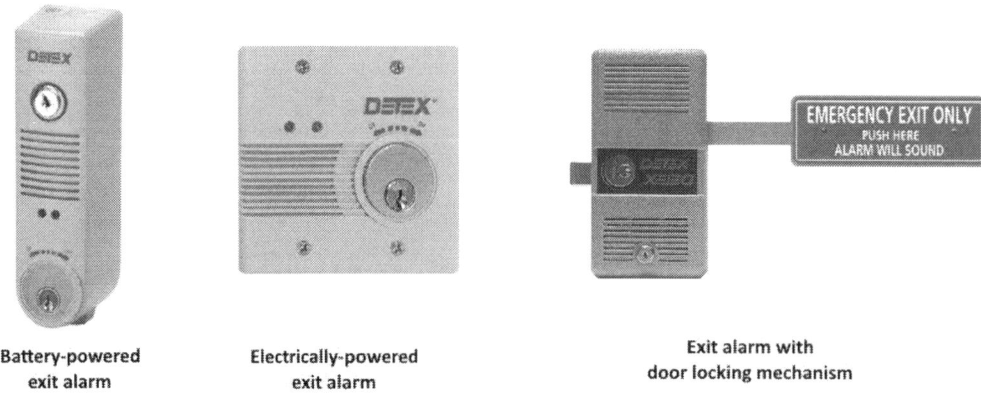

Figure 13-6 - Types of Exit Alarms

Exit alarms are available in both battery-powered and electrically-powered versions. Battery-powered exit alarms are less expensive and easier to install, but there is a need to frequently change batteries, especially in locations where the door is misused often. At multifamily properties, it is common to find exit alarms with dead batteries. This is usually caused by someone exiting through the door, causing the alarm to sound and continue to sound until the battery is dead. When the door is eventually closed, no one thinks to replace the battery, leaving the exit alarm inoperative.

Electrically-powered exit alarms are powered from a building electrical circuit, either directly, or through a low voltage power supply. Electrically-powered exit alarms are more expensive than battery-powered exit alarms, but eliminate the need to change batteries.

Exit alarms are available with mortise lock cylinders that can allow the exit alarm to be turned on and off from either or both sides of the door using a key. These lock cylinders can be used by property management staff or residents when it is necessary to open the door without setting off the alarm.

When an egress door with an exit alarm needs to be used frequently, using a key to bypass the alarm can become cumbersome. A more convenient solution is to use an access card to bypass the alarm. This is accomplished by installing a card reader on one or both sides of the door, and connecting the building's access control system to the exit alarm. When a user needs to pass through the door, he or she presents an access card to the card reader, temporarily bypassing the alarm.

Door-Propped-Open Alarms

Door-propped-open alarms are used to monitor the status of a door and sound an alarm when the door has been open longer than a predetermined period. Door-propped-alarms can be useful at buildings where residents frequently leave exterior doors propped open either deliberately or accidently.

For example, a door-propped-open alarm might be used on the exterior door to a building lobby. Residents and visitors could come and go throughout the day without setting off the alarm. However, if a resident propped open the door to load groceries, and then failed to close the door afterwards, the alarm would sound after the predetermined time period. The time that the door can be held open is adjustable and is typically set at between one and three minutes.

Door-propped open alarms are available as self-contained units that can be powered by a battery or external power supply. If the door is controlled by an access control system, it is usually possible to monitor the status of the door through the system rather than having to install a separate door-propped-open alarm device.

Alarm Notification Options

When an alarm system detects an abnormal condition, there are three methods of notification that can be used:

Local Alarm Notification

Local alarm notification is when signaling devices such as electronic sirens, digital voice announcers, and strobe lights are used as the only means of communicating that an abnormal condition exists. An example would be an intrusion alarm system that was not connected to an off-site alarm monitoring center and the user was relying exclusively on the electronic siren as the notification device.

For an intrusion alarm system, the primary goal of local alarm notification is to scare away the intruder. A secondary goal is to alert people in the vicinity that the alarm is activated. This allows them to observe any unusual activity that is going on, and gives them the opportunity to notify a responsible party if they are so inclined. For example, a resident may hear the sound of a siren coming from a neighbor's apartment and choose to call an on-site security officer or the police.

Off-Site Alarm Monitoring

Off-site alarm monitoring is when the alarm control panel communicates with an off-site alarm monitoring center when an abnormal condition exists. Off-site alarm monitoring centers are private businesses that specialize in monitoring alarm systems for a fee. Most alarm monitoring centers operate nationally and may monitor hundreds of thousands of different accounts.

When an alarm is activated, a signal is sent to the monitoring center. Depending on how the alarm system was designed, the signal sent may be very general or very precise. For example, a generalized signal would notify the monitoring center that an alarm was coming from the "Clubhouse", while a more precise signal would notify the monitoring center that the alarm was coming from the "Clubhouse North Entry Door".

When an alarm monitoring center receives an alarm signal, they follow a specific set of instructions that were provided by the property owner or manager. For example, when a panic button is pressed, the monitoring center would likely be instructed to immediately notify the police. For other types of alarms, such as water leak alarms, the monitoring center would likely be instructed to call a maintenance technician or other member of the property management team. The instructions given on how to respond to intrusion alarm systems can vary greatly depending on where the property is located.

Most law enforcement agencies are overwhelmed with false alarms and have instituted policies regarding if and how they will respond to intrusion and panic alarm systems. Most agencies consider panic alarms to be a high priority and will respond as soon as possible when a panic alarm is activated. Some agencies require that the monitoring center call the premises to verify the validity of the panic alarm before they will respond.

Policies on intrusion alarm systems vary greatly from agency to agency. Some agencies will respond to intrusion alarms without restriction, others may require that the alarm be verified by telephone or video camera before they will respond, and some may refuse to respond to intrusion alarms entirely. Agencies who do choose to respond may consider intrusion alarms to be a low priority and it may take 30 minutes or longer for an officer to respond. Many law enforcement agencies issue fines for false alarms and may refuse to respond to an intrusion alarm if false alarms exceed a certain number over a specific period of time.

If police response to intrusion alarm systems is not an option, the best alternative is to use a private security officer to respond to alarms. If the property does not have on-site security officers, it is usually possible to subscribe to a security patrol service that will respond to alarms when notified by the alarm monitoring center.

At multifamily properties, there are several types of alarms where asking the police to respond would be inappropriate, regardless of their response policies. This would include exit alarms on egress doors, object protection alarms on items within the building, and most types of outdoor protection alarms. Response to these types of alarms is best done by a security officer who can evaluate the situation and then call the police if an actual crime is being committed.

Proprietary Monitoring

Proprietary monitoring is when alarms are monitored by in-house property management or security staff. This monitoring is typically performed at a location that is staffed at all times, such as a gatehouse or concierge desk that is manned 24/7. Alarms are commonly monitored using an access control system client workstation that provides an alert when an alarm is activated, displaying the type of alarm and the location that it is coming from. The staff member monitoring the alarm can then take the appropriate action, such as notifying the on-site security officer.

At properties that do not have a location that is continuously staffed, there are several methods that can allow alarms to be monitored by on-site property management or security staff. Many server-based access control systems have the ability to send alarm messages via email. These messages can be sent to the cell phones of on-site staff members.

If the property does not have an access control system, or if the access control system lacks email capability, there are external devices known as alarm dialers that can send text, email, or voice messages to cell phones. At properties that use two-way radios, there are devices that allow pre-recorded messages to be automatically broadcast over the two-way radio system when an alarm is activated.

The best type of alarm notification method to use depends on the resources available at the property and the criticality of the alarms being monitored. Smaller multifamily properties without an on-site staff will probably need to rely exclusively on the use of local alarm notification and off-site alarm monitoring. Properties with an on-site security staff will likely choose to monitor some or all of their alarms on-site using the proprietary monitoring method.

It often works well to use two or more methods of alarm notification at the same time. For example, when using an outdoor protection system, local notification should be provided to scare the intruder away, and off-site or proprietary notification used to notify the appropriate people that an intrusion is taking place.

As a general rule, critical alarms such as panic alarms are best monitored at an off-site monitoring center. If proprietary monitoring is used for critical alarms, it is sometimes beneficial to use redundant monitoring, where alarms are monitored both on-site and by an off-site alarm monitoring center.

Alarm notification made exclusively by voice message or email to a cell phone is not recommended for panic alarms and other critical alarms. This is because of the potential for a missed message caused by network problems or dead spots in cell phone coverage areas.

Chapter 14: Video Surveillance Systems

What is a Video Surveillance System?

A video surveillance system is an electronic system that is used to capture, display, and record visual images. Video surveillance systems were once commonly called closed circuit television (CCTV) systems.

Video surveillance systems can play an important part in the overall security program at a multifamily property. Some of the primary functions of a video surveillance system include:

Real-Time Viewing

A video surveillance system can be actively monitored by staff, allowing staff to observe and react to unusual activity that may pose a threat to the property. For example, a video surveillance system might be installed to allow the viewing of an outdoor parking lot area from a concierge desk. The concierge sitting at the desk could observe activity in the parking lot, and take action if something suspicious was spotted.

Real-time viewing of video surveillance systems at multifamily properties is rare because few properties have the staffing resources necessary to monitor the system on a continuous basis.

Assessment

A video surveillance system can be used as a tool to remotely assess a situation in order to decide an appropriate course of action.

One example would be where a video surveillance system was installed to allow the viewing of a perimeter fence that was equipped with an intrusion alarm system. When the alarm on the fence was activated, the person monitoring the system could determine if it were an actual intrusion (an intruder climbing over the fence), or something more innocent (a landscaper trimming a bush next to the fence).

Another example would be where a video surveillance system was used to view an exterior loading dock door from a concierge desk. When a call was received from the intercom station at the door, the concierge could use the video surveillance system to verify the identity of the caller before deciding to admit him or her into the building.

When the video surveillance system is used for assessment purposes, it is not necessary to monitor the system continuously, but only when an event occurs. This type of monitoring is called "event monitoring". Event monitoring makes effective use of staffing resources and is frequently used at larger multifamily properties that have an on-site staff.

Recording

A video surveillance system can be used to record activity to allow the after-the-fact investigation of security and safety incidents. For example, if a theft occurred in a lobby that was monitored by a video surveillance system, the video recordings could be examined to determine when the theft occurred and hopefully identify who committed it. Video recordings can also be used to investigate accidents and safety incidents, such as slips and falls occurring on the property.

The video recording capability can be used in conjunction with the real-time viewing and assessment capabilities of the video surveillance system. Video recording is by far the most common reason that multifamily properties install video surveillance systems. Multifamily properties of any size can benefit from the video recording feature.

Components of Video Surveillance Systems

The basic components of a simple video surveillance system include video surveillance cameras, video monitors, and video recorders. Within these basic components, there are numerous varieties of equipment that can be used depending on the requirements of the specific property where the video surveillance system is used. There are also many accessories that can be used to enhance the performance of the system.

Video Surveillance Cameras

Video surveillance cameras are the primary component of any video surveillance system. Video surveillance cameras capture a full-motion image and convert it to a format that can be transmitted electronically to video viewing and recording devices. Video surveillance cameras vary widely in capabilities, performance, and cost.

The following are some of the factors that differentiate video surveillance cameras:

Camera Technology

The original video surveillance technology was known as analog video technology. This technology was based on the original NTSC (National Television System Committee) standards for broadcast television introduced in the 1940's. Analog video technology was widely used for security video surveillance systems up until the mid-2000's. Many analog video surveillance systems remain in use, and it is still possible to purchase analog cameras today. Many low-cost camera kits and some specialty cameras continue to use analog technology.

Analog cameras convert images into what is known as a composite video output. This output is then connected to a coaxial cable [16], which is in turn home-run to a video monitor or recording device. Each camera requires its own coaxial cable. A building that has hundreds of analog cameras would have hundreds of coaxial cables running throughout the property.

In the late 1990's, a new type of camera known as the IP (Internet Protocol) network camera, or simply "IP camera", was introduced. Adoption of IP cameras was slow, but began to gain momentum in the mid-2000's.

IP cameras convert images into data packets rather than composite video signals. The IP camera, acting as a small computer, transmits these packets over a standard data network. This can be the regular data network used at the property, or a separate data network that is installed specifically for the video surveillance system. The use of a data network eliminates the need to run individual coaxial cables to each of the cameras, as the signal from all cameras is transmitted over the network.

IP cameras, unlike their analog predecessors, are not constrained by the limits of the NTSC standard and can provide images that are of significantly higher quality than that provided by analog cameras. IP cameras contain a microprocessor and memory that allows them to act

[16] Coaxial cable is the most common method used to connect analog cameras, but connections can also be made using fiber-optic cable and twisted-pair cable if the correct converters are used.

intelligently. IP cameras can both send and receive data. Each IP camera has its own "IP address", allowing it to be individually monitored, controlled, and programmed over the network.

Because of the many benefits of IP cameras, they have become the most predominate type of camera used in video surveillance systems today. While there are some alternative technologies that compete with IP cameras, these are not widely used and command only a tiny percentage of the overall market.

Form Factor

Cameras are available in a number of different types of physical configurations, known as "form factors". The following are some common types of camera form factors:

Dome Cameras:

Dome cameras consist of a semicircular shaped camera body that includes both camera and lens. Dome cameras can be mounted directly to a wall or ceiling, or can be mounted using an external bracket. Dome cameras are the most popular type of camera used today.

Figure 14-1 - Dome Camera

Bullet Cameras:

Bullet cameras consist of a tubular enclosure that includes both camera body and lens. Bullet cameras come with an integrated bracket that allows them to be mounted to the wall or ceiling.

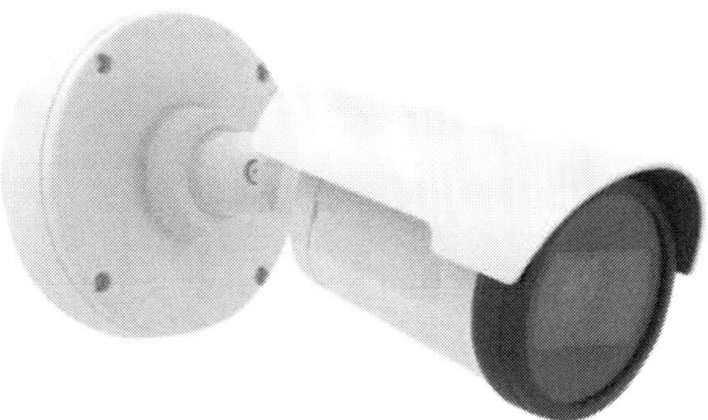

Figure 14-2 - Bullet Camera

Box Cameras:

Box cameras consist of a rectangular-shaped camera body with a detachable camera lens. Box cameras are mounted using a bracket at the bottom or top of the camera body. Box cameras are commonly installed within a separate protective camera housing, but can be installed without a housing when used indoors. Once the most popular type of camera, the use of box cameras has fallen off today because of user preference for dome or bullet cameras.

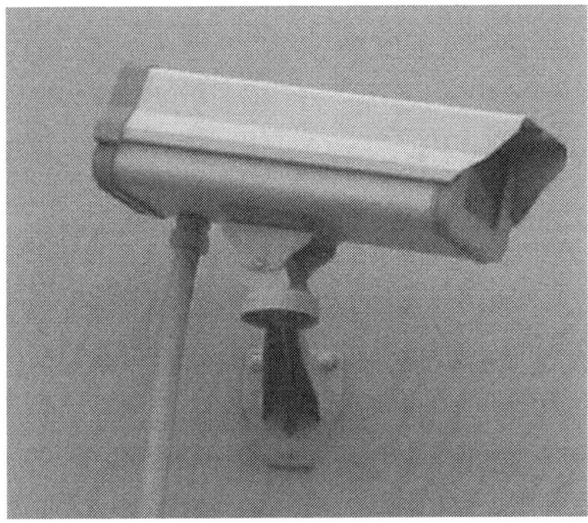

Figure 14-3- Box Camera

Multi-Sensor Cameras:

Multi-sensor cameras have multiple camera sensors and lenses that can each be pointed in separate directions. Multi-sensor cameras consist of either three or four separate sensors and lenses packaged into a single domed housing. Multi-sensor cameras are relatively new and are becoming popular because of their ability to allow a single camera to serve the function of multiple cameras.

Figure 14-4 - Multi-Sensor Camera

Fisheye Cameras:

Fisheye cameras provide a panoramic 360 degree view of an area and are used to view small, confined areas such as lobbies. Fisheye cameras must typically be used with special software that allows the images to be correctly displayed.

Figure 14-5 - Fisheye Camera

Pinhole Cameras:

Pinhole cameras are designed to view through a very small hole, usually 1/4" or less, and are used in special applications where space for another type of camera is not available. One common use of pinhole cameras is at intercom stations, where the camera is built-into the face of the intercom station itself. Another use of the pinhole camera is for covert surveillance, where the camera can be hidden so that its presence is not obvious.

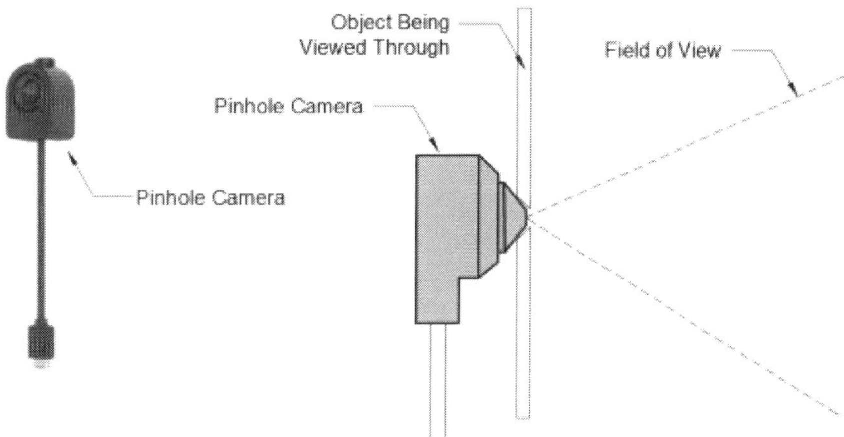

Figure 14-6 - Pinhole Camera

Pan-Tilt-Zoom (PTZ) Cameras:

Unlike other camera types that provide a view of a fixed area, PTZ cameras have the ability to move from right-to-left (pan), up and down (tilt), and focus near and far (zoom). To accomplish this, PTZ cameras have remotely controlled mechanisms that allow the camera to be moved as well as lenses that allow the camera image to be zoomed in and out. PTZ cameras are best used for real-time viewing and assessment purposes because they require the use of a human operator to make the most effective use of the camera.

Figure 14-7- Pan-Tilt-Zoom (PTZ) Camera

Most camera form factors permit the mounting of the camera in a variety of ways, including wall mounting, ceiling mounting, and pole mounting. Most camera form factors are available in both indoor and outdoor versions.

Resolution

The image that a camera sees is captured by an electronic component known as a camera sensor, sometimes called an imager. The sensor has a rectangular shaped array that is made up of thousands of individual sensing elements known as pixels. These pixels are arranged in horizontal and vertical rows. Camera resolution is specified by stating the number of horizontal pixels in each row by the number of vertical pixels in each row. For example, a camera may be said to have a 1920 x 1080 resolution, which means it has 1920 horizontal pixels by 1080 vertical pixels.

The total number of pixels in the camera sensor is often used as a shortcut when specifying camera resolution. This is calculated by multiplying the number of horizontal pixels by the number of vertical pixels. In the case of a 1920 x 1080 sensor, the total number of pixels would be 2,073,600 pixels. This is rounded off to an even number and stated in megapixels (millions of pixels), abbreviated as MP. So, a camera with a 1920 x 1080 resolution would be called a two megapixel or 2 MP camera.

IP cameras are available in a variety of resolutions starting at below 1 MP and going up to as high as 40 MP or more. Commonly used camera resolutions in video surveillance systems today are 1 MP, 2 MP, 3 MP, and 5 MP.

Terminology that is used in the consumer electronics industry is sometimes applied to cameras used for video surveillance. For example, the term "HD" may be used to describe a 2 MP camera, or the terms "4K" or "Ultra HD" may be used to describe an 8 MP camera.

In general, the greater the number of pixels a camera has, the more detail that the camera image will provide. Camera resolutions in video surveillance systems have been gradually trending upwards, with higher resolution cameras being used each year.

The amount of data that a camera transmits corresponds directly with the resolution of the camera sensor. For example, a 2 MP camera would transmit more data than a 1 MP camera, a 5 MP camera would transmit more data than a 2 MP camera, and so on. The term "bandwidth" is used to specify the rate of data transmitted by a camera. The higher the MP rating of a camera, the more bandwidth that it consumes. Bandwidth has an impact on both the transmission capacity of the data network, and the amount of disk or memory storage space required to store camera images.

Aspect Ratio

Aspect ratio refers to the ratio between the width and height of the imager. Older video surveillance cameras used an aspect ratio of 4:3, which has an image size that was 4 units wide and 3 units high. Modern video surveillance cameras use an aspect ratio of 16:9, which has an image size that is 16 units wide and 9 units tall. Most modern cameras can also be programmed to use the older 4:3 aspect ratio.

Many modern cameras also support what is known as corridor mode or hallway mode, where the aspect ratio is flipped 90 degrees, providing a 9:16 aspect ratio. This can be useful when viewing long narrow scenes such as hallways and alleyways.

Camera Lens

Camera lenses are optical devices that are used to gather light images and project these images on to the camera sensor. Camera lenses have two main parameters, their focal length, and their aperture. In video surveillance systems, focal length is of primary concern because it is the main factor in determining what the camera sees.

Focal length is measured in millimeters (mm). The lenses used with video surveillance cameras typically have a focal length of between 2 mm and 10 mm, although there are some lenses 150 mm or longer used for special applications. The focal length affects how wide or narrow the camera's field of view is. Lenses with shorter focal lengths provide a wider field of view, while lenses with longer focal lengths provide a narrower field of view.

Lenses can have a fixed or variable focal length. Fixed focal length lenses have a single focal length, such as 2 MM. Variable focal length lenses, sometimes called "varifocal" lenses, allow the focal length to be adjusted within a certain range, such as between 3 MM and 9 MM.

There are lenses available that provide an even greater range of focal lengths, often ranging from as short as 4 MM to as long as 150 MM or more. These lenses are most commonly capable of being controlled remotely and are used as a part of a pan-tilt-zoom (PTZ) camera.

The amount of light that is transmitted through a lens is determined by the size of its aperture, which is controlled by a device known as an iris. The iris can be opened or closed to allow more or less light to pass through. Lenses are available with either fixed or automatic irises. Fixed irises are manually adjusted at the time the camera is installed. Automatic irises are electrically controlled and automatically adjust to compensate for changing light levels. Fixed iris cameras work well in indoor areas where the level of lighting is constant. Automatic iris lenses are used outdoors and in other areas where light levels are expected to frequently change.

The box cameras that were widely used in the past allowed the camera and the camera lens to be selected separately, allowing many types of different lenses to be used with cameras. Most of the dome, bullet and multi-sensor cameras that are used today come with a built-in lens that cannot be changed. This is not a problem in most cases, because the lens provided with the camera works well in the majority of applications. However, if there is a need for a special lens, such as one capable of viewing a very long distance, it will probably be necessary to use it in conjunction with a box camera.

Sensitivity

Camera sensitivity is the amount of light that must be projected on the camera sensor in order to produce a usable image. There are a number of factors that affect camera sensitivity, including the camera lens and the characteristics of the camera sensor itself. Camera sensitivity is specified in a unit of measure known as the Lux.

Because it takes considerably more light to produce a color image than a black and white image, most quality cameras have a feature known as "day/night mode". This feature allows the camera to produce a color image when there is sufficient lighting, but revert to a black and white image when light falls below a certain level. The sensitivity of cameras with the day/night feature are often specified using two figures, one that indicates the amount of light required to produce a color image, the other that indicates the amount of light needed to produce a black and white image. For example, the specifications on a camera might say that it takes 0.05 Lux to produce a color image, but only 0.01 Lux to produce a black and white image.

Many cameras are available with IR (infrared) illuminators built-into the camera. These illuminators shine light on the scene being viewed by the camera. This light is just above the visible spectrum and cannot be seen by humans, but can be used by the camera sensor. IR illuminators allow cameras to work in areas with no visible light, so the specifications for cameras with built-in illuminators sometimes may say the camera is capable of operating at 0.00 Lux.

<u>Light Processing Capabilities</u>

Cameras produce the best quality images when viewing well-lit areas that have a consistent amount of light throughout the camera scene. Cameras face challenges when lighting is inconsistent within the scene, such as when there are some areas that are very dark and some areas that are very light. This could occur when a camera was viewing a relatively dark lobby area that had an exterior window with sunlight shining through it. The window would appear very bright and dominate the image, while the rest of the lobby would appear very dark, making it difficult to observe activity occurring here.

Another example would be when a camera was used to observe vehicles approaching a driveway entrance at night. The headlights on the vehicle would be very bright, while the rest of the vehicle would be very dark. This can make it difficult to accurately identify a vehicle or capture a license plate number.

To overcome these challenges, camera manufacturers have developed several different techniques to deal with variations in lighting in the camera scene. Depending on manufacturer, these may be called backlighting compensation, wide dynamic range (WDR), digital wide dynamic range (DWDR), or something else.

One widely used technology for dealing with light variations is WDR. This technology works by taking multiple images at different exposure levels and then combining them together to produce the final image. Some manufacturers may use other software techniques to alter the contrast and tone of the image.

Because different manufacturers use different techniques and different terminology to describe and measure light processing capabilities, it is difficult to compare cameras using written documentation alone. It is often best to test the actual cameras being considered in the environments where they will be used.

Frame Rate

Camera video images are created by streaming a series of still video images, also known as frames. The rate in which these frames are streamed is known as the frame rate, and is specified in FPS (frames per second). The analog cameras originally used for video surveillance followed the NTSC broadcast standard of 30 FPS.

IP cameras are capable of streaming at various frames. Most cameras allow the frame rate to be individually set at a rate between 1 and 30 FPS. Some specialty cameras are capable of streaming at as high as 60 FPS. Some types of very high resolution or multi-sensor cameras have a maximum frame rate below 30 FPS. The frame rate used affects the bandwidth that the camera uses, with higher frame rates consuming correspondingly larger amounts of bandwidth. This translates into more traffic on the data network and more storage space required for video recording.

While 30 FPS was once considered the standard, security experts have determined that frame rates as low as 5 FPS provide video that is perfectly acceptable for investigative purposes at multifamily properties. Setting cameras at a reduced frame rate can reduce network traffic and reduce the storage space needed for video recording.

Camera Power

Most IP cameras are powered over the same data cable that is used to connect them to the network. This technology is known as POE (Power-Over-Ethernet) and eliminates the need to run separate wiring for camera power in the majority of cases. Some outdoor cameras may have heaters, blowers or infrared illuminators that draw power in excess of what can be provided by a standard POE connection. This can require the use of higher-powered POE (POE +) or the use of extra cabling to supply the additional power.

Application Programs

Because IP cameras are actually small computers, they can run computer programs that perform various functions at the camera itself. Some of these programs come built into the camera, while others have to be purchased separately and installed on the camera.

The most basic program installed in cameras is simple motion detection, which allows the camera to take actions when motion is detected in the camera scene. This program comes by default in most IP cameras and can be used to start recording of camera images when motion is detected. Other more sophisticated programs can be used for people counting, license plate recognition, and many other purposes.

Audio Capabilities

Some IP cameras are capable of transmitting either one-way or two-way audio signals and come equipped with a built-in microphone, speaker, or both. Other cameras support the use of audio, but require that external microphones or speakers be used.

Care should be taken to observe privacy laws when using cameras to record audio. The laws concerning the recording of audio can be much stricter than those that apply to the recording of video.

Determining What A Camera Will See

The image that a camera sees is determined by a variety of factors, the most significant of which are the camera's resolution, the size and aspect ratio of the camera sensor, the field of view of the camera lens, and the distance between the camera and the objects being viewed.

The field of view is the most important factor in determining what the camera sees. Wider fields of view cover more area, but provide less detail, while narrow fields of view cover a smaller area, but provide more detail. The greater the size of the area that a camera covers, the less detail that it can provide.

Field of view is specified by stating the angle of the camera's horizontal view. A camera with a variable focal lens might have a focal length that is adjustable between 3.4 mm and 8.9 mm. With the lens set at the 3.4 mm setting, the lens would provide a horizontal viewing angle that was approximately 100 degrees. With the lens set at the 8.9 mm setting, the lens would provide a horizontal viewing angle that was approximately 36 degrees. So, this lens could be set to provide a viewing angle of anywhere between 36 degrees and 100 degrees.

The area that the camera sees is based on both the viewing angle and the distance between the camera and the objects being viewed. For example, if a wall were 20' away from the camera, and the viewing angle was set to 90 degrees, the camera would view an area of the wall that was approximately 40' wide. If the viewing angle on this camera was changed to 40 degrees, the camera would view an area of the wall that was approximately 15' wide.

One measurement commonly used to specify the level of detail provided in a camera image is known as "Pixels-Per-Foot" (PPF). This measurement divides the number of horizontal pixels in the camera's image sensor by the total width of the camera image.

For example, a 2 MP camera with a 1920 x 1080 resolution would have 1,920 horizontal pixels. If the camera lens were set to a 90 degree viewing angle, the width of the horizontal viewing area would be 40 feet. 1,920 pixels divided by 40 feet gives a result of 48 PPF resolution at the wall. Changing the viewing angle to 40 degrees on this same camera would produce a horizontal viewing area that was 15', yielding a resolution of 128 PPF at the wall. (1920 pixels divided by 15').

Examples of camera coverages with 90 degree and 40 degree viewing angles are shown in Figure 14-8 and Figure 14-9 below. As can be seen, the camera with the 90 degree viewing angle gives coverage of a wider area, but provides less PPF at the objects being viewed than the camera with the 40 degree viewing angle.

Please note that the above calculations are used as an example to illustrate the tradeoff between the amount of area that a camera can cover, and the level of detail provided in the camera image. The exact viewing angles, viewing areas, and PPF will vary depending on the type and size of the imager being used and other factors.

In simplified terms, a camera can either allow viewing of a very wide area with very little detail, or can view a smaller area with greater detail, but not both. The failure to understand this concept often results in disappointment. For example, a property owner may install a single camera to view a large parking lot and is then unhappy when the quality of the recorded video image does not allow a person to be identified or for a license plate number to be read.

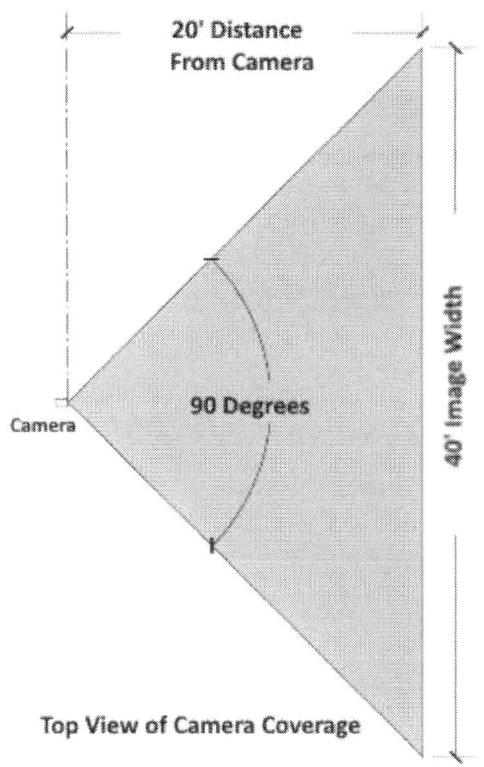

Camera View Seen on Screen

2 MP camera, 1920 x 1080 pixels, 90 degree viewing angle, 20' distance between camera and objects being viewed. 48 PPF at objects.

Figure 14-8 - Camera Coverage with 90 Degree Viewing Angle

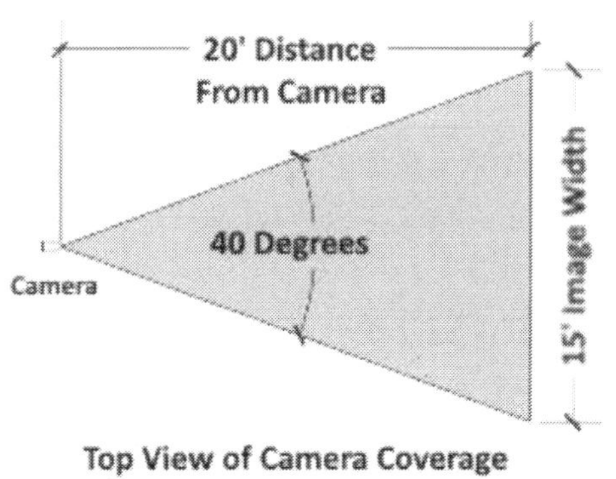

Camera View Seen on Screen

2 MP camera, 1920 x 1080 pixels, 40 degree viewing angle, 20' distance between camera and objects being viewed. 128 PPF at objects.

Figure 14-9 - Camera Coverage with 40 Degree Viewing Angle

The PPF required in a camera coverage area depends on the intended goals of that specific camera.

The goal of some cameras may be to just allow general observation of activity in an area without any particular need to identify a person or vehicle. In these cases, a camera that provided an image with a relatively low PPF could be used. The goal of other cameras might be to allow positive recognition of people or license plates. This would require that these cameras provide an image that had a much higher PPF.

Security experts have differing opinions on the exact number of PPF required to achieve the intended goals of a video surveillance system, however the following guidelines are commonly used:

Security Goal	***Level of Detail***	***PPF Required***
Detection	Image provides sufficient detail to allow a person or vehicle in motion to be seen and distinguished from the surrounding background.	10 to 15 PPF
Observation	Image provides sufficient detail to allow a viewed object to be positively identified as a person or vehicle rather than something else. Image provides general information on type of vehicle (car or truck), number of people, and direction of movement.	15 to 40 PPF
Recognition	Image provides sufficient detail to allow people already known to be recognized. Image allows type of clothing worn and objects being carried to be generally identified. Vehicle type, color and model can generally be determined.	40 to 60 PPF
Identification	Image provides sufficient detail to allow the identity of a person to be established beyond a reasonable doubt. Details concerning clothing being worn, items being carried, and activities being conducted can usually be determined. Detailed description of vehicles available. Vehicle license plates can be reliably read.	60 to 100+ PPF

While PPF is the most commonly used measurement to specify the level of detail provided in a camera image, it is by no means the only consideration. The amount and uniformity of lighting illuminating the camera scene can have a big impact on image quality. As a general rule, the less light available, the greater the PPF required to identify a person or object. Glare in the camera scene can also make it difficult to positively identify faces or license plates.

The PPF provided by a camera can be increased by moving the camera closer to the objects being viewed or by decreasing its viewing angle. A higher resolution (greater MP) camera can also be used, but this is not always as beneficial as it may first seem. For example, using a 5 MP camera instead of a 2 MP camera only increases PPF by about 33%.

Where To Place Cameras at Multifamily Properties

Design Strategy

If security were the only consideration, video surveillance systems would be designed so that every square foot of the common areas at a multifamily property was viewed by a camera. In the real-world, this would be prohibitively expensive and probably create a "big brother" atmosphere that was considered offensive by residents and visitors.

A more practical approach is to design a video surveillance system to view the areas where criminal activity is most likely to take place. These are known as "crime hotspots". At multifamily properties, typical crime hotspots can include resident storage rooms, bicycle rooms, mail and package rooms, and parking garages. Crime hotspots are one important place to install cameras at a multifamily property.

In some cases, crime hotspots can be so large that providing complete camera coverage throughout them is not cost effective. For example, a condominium building may have a multi-level parking garage that has 50,000 square feet of floor space. Providing camera coverage throughout the entire 50,000 square feet would require many cameras and be very costly.

Rather than to try to cover the entire garage, one approach is to provide cameras at strategic "chokepoints" – locations where the criminal is likely to have to pass in order to carry out a crime. Typical chokepoints at a parking garage would be at the garage exterior doors, garage stair doors, doors between the garage and the building, and at the garage elevator lobbies.

Placing cameras only at crime hotspots and strategic chokepoints throughout the property can reduce the number of cameras needed while still achieving the intended goals of the video surveillance system.

Locations of Cameras

The locations where cameras should be installed can vary greatly from property to property depending on property type, size, and location. The number of cameras used and the locations where they should be placed will also vary depending on the level of security risk that the property faces.

Camera locations should be specifically determined for each property based on needs and budget. Camera locations should be prioritized, with cameras installed at high priority locations first, and then installed at lower priority locations as desired or as funding becomes available.

The following are some recommended priorities for camera placements at multifamily properties:

Priority 1

- Exterior site entrances.
- Exterior building entrances, including overhead doors and pedestrian doors.
- Main building lobbies.
- Interior garage to building doors.

Priority 2

- Stairways.
- Elevator lobbies.
- Mail and package rooms.
- Resident storage rooms.
- Bicycle rooms.
- Amenity areas such as fitness centers, party rooms, media rooms, etc.
- Pathways between buildings and parking lots.

Priority 3

- Trash and recycle rooms.
- Exterior courtyards.
- Exterior parking lots.
- Interior of parking garages.
- Mechanical and electrical rooms.
- Within elevator cars.

Video Recording

Video recording is a crucial component of a video surveillance system used for security purposes. Prior to the year 2000, video cassette recorders (VCRs) were used to record video. These recorders required the use of video cassette tapes that had to be periodically changed. To get 30 days' worth of video recording often required boxfuls of tapes.

In the early to mid-2000's, the use of computer-based storage systems began to gradually replace the use of VCRs. These systems stored video on computer disks and eliminated the need to use video cassette tapes.

Video recording systems have continued to evolve, providing better quality video recordings, greater storage capacity, and features that make the retrieval and display of video recording easier and faster.

The following are some of the types of video recording systems in use today:

Digital Video Recorders

Digital video recorders (DVRs) were the first type of recorder used to replace VCRs. DVRs are a self-contained appliance that provides video processing and storage capabilities. DVRs are typically available in versions that support either 4, 8 or 16 analog cameras. Each camera connects to the DVR with a coaxial cable.

The DVR takes the analog signal from each camera and converts it to a digital format that can be stored on an internal hard disk drive. Most DVRs allow additional internal disk drives to be added to increase storage capacity. The more disk space available, the longer the recording time.

A video monitor, mouse and keyboard can be directly connected to the DVR to allow direct viewing and control of cameras. At smaller properties, the DVR is typically placed in an office or electrical room and used as the central hub of the video surveillance system.

Most newer DVRs include a network connection that allows them to be controlled remotely using special software provided by the manufacturer. This software allows the viewing of live and recorded video as well as the programming of the DVR using a computer or smartphone.

In recent years, property owners have been moving away from analog cameras in favor of IP cameras. Recognizing this, some manufacturers have produced "hybrid" DVRs that support both analog cameras and IP cameras. These can be useful when transitioning to IP cameras, but the total number of IP cameras supported by hybrid DVRs is usually small and the features provided are limited.

The use of DVRs is declining rapidly as the use of IP cameras continues to grow. However, many low-cost camera kits continue to use DVRs, and there are still many existing DVRs in use in older video surveillance systems.

Network Video Recorders

Network video recorders (NVRs) are similar to VCRs, except are designed to work with IP cameras rather than analog cameras. Unlike DVRs which require a separate connection for each camera, all cameras connect to the NVR using a single network connection [17]. Because there is no physical limitation on the number of cameras that can be connected to an NVR, its capacity is limited only by its processing power, storage capacity, and any licensing requirements imposed by the manufacturer.

A large number of different types of NVRs are available, ranging from simple NVRs designed to support a building with only a few cameras, to more sophisticated NVRs designed to support a multi-building campus with a large number of cameras.

Simple NVRs provide connections for a video monitor, mouse, and keyboard, allowing them to be used just like a DVR. These NVRs are typically placed in an office or electrical room and used as the central hub of the video surveillance system. More sophisticated NVRs can usually only be controlled over the network and are typically mounted in a rack in an electrical or telephone room.

NVRs use internal disk drives to store video. Some NVRs also allow the use of external disk drives or storage devices attached to the network. The recording capacity of an NVR is calculated based on the total number of days of recorded video that can be stored. For example, if an NVR had a recording capacity of 30 days, recorded images from cameras would be available for up to 30 days prior to the present date. If an event occurred more than 30 days ago, recorded video would not be available.

The NVR's recording capacity is determined by a number of factors, including total number of cameras, resolution of each camera, frame rate of each camera, and the encoding and compression schemes used by the cameras and NVR. The use of high-resolution cameras

[17] High-capacity NVRs may use more than one network connection to provide a larger data "pipeline" between the NVR and the network.

operating at high-frame rates can quickly consume NVR capacity and increase the amount of disk storage space needed to provide the desired number of days of storage.

When large numbers of high-resolution cameras are used, the NVR's processing power also becomes a factor, limiting the number of cameras that each NVR can support. At larger properties, it is often necessary to install multiple NVRs in order to provide the processing power and storage capacity needed.

Edge Recording

Many IP cameras allow the use of memory cards to record video on the camera itself. This is known as "edge recording". As manufacturers continue to develop memory cards with more and more memory, the amount of video that can be stored on a camera has also increased. Many cameras today are capable of providing 90 days or more of recording capacity, and this is only expected to increase as better memory cards are introduced.

Edge recording is commonly used in two different ways. The first way is to use edge recording to eliminate the need for an NVR entirely. This can work well in some applications, but when storage is done only at the camera, there is some risk that it could be lost if the camera were destroyed or stolen.

The second way is to use edge recording to provide redundancy to the NVR in case the network connection is lost. When the camera was connected to the network, recording would be done at the NVR. When the network connection was lost, video would be recorded on the camera's memory card. When the network connection was restored, video from the memory card would automatically be uploaded to the NVR.

Cloud-Based Recording

Cloud-based recording is when video recording is performed at an off-site location managed by a service provider. This service provider charges a subscription fee and is responsible for providing and maintaining the video storage devices. All cameras on the property are connected to the service provider using an internet connection. There is no NVR or other type of recording device needed at the premises [18].

Authorized users are assigned a username and password that allows access to the cloud-based recording system. After signing on, the user can view both live and recorded video and change system settings.

Cloud-based recording systems can work at smaller properties where users do not want to install or maintain their own NVR. One of the primary weaknesses of cloud-based recording systems is their dependence on an internet connection. When a connection is lost, the recording stops. This weakness can be overcome through the use of cameras that have edge recording capability.

Cloud-based recording systems are usually not a good choice for use at larger properties with a large number of cameras because of the significant bandwidth needed to transmit the camera signals over the internet. The service provider also typically charges a "per camera" fee for each camera and this fee can become substantial when large numbers of cameras are involved.

---

[18] Some cloud services require the use of a "gateway" at the premises. This gateway usually has some recording capacity and acts as a buffer when network communications is lost.

Recorder Capabilities

Most DVRs and NVRs contain built-in software that allows them to be used as a platform for video surveillance at a property. This software allows the programming of system settings, such as when the system will record, and provides alerts when something goes wrong with the system. This software can include the following features:

- Ability to view both live and recorded video in full screen mode, or in arrangements of 4, 8, 16 or 32 cameras per screen.
- Ability to control pan-tilt-zoom (PTZ) cameras using on-screen controls.
- Ability to view and record cameras at different resolutions and different frame rates.
- Ability to record only on specific days and during specific times.
- Ability to record camera images only when motion is detected.
- Ability to provide an enlarged view of portions of the camera image.
- Ability to search recorded video by time and date.
- Ability to export video recordings and still video images.

The DVR's or NVR's built-in software is usually all that is needed to manage video surveillance systems at smaller properties.

Video Management Systems

While a DVR or NVR is usually all that is needed at a smaller property, using these devices alone can become cumbersome when a property has a large number of cameras, multiple NVRs, and the need to monitor cameras from multiple locations.

Video management systems (VMSs) were created to meet the needs of larger and more complicated video surveillance systems. VMSs are created by installing special VMS software on standard personal computers. VMS software provides the ability to better manage large video surveillance systems and offers numerous benefits. Some of these benefits include:

- Ability to support large numbers of cameras and video viewing workstations spread across multiple buildings and campuses.
- Ability to manage multiple NVRs and cameras with edge-based recording using a single user interface.
- Ability to display and control cameras using a graphical map display.
- Ability to support mobile viewing devices such as smartphones and tablets.
- Ability to view and control cameras over internet using standard web browser.
- Ability to use standard personal computers and storage devices to serve as NVRs.
- Ability to provide redundancy in case of system failure.
- Ability to provide automatic backups and archiving of recorded video.
- Ability to integrate with access control systems, intrusion alarm systems, and security intercom systems.

VMS software and the computers necessary to run it are purchased in addition to the cameras, NVRs [19] and other equipment necessary for the video surveillance system. VMS software is usually sold on a "per channel" basis, meaning that a separate software license is required for each camera. There is also typically an annual fee charged to provide support and upgrades to the VMS software.

Video System Monitoring

The ability to monitor live and recorded video is the desired end result of the video surveillance system. There are several options for viewing video:

Attached Video Monitors

Video can be viewed using computer monitors directly attached to the DVR or NVR. A mouse and keyboard are typically provided to allow camera selection and control. This arrangement is commonly used on smaller systems where the NVR serves as the hub of the system.

Video Viewing Workstations

Video viewing workstations are created by installing the NVR or VMS manufacturer's viewing software on a standard personal computer. This is often called "client software" and connects with the NVR or VMS over the network. Once connected, this software provides the ability to view both live and recorded video as well as to control the system.

In smaller systems, the computer used for the video surveillance workstation may continue to be used for other purposes such as word processing and email. In some cases, a second video monitor may be added to the computer just for video surveillance purposes.

In larger systems, a dedicated computer is usually provided for use as a video viewing workstation. This computer is equipped with multiple video monitors, allowing large numbers of cameras to be viewed at once. Viewing many video images at once can require extensive computer resources, so computers with high-performance processors and large amounts of memory are typically required.

More than one video viewing workstation can be used with the NVR or VMS at the same time. Workstations used for live video monitoring and assessment would typically be left on at all times, while workstations used exclusively to investigate incidents and retrieve recorded video may only be used infrequently.

Figure 14-10 - Video Viewing Workstation

[19] Some NVRs may come with a specific number of VMS software licenses included.

Web Browser Viewing

A standard web browser can be used to view and control the video surveillance system. This is the primary method used to connect to a cloud-based video recording service, and most VMS and some NVRs also support the use of a web browser interface. To establish a connection, the user enters an IP address, username, and password, and then has access to the system.

Web browser viewing is great for viewing the video surveillance system from an off-site location and also works well for users who only need occasional access to the system. For example, at a condominium, HOA Board members may have a need to view video recordings from time to time.

Mobile App Viewing

Many VMS, NVRs, and cloud-based services allow the viewing and control of the video surveillance system using a smartphone app. This app can be used to view live and recorded video and control some system functions.

Standalone Video Monitors

There are cases when there is a need to view only a single camera on a monitor and it is not practical to install a video viewing workstation. For example, there may be a need for a concierge to monitor a loading dock door from the concierge desk, but there is no space in which to install a computer and monitor.

To meet this need, it is possible to use a device known as a video decoder combined with a standalone video monitor. The video decoder connects to the network, decodes the signal from a specific IP camera, and displays it on a video monitor.

The monitor used can be as small or as large as needed to serve the intended purpose and fit the space available. Monitors are available with video decoders that are built-in, or a separate decoder and monitor can be used.

Off-Site Video Monitoring Services

There are services available that will remotely monitor video surveillance systems from an off-site location. These services have operators that can watch cameras on the property and take the appropriate actions if suspicious activity is observed. In some cases, the operator is alerted to activity using the camera's motion detection feature. In other cases, the operator simply looks at the monitor occasionally in an attempt to spot something unusual.

These services can work well when used to view an unoccupied area, such as a swimming pool that is closed at night or a rooftop that is supposed to be unoccupied. In these cases, a camera's motion detection capability can be used to alert the operator, who can then use the camera to assess the situation and take the appropriate action.

However, these services have a limited ability to assess activity in an occupied area where there is a lot going on. For example, using a camera to view a busy lobby or parking garage and expecting the operator to be able to tell what is normal and abnormal is probably unrealistic. The effectiveness of using off-site monitoring services for this purpose has often been oversold, sometimes creating false expectations on the part of property owners and managers.

The cost of off-site video monitoring services is usually directly related to the hours that the system will be monitored and the level of activity at the property. If used many hours per day, the cost of off-site video monitoring can approach the cost of using an on-site security officer.

Video Analytics

Video analytics is the capability of a video surveillance system to analyze what is seen within a camera scene and to make intelligent decisions about it. Simply put, video analytics makes the video surveillance system smart and capable of making decisions and acting on its own, without the need for human intervention. Video analytics is sometimes considered to be a form of Artificial Intelligence, also known as "AI". Video analytics has the potential to greatly improve the efficiency of a security monitoring operation – people no longer must continuously watch video monitors to detect unusual events – the system can do it for them.

Video analytics software can be directly installed on many IP network cameras allowing decisions to be made at the camera. Video analytics software can also be installed at the VMS server or on a separate server or appliance specifically installed to support analytics.

Video analytics systems are most commonly used to detect motion within a camera scene but can detect many other types of events. These events include objects leaving or entering an area, objects stopping within an area, objects moving in the wrong direction, objects being left in or removed from an area, objects loitering, and many more.

While video analytics can be useful in many applications, it does have its limitations. Many manufacturers have greatly oversold the capabilities of their video analytics systems, leaving users disappointed. In particular, systems that claim to be able to tell the difference between a person who is a legitimate user of a property (resident or visitor), and a criminal should be viewed with great skepticism. This is one of those cases where if it seems to be too good to be true, it probably is.

Video System Communications

An IP based video surveillance system uses a data network to communicate between each of the components in the system including cameras, NVRs, and video viewing workstations. The hub of the network is the network switch, which routes communications between all components. Larger systems may have multiple network switches, all of which are interconnected together.

Components are most commonly connected to the network switch using twisted-pair cabling. This cable is rated based on the bandwidth that it can carry. Cat 5e or Cat 6 cabling is most commonly used. Some very large systems spread out over a large campus may use fiber-optic cable between network switches.

At existing properties that are upgrading from an analog video surveillance system to an IP video surveillance system, it is possible to reuse the existing coaxial cable. This requires the use of "IP over Coax" conversion devices. These can eliminate the need to install new cabling but can add cost and complexity into the system. In some cases, it can be better in the long run to replace the existing cabling rather than trying to reuse it.

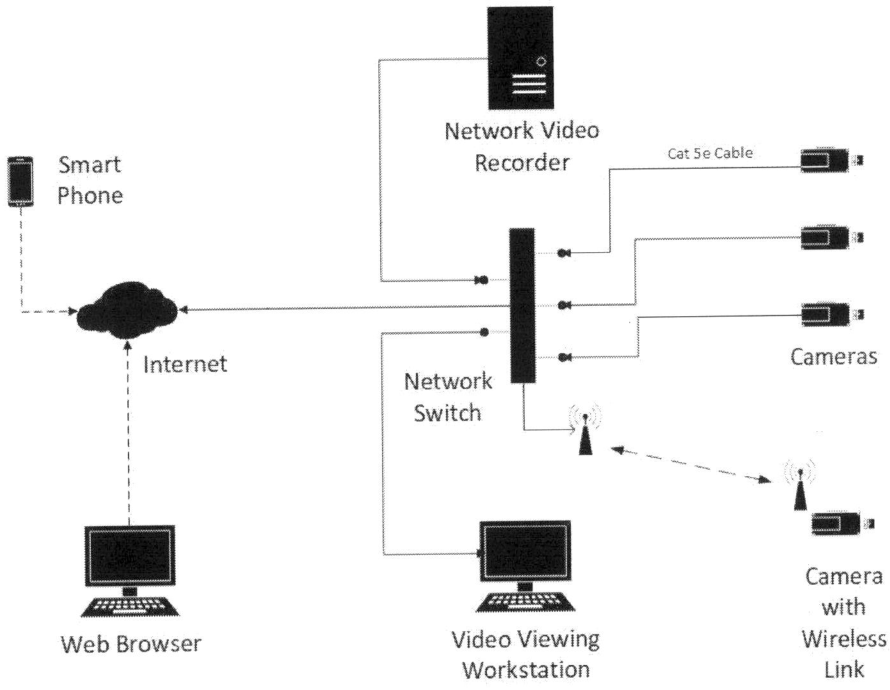

Figure 14-11 - Block Diagram of Simple Video Surveillance System

Wireless Communications

Wireless communications systems provide the ability to transmit data without using cabling. Most wireless communications systems use radio signals to transport the data, although systems that use infrared light or other technology are sometimes also used.

Many users love the concept of wireless communications as it can eliminate the need to run cabling throughout the property. However, most professional-grade video surveillance systems make very limited use of wireless communications. While some consumer-grade cameras come in wireless versions, most professional-grade cameras do not. The complexities of transmitting wireless signals throughout a multifamily property, and the bandwidth required to support large numbers of cameras, makes the use of all-wireless video surveillance systems impractical in the majority of cases. Because of this, most video surveillance systems at multifamily properties continue to use cabling to connect the majority of cameras.

Where wireless communication is useful is in transmitting video data between locations where the installation of cabling is impractical or would be prohibitively expensive. An example would be a pole-mounted camera installed in a parking lot, where a wireless link could be used to transmit the signal from the camera pole to the nearest building. Wireless links can also be used to transmit signals between buildings where no cabling pathway exists, and to connect cameras located at gates at the perimeter of the site.

Cybersecurity of Video Surveillance Systems

Most IP based video surveillance systems use standard computer hardware and standard data networking equipment. Most systems are connected to the Internet to allow remote viewing and control using mobile devices such as smartphones and tablets. Because of this, IP based video systems can be vulnerable to the risk of hacking and other types of cybersecurity attacks.

Property managers should make it clear to the installer of the video surveillance system that cybersecurity is important and that proactive steps should be taken to assure the security of the system. Strong passwords rather than default passwords should be used on all cameras and other devices. Unused network ports and services should be disabled. The use of other security enhancements such as firewalls, VLANS, and MAC address filtering should also be considered.

Video surveillance manufacturers often issue software patches when a vulnerability in their hardware or software is discovered. These patches should be installed promptly as they are issued.

Limitations of Video Surveillance Systems

Many property managers think that video surveillance systems are a "magic bullet" and rush out to buy them in response to a crime problem at the property that they manage. While video surveillance systems can be a useful tool as part of a comprehensive security program, they are not a security solution in themselves.

One thing that is greatly overrated is the deterrent effect of cameras. It is a common misconception that criminals will see the presence of cameras at the property and choose to commit their crimes elsewhere. Despite this commonly held belief, there are few scientific studies to support the theory that cameras are a deterrent.

While more independent studies are needed, the evidence at this point suggests that security cameras rarely prevent crimes from occurring, and almost certainly don't deter crime to the degree that is implied by many sellers and installers of video surveillance equipment.

The following should be considered when contemplating the deterrent effect of video surveillance cameras:

- Most people who engage in criminal behavior don't have the same thought processes that honest people do and don't consider the long-term consequences of their actions.
- Many people who commit crimes aren't thinking rationally at the time they commit them. They may be drunk, high on drugs, or suffering from some form of mental illness.
- Smart criminals are well-aware of the limitations of video surveillance systems and may plan their crimes around them. They may commit crimes just outside of the range of cameras, or wear simple disguises to conceal their identity.
- People become desensitized to the presence of video cameras after a short time. While there may be an awareness of cameras when they are first installed, they soon become part of the environment, making regular occupants of the area almost oblivious to their presence.
- Many law enforcement agencies lack the resources to investigate and prosecute minor property crimes, even if good images of the perpetrators are available. Many criminals know this and blatantly commit crimes in front of video cameras, knowing that there is little chance that they will be caught or prosecuted.

Part III – Security Strategies

Chapter 15: Securing the Perimeter of the Site

Importance of Site Security

Site security is the first line of defense against intrusions and serves as the outer layer of your protective circles [20]. In addition to their practical value, the types of site security measures used can set the tone for your property's overall security program.

This chapter provides strategies for securing the site perimeter at multifamily properties.

Developing a Plan for Site Security

The following basic questions should be asked when developing a plan for site security:

Will the Site Be Open or Closed?

One of the most important questions to be asked is whether the site will be open or closed. An open site is one where people can freely come and go with little or no restrictions. A closed site is one in which access is controlled and only authorized people are allowed to enter the site.

There is a balancing act between providing an adequate amount of site security and maintaining a pleasant and welcoming environment for residents and visitors. At one end of the spectrum would be a site that is completely open and has no physical barriers of any type. This site would be aesthetically pleasing and create a welcoming environment for residents and visitors, but would provide little or no security.

At the other end of the spectrum would be a site that is heavily fortified with many physical barriers. This site would provide excellent security, but might create a "prison-like" living environment that was unacceptable to all but the most security conscious of residents.

The degree and types of site security measures used should correspond to the level of security risk that the property faces. Properties that face low security risks can generally get away with having an open site, while properties with medium or high security risks almost always benefit from having a closed site.

What Types of Barriers Will Be Used?

If a decision is made to have a closed site, the types of security barriers that will be used at the perimeter of the site needs to be determined. This is determined by a combination of factors, including security risk, budget, local code restrictions, and the type of image that the property wishes to portray to residents and visitors.

Ornamental iron fencing, manufactured metal fencing, masonry walls, and hedges are commonly used when the appearance of the property is important, and an ample budget is available. Less expensive materials, such as chain-link fencing, are often used when controlling costs is important and appearance is less of a consideration.

It often works best to use a combination of types of physical security barriers at the perimeter of the site. For example, ornamental iron fencing might be used along the main roadway in front of a site, wood fencing used on the sides of the site that face neighboring

[20] See Concentric Circles of Protection concept in Chapter 3.

residential properties, and chain-link fencing used on the back side of the site that faces a commercial property.

The height of the security barriers used has an impact on their effectiveness, appearance, and cost. For lower risk properties, a minimum height of 6' is recommended for all perimeter barriers. For higher risk properties, heights of 7' or higher are recommended.

Barriers less than 6' high provide only a minimum amount of security, but can be used to define the boundaries of the property and to direct the flow of traffic to designated entrance points.

How Many Points Of Vehicle And Pedestrian Access Will Be Provided?

If the site will be closed, it is necessary to determine how many points of vehicle and pedestrian access will be provided. While providing many access points may seem convenient, having too many entrance points increases costs and increases the number of potential places where an intruder can enter.

The number of pedestrian and vehicle entrance points should be kept to a minimum. Unless a site is exceptionally large, it is best to have only one or two entrance points.

Tips for Good Site Security

- Fences and walls intended for use as security barriers should be designed so that they are not easy to climb. The use of horizontal pickets and design features that can be used as hand or foot holds should be avoided. If the fence looks like a ladder, it can probably be used as one.
- If a decision is made to have an open site, it can still be beneficial to direct the flow of vehicle and pedestrian traffic to designated entrance points. These entrance points should be in locations that allow residents to observe incoming and outgoing traffic. This can lessen the number of people passing through the site, reducing the property's exposure to crime.
- Some boundaries of a site may face natural obstacles that make the use of additional security barriers seem unnecessary. These obstacles can include steep hillsides, dense shrubbery or bushes that seem impenetrable. Part of the site perimeter may face a body of water such as a river or lake and it may seem like the chances of an intruder entering by water is unlikely. It is acceptable to make a decision not to install barriers along these portions of the site provided that the risks involved are understood. However, special precautions should be taken at the locations where security barriers connect with these portions of the site. An example would be a fence that stops at the shoreline of a lake, allowing an intruder to step around the fence at the water.
- Good lighting should be provided on both sides of all site entrances. A minimum light level of between 30 and 50 Lux is recommended.
- "No Trespassing" signs should be provided at all site entrance points and at intervals not to exceed 100' around the entire perimeter of the property.
- At higher-risk properties, consider the use of perimeter intrusion detection systems along the perimeter boundaries of the site.

Common Points of Weakness in Site Security

Tailgating

"Tailgating" is when vehicles or pedestrians enter a closed site as a resident enters or exits. This most commonly occurs at vehicle gate entrances to a site, where the intruder waits just outside of the gate and enters while the gate is still open after a resident drives off. Tailgating is considered to be the number one security vulnerability at most multifamily properties.

The following are some suggestions to reduce tailgating at site entrances:

- Require residents to wait for the gate to fully close behind them before driving off. Educate residents on the importance of this during security awareness training sessions. Provide "*Wait for Gate to Close*" reminder signs on both sides of gate. Consider imposing fines or other penalties on residents who repeatedly fail to comply with this policy.
- Adjust the timer on automatic gates to close the gate as soon as possible after a vehicle passes through.
- Discourage pedestrians from using automatic vehicle gates to walk on and off the property.
- Trim landscaping around gate entrances to eliminate potential hiding places for intruders.

Bypassing Pedestrian Gates

Many pedestrian gates used at multifamily properties are poorly designed and fail to close or lock reliably. In many cases, it is possible to easily reach around the gate, grab a lever, and unlock the gate from the outside.

To reduce these vulnerabilities, pedestrian gates should be modified so that they close and lock properly and are difficult for an intruder to compromise. Guidelines for good gate design are provided on page 41 in Chapter 5.

Poorly Maintained Fencing

The fencing at many multifamily properties can quickly fall into disrepair and no longer serve as an effective security barrier. Fencing can be damaged by vehicles, landscapers, or falling trees. High winds may cause fences to fall down. Heavy rains can erode the soil underneath of the fence, creating a gap large enough to crawl under. Intruders may cut through the fence, leaving an opening that can be used to enter the property repeatedly. Residents and contractors may stack items next to the fence that makes it easy to climb over.

A proactive approach must be taken to reduce these vulnerabilities. Property management or maintenance staff should make physical inspections of the entire fence line on a scheduled basis. Any problems identified during these inspections should be promptly corrected.

Use of PIN Codes at Gates

Many multifamily properties allow the use of PIN codes to gain access to the site. These are often used at the telephone entry systems at vehicle gate entrances, and at mechanical or electronic keypad locks at pedestrian gates.

PIN codes can easily fall into the wrong hands and become widely known by criminals in the community. The vulnerabilities of PIN codes should be recognized and alternative types of access control devices (such as card readers or long range RFID readers) should be used in place of PIN code access whenever possible. (See page 271 for more information on PIN codes.)

<u>Manipulating Postal Lock Switches</u>

Many telephone entry systems are equipped with what is known as a "postal lock switch". The postal lock switch uses a lock supplied by the United States Postal Service. All postal delivery employees are issued a key that operates this lock. When this key is used in the postal lock switch, it activates the gate, allowing the postal employee to gain entry.

It is possible to manipulate the postal lock switch or its wiring to gain entry to the site. This requires that the locked cover on the telephone entry system be opened to gain access to the switch. Many manufacturers use a standard lock on the cover of all telephone entry systems that they produce. This means that a key to one system will work on any other system of the same brand.

Criminals have learned to exploit this vulnerability by obtaining keys to popular brands of telephone entry systems. These can be purchased online and essentially give the criminal a "master key" to most properties that use a telephone entry system. Criminals without a key can also gain access to the postal lock switch by prying open the cover on the telephone entry system.

To make it more difficult to gain access to the postal lock switch, the standard factory lock on the cover of the telephone entry system should be replaced with a high-security cam lock. This lock should be uniquely keyed to the property.

At properties that face a higher level of risk, a supplemental lock can be installed on the front of the telephone entry system to provide additional protection. For maximum security, a protective shroud can be installed to cover the entire telephone entry system, leaving only the display and keypad exposed. This shroud would be fastened in place with tamper-resistant fasteners and only removed when it was necessary to service the system.

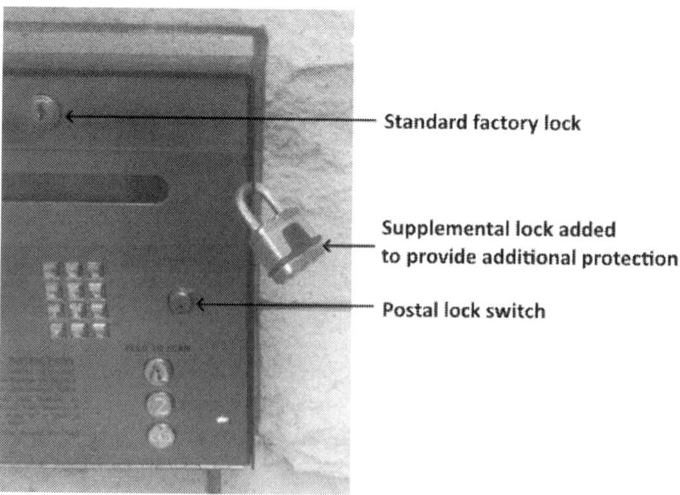

Figure 15-1 - Supplemental Lock Added to Telephone Entry System

Using Default Codes on Telephone Entry Systems

Many telephone entry systems come from the factory with default programming codes. These codes are used by the installer to program the system at the time that it is installed and are intended to be changed to a different code when the installation is complete.

Unfortunately, many installers fail to do this and leave the default code in place. Some smarter criminals are aware of this and often try default codes on telephone entry systems to see if they will work. A surprising number of times, they do. This allows the criminal to manipulate the system to gain access to the property. In some cases, the criminal can program an access code that allows him or her to make repeated entries to the property over an extended period of time.

The obvious solution to this problem is to change the default programming code to something that is unique to the property. When a new telephone entry system is installed, the installer should be specifically asked if all default programming codes have been changed.

Manipulating Key-Operated Switches

Key switches are simple electrical switches that provide either a normally-open switch contact, normally-closed switch contact, or both. Most of the time, a normally-open switch contact is used.

Anyone who has even a slight amount of electrical knowledge can bypass a key switch by simply removing it from the wall, and placing a jumper wire across the switch contacts. In most cases, this is easy to do, as standard slotted-head or Phillips-head screws have been used to fasten the key switch faceplate to the wall.

Many intruders are aware of the vulnerability of key switches and use the technique described above to commit burglaries. In many cases, the intruder reassembles the key switch after he or she has gained entry, so that the property owner may not even be aware that a burglary has occurred.

Here are some tips for providing improved security of key-operated switches:

- Confirm that the key switch is really needed in the first place. In some cases, key switches are rarely used, and the benefits of having them are outweighed by the security risks. If not needed, the key switch should be removed.
- Use tamper-resistant security screws to mount the key switch faceplate.
- Protect the wiring that goes to the key switch. Use conduit to protect the wiring when it cannot be concealed within the wall.
- If the key switch must be surface-mounted, try to use an electrical box that has no 'knock-outs". (These can give an intruder access to the key switch wiring by removing a knock-out.) If the box you are using does have knock-outs, permanently seal them by tack welding them or by using epoxy to prevent them from being removed.
- If the property has an intrusion alarm system or access control system, provide a tamper switch on the key switch, and connect it to this system. This will allow property management or security staff to be notified if the key switch is tampered with.

Chapter 16: Securing Outdoor Areas

Importance of Securing Outdoor Areas

Outdoor areas are the portions of the property that are located outside of the buildings on a multifamily property site. These areas include parking lots, walkways, courtyards, and outdoor amenity areas such as swimming pools and playgrounds. These areas will vary depending on the type of property; a multi-building apartment complex or gated community may have many outdoor areas, while a high-rise condominium located in an urban area may have none.

Properly securing outdoor areas provides better protection of residents and visitors, reduces thefts and vandalism, and discourages improper activity that may detract from full enjoyment of the property.

Parking Lots

Outdoor parking lots often experience high levels of theft and vandalism, frequently making them a trouble spot at many multifamily properties. Here are some tips for improving the security of parking lots:

- Parking lots should have defined perimeter boundaries with designated entrance points rather than being accessible from all sides. It is recommended that this apply to all parking lots, even if the parking lot is located within a secured site. These boundaries can consist of buildings, fencing, walls, or landscaping.

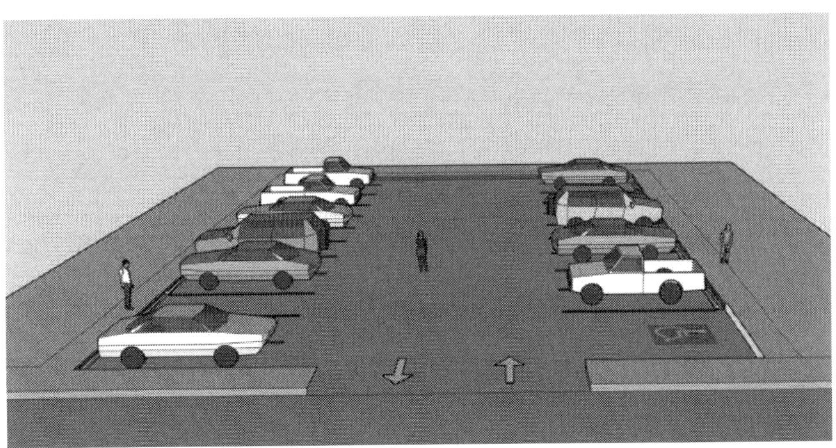

Figure 16-1 - Open Parking Lot with No Defined Perimeter Boundaries

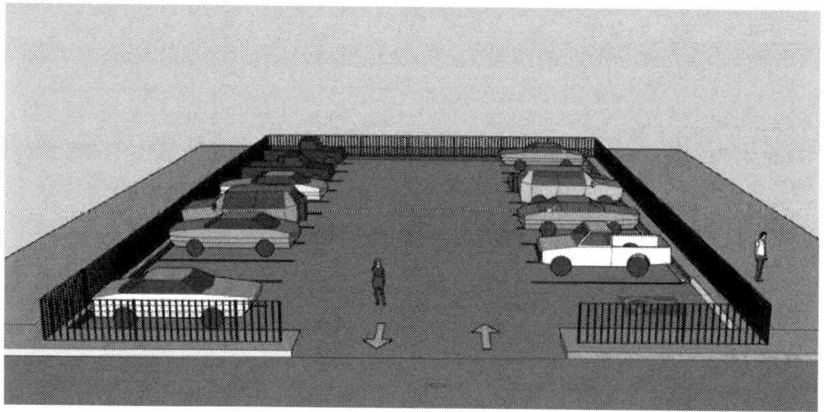

Figure 16-2 - Parking Lot with 4' High Fencing Used to Define Boundaries

- At lower-risk properties, the barriers used at the parking lot boundaries are intended primarily to direct the flow of people to designated entrance points and can be at a lower height (5' or less). At higher-risk properties, the barriers used should be at a height that discourages climbing (6' or higher).
- The number of vehicle entrance points should be kept to a minimum. At lower-risk properties, the entrance points can be left open. At higher-risk properties, the use of access-controlled vehicle and pedestrian gates at the parking lot entrances should be considered.
- Good lighting should be provided in the parking lot. A minimum light level of between 10 and 40 Lux is recommended. The lighting uniformity ratio should not exceed 4:1.
- Any landscaping used in the parking lot should be maintained in accordance with CPTED guidelines so that clear lines of sight are maintained. Landscaping should also be trimmed so that it does not block lighting or create places where criminals can hide.
- Provide "No Trespassing" signs at all parking lot entrances and at 50' intervals within the parking lot itself.
- If there is a need to identify parking stalls, each stall should be numbered with a sequential stall number. For the safety of residents, the parking stall numbers should not correspond with the residential unit numbers. For the same reasons, stalls should never be identified with resident names.
- Parking lots should not be used as outdoor storage areas and the items other than vehicles that are allowed to be kept in the parking lots should be strictly limited.
- Junk vehicles, abandoned vehicles, and vehicles that are clearly not operational should be promptly removed from the parking lot.
- Parking lots should be well-maintained. Trash should not be allowed to accumulate, and the lot should be regularly swept. Any graffiti painted on fencing or walls in the parking lot areas should be promptly removed.

Carports

Carports are often used at multifamily properties either in place of or in addition to outdoor parking lots. Carports have many of the same security risks that outdoor parking lots do, but have a few unique security risks of their own.

Carports that have side walls offer additional places of concealment where a criminal can hide or commit a crime unobserved. Carports also provide shelter from the weather and can be an attractive place for the homeless to camp or for criminals to commit illicit acts.

Here are some tips for improving the security of carports:

- When possible, carports should be constructed so that they are open on all sides to permit visibility into the carport from all directions.
- Good lighting should be provided on the ceiling of carports. For even light distribution, it is better to use multiple lower-intensity luminaires spaced evenly throughout the carport rather than to try to illuminate the entire carport with only one or two high intensity luminaires. A minimum light level of between 10 and 40 Lux is recommended throughout the carport. The lighting uniformity ratio should not exceed 4:1.
- To increase visibility and improve the effectiveness of lighting in carports, consider painting the walls, support columns and ceiling a bright reflective color.
- Avoid locating storage cabinets or lockers in carports as they tend to attract crime. If storage cabinets or lockers are used, they should be well-constructed and locked using high-quality lock hardware.

Walkways

Walkways include the pathways and sidewalks that pedestrians use to travel to and from the buildings on the property.

To the greatest extent possible, the entire length of walkways should be clearly visible from the windows of the adjacent residential units and the surrounding streets. The landscaping used in the areas adjacent to the walkways should be maintained in accordance with CPTED guidelines so that clear lines of sight are preserved. Landscaping and other site features should not create places near the walkway where criminals can easily hide.

Good lighting should be provided along the entire length of the walkway. A minimum light level of between 10 and 40 Lux is recommended. The lighting uniformity ratio should not exceed 4:1. The low-mounted luminaires typically used to light pathways usually do not provide lighting that is adequate for security purposes. These should be supplemented with other types of luminaires as needed to achieve the desired illumination level.

Directional signage should be provided along the walkways as needed to direct people who are not familiar with the property to the correct building entrances.

Outdoor Mailboxes

Outdoor mailboxes are used at many multifamily properties to receive mail from the United States Postal Service. These mailboxes may be located on the outside of the buildings, or freestanding cluster mailbox units may be used.

To provide for the safety of residents and to prevent the theft of mail, outdoor mailboxes should be located in highly visible places and not tucked away in hidden locations. If a mailbox shelter is used, it should be designed so that it is open on all sides and does not create a place for criminals to hide or to work without being seen. Mailbox clusters should be arranged in a single row or placed back-to-back rather than facing each other to avoid creating a concealed area between clusters. Any landscaping used in the vicinity should be well-maintained so that it does not obstruct views of the mailboxes.

The entire mailbox area should be well-lit. A minimum light level of between 50 and 100 Lux is recommended. The lighting uniformity ratio should not exceed 4:1.

Trash and Recycle Areas

Trash and recycle areas are provided outside of the buildings at many multifamily properties. These may be located directly adjacent to the buildings, or in freestanding shelters located away from the building.

Because trash and recycle containers can be an eyesore, they are often placed in out of the way locations or concealed behind walls. This can create hidden places where criminals can hide or where the homeless can camp.

Arsonists have been known to deliberately set fires in trash and recycle containers. This poses a particular risk when containers are located close to buildings or under carports, as the fire can easily spread to the structure itself.

Illegal use of trash containers by non-residents can be a problem when trash containers are located on an unsecured site. This can increase disposal costs and frustrate residents when they find that containers are overflowing when they go to empty their trash.

Here are some tips for improving the security of trash and recycle areas:

- Locate trash and recycle containers away from the buildings and carports to reduce the potential damage that could be caused if they were set on fire.
- When fenced or walled enclosures are built-around trash and recycle containers, the fence or wall material should allow some visibility into the enclosure, permitting people in the trash and recycle area to be observed from the outside.
- Provide good lighting of the trash and recycle area and the pathways leading up to it. A minimum light level of between 10 and 40 Lux is recommended. The lighting uniformity ratio should not exceed 4:1.
- At properties where illegal dumping is a problem, consider locking trash and recycle containers or providing a locked enclosure around the entire trash and recycle area. Also provide signs stating that illegal dumping is prohibited and that violators will be prosecuted under the applicable laws.

Swimming Pools

Outdoor swimming pools at multifamily properties create a number of security challenges. There is the potential for swimming pools to be misused by both residents and their visitors, and people not associated with the property can gain unauthorized access to the pool. There are also significant safety issues associated with swimming pools, and potential legal liabilities if property owners don't take the right steps to properly secure their pools.

Here are some tips for improving the security of outdoor swimming pools:

- Access to the swimming pool area should be separately controlled, even if the pool itself is located on a secured site. A fence or other barrier should be installed around the entire swimming pool. This fence or barrier should be at least 6' high.
- All gates and doors that lead into the swimming pool area should be kept locked so that only residents and authorized staff have access to the pool. Gates and doors should be kept locked at all times and never left unlocked or propped open. The use of an access control system on the doors and gates that allow entry to the pool is highly recommended.
- The pedestrian gates used at many swimming pools often don't close and lock reliably, and many pool gates are notoriously easy to open from the outside. To reduce these vulnerabilities, pool gates should be modified so that they close and lock properly and are difficult for an intruder to compromise. (See page 41 for more on pedestrian gates.)
- Many state and local governments have specific safety and security regulations concerning swimming pools. Be sure that your property is in compliance with all applicable regulations.
- Consider providing an auto-dialing telephone for use as an emergency phone in the pool area. This is required by code in some locations, but is recommended even if not required by code. The auto-dialing phone should be programmed to automatically dial 911. Signs should be provided that clearly indicate the location of the emergency phone. The emergency phone should be easily accessible and not be blocked by items such as pool furniture.
- Consider the use of an automatic pool cover to cover the pool when not in use.
- At properties where after-hours use of the pool by residents or unauthorized parties is a problem, consider the installation of an outdoor intrusion alarm system. (See page 157.)

Courtyards

Courtyards are shared outdoor open spaces located outside of multifamily housing buildings. Courtyards may be completely surrounded by buildings and accessible from only the inside, or may have one or more sides that face a public space or an adjacent property.

Courtyards often contain gardens, walkways, and features such as benches, picnic tables and outdoor barbeques. Courtyards may also contain larger amenity areas such as swimming pools or cabanas. Courtyards that are completely surrounded by buildings and not accessible from the outside generally have few security risks. Courtyards that are accessible from the outside can be problematic from a security standpoint and require more attention.

A special problem exists when building codes require that the doors between the courtyard and the interior of the buildings be left unlocked to permit emergency egress. This condition can occur when the courtyard is large and at least two means of egress out of the courtyard is required. This often requires an egress door between the courtyard and the building.

An example of such a door is shown in Figure 16-3 below. This door is located off a courtyard that is enclosed only with a short fence. The door is equipped with an exit sign, indicating that it is an emergency egress door, and the exit device installed on the door allows free entry into the building at all times. This essentially allows anyone who gains access to the courtyard to have free access to the building.

Figure 16-3 Courtyard Door that Allows Free Access to Building

Here are some tips for improving the security of courtyards:

- The exterior boundaries of courtyards that face public spaces or adjacent properties should be treated the same as a site perimeter and should use the same security measures.
- When permitted by code, all doors between the courtyard and the buildings should be kept locked. If the doors must be left unlocked to permit emergency egress, consider the use of exit alarms on these doors. These alarms should be designed so that residents can freely pass through the door without setting off the alarm by using their key or access card, but anyone entering without a key or card would cause the alarm to sound.

Playgrounds and Sport Courts

Some multifamily properties have private playgrounds or sport courts located within the boundary of the property. These are intended for use exclusively by residents and their visitors, but sometimes unintentionally become facilities that are used by the general public.

In higher crime neighborhoods, private playgrounds and sport courts can become places where gang members congregate, and criminal activity such as drug dealing occurs. In areas where homelessness is a problem, private playgrounds can become places where the homeless set-up camps.

Here are some tips for improving the security of playgrounds and parks:

- Playgrounds and sport courts should be designed using CPTED principles to allow natural surveillance, natural access control, and territorial reinforcement.
- Provide good lighting of playgrounds and sports courts. A minimum light level of between 10 and 40 Lux is recommended for security. Higher lighting levels may be required to allow certain types of sports to be played at night. The lighting uniformity ratio should not exceed 4:1.

- If possible, the perimeter boundaries of the playground or sport court should be enclosed using a fence or other barrier. Gates that control access should be provided. These gates can be left open during daytime hours, but closed and locked at night.
- Signs should be provided that clearly state that the facilities are private and intended exclusively for use by residents and their accompanied visitors.

Minimizing Hiding Places

Multifamily property sites are often designed in such a way that creates convenient places for trespassers to hide. Examples of such hiding places include:

- Exterior areas located between adjacent buildings or between different wings of a building.
- Long exterior passageways that lead out from emergency exit doors.
- Recesses in the building where utility meters or mechanical equipment are located.

Hiding places are often located in areas that are not frequently viewed by residents or employees, allowing trespassers to linger there for long periods of time without being observed. Designers will often deliberately place landscaping in front of these areas to conceal what is behind them, making them an even better hiding place. This provides an ideal location to consume drugs or alcohol or to set-up a temporary camp. Attackers can also linger in these places waiting for a resident or visitor to pass by.

Figure 16-4 - Example of Potential Hiding Place

Here are some tips for minimizing hiding places:

- Enclose potential hiding areas with fencing to discourage them from being used by trespassers. Provide manual gates in fencing as required for service access and to allow egress from emergency exit doors.
- Trim landscaping to allow natural surveillance of the area using CPTED principles.
- Provide good lighting of potential hiding areas. A minimum light level of 10 Lux is recommended. The lighting uniformity ratio should not exceed 4:1.

Reducing Graffiti

Here are some tips for reducing graffiti at multifamily properties.

- Provide good exterior lighting in graffiti-prone areas. A minimum light level of 10 to 20 Lux is recommended.
- Use CPTED principals to allow good visibility of exterior areas.
- Control access to exterior stairways and roofs.
- Promptly remove graffiti to minimize the time that it is exhibited, thwarting the goal of the "tagger" who wishes his or her work to be on display for as long as possible. Promptly removing graffiti also shows that the property is actively cared for and that improper activity will be quickly noticed.
- Consider use of anti-graffiti wall coatings to allow quick removal of graffiti.
- Consider the use of anti-graffiti film to protect windows.
- Consider painting murals on walls. Many self-proclaimed "graffiti artists" are surprisingly respectful of the work of other artists and won't tag it.
- Consider blocking wall surfaces with thorny bushes or other landscaping
- Consider replacing solid fences with ornamental iron or chain-link fences to minimize the surface area where graffiti can be applied.

Benches and Tables

Outdoor benches and tables should be securely fastened to the ground to prevent theft and to discourage improper use. In areas where homelessness is a problem, benches should be compartmentalized or equipped with armrests to discourage them from being used as a place to lie down.

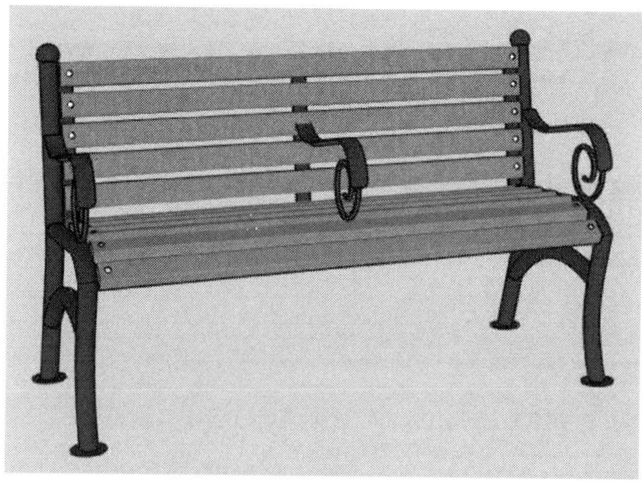

Figure 16-5 - Bench with Center Armrest

Bicycle Racks

Outdoor bicycle racks should be located in places that are highly visible and not tucked away in places where criminals can work without being seen.

Bicycle racks should be constructed of heavy-gauge metal (10 gauge or thicker). Bicycle racks constructed using rectangular tubing are preferred over those that use round tubing as they are more difficult to cut with a tubing cutter – a favorite tool of many bicycle thieves.

When possible, the posts of bicycle racks should be embedded into a concrete base rather than bolted to the surface. For extra security, consider installing a length of heavy steel chain within the tubing. The ends of this chain would be embedded into the concrete base when the racks were being installed and prevent removal of the bicycle lock even if the rack tubing were cut through. (See Figure 16-6.)

If the bicycle rack posts cannot be imbedded, tamper-resistant security fasteners should be used to attach the base of the rack securely to the ground.

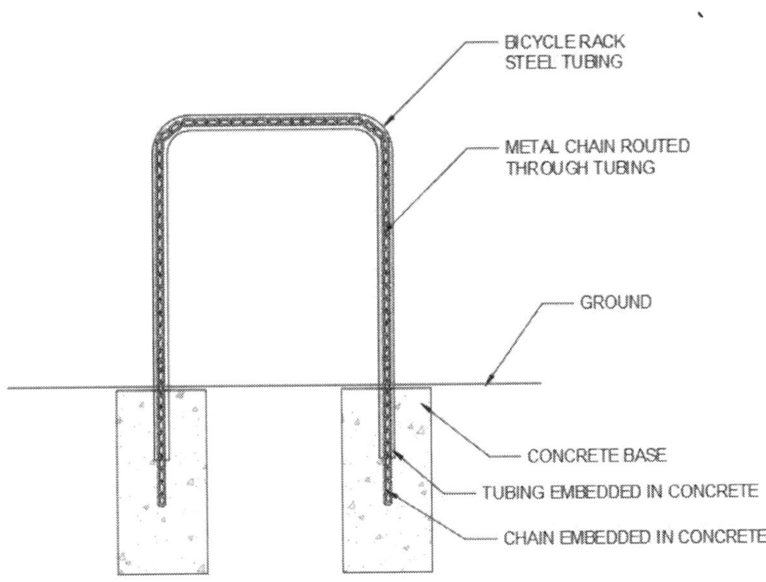

Figure 16-6 - Outdoor Bicycle Racks

Skate Deterrents

Retaining walls, railings, edges of stairwells and other site features can be attractive targets for skateboarders to use in performing their stunts. This can cause damage to the property and create safety hazards for both the skater and people who are nearby.

To deter unauthorized use of the property by skateboarders, skate deterrent devices should be added to the edges of retaining walls, planters, and other site features that could be used by skateboarders. The devices should also be provided along handrails where needed.

It may also be helpful to provide signs that direct skaters to nearby skateparks and other legitimate places that are more appropriate for skating.

Amenity Buildings

Amenity buildings are detached structures on the site that contain laundry facilities, recreational facilities, workshops, and other amenities intended for use by residents. Although securing amenity buildings is often not considered as high a priority as securing residential buildings, they can face an equal or greater risk of crime.

All amenity buildings should be kept locked at all times. Residents should be required to use their key or access card to gain entry. An exception can be made when a scheduled event (such as a party) is taking place at a recreational building.

Here are some tips for improving the security of amenity buildings:

- The doors to amenity buildings should be secured using the best practices for securing doors described in Appendix A.
- To provide improved accountability and control, doors to amenity buildings should be controlled by an access control system rather than a standard lock.
- Provide "No Trespassing" signs at all entrances to amenity buildings.
- If the windows of an amenity building must be left open to provide ventilation, consider installing security screens or window bars on the windows.
- At higher-risk properties, consider installing an intrusion alarm system that can be turned on when the building is closed.

Utility Buildings

Utility buildings are standalone buildings on the site that contain equipment such as generators, fire pumps, and other types of mechanical and electrical equipment.

Utility buildings are frequently targeted by thieves seeking to steal copper wiring and piping that can easily be sold for its scrap metal value. Utility buildings are also attacked by vandals who wish to cause harm to a property. In some cases, homeless people have been known to break into utility buildings and use them as places to sleep.

Here are some tips for improving the security of utility buildings:

- The doors to utility buildings should be secured using the best practices for securing doors described in Appendix A.
- Provide "No Trespassing" signs at all entrances to utility buildings.
- At higher-risk properties, consider installing an intrusion alarm system on utility buildings. This alarm system should be left turned on at all times except when authorized people require access.

Outdoor Storage

Care should be taken when storing items in outdoor areas, regardless of whether or not the site perimeter is secured. Even items that are of low value can attract the attention of criminals and cause them to be drawn to the property. Some items stored outdoors can be used as aids to help the criminal make forced entry into a building. These items may actually tempt the criminal to commit an act that he or she may not have originally thought of.

Here are some tips for properly storing outdoor items:

- Residents and maintenance staff should be strongly encouraged to store items within a secured building rather than outdoors. If items must be stored outdoors, they should be placed in areas where they cannot be easily seen from outside of the property.
- Garden tools such as shovels, picks and axes can be used as burglary tools and should never be stored openly in outdoor areas.
- Ladders can be used by criminals to gain access to balconies and open windows on upper floor units. Preferably, all ladders should be stored inside of a building. If ladders must be stored outdoors, they should be securely fastened to a fixed object using a heavy-duty chain and padlock.
- Criminals often use items such as flowerpots, statues, and boulders as a means to smash windows to gain entry. Avoid having these items near the entrances if possible. If items must remain, take steps to securely fasten them so that they cannot be easily removed.

Outdoor Electrical Receptacles

In areas where homelessness is a problem, outdoor electrical receptacles can attract trespassers to the property. People living on the street often use outdoor electrical receptacles to charge their cell phones or other mobile devices. In some cases, outdoor outlets are used to power hotplates for cooking or space heaters to keep warm.

The first step is to confirm that outdoor receptacles are actually needed. In some cases, receptacles were installed at the time that the building was constructed and are seldom if ever actually used. If this is the case, the receptacles should be removed and covered with a blank cover plate.

If outdoor receptacles are needed, they should be equipped with a lockable receptacle cover. These covers have tabs that allow them to be secured with a padlock when the receptacle is not in use. Covers constructed of plastic are primarily intended to provide protection against weather and can easily be removed. Use a heavy-duty outlet cover constructed of metal and use a high-quality padlock to secure it.

Figure 16-7 - Lockable Cover for Electrical Receptacle

Outdoor Water Faucets

Like outdoor electrical receptacles, outdoor water faucets (also called hose bibbs) can attract trespassers to the property. People living on the street often use outdoor faucets to fill water containers or for bathing. In some cases, a water faucet can be either accidentally or intentionally left on, which can create flooding. Vandals have also been known to insert hoses through windows or mail slots and turn on the water.

Outdoor water faucets should be equipped with faucet locks. These are available in several different types and require the use of a key in order to use the faucet. Once faucet locks are installed, it is important that landscaping staff and others be instructed to always reinstall the lock after the faucet has been used. It is common to see faucet locks sitting on the ground near the faucet because staff has neglected to replace them.

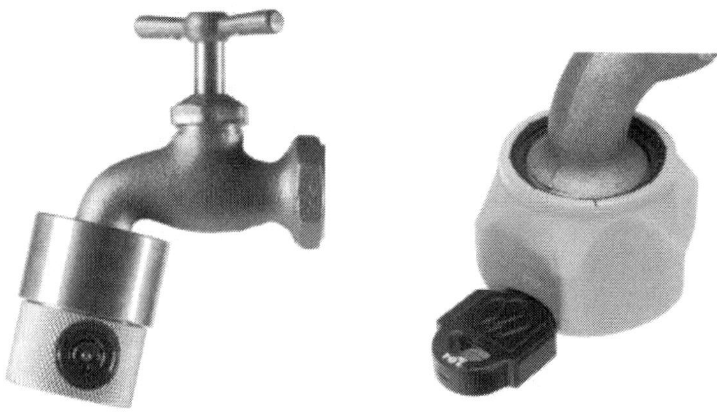

Figure 16-8 Faucet Locks

Outdoor Water Features

Outdoor water features include decorative pools and fountains that are intended to enhance the appearance of a property. Outdoor water features can be the target of vandalism and can sometimes pose a safety hazard to small children.

When possible, decorative fencing or low shrubbery should be placed around water features to limit access by children and trespassers. Strategically placing boulders around the water feature can also create a barrier to restrict access.

The depth of decorative pools should be kept to a minimum to reduce the chances of a child drowning. One way to accomplish this is by adding stones just beneath the water to effectively raise the bottom of the pool.

Chapter 17: Securing the Perimeter of the Building

Importance of Building Security

Many properties do not allow the site to be secured, making the buildings themselves the first line of security defense. Even when a site is secured, it is sometimes possible for a motivated intruder to compromise site security measures with little effort. Because of this, the security of the building perimeter is of utmost importance in the overall security of the multifamily property.

This chapter provides strategies for securing the commonly shared building perimeter at multifamily properties.

Building Entrances

Building entrances are the most vulnerable point of entry at the building perimeter and the place where intruders most frequently enter. Here are some tips for properly securing the common building entrances at multifamily buildings:

- Establish designated doors that can be used as building entrances by residents and visitors. Keep the number of entrance doors to a minimum. Not every exterior door needs to be accessible to residents from the outside. As a general rule, the fewer entrances, the better the security of the building.
- Doors not used as designated entrances, but which still must be available for emergency egress, should be equipped with exit alarms. Signs should be provided that indicate that the door is for emergency use only and that an alarm will sound when the door is opened.
- Provide high-quality (ANSI Grade 2 or better) door lock hardware on exterior doors and equip these doors with protective devices to make forced entry more difficult. Install security window film to protect any glass panes that may be installed in the door or beside it. (See Appendix A for best practices for securing doors.)
- Consider the use of an access control system on building entrance doors and issue access cards to residents instead of exterior door keys. The more residents a property has, the more beneficial it is to use an access control system.
- Provide "No Trespassing" signs at all designated building entrances.
- Good lighting should be provided at all building entrances. A minimum light level of between 30 and 50 Lux is recommended.
- Trim landscaping around building entrances to eliminate potential hiding places for intruders.
- Consider the use of door-propped open alarms on entrance doors at buildings where doors are frequently found propped open.
- Minimize or eliminate key boxes at exterior entrances.

Windows in Common Areas

Glass windows are considered the second most likely point of entry by an intruder. Here are some tips for properly securing windows at a multifamily property:

- Review the need to have operable windows (windows that can be opened) in the common areas of a multifamily building. The security risks created by operable windows can outweigh their benefits, particularly in buildings that are air conditioned.
- If operable windows will be used, consider installing stops that allow the window to be opened wide enough to allow ventilation, but not wide enough to allow an intruder to enter.
- Install supplementary locking devices on windows that do not have an effective lock. These are often needed on older windows where the factory-supplied lock is inadequate.
- Consider the use of security window film to strengthen the glass at windows in vulnerable locations. At higher risk properties, consider replacing window glass with polycarbonate glazing or installing security window screens or window bars.
- Don't forget to properly secure windows on upper floor decks and patios. Many criminals have no problem at all in climbing up to a window that the average person might consider inaccessible.

Ventilation Grilles

Ventilation grilles are sometimes installed on the exterior of the building to allow the flow of air in or out of the structure. These grilles can be installed on the ground above floors that are below grade, in exterior walls, and in the doors to mechanical, electrical and trash rooms.

Ventilation grilles are usually attached with fasteners that can be easily removed with a wrench or screwdriver. Criminals have been known to remove ventilation grilles to gain access to the building to commit crimes. In some cases, the grille is replaced after the criminal enters, concealing the fact that entry has been made at all.

Figure 17-1 - Ventilation Grille on Ground Above Below-Grade Floor

The following tips are recommended to reduce the chances of entry through ventilation grilles:

- Ventilation grilles should be fastened using tamper-resistant security screws or bolts.
- Where conditions permit, consider tack welding the ventilation grille in place.

- Ventilation grilles on doors should be secured using a carriage bolt that extends through the door and attaches both the inside and outside grille. (See Figure 17-3.)
- If a ventilation opening cannot be properly secured, consider installing a supplemental set of ornamental iron security bars over the opening.

Figure 17-2 - Ventilation Grille in Exterior Door

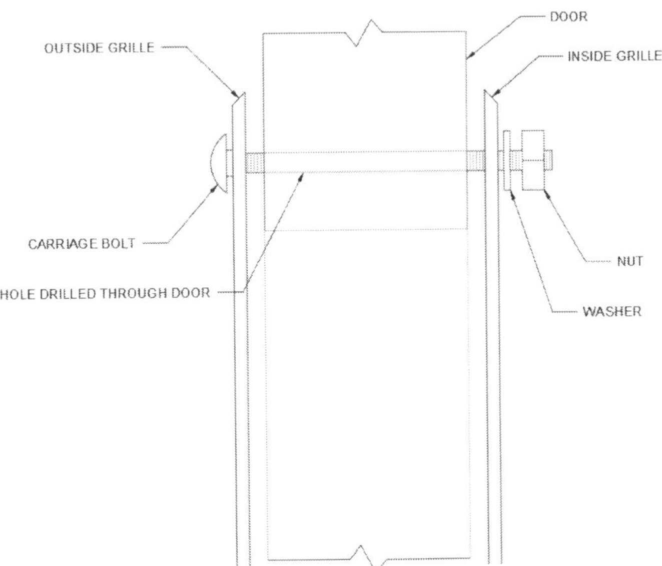

Figure 17-3 - Using Carriage Bolt to Secure Ventilation Grilles to Door

Exterior Rooms

Many buildings have rooms that are accessible from the exterior, but which do not allow access to the interior of the building. These can include mechanical and electrical rooms, trash and recycle rooms, and storage rooms.

Although these rooms cannot be used to gain access to the building, it is important that they be properly secured to prevent theft, vandalism, and arson. In areas where homelessness is an issue, rooms of this type are also often used as sleeping places by the homeless.

Doors to exterior rooms should be treated similarly to building entrances and equipped with the same types of locking hardware. (See Appendix A for best practices for securing doors.)

Roof Access

Doors and hatches are often used to provide access to the roof. In many cases, access to the roof is only needed by maintenance personnel. In these cases, the door to the roof should be kept locked at all times and keyed so that only authorized people have access. If roof hatches are used, they should be locked using a heavy-duty padlock.

For safety and to comply with building codes, the locks on roof doors should control access to the roof, but allow people to freely exit from the roof back into the building. This can create a security vulnerability when it is possible to gain access to the roof from an adjacent building or by other means. One way to solve this problem is to use an outdoor intrusion alarm system. (See page 157.)

In some cases, portions of the roof may contain amenity areas such as rooftop decks that are accessible to residents. In these cases, the amenity areas should be physically separated from other portions of the roof using fencing or other type of barrier. The door that provides access to the roof should be treated the same as the door to any other amenity area and controlled with a common area key or card reader.

Figure 17-4 - Roof Hatch

Drop Slots

Some buildings have drop slots on exterior walls or doors that are used for mail or newspaper deliveries. Drop slots are also often used to allow the drop-off of payments or paperwork such as rental applications.

Drop slots located in or near entrance doors can sometimes be used by intruders to manipulate the lock hardware on the doors, allowing entry. Vandals have also been known to insert hazardous or obnoxious items through a slot or to place a garden hose through the slot and turn on the water.

The best solution is to eliminate the use of drop slots entirely. If a drop box is needed, the use of a separate, fully-enclosed box on the exterior of the building is recommended.

If through-wall drop slots will continue to be used, an enclosure should be built around them on the inside. This enclosure should be large enough to accommodate the items being received but reduce the damage that could be caused if harmful items were inserted into the slot. Drop slots located in doors are difficult to protect, and should be equipped with barriers that make it difficult to manipulate the lock hardware on the door to gain entry.

Figure 17-5 - Drop Slot

Common Points of Weakness in Building Security

Tailgating

"Tailgating" is when an intruder enters the building as a resident enters or exits through an exterior door. This is especially easy at busy buildings where many people are coming and going, allowing intruders to quickly gain entry.

Tailgating can be one of the most challenging security problems to solve at a multifamily property. The best solution is to encourage residents to be aware of who attempts to enter the building as they enter or leave and to challenge people that they do not know. This can be accomplished through ongoing security awareness training for residents. It can also be helpful to post signs at the building reminding residents not to let people that they do not know into the building.

Use of PIN Codes

Many buildings allow the use of PIN codes to gain access at the building entrances. This is often accomplished using the keypad on the telephone entry system.

PIN codes can easily fall into the wrong hands and become widely known by criminals in the community. (See page 271 for more on PIN codes.)

Unprotected Door Latches

The door latch on many exterior doors is unprotected and can be easily forced open by an intruder. This is a particular problem on doors with electric strikes used with telephone entry and access control systems. The door latch often does not properly align with the electric strike, making it simple to push back the latch using a knife or screwdriver.

The solution to this problem is to install a latch guard or astragal on the exterior of the door. These will provide better protection of the door latch, making it more difficult to force open the door. (See best practices for securing doors in Appendix A.)

Manipulating Postal Lock Switches

The postal lock switches on telephone entry systems can often be easily manipulated to allow entry into the building. (See page 192 for more on manipulating postal lock switches.)

Using Default Codes on Telephone Entry Systems

Default entry codes on telephone entry systems can sometimes be used to gain entry into the building. (See page 193 for more on default entry codes.)

Key Boxes

Key boxes are commonly used on the exterior of the building to allow access by contractors, utility companies, and emergency responders. Key boxes typically contain keys or access cards that allow entry through exterior entrance doors.

Many key boxes are poorly constructed and can be easily compromised by a criminal. Once entry to a key box has been made, the intruder can remove the key or access card and use it to gain entry to the building. (See page 107 for more on key boxes.)

Exit Motion Detectors

When electromagnetic locks are used to secure exterior doors, motion detectors are commonly used to unlock the door from the inside when people approach to exit. These motion detectors are known as "request-to-exit" detectors.

It is often possible to activate the request-to-exit motion detector from outside of the door. This can be accomplished by inserting an object in the gap above or between the doors and using it to trigger the motion detector. The motion detector can sometimes also be triggered by blowing smoke or compressed air through gaps above or between the doors.

To reduce this vulnerability, request-to-exit motion detectors should be adjusted so that they detect people approaching the door from the inside, but are difficult to trigger from outside. This can sometimes require moving the motion detector to another location.

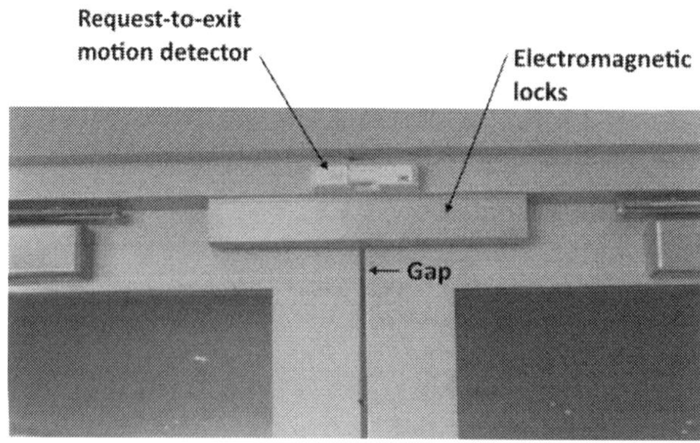

Figure 17-6 - Request-To-Exit Motion Detector

Tampering With Wiring to Electric Lock Hardware

In some cases, the wiring to electric lock hardware is installed on the non-secured side of the door. For example, the wiring on an access controlled door at a parking garage elevator lobby may have been installed on the garage side rather than on the lobby side. This would allow an intruder to gain access by tampering with the wiring. This is a particular problem when using fail-safe devices such as electromagnetic locks where simply cutting the wires would allow access.

The best solution is to always install all wiring to access control devices on the secured side of the door. If wiring must be installed on the unsecured side, it should be installed in conduit. The covers on any junction boxes used should be fastened using tamper-resistant fasteners.

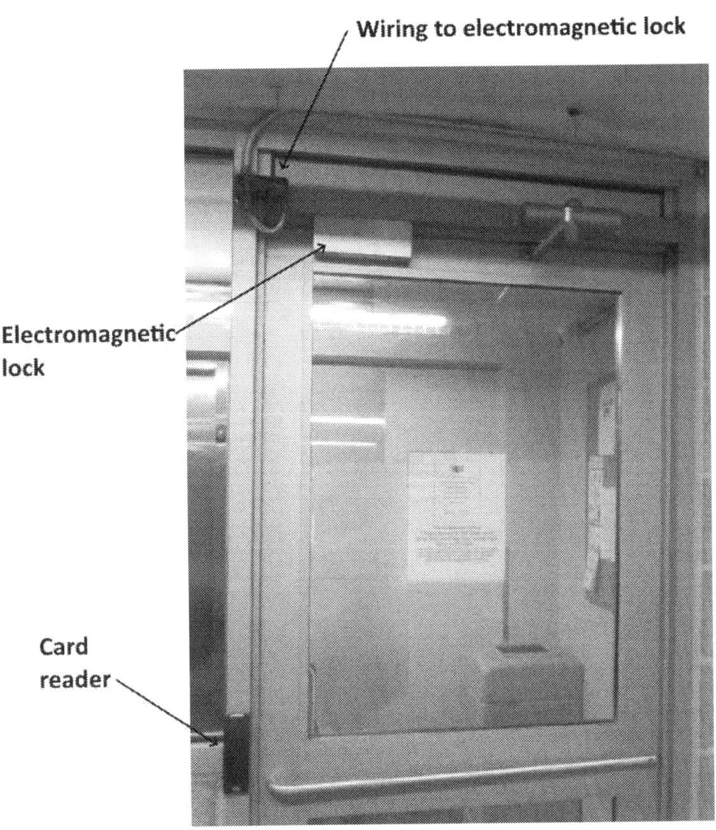

Figure 17-7 - Wiring to Electric Lock Hardware on Unsecured Side of Door

Use of Under-Door Tool

When locksets with lever handles are used on doors, it is often possible to open them from the outside using a device known as a "under-door tool". This device is inserted in the gap underneath of the door and used to grab the inside handle of the lock, allowing entry.

The use of an under-door tool can be made more difficult by reducing the size of the gap under the door. This can be accomplished by installing a threshold and door bottom under the door. The door bottom should provide a tight seal against the threshold that prevents the insertion of an under-door tool. (See page 97 for more on door bottoms and under-door tools.)

Use of Double-Door Tool

When exit devices are used on double doors, it is often possible to open them from the outside using a device known as a "double-door tool". This tool can be inserted in the gap between the door leaves and used to activate the exit device push bar, allowing entry.

The use of the double-door tool can be prevented by installing an astragal to cover the gap between the door leaves. (See page 95 for more on astragals and double-door tools.)

Chapter 18: Securing the Interior of the Building

Importance of Securing Indoor Areas

Indoor areas are the portions of the property that are located inside of the buildings on a multifamily property site. Indoor areas include lobbies, hallways, stairways, mail rooms, storage rooms, amenity rooms, building offices, and other common areas of the building.

Properly securing indoor areas provides a second line of defense against intruders who may have made their way past the building perimeter. This is consistent with the Concentric Circles of Protection concept described in Chapter 3 which recommends that multiple layers of security be provided in order to effectively protect assets.

Properly securing indoor areas also provides better protection against crimes committed by "insiders" – people who have legitimate access to the building but misuse this privilege to carry out criminal acts. Insiders may include current or former residents, visitors, delivery drivers, contractors, employees, and others.

Building Lobbies

Building lobbies are the formal point of entry to the building. Depending on size and layout, a property may have one or more building lobbies.

Building lobbies should be clearly marked from the outside so that first-time visitors and delivery drivers can easily find them.

The interior of lobbies should be well-lit, with a minimum light level of 10 to 35 Lux provided uniformly throughout the lobby area. There should be clear lines of sight within the lobby, with a minimum number of places where a person could hide.

Unattended Building Lobbies

Unattended lobbies are lobbies that are not staffed by a concierge or other employee.

In lobbies that are unattended, the types of furnishings used should be limited to those that provide a practical purpose and kept as simple as possible. The use of expensive furniture or artwork in lobbies can invite theft by both insiders and outsiders and should be avoided.

Where the theft of furniture or artwork from the lobby is a potential problem, the items should be secured to the wall or floor using security fasteners. An object protection alarm system can also be used to detect when an attempt is made to remove furniture or artwork. (See page 157).

Clutter in the lobby should be kept to a minimum. Packages and newspapers should be delivered to a mailroom or package room and not left in the lobby.

At higher-risk properties, a second interior door within the lobby can be used to provide additional security. This door would separate the main lobby area from the secured interior portion of the building, providing an additional layer of security and reducing the risks of tailgating. Residents entering through the lobby would be required to use their key or access card twice: once to enter through the exterior lobby door, and then again to enter through the interior lobby door.

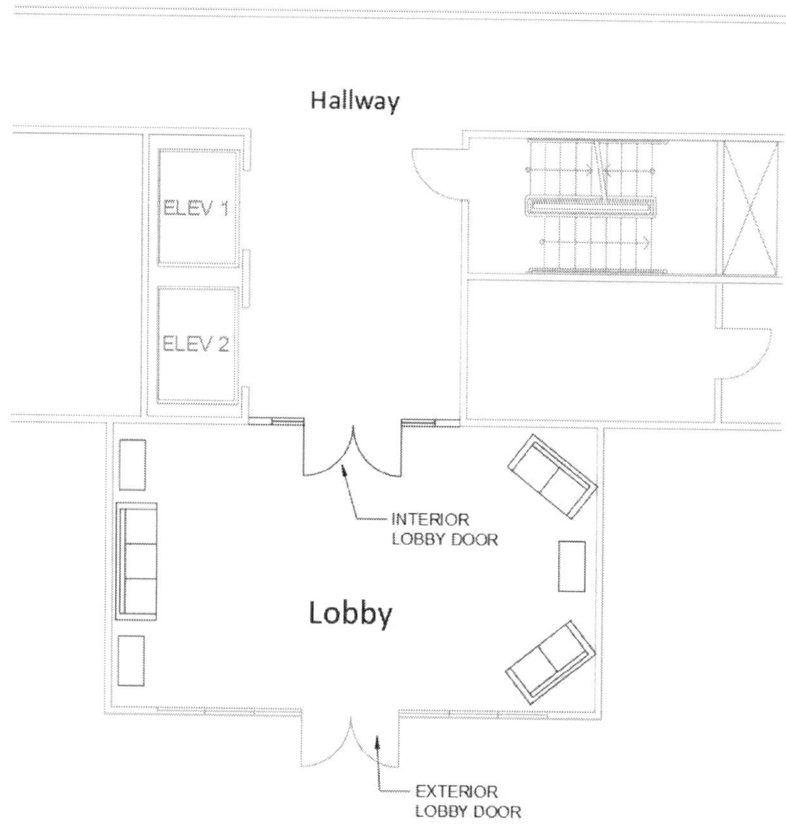

Figure 18-1 - Unattended Lobby with Interior Door

Attended Building Lobbies

Attended lobbies are those that are staffed by a concierge at all times. The proper design of these lobbies is essential in order to get maximum value from the concierge and to provide the best service to residents. Here are some tips for providing improved security at attended building lobbies:

- The concierge desk should be positioned so that it allows clear observation of the building entrance and lobby. The desk should be located in front of any elevators, stairways, and corridors so that it is necessary to pass by the desk in order to enter the secured portion of the building.
- A barrier wall and door should be provided to separate the main lobby area from the secured interior portion of the building. The door should be equipped with a card reader, requiring residents to use their access card to enter. A remote door release button should be provided at the concierge desk to allow the door to be opened for visitors.
- The concierge desk should be fully enclosed from the lobby side to prevent people in the lobby from getting behind the desk. A lockable door should be provided that allows authorized staff to enter the area behind the desk. (See Figure 18-2).
- The concierge desk should have two worksurfaces, a higher level on the lobby side, and a lower level on the concierge side. The worksurface on the lobby side should be between 38" and 42" high. The worksurface on the concierge side should be approximately 30" high.

- At higher-risk properties, additional steps should be taken to prevent people from climbing over the desk or physically attacking the concierge. This can be done by extending the height of the desk on the lobby side to at least 60" and creating one or more service windows. (See Figure 18-3.) The width of the windows (dimension "A") can vary depending on how much security is desired. Wider windows (32" to 40") provide a more open and friendly environment, while narrower windows (18" to 24") provide better protection.
- A panic button should be provided at the concierge desk. This panic button should send a silent alarm signal to an off-site monitoring center when the button is pressed.
- The exterior lobby door should be capable of being locked. Depending on the level of security risk at the property, the door can be kept locked at all times, or left open during daytime hours and locked only at night. The door should be equipped with a card reader to allow residents to enter. An intercom system should be provided between the outside of the door and the concierge desk to allow visitors to contact the concierge when the door is locked.
- If the concierge will have the capability to monitor the building access control and video surveillance systems, the monitors for these systems should be carefully integrated into the design of the concierge desk. Monitors should be arranged in such a manner that they can be comfortably seen by the concierge without blocking the view of the building entrance and lobby.
- If there are ever times that the concierge desk will be left unattended, all drawers and cabinets should be equipped with locks. Provisions should also be made to secure all computers and monitors that are located at the desk.

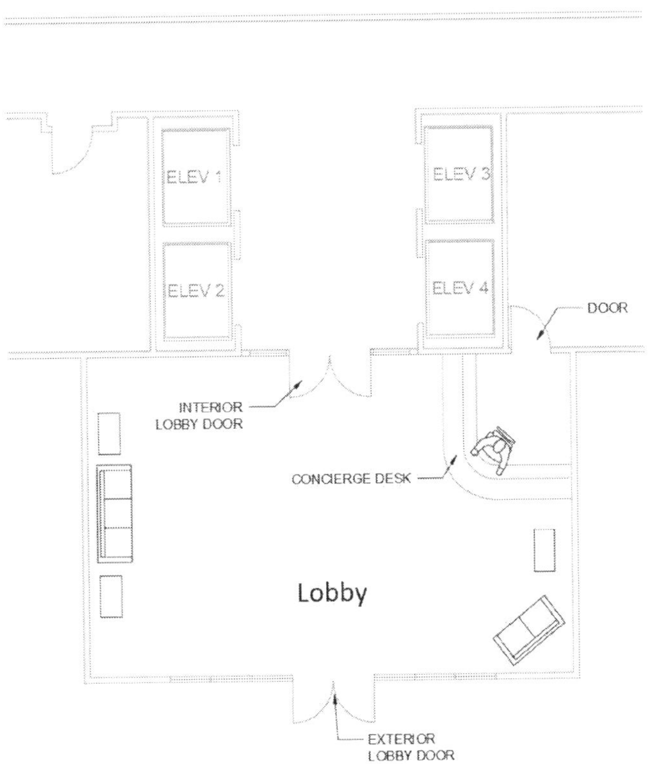

Figure 18-2 - Attended Building Lobby with Concierge Desk

Figure 18-3 - Concierge Desk with Service Window

Hallways

Hallways should be well-lit, with a minimum light level of 10 to 35 Lux provided within the hallway. Light fixtures should be spaced so that lighting is uniform along the length of the hallway, avoiding conditions where some parts of the hallway are very bright and other portions are very dark. When possible, hallways should be painted a bright reflective color to maximize the effectiveness of the lighting and to increase visibility.

Policies should be established to limit the types of items that residents can place outside of their residential units to avoid clutter and to maintain an unobstructed path of travel down the hallway. Good housekeeping practices should be used to keep the hallways clean and litter-free at all times.

Stairways

In multistory buildings, stairways are a code-required means of egress from the building. Depending on the size and configuration of the building, two or more stairway exits are typically required off of each floor. In addition to being used for emergency egress, stairways are sometimes used by residents as a means to routinely travel between floors.

Stairways can pose a major security risk at many multifamily properties. First, free access must be allowed into the stairways at all times for exiting purposes. This allows anyone to enter the stairway at any time. Second, many stairways are infrequently used, making them an ideal place for trespassers to hide, to consume drugs or alcohol, or to lay in waiting for an unsuspecting victim. In areas that have a homeless problem, it is common to find people using the stairwells as a place to sleep at night.

There can be a particular problem when the same stairways are used for the parking garage levels and residential levels of a multistory building. An intruder who sneaks into the parking garage can enter a stairway and use it to travel up to a residential floor.

A similar problem can exist in mixed-use buildings when retail shops use the same stairways that are used by the residential floors above. People exiting into a stairway from a retail area can gain access to the residential floors.

Here are some tips for providing improved security in stairways:

- If possible, separate stairways should be provided for residential floors, parking garage floors, and floors with retail shops. These stairways should allow exiting to the street without permitting access to other secured areas. Providing separate stairways can be easily accomplished when a building is being designed, but can be prohibitively expensive or impossible to achieve once a building has been constructed.
- If separate stairways cannot be provided, the use of an internal gate within the stairway itself should be considered. This gate should be placed in the stair just beyond the exit door to the street. This would allow people from both above and below to exit, but prevent people from the lower floors from entering the upper floors. If desired, the gate can be equipped with a key operated lock or card reader to allow authorized residents to enter the upper portion of the stairway. Before installing a gate in an existing stairway, be sure to obtain permission from local building officials. In some cases, installing a gate may reduce the required clearances within the stairway and may not be allowed.

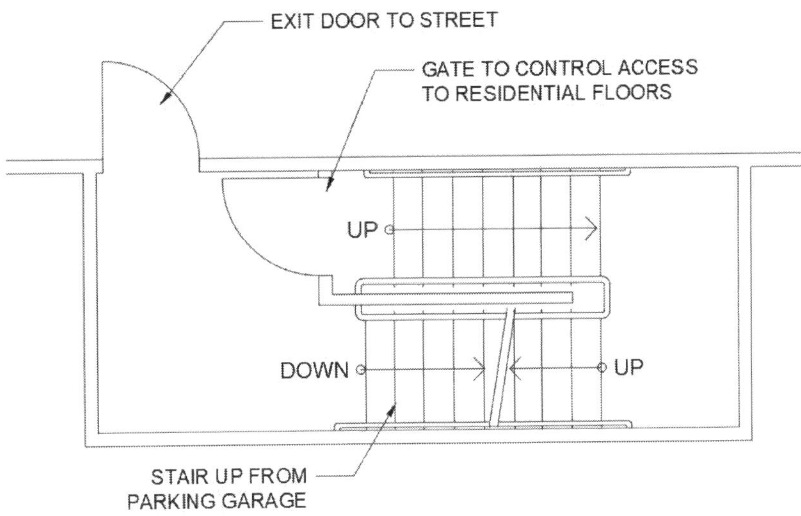

Figure 18-4 - Gate in Stairway at Street Level

- For additional security, the doors between the stairway and the residential floors should be kept locked. Depending on the height of the building and where it is located, building codes may require that special systems be put into place in order to lock the stairway doors. This can include providing electric locks connected to the fire alarm system and providing emergency communications systems at the stair landings. Local building codes should be reviewed to determine the specific requirements that may apply to your building. If desired, the doors between the stairways and the floors can be equipped with a key-operated lock or card reader to allow authorized residents to enter from the stairway.
- If routine travel through a stairway door is not required, signs should be provided indicating that the door is for emergency use only. As a further deterrent, an exit alarm can be added to the door. (See page 160.)
- Stairways should be well-lit, with a minimum light level of 30 to 50 Lux provided within the stair. When possible, stairways should be painted a bright reflective color to maximize the effectiveness of the lighting and to increase visibility.

- There is often a space under the stairs at the lowest level of the stairway. This space can be a popular place for people to sleep or hide. To prevent this, the space should be enclosed with a wall or fence to prevent access.
- Good housekeeping practices should be used to keep the stairways clean and litter-free at all times. Stairways should not be used for storage of any kind.

Elevators

Elevators are the most frequently used means of travel between floors in most multistory buildings. Here are some thoughts on providing improved security in elevators:

- Card readers can be used in the elevators to provide an additional layer of security. When this is done, a valid access card should be required to travel to any floor but the main lobby. However, it should be understood that card reader controlled elevators provide only a moderate level of security and can be compromised. (See page 141 for more on elevator control.)
- Video surveillance cameras can be installed within the elevator car and can be used to capture images of people using the elevators. These cameras can also be useful in capturing images of people who may be vandalizing the elevator itself. However, in some cases, residents may consider cameras in elevators to be intrusive as they feel that they have a right to privacy when riding in an elevator. In these cases, the need for security should be balanced with resident's concerns.

Resident Storage Spaces

Resident storage spaces provide additional storage for residents outside of their residential units. Resident storage spaces can be a single room or closet to which the resident has exclusive access, or may be a closet or locker located within a larger storage room that is shared with other residents. Resident storage spaces can be located inside or outside of the building.

Burglaries of resident storage spaces is one of the leading security problems at many multifamily properties. Here are some tips for providing improved security at resident storage spaces:

- If individual storage rooms or closets are used, the doors to these rooms should be secured using the best practices for securing doors described in Appendix A.
- If storage closets or lockers are located within a common storage room, the doors to that room should be secured using the best practices for securing doors described in Appendix A. To provide improved accountability and control, the doors to common storage rooms should be controlled by an access control system rather than a standard lock.
- The type of storage locker system used directly affects the level of security that it provides. Figure 18-5 shows the types of storage locker systems commonly used at multifamily properties. Upgrading the locker system to a higher security type is often the best solution at properties that are experiencing a large number of storage locker burglaries.

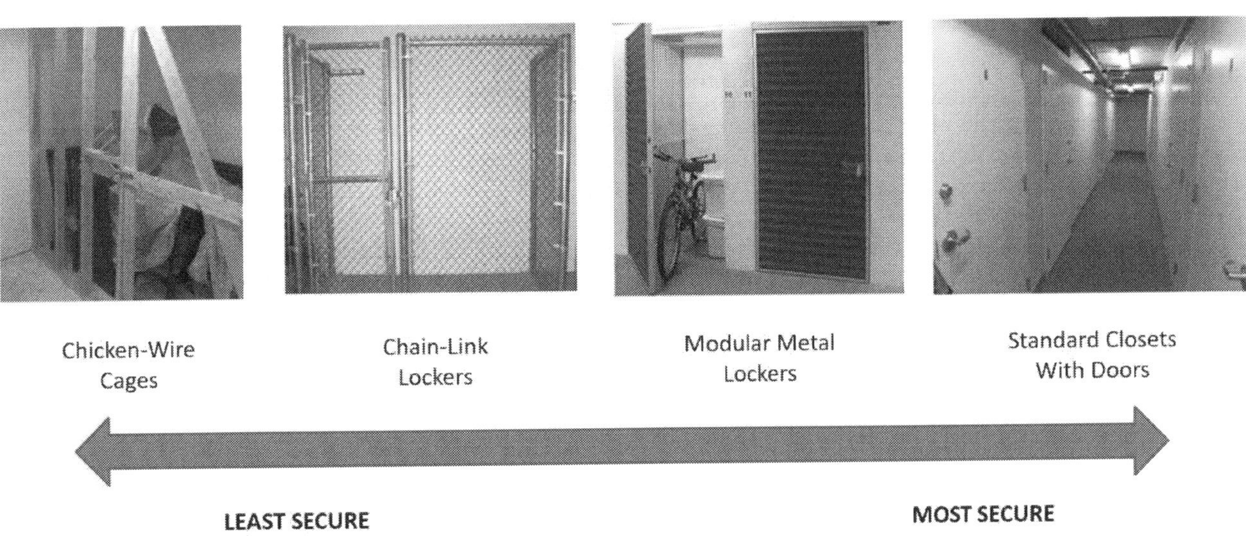

Figure 18-5 - Commonly Used Types of Storage Locker Systems

- Signs that indicate where resident storage spaces are located should be removed and replaced with a sign that provides just a room number. Residents should know where their storage space is located and there is no need to advertise the locations of these rooms to would-be burglars.
- If residents provide their own padlocks for storage lockers, they should be encouraged to use a high-quality, discus style padlock that is operated by a key. For additional protection, the use of a high-security padlock should be considered. Most inexpensive padlocks and combination padlocks can be easily compromised by a burglar.

Figure 18-6 - Example of Discus Style Padlock

- When a property has multiple shared storage rooms, residents should only be given access to the specific room in which their locker is located. This can be accomplished by keying the locks to each storage room differently. If an access control system is used, then each resident's access card should be programmed to only allow access to the room that contains their locker.
- No matter what precautions are taken, resident storage spaces are not suitable for the storage of high-value items such as expensive jewelry or artwork. Residents should understand the limits of the security that can be provided in resident storage spaces and advised not to store high-value items there.

Bicycle Storage

Bicycle storage areas are provided at many multifamily properties for use by residents and visitors. Bicycle storage facilities can include floor and wall-mounted bicycle racks which are installed in interior areas of the building, and enclosed bicycle storage rooms or cages.

Bicycles are considered a highly attractive target by thieves. Many bicycles have a high resale value and can easily be sold to individuals or bicycle dealers. Many bicycle thieves operate in organized groups and have developed techniques for entering a property and making off with large numbers of bicycles in a short time.

Indoor Bicycle Racks

Indoor bicycle racks can be located in open areas within the building, or within enclosed bicycle rooms or bicycle cages. Here are some tips for providing better security at bicycle racks:

- The types of bicycle racks used should have been specifically designed with security in mind. Many inexpensive bike racks are constructed of thin metal material that can be easily cut-through. Many racks are assembled using standard nuts and bolts that allow the rack to be easily disassembled.
- Bicycle racks should be securely fastened to the wall or floor using tamper-resistant security fasteners. Any nuts and bolts that are used to assemble the racks should be tack-welded to prevent the rack from being disassembled.
- A secure attachment point should be provided at each bike rack to allow the attachment of bicycle locks. If the rack itself does not provide a suitable attachment point, then an external bicycle lock anchor should be used. (See Figure 18-7).
- When residents are allowed to park their bicycles adjacent to their parking space in parking garages, the use of a wall mounted rack on the wall in front of the parking space is recommended. If a bicycle rack will not be used, then a bicycle lock anchor should be provided to allow the bike to be locked to the wall or floor.
- When possible, indoor bicycle racks should be placed so that they cannot easily be seen from outside of the building through a window or when an overhead door is opened. This reduces the chances that a would-be bicycle thief would be tempted when passing by the building.

Figure 18-7 - Bicycle Lock Anchor

Bicycle Rooms

Bicycle rooms are rooms within the interior of the building that are used for the storage of bicycles. These rooms may be accessible from inside of the building, outside of the building, or both. Bicycle rooms provide an additional layer of security and are especially recommended for use at higher-risk properties.

The doors to bicycle rooms should be secured using the best practices for securing doors described in Appendix A. To provide improved accountability and control, doors to bicycle rooms should be controlled by an access control system rather than a standard lock.

Ideally, bicycle rooms should have no windows. If the room has windows, they should be covered with opaque window film to prevent bicycles from being seen from outside of the room. Signs or artwork that indicates where bicycle rooms are located should be removed and replaced with a sign that provides just a room number.

Bicycle Cages

Bicycle cages are similar to bicycle rooms except are constructed using fencing material rather than traditional walls and doors. Bicycle cages are commonly installed in open areas of parking garages and are sometimes added to a building after it has been built in an attempt to reduce bicycle thefts.

Bicycle cages are typically constructed of chain-link fencing material or ornamental iron fencing material. Chain-link fencing material costs less than ornamental iron fencing material but is easier for an intruder to penetrate. Ornamental iron fencing material costs more but provides better security.

All gates that provide access to bicycle cages should be secured using the construction guidelines for pedestrian gates. (See page 41.)

Amenity Rooms

Amenity rooms include party rooms, libraries, business centers, fitness centers, indoor pools and spas, and other such spaces intended for common use by residents. Amenity rooms should be kept locked so that access is restricted to only residents and their authorized visitors.

To provide improved accountability and control, doors to amenity rooms should be controlled by an access control system rather than a standard lock.

Building Office

Most larger multifamily properties have an office where the business of the property is conducted. Depending on the type of property, these offices may be known as the Management Office, Leasing Office, Homeowners Association Office, or by other names.

Offices of this type can contain confidential information about residents, as well as keys and access cards that can be used to compromise the security of the buildings or individual residential units. The staff working in these offices can also face risks from disgruntled people that they come into contact with.

Here are some tips for providing improved security at building offices:

- The doors to offices should be secured using the best practices for securing doors described in Appendix A.

- If possible, a room within the interior of the office should be used for the storage of confidential files, keys, and access cards. This "room within a room" should have a door equipped with a deadbolt lock and be kept locked at all times when the office is unoccupied.
- All files that contain confidential information should be stored in a locked file cabinet, even if the cabinet itself is in a locked room. Most standard file cabinet locks can be easily bypassed and provide very little security. To provide better protection, install a file cabinet locking bar on the file cabinet and lock it using a high-security padlock. (See Figure 18-8.)
- Offices that handle significant amounts of cash should be equipped with a safe that has an Underwriters Laboratories (UL) TL-15 rating or better.

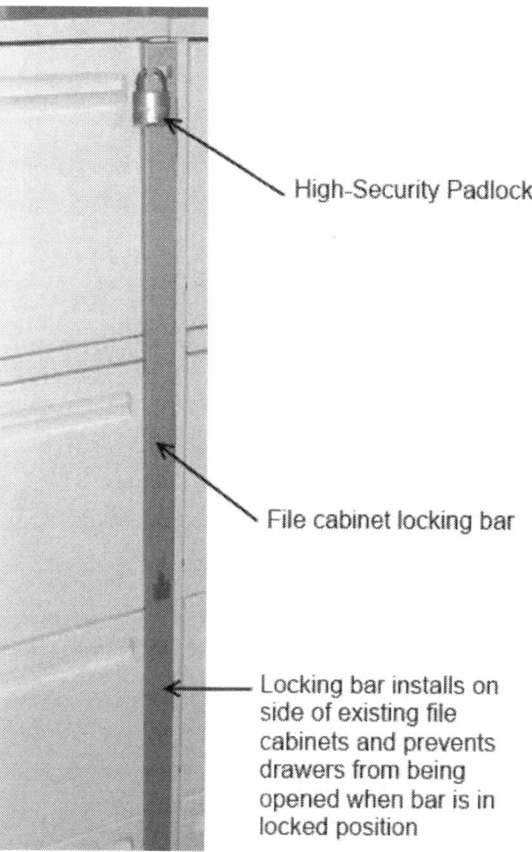

Figure 18-8 - File Cabinet Locking Bar

The following should also be considered for offices at higher-risk properties:

- The exterior windows of offices located on the ground floor should be equipped with security window film.
- The office should be equipped with an intrusion alarm system. This system should be turned on at times when the office is unoccupied
- Panic buttons should be provided at the desks of employees. These panic buttons should be connected to the intrusion alarm and send a silent alarm signal to an off-site monitoring center when a panic button is pressed.

Indoor Mailboxes

Indoor mailboxes are used at many multifamily properties to receive mail from the United States Postal Service. These mailboxes are grouped into clusters and provide individual boxes for each resident. Indoor mailboxes are sometimes located in or directly adjacent to the building lobby. There may be more than one location where indoor mailboxes are located depending on the size of the property.

Mailboxes should be located in highly visible locations and not tucked away in obscure areas. At buildings that are attended by a concierge, having mailboxes located where they can be seen from the concierge desk is desirable.

At higher-risk properties, mailboxes should be located in a locked mailroom. The door to the mailroom should be secured using the best practices for securing doors described in Appendix A. To provide improved accountability and control, the door to the mailrooms should be controlled by an access control system rather than a standard lock.

At buildings that don't have on-site staff, it is common for carriers such as Amazon, FedEx, and UPS to deliver packages and place them near the mailboxes. This leaves the packages exposed to theft, particularly if the mailboxes are not located in a locked mailroom.

One relatively inexpensive option to solve this problem is to install a simple locker that has a door equipped with a mechanical combination lock. The combination for this lock would be given to both delivery drivers and residents. When delivering packages, the driver would use the code to open the locker and place the package inside. The driver would then relock the locker and leave a delivery notice on the mailbox of the package recipient. Residents would use the code to open the locker and retrieve their packages.

The code to the locker should be changed periodically and when it is suspected that the code has fallen into the wrong hands. While this system is not perfect, it does provide better security than simply leaving packages unsecured next to the mailboxes.

Automated Package Locker Systems

The use of automated package locker systems has become popular at multifamily properties. These systems fully automate the receiving of packages and can be used at both unattended and attended buildings.

At unattended buildings, automated package lockers provide a convenient, secure way for residents to receive packages. At attended buildings, automated package lockers allow the majority of packages to be processed without the involvement of staff, greatly reducing their workload, and allowing them to focus on other more productive activities.

Figure 18-9 - Automated Package Locker System

Here is how an automated package locker system works:

1. Automated package lockers are installed at the property. The package locker systems can be installed in the existing mailrooms in individual buildings, or a package locker system for all buildings can be installed in a central location such as a parking garage. The package locker system requires electrical power and an Internet connection.
2. Delivery services such as UPS and FedEx are issued codes that allow them to gain access to the place where the package locker system is located. This can be done using the building's telephone entry system, or a separate keypad can be provided to allow access.
3. When arriving at the building, the delivery driver uses the assigned code to enter the building.
4. Once in the building, the driver proceeds to the place where the package locker system is located. A passcode is then entered to gain access to the system.
5. Using a touchscreen on the locker system, the driver looks up the name of the resident receiving the package using a pulldown menu. A name is selected, causing a locker door to automatically open. The driver then places the package inside the locker and closes the door.
6. When the locker door is closed, a text or email message is automatically sent to the package recipient. This message advises the resident that a package has arrived, and provides a temporary access code.
7. The resident goes to the locker system and enters the access code. This causes the door on the appropriate locker to unlock, allowing the resident to retrieve the package.
8. Video cameras are provided that document all activity occurring at the locker system, including package delivery by the carrier and package pick-up by the resident.

Automated Parcel Rooms

Automated parcel rooms are similar to automated package lockers except use a single secured parcel room to store packages rather than individual lockers. There are shelves within this room where packages are stored. Delivery drivers use a code to enter the building and parcel room.

Once in the room, the driver enters information on a special keypad. The automated system then tells the driver on which shelve to place the package. A text or email message is then sent to the resident. The resident then uses a code to enter the parcel room and to retrieve their package from the designated shelve.

If a person attempts to remove a package from the wrong shelve or without entering the proper code, an alarm will sound, and an off-site monitoring center will be notified. There are cameras within the parcel room that allow the monitoring center to remotely observe and record activity occurring within the room.

Figure 18-10 - Automated Parcel Room

Chapter 19: Securing Parking Garages

Importance of Securing Parking Garages

Crime problems in parking garages are often one of the biggest problems that the property manager must face. The vehicles parked in garages and their contents are subject to theft and vandalism, often at alarming rates. While most crimes involving vehicles don't usually cause high dollar value losses, these crimes are significant to the residents that are victimized and create dissatisfaction with the property and its management. Chronic thefts from vehicles can cause residents to move out and result in negative reviews being posted at online review sites. Too many negative reviews can affect the rentability of rental properties, and in some cases, can make it more difficult to sell an owned residential unit.

Crimes of a more serious nature can also occur in parking garages. Residents and visitors can become victims of robbery or physical or sexual assaults. Many parking garages have few people in them at certain times of the day and provide numerous places for a criminal to hide. This makes them a perfect place to lay in waiting for an unsuspecting victim.

Because of these factors, the security of parking garages must be taken very seriously.

Types of Parking Garages

Parking garages can be located within a multifamily building, or can be located in a separate detached parking structure. Parking garages can be open or enclosed.

Open parking garages are those constructed with few exterior walls or doors, allowing them to be freely accessed, often from multiple sides. Open parking garages allow natural ventilation and lighting from the outside. Aside from the structural columns that hold up the building, there are few physical barriers to prevent entry from the outside. Open parking garages have no overhead doors but may use barrier arm gates to control traffic in and out. Pedestrian entrances may consist of just an opening rather than a door.

Enclosed parking garages are those that have exterior walls around the outside perimeter of the garage at the ground level. All vehicle and pedestrian entrances have doors which can be kept closed and locked at times when desired. While fully enclosed at the ground level, many enclosed garages may be fully or partially open on the upper levels. For example, it would be common to find a four-story parking garage where the first level is fully enclosed, the second and third levels are partially open, and the fourth level is completely open.

As you can imagine, open parking garages are significantly more difficult to secure than enclosed parking garages and can create serious security challenges. When new multifamily properties are being designed, most security professionals would almost always recommend that an enclosed parking garage rather than an open parking garage be used.

It should be kept in mind that an enclosed parking garage can always be left open by keeping overhead doors raised and leaving pedestrian doors unlocked, but that the reverse is not true – it is difficult or impossible to restrict access to an open parking garage.

Often, the architect designing the building gives no thought to security when choosing to use an open parking garage concept. Or, if security was considered, the rate of crime at the location was so low at the time that the use of an open parking garage was thought to be acceptable. However, as time has gone by, the rate of crime at the location has increased exponentially, and the use of an open parking garage now creates unacceptable security risks.

While the use of measures such as security patrols and video surveillance systems may provide some benefits at open parking garages, the best solution is to make changes to the structure to convert it into an enclosed garage. This usually requires:

- Installing partitions between the structural columns at the exterior walls. Ornamental iron panels are commonly used in this application as they provide security while allowing natural lighting and ventilation.
- Installing doors or gates at the pedestrian entry points to the garage. All doors and gates should allow free egress from the garage to comply with code requirements.
- Installing overhead doors at the vehicle entry points to the garage. If the garage has multiple vehicle entrance points, consider reducing the number of entrances to only one or two to reduce both initial costs and ongoing maintenance costs.

While converting an open garage to an enclosed garage can be expensive, it is often the only real way to reduce chronic crime problems in garages at higher-risk properties.

Garage Overhead Doors

Overhead doors with automatic operators are most often used at the vehicle entrances to parking garages. Overhead doors are often a weak spot in parking garage security and should be given careful attention.

Here are some suggestions:

- A high-quality overhead door and door operator should be used. The door and door operator should be rated to handle the number of opening and closing cycles expected – often 1,000 cycles or more per day at a larger multifamily building.
- Consider the use of a high-performance overhead door to greatly reduce the chances of “tailgating”. (See page 75.)
- The area outside of parking garage entrances should be kept clear so that people lingering outside the door can be seen. Trim or remove any trees or shrubbery that may create a place near the door for a potential intruder to hide.
- Good lighting should be provided at all garage entrances. A minimum light level of between 30 and 50 Lux is recommended.
- Adjust the time that the door stays open to an absolute minimum. Keep in mind that the door timer only begins its countdown after the vehicle clears the door’s safety devices.
- Provide signs on both sides of the overhead door to remind residents to wait for the door to close before driving off.
- For safety reasons, pedestrians and bicyclists should use pedestrian doors, not the overhead door, to enter and exit. People driving in and out of a garage can be caught off guard when a pedestrian unexpectedly appears in their path.
- If the overhead door has open panels that can easily be cut through, consider installing metal bars or perforated metal sheeting across the panel openings. (See page 74.)

- If the overhead door has an emergency release mechanism, be sure that it cannot be activated from outside of the garage. This can be accomplished by installing shields specifically made to protect the release, or by removing or tying back the cord that pulls upon the release. (See Figure 19-1.)

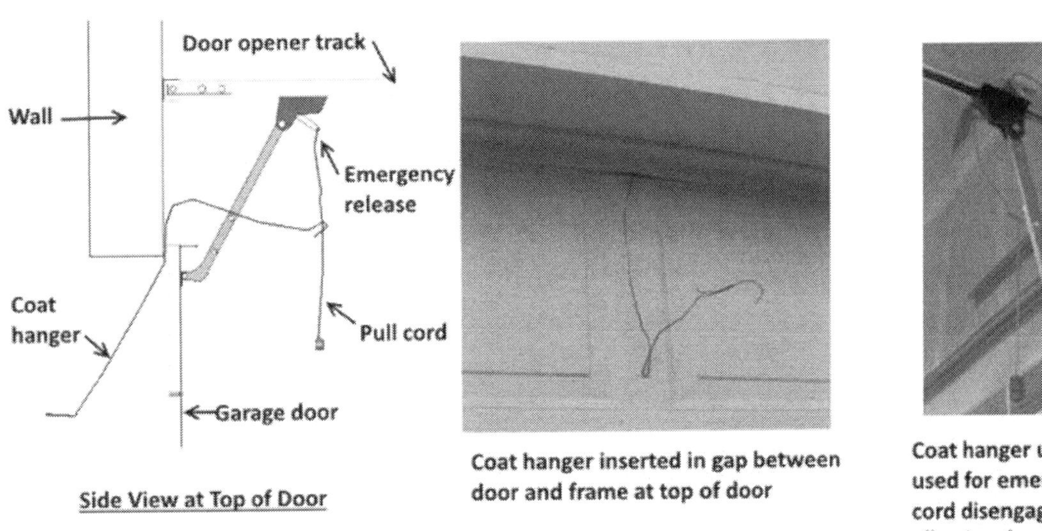

Side View at Top of Door

Coat hanger inserted in gap between door and frame at top of door

Coat hanger used to grab pull cord used for emergency release. Pulling cord disengages door from opener, allowing door to be opened

Figure 19-1 - Method That Can Be Used by Intruder to Activate Emergency Release

Garage Door Controls

Garage door controls are the devices used to open the garage overhead doors. These can include long-range RFID readers, card readers, wireless radio controls, motion detectors, manual button stations, and other devices. If used improperly, garage door controls can compromise the security provided by the overhead door.

Here are some suggestions for properly using garage door controls:

- If using radio controls, a high-quality rolling code type of system should be used. These require the use of a rolling code radio receiver at the overhead door, and the issuance of rolling code wireless transmitters to residents. The older fixed-code type of radio controls can be easily compromised. Consider upgrading these older controls if you have them at your building. (See page 138 for more on radio controls.)
- Many radio controls have the capability to open the door from several hundred feet away. Some residents take advantage of this capability so that the door is fully open when they reach it, avoiding the need to wait. This gives intruders standing outside the garage door an opportunity to quickly sneak in without being observed. Residents should be instructed to only open the overhead door when it is actually in their sight. To help enforce this, the range on radio controls can often be adjusted by trimming or repositioning the receiving antenna.
- Motion detectors are often used to allow vehicles to open the overhead door automatically when they drive up to it from the inside. These motion detectors can be activated accidently as people walk by the door on the inside. This creates additional opportunities for intruders to

sneak in. For better security, consider eliminating the motion detector and requiring residents to use their wireless transmitter to both enter and exit the parking garage.

- Button stations are typically provided on the inside of overhead doors. These buttons can encourage the improper use of the door by pedestrians and bicyclists and can create security vulnerabilities. Consider replacing the button station with a key-operated switch or card reader so that only authorized people can open the door.
- If button stations are used, be sure that they cannot be activated from outside of the garage. In some cases, there are openings on the exterior of the garage that can permit an intruder to insert an object and use it to activate the button station. This problem can be solved by filling-in the opening, moving the button station, or by providing a protective shield around the button station that makes it difficult to activate from the outside.

Garage Pedestrian Doors

The exterior doors to parking garages should be treated the same as the exterior doors to the buildings. Provide high-quality (ANSI Grade 2 or better) door lock hardware on these doors and equip them with protective devices to make forced entry more difficult. (See Appendix A for best practices for securing doors.)

To provide improved accountability and control, the exterior doors to the garage that will be used as entrances should be controlled by an access control system rather than a standard lock.

Lighting in Parking Garages

Good lighting in parking garages is crucial. A minimum light level of between 20 and 70 Lux is recommended within the interior of the garage. The lighting uniformity ratio should not exceed 4:1. LED light fixtures that provide a clear white light can be ideal for use in parking garages.

Motion-activated lighting in parking garages is great from an energy saving perspective, but can create security challenges when a garage is left completely in the dark. Consider using a combination of motion-activated lights and lights that are always left on.

To improve the effectiveness of the lighting, the walls, structural columns, and ceilings within the garage should be painted white or other reflective color. This can also create an environment that makes it easier to spot people in the garage and can make residents feel safer.

Parking Stalls

If assigned parking spaces are used, parking stalls should be numbered with a sequential stall number. For the safety of residents, the parking stall numbers should not correspond with the residential unit numbers. For the same reasons, stalls should never be identified with resident names.

Residents should not be allowed to store items openly and unsecured within their parking spaces. This creates clutter in the garage and makes it more difficult to quickly spot abnormal conditions such as signs of a car break-in. If a storage space is needed, a wall-mounted storage cabinet that can be kept locked should be provided on the wall near the parking stall. If bicycle storage within parking stalls is permitted, a bicycle rack or bicycle lock anchor should be provided to allow bicycles to be securely locked.

Housekeeping

Good housekeeping practices should be used within parking garages. The garages should be regularly swept and kept free of trash and debris. The walls, ceilings, and structural columns should be regularly cleaned and repainted when necessary.

Property management staff and residents should avoid storing items in unsecured locations within the parking garage. Too often, the garages at multifamily properties become a gathering place for unused items that should be recycled or disposed of rather than kept forever in the garage. If storage in the garage is needed, a locked storage room or fenced cage should be provided to permit items to be stored securely.

Video Surveillance Cameras

If the property is equipped with a video surveillance system, the use of cameras in the parking garage should be considered.

Because of the structural columns and the many nooks and crannies that exist within most parking garages, they can be a challenge to efficiently cover with cameras. Providing complete coverage of all areas can be prohibitively expensive. The best strategy is often to place cameras at key "chokepoints" such as at the garage exterior doors, garage stair doors, doors between the garage and the building, and at the garage elevator lobbies.

It is important that both residents and property management staff have realistic expectations about what cameras in the garage can and cannot do. Cameras that are not monitored on a real-time basis can do little to prevent crime and this should be clearly understood before they are installed. (See page 186 for more on the limitations of video surveillance systems.)

Emergency Callboxes

Emergency callboxes are sometimes used in the parking garages at multifamily properties. The purpose of these callboxes is to provide a means for residents and visitors to summon help in the event of an emergency. Cell phones often don't work reliably in parking garages, particularly if they are underground.

Emergency call boxes most commonly use autodialing telephones. These phones can be programmed to call 911 or a Security Operations Center (SOC) located on site when help is needed. Emergency call boxes usually also have a flashing light that flashes when the phone is activated and emergency signage that allows the callbox to be quickly located.

Before installing emergency callboxes, it is imperative to know who they will call and what type of response can be expected. Before programming autodialing phones to call 911 or other emergency number, be sure to check with the local authorities to confirm that this is acceptable.

Many 911 call centers have the ability to determine the location of where a call is coming from based on a telephone number. However, depending on the way that the call boxes are connected, this information may or may not be accurate at a multifamily building. To allow callers to give an accurate location, a sign should be provided at each call box that indicates the street address of the building and the floor and location where the call box is located (for example: "101 Main Street, 4th Floor, Southeast Corner").

If the call box will be programmed to call an in-house number rather than 911, it is essential that this number be answered at a fixed-location such as a Security Command Center that is staffed at all times. It is not acceptable to have a call box dial a cell phone or a phone at a location that is not continuously staffed. For example, having a call box dial a concierge desk where the concierge occasionally steps away to deliver packages is totally unacceptable.

Emergency call boxes should be tested on at least a monthly basis to confirm that they are working properly. If a call box is not operational, it should be covered, and an "out-of-service" sign placed on it until it can be repaired.

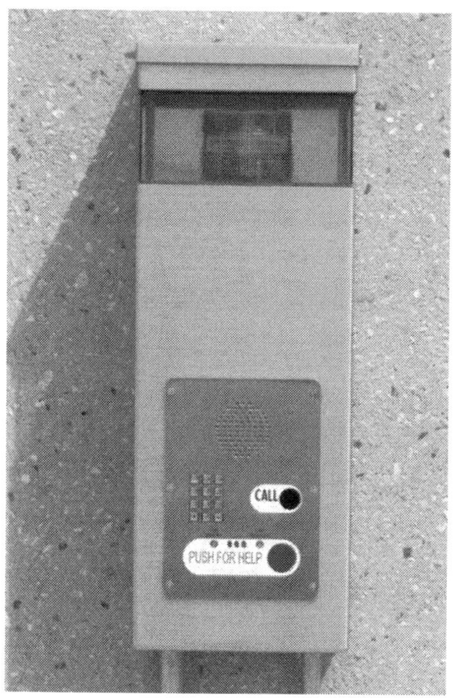

Figure 19-2 - Emergency Callbox

Chapter 20: Securing Residential Units

The Need to Secure Residential Units

The place that residents call their home is one of the most important areas to protect at a multifamily property. Even when a building or site is secured using the best of security measures, there is still a need to secure each of the individual residential units. Many residents are oblivious to this fact, and feel so secure within a property that they fail to take steps to secure their own unit. In their mind, their home is located within a protective bubble that no intruder can penetrate. This is rarely the case.

Responsibility for Security of Residential Units

The responsibility for security of individual residential units varies depending on property type. At most condominiums and homes within a gated community, the homeowner is usually entirely responsible for the security of their individual homes. For these properties, the property manager can provide guidance to residents on the most effective types of security measures to utilize, but has no authority to mandate their use.

At rental properties, the property manager has greater control over the types of security measures that can be used and has greater responsibilities. In many jurisdictions, local laws require that the property provide certain basic security measures at rental units. Ignoring these laws can place the property in legal jeopardy.

Some owners of rental properties may choose to only comply with the minimum legal requirements for security. Other owners may choose to offer enhanced security features to provide better protection of their residents and to increase the marketability of their property. Many renters appreciate enhanced security features and may choose to live at a property specifically because these features are available.

Risks Faced by Residential Units

The level of security risk faced by residential units can vary greatly depending on the location where the multifamily property is located. If the property itself is in a higher-crime area, then the residential units located within this property probably face greater security risks.

Risk can also vary depending on the type of property and where the residential unit is situated within the property. For example, ground floor units in a multistory building often face greater risks than the units on the upper floors. Units in garden style apartments that are spread out over a large property usually face greater security risks than units located in a high-rise condominium building.

The types of security measures implemented at a residential unit should be directly proportional to the level of risk as determined by the security risk assessment and the location of the unit within the property.

Exterior Doors

The front door to a residential unit is the most popular point of entry chosen by burglars. In almost every case, exterior doors are the weak link in security and should be one of the first places where improvements should be made to increase the security of the home.

The type of materials used to construct the door and door frame greatly affect the security of the door. Hollow-metal doors and frames offer greater security than wood doors and frames. Solid-core wood doors provide more security than hollow-core wood doors. Doors without windows provide better security than doors with windows.

However, in many cases, it is impractical to replace the type of door being used. In these cases, steps should be taken to improve the security of the door that already exists. Here are a few suggestions:

- Wood doors and frames should be reinforced using an extended length strike plate or door and frame reinforcement kit to make them more difficult to force open. (See page 100.)
- A high-quality (ANSI Grade 2 or better) deadbolt lock should be used on the door. If possible, the lock should use a high-security lock cylinder.
- A peephole viewer should be provided to allow residents to see who is outside of the door before opening it.
- At higher-risk properties, the use of protective devices such as latch guards or astragals should be considered. (See page 94.)

Windows and Glass Sliding Doors

Windows and glass sliding doors at ground level are another popular point of entry used by burglars. Here are some suggestions for improving the security of windows and sliding doors:

- The factory-provided lock hardware on newer windows and sliding doors usually provides good security, however the hardware used in older windows and doors does not. Supplemental lock hardware should be installed to improve the security of older windows and sliding doors.
- Windows and sliding doors should be kept closed and locked when the resident is away or has retired for the evening. While units at ground level are most vulnerable, residents should keep in mind that many burglars have no problem at all in climbing up to a window or deck located on an upper floor.
- If windows must frequently be left open to provide ventilation, then security window screens or bars should be provided to discourage entry by burglars.
- At higher-risk properties, the use of security window film on all ground floor windows should be considered. This includes the windows in and around the exterior doors. Security film makes it more difficult to enter through a broken window and can slow down a burglar.

Exterior Areas Outside of Ground Floor Units

The exterior areas outside of residential units on the ground floor should be secured using the Crime Prevention Through Environmental Design (CPTED) principals discussed in Chapter 3. These include maintaining landscaping to allow natural surveillance and to eliminate hiding places, and providing barriers to control access and to define private spaces.

Storage on Decks and Patios

Residents should be discouraged from storing high-value items such as expensive bicycles and sporting equipment on their decks and patios. If such items are stored here, they should be secured to a fixed anchor point with a chain and padlock.

Any storage closets located on or adjacent to a deck or patio should be kept locked. This applies to both units located on the ground level and to units on upper floors that could be reached by a motivated criminal.

Lighting

Good lighting should be provided outside of the entrances to the residential units. A light level of 10 to 20 Lux at each entrance is recommended.

Lights should be left on inside of the home during hours of darkness when the occupants are away. Timers should be used to automatically turn the lights on and off. Timers that turn the lights on and off at random rather than fixed times can be used to better create the illusion that the occupants are at home.

Outside Key Storage

Many residents keep a spare key outside of their residential unit to allow entry in the event that they lose their key. This can also provide a way for family members, friends, or contractors to gain access to the unit when the resident is away.

One method used is to simply hide a key: under a rug, in a planter, or on top of a ledge near the door. Another method is to use a key box with a combination lock mounted on an outside wall or on the door itself.

Here are a few thoughts on storing a key outside of a residential unit:

- There are a limited number of places where a key may be hidden. Criminals often have an uncanny way of finding keys, no matter how well-concealed that they may seem to the person who hides them. If one person can think of it, so can someone else.
- Most exterior key boxes can be easily compromised using tools and techniques shown in online videos. Burglars familiar with these techniques can open a key box, remove the key, and use it to enter the residential unit. For these reasons, residents should be discouraged from using key boxes on the exterior of their units. (See page 107 for more on key boxes.)
- The best solution is to not store a key outside of the unit at all. If access is needed, arrangements to gain entry can be made with the on-site manager or a trusted friend or neighbor.
- If there is a frequent need for non-residents (housekeepers, contractors, etc.) to enter the unit, consider using an electronic keypad lock on the door. Codes can be issued to non-residents for a limited duration and then can be quickly deleted when access is no longer needed. The electronic lock should be used in conjunction with a deadbolt lock, not in place of it. The

deadbolt should be bolted at times when the resident is at home and at times when a non-resident should not have access to the unit.

Locks on Interior Doors

One relatively inexpensive way to improve security at residential units is to install locks on one or more interior doors. Locking interior doors creates an additional "layer" of security and is consistent with the Concentric Circles of Protection concept described in Chapter 3.

For example, installing a deadbolt lock on a master bedroom door and locking it while away can greatly slow down a burglar and provide better protection of any assets stored in the room. If a second lock were to be installed on the door to a closet within the master bedroom, yet another security layer would be created, providing even more protection for any assets stored in the closet.

A locked interior room can also provide a temporary place to hide if an intruder were to force his or her way into the unit. While certainly not as secure as a "safe room" or "panic room" built specifically for the purpose, a locked interior room may delay an intruder long enough for the police to arrive.

Safes

Safes can be used to provide an additional level of protection for items such as jewelry, precious metals, coin or stamp collections and irreplaceable documents.

The type of safe chosen should correspond to the value of the assets being protected and the level of security risk expected. In general, the better protection a safe provides, the more it costs. While it would be foolish to protect a million dollars' worth of jewelry in a $100 safe, it also doesn't make sense to spend $5,000 for a safe that will be used to store $100 in cash.

There are two general categories of safes: burglar safes, and fire safes. Burglar safes are designed to provide protection against burglary, and fire safes are designed to provide protection against fire. While some burglar safes provide a limited degree of protection against fire, and some fire safes provide limited resistance to burglary, a specialized safe of one type or the other is generally needed to provide the best protection against either fire or burglary.

Underwriters Laboratories (UL), a has developed a rating system for both burglary and fire safes. Popular UL ratings for burglary safes include RSC, TL-15, and TL-30.

RSC stands for Residential Security Container. Safes with the RSC rating provide a moderate level of protection and are commonly used to store assets of a low to medium value. Safes with a TL-15 rating provide considerably more protection and are commonly used to store higher value assets such as expensive jewelry. Safes with a TL-30 or higher rating provide the very best protection of all and are typically used to protect extremely high-value assets.

The following are some tips when considering a safe:

- The resident's insurance company should be consulted to determine if they have minimum requirements for safes and to determine if insurance discounts are available if certain types of safes are used.
- For best results, a safe with a recognized UL rating should be chosen. Watch out for unrated safes and safes that make claims of burglary-resistance or fire resistance that are not substantiated by a specific UL rating.
- The safe should be purchased from a well-known and reputable supplier, not just someone found on the internet that has the lowest price. Buying a safe from a reputable local dealer in

the community has many advantages, not the least of which is the dealer's ability to provide prompt on-site service in the event of a problem. (Do you really want to ship a 500 pound safe back to the factory for service?)

- Many inexpensive safes sold through retail stores and big box stores are fire-rated (if rated at all) and provide minimal protection against burglary.
- The safe should be installed in a concealed location and not be visible from outside of the unit. The safe should be securely fastened to the wall or floor to prevent it from being removed.

Intrusion Alarm Systems

The use of intrusion alarm systems in residential units should be considered at higher-risk properties and when the units contain assets of above average value. At a minimum, intrusion alarm systems should include magnetic contact switches on the exterior doors and motion detectors in one or more interior areas of the unit.

Most residential intrusion alarm systems also include a panic alarm feature that allows the resident to summon help in an emergency by pressing a button on the alarm keypad. Portable wireless panic buttons can also be added to the system at a moderate cost.

Intrusion alarm systems in residential units at multifamily buildings can have an impact on people other than the resident that occupies the unit. For example, a false alarm in one unit can disturb residents in other units. Intrusion alarm systems may also create challenges for management and maintenance staff when access to the unit is needed.

If intrusion alarm systems are used in residential units, the property manager should establish a written policy regarding their use. This policy should address how the system will be installed, who will respond when the system is activated, and how maintenance and management staff can gain access when needed.

Video Doorbells

Video doorbells provide a convenient and secure way for residents to see and communicate with a person standing outside of their entry door before opening the door to greet them. Video doorbells are installed in place of the doorbell button and work in conjunction with an app installed on the resident's smartphone. (See page 150 for more on video doorbells.)

Inventory of Home Assets

A complete written inventory that lists all major assets (furnishings, antiques, equipment, jewelry, etc.) in the home should be created. This inventory can be used to provide information to law enforcement agencies and insurance companies in the event that assets were stolen or destroyed.

The inventory should list assets by type and include make, model number, and serial number of each asset. A picture of each asset should also be taken. Pictures are particularly valuable to enable the identification of items such as jewelry or antiques which may not have a serial number and may be difficult to describe. Copies of the inventory and pictures should be stored in secure locations both on and off the premises. Making a video recording of the home inventory is also a good idea, but should be done in addition to, not in place of, the written inventory and pictures.

The inventory should be periodically reviewed and updated to add items that have been recently purchased and to delete any items that may have been disposed of.

Family Emergency Plan

Families should prepare an emergency plan. At a minimum, this plan should include:

- What family members should do when the burglar alarm, fire alarm, or carbon monoxide alarm sounds.
- How the family will evacuate or shelter-in-place during various types of emergencies (fire, home invasion, earthquake, etc.)
- The places that family members will gather in case they are separated during an emergency.
- Where fire extinguishers are located and how to use them.
- How to shut off the power, water, and natural gas.
- How to call for help in the event of an emergency.

The entire family should review and practice the emergency plan regularly. In some cases, children may be too young to understand all aspects of this plan, but it is amazing how much information even very young children can absorb and retain. Parents should not be afraid to talk to children about this topic and not underestimate their abilities to prepare for different types of disasters. Kids are often better able to handle the stress of a crisis when they know what to expect.

Bringing it All Together

Good security for residential units is best provided by using a combination of different types of security measures. This is consistent with the Balanced Approach to security discussed in Chapter 3 and avoids placing reliance on any one thing to protect the resident's home.

For example, an effective security program for a residential unit could include good locks on exterior doors and windows, and a locked interior room to store high value assets. Adding a safe within that room and installing an intrusion alarm system would provide an even greater level of protection.

The types of security measures used in residential units should be based on the level of security risk that the property faces and the location where the unit is located. Basic security measures, such as good locks on doors and windows, should be used at every type of property, while enhanced security measures, such as safes and intrusion alarm systems, may only be needed at higher-risk properties.

Chapter 21: Securing Gated Communities

Definition of a Gated Community

A gated community is commonly defined as a group of homes that is accessible only to residents and their visitors. These homes can be single family residences, townhomes, residential units located within a multistory building, or some combination of all of these.

Gated communities provide controlled access, limiting the number of unauthorized people who have access to the property. These people can include curious individuals just wanting to drive through the neighborhood, door-to-door salespeople, and solicitors for charities. On a more serious note, unauthorized people can include stalkers and criminals who wish to commit a burglary or robbery.

Residents most often choose to live within a gated community for increased security and privacy. Many celebrities and other high-profile individuals prefer to live in gated communities to reduce their exposure to both well-meaning admirers and individuals who may wish to do them harm.

Types of Gated Communities

There are a wide range of different types of gated communities.

At the lower end of the spectrum would be a simple gated community that was created by installing an automatic gate across the driveway entrance to a small group of single-family homes. This gated community would be unstaffed and provide a minimal level of security.

At the other end of the spectrum would be a very large community consisting of hundreds or thousands of homes, multiple staffed security entrances, a central security operations center, and a large number of highly trained security officers. The security department here might more closely resemble a small police department than a traditional private security operation. This gated community would provide a relatively high level of security.

Most gated communities will probably fall somewhere in between these two extremes, perhaps having one or two security entrances, and a small security staff. The primary emphasis of this chapter will be on communities of this type, however some of the items discussed here can also be applied to larger or smaller communities with or without a security staff.

Developing a Security Plan for a Gated Community

The type of security measures used at a gated community will vary greatly depending on the size of the community, the level of security desired, and the financial resources available to implement and operate the security program. Some questions to be asked when planning security for a gated community include:

1. Will only vehicle access to the site be controlled, or will pedestrian access also be controlled?
2. Will access be controlled in just one direction (entry), or in both directions (entry and exit)?
3. Will entry and exit be controlled by security staff, by electronic access control systems, or a combination of both?
4. How many vehicle entrances and pedestrian entrances will be provided?
5. Will entrances be attended by a security officer? If so, which entrances and during what hours?

6. Will the entire perimeter of the site be monitored to detect intrusions?
7. What enhanced services will the security officers provide?
    a. Handling of packages and deliveries?
    b. Making security patrols within the community?
    c. Enforcement of traffic and parking regulations?
    d. Monitoring of resident's home alarm systems?
    e. Responding to alarms and security incidents at individual homes?
    f. Unlocking of homes for contractors and service providers?
    g. Making periodic checks of homes when residents are away?

Answering these questions will help to develop an overall security plan and to determine what types of systems, procedures, and staffing will be required to successfully operate the security program.

Site Design

The perimeter of gated communities should be designed using the principals outlined in Chapter 15 Securing the Perimeter of the Site.

In general, a gated community should be designed with as few as possible vehicle and pedestrian entrance points. This will reduce both initial installation costs and ongoing operating costs and provide a better overall level of security.

Unattended Vehicle Entrances

Unattended vehicle entrances are entrances that are not staffed by a security officer and rely solely on automated devices to control access to the site.

Unattended entrances typically include:

1. Automatic vehicle gates across the driveway entrances to the site. If the driveway has both entrance and exit lanes, a separate gate for each lane is recommended to improve traffic flow and to reduce tailgating. The gates should use a full height gate panel that prevents both vehicles and pedestrians from entering.
2. An electronic access control system to allow resident access through the automatic gates. The preferred solution for gated communities is an access control system that uses long-range RFID readers. These allow the gate to automatically open when a resident's vehicle approaches and can greatly speed up traffic flow. Pedestal mounted card readers can also be used, but these require that the resident stop, roll down their window, and present their access card in order to gain entry. This can cause traffic backups at heavily used gates.
3. A telephone entry system. This provides a means for visitors, delivery drivers, and contractors to gain entry to the site.
4. Emergency access devices. These devices are used by the fire department and other emergency responders to gain access through the gate.
5. Video surveillance cameras. These should be provided to record activity through the entrance and exit gates. These cameras should be recorded to provide a visual record of who entered

and exited the property and when. At properties that have an on-site security staff, these cameras may also be monitored on a real-time basis.

Figure 21-1 - Unattended Vehicle Entrance

Attended Vehicle Entrances

Attended vehicle entrances are entrances that are continually staffed by a security officer or gate attendant.

Attended vehicle entrances typically include:

1. A gatehouse building. This is typically located in the center of the roadway between the entrance and exit lanes, although it can also be located beside the entrance.
2. Barrier arm gates across entrance and exit lanes. At busier entrances, two lanes in each direction should be provided. The lanes closest to the gatehouse should be used by visitors and contractors, while the lanes furthest away from the gatehouse should be used exclusively by residents.
3. An electronic access control system to allow resident access through the gates on the resident-only lanes. This system should use long-range RFID readers, allowing the gates to automatically open when a resident's vehicle approaches to enter or exit.
4. Manual gate release buttons. These should be provided in the gatehouse and allow the security officer to raise the gates on the visitor/contractor lanes once a vehicle is cleared for entry.
5. Video surveillance cameras. These should be provided to record activity through all entrance and exit gates. These cameras should be recorded to provide a visual record of who entered and exited the property and when.

Barrier arm gates rather than full height gates are typically used at attended vehicle entrances. Barrier arm gates open and close very fast and can handle large volumes of traffic. While it is possible for a pedestrian to walk around a barrier arm gate, this is not normally a problem at an entrance that is continuously staffed by a security officer.

Some communities may choose to staff a gatehouse only during certain hours and not all of the time. If an attended entrance will not be staffed during certain times, then a second set of full-height gates should be installed at the property perimeter just beyond the gatehouse. These gates can be left fully open at times when the gatehouse is staffed, but closed when the gatehouse is unattended. The gates should be equipped with RFID readers connected to the access control system to allow residents to open them when they are closed.

Some properties may feel that the appearance of gates does not portray the proper image for an upscale residential community. These properties choose to install a gatehouse, but not to install gates of any kind. This provides a much more open appearance, but provides no means to prevent a vehicle from driving past the gatehouse without stopping. This can create a security vulnerability, particularly at very busy entrances. The security officer who is processing one vehicle can do little or nothing to stop another vehicle who chooses to enter without stopping at the gatehouse.

Along the same lines, some communities may feel that the use of an automated system to control resident access is too impersonal and would prefer to have the officers personally identify and greet each resident as they enter. While this can work at smaller communities, it is unrealistic to expect a security officer to personally recognize each and every resident vehicle at larger communities. While identification stickers placed on vehicles can help, such stickers can be difficult to see, and most can be easily counterfeited.

Figure 21-2 - Attended Vehicle Entrance

Service Entrances

At larger gated communities, there can be a substantial number of delivery drivers, landscapers, housekeepers, contractors, and other service providers coming to the site on a daily basis. This results in a large number of vehicles coming and going during peak periods, creating traffic backups at the entrance, and causing delays for residents and their visitors. To manage these traffic volumes more efficiently and to avoid inconveniencing residents and visitors, some larger gated communities can benefit by providing a dedicated service entrance.

The dedicated service entrance would be in addition to the regular entrances used by residents and visitors, and used exclusively by delivery drivers, contractors, and other service providers. Service entrances of this type are typically staffed only during daytime business hours and are closed at night and on weekends.

Pedestrian Entrances

Pedestrian entrances are used to allow residents and visitors to walk on and off of the site. Pedestrian entrances are commonly located next to vehicle entrances, but can also be located at other points along the perimeter of the site, such as on a path to a bus stop or a public park.

Pedestrian entrances typically include:

1. A pedestrian gate to allow residents to enter and exit the site.
2. A card reader and electric lock hardware to allow residents to enter using an access card.
3. A telephone entry system. This is optional and would only be used if visitors arriving on foot are expected frequently.
4. A video surveillance camera. This camera should be recorded to provide a visual record of who entered and exited the property through the gate and when.

Gatehouses

Gatehouses, sometimes also called guardhouses or security booths, are located at attended vehicle entrances. There are a wide variety of different types of gatehouses, ranging from simple premanufactured metal booths to elaborate custom-built buildings.

The type of gatehouse used should be determined based on the functions that will be performed there, the architectural appearance desired, and budget. Space limitations and local building code restrictions can also be a factor when designing a gatehouse.

Some issues that should be considered when planning a gatehouse include:

- Number of security officers that will occupy the gatehouse.
- Types of security and surveillance systems that will be monitored from this location. (Intrusion alarm systems, fire alarm systems, video surveillance systems, etc.)
- Types of communication systems that will be used. (Telephones, intercoms, two-way radios, paging systems, etc.)
- Numbers and types of computers and printers that will be used.

- Need for storage:
  - Keys and access cards.
  - Packages for residents received at gatehouse.
  - Supplies.
  - Emergency equipment (traffic cones, first aid kits, fire extinguishers, etc.)
  - Security officer uniforms and equipment, including foul weather gear.
- Need for toilet and sink.
- Need for refrigerator, microwave oven, and coffee maker.
- Heating and air conditioning requirements.

The gatehouse should be designed to provide an efficient work environment for the security officers who work there. If the building will be used to monitor security and surveillance systems, then the equipment should be arranged in a manner that allows the comfortable viewing of all equipment.

A common mistake is to provide a building that is just barely large enough in the beginning to keep costs down. Equipment and functions are then gradually added over the years until the point that the gatehouse is filled beyond its capacity, making working conditions intolerable.

If an existing gatehouse is at overcapacity, carefully review the functions currently being performed there. In many cases, a function is being performed at the gatehouse that could just as easily be performed somewhere else.

There are also cases where several independent systems have been installed at the gatehouse that could be consolidated. For example, there may be separate computers, keyboards and monitors for an access control system, video surveillance system, and building management system, as well as a general purpose computer used for email and report writing. It may be possible to consolidate some or all of these systems, allowing fewer computers, monitors, and keyboards to be used.

Turnarounds and Holding Areas

When designing an attended vehicle entrance and gatehouse, thought should be given to how vehicles who are denied entry will be turned around. Examples would be vehicles who have mistakenly come to the wrong address, or door-to-door salespeople who were denied entry because of community policy.

If space allows, it is best to provide a turnaround lane that is just beyond the gatehouse, but ahead of any gate that exists. This allows vehicles to turn around without entering the site. If this is not possible, then a turnaround lane should be provided as close as possible inside of the gate to allow the officer to observe whether the vehicle actually turns around or decides to proceed into the community instead.

There can be delays when a vehicle arrives at the gatehouse, but a resident cannot be immediately reached to authorize access. This can create traffic backups at the entrance. The best solution is to provide a small holding area where vehicles can wait until access is either approved or denied. Ideally, this holding area would be located outside of the site perimeter, but if located inside, should be placed where it can be observed by the security officer.

Security Operations Center

In larger gated communities, the security monitoring and dispatch operation may require space that goes well beyond what can be provided at a gatehouse. There may also be concerns about locating the security monitoring operation in a location where it could easily be compromised by a more capable and motivated criminal.

In these situations, the best solution is to create a separate Security Operations Center (SOC). The SOC should be used as the central monitoring and control facility for the gated community. All alarm and video surveillance systems should be monitored at the SOC, and all calls for security services should be received at the SOC. The SOC should be staffed by at least one security officer at all times.

The SOC should be situated in a secure, restricted access location. Often, it works well to locate the SOC in a separate room in or adjacent to the business or leasing office for the community. Access to the SOC should be limited to only authorized personnel. The SOC should not be generally accessible to residents or the general public.

The minimum recommended size for a SOC is 300 square feet. A larger sized SOC may be needed depending on the number and type of security systems to be monitored, the types of functions to be performed in the SOC, and the number of security officers that will be operating the SOC.

Visitor Management Systems

At gated communities, all visitors to the site, including contractors and service providers, should be required to check-in at the gatehouse. Visitors should be asked to sign-in, and all information such as visitor name, vehicle description, license plate number, and date and time should be recorded in a visitor log.

While this process can be performed manually using paper sign-in sheets, it is strongly recommended that a computer-based software program be used to track visitors and contractors. There are software programs designed specifically for gated communities that allow visitors and contractors to be quickly signed in and out. These systems accurately track all information and allow reports of access activity to be quickly created.

Video Surveillance Systems

Video surveillance systems are used at gated communities to provide a record of activity occurring at the site and to leverage the capabilities of the security officers. At a minimum, video surveillance cameras should be provided to record all activity at the vehicle and pedestrian entrances to the site.

At higher-risk properties, it can be highly desirable to also use video surveillance systems to monitor the exterior perimeter of the site. This can be extremely expensive at properties whose perimeter boundaries can extend for miles. In these cases, it may be most cost-effective to use cameras to observe the boundaries where intruders are most likely to enter (such as those facing public streets), and omit cameras on boundaries where entry is less likely (such as those facing a steep hillside or cliff.)

Another strategy is to use video surveillance cameras to view the locations where major roadways within the community intersect. This can provide some ability to track vehicles and people traveling throughout the property using a minimum number of cameras.

Perimeter Detection Systems

Not all intruders will come through the entrance gates.

If the site is fenced or walled, intruders can gain entry by climbing over the wall or fence or by cutting through the fencing material. In cases where no perimeter barrier exists, intruders may be able to simply walk on to the site. Sites that border bodies of water face additional risks as intruders can also enter the site from the water.

Perimeter detection systems can be used at higher-risk properties to detect intruders entering the property at the perimeter of the site. Commonly used perimeter detection systems at gated communities include fiber-optic fence detection systems, photoelectric or microwave beams, buried in-ground sensors, and video analytics systems. In many cases, it is necessary to use a combination of these systems in order to effectively protect a property.

Perimeter detection systems work best when a security officer is available to monitor them full-time from an on-site SOC. Attempting to have these systems monitored remotely at an off-site monitoring center or by an officer with other responsibilities is usually not effective.

Perimeter detection systems are most effective when used in conjunction with video surveillance cameras. When an intrusion is detected, the perimeter detection system will alert the security officer at the SOC. The officer can then use video cameras to assess the situation to determine if there is an actual intrusion, or if it is a false alarm. If the alarm is real, then the officer at the SOC can dispatch the appropriate response to the location where the alarm occurred.

The perimeter detection system should be divided into zones, each zone representing a length of the site perimeter. Each detection zone should be 300' or less in length. This allows the location of the alarm to be more precisely identified and assessed, and if necessary, for a security response to be quickly dispatched to the correct location.

Perimeter detection systems require a significant investment but can greatly increase security at a gated community. They are best suited for use at communities where residents have greater than average concerns about security and have the resources available to fund the installation, operation, and maintenance of this type of system.

Each perimeter detection system should be custom-designed by a qualified security consultant or security systems integrator to meet the needs of the specific community in which it is installed.

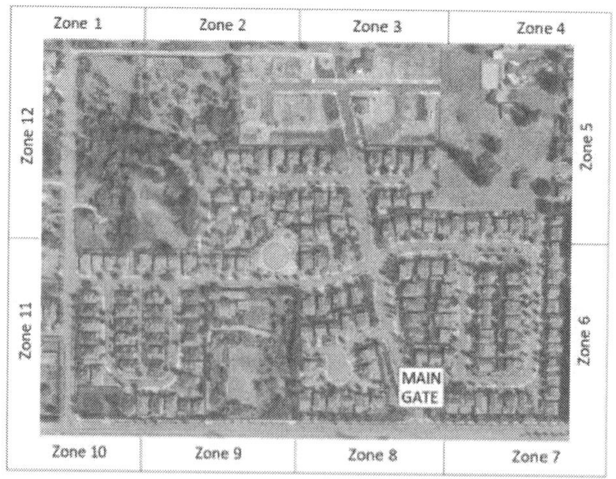

Figure 21-3 - Example of Perimeter Intrusion Detection Zones

Providing Alarm Monitoring Services

Most residential alarm systems are programmed to communicate with an off-site alarm monitoring center when the alarm is activated. The monitoring center then notifies the local police or fire department as appropriate. If the residence is located in a gated community, the monitoring center may also notify the security staff at the community.

Some gated communities may choose to monitor residential alarm systems directly, eliminating the need for residents to contract with an off-site monitoring center. This is typically offered as a value-added service and is usually very well-received by residents.

Before agreeing to provide this service, property managers need to carefully consider the legal ramifications of this decision. Monitoring intrusion and fire alarm systems is a serious business, and failing to respond to alarms in a timely manner can create serious legal liabilities. This issue should be carefully reviewed with both your attorney and insurance broker to confirm that it does not create unacceptable risks.

If a decision is made to offer alarm monitoring services, then the following should be considered:

- A professional grade alarm receiver should be provided at the SOC. This receiver should be capable of receiving alarm messages in the most popular alarm communications formats. The receiver should be capable of receiving alarms using both IP (Internet Protocol) and PSTN (Public Switched Telephone Network)[21] line cards.
- A backup strategy for managing the failure of the primary alarm receiver should be developed. This strategy can include having a back-up alarm receiver, a complete spare parts package, and the ability to divert alarms to an off-site location in the event of failure.
- An uninterruptible power supply with emergency generator backup should be provided for the alarm receiver and communication systems.
- All residents should be required to sign a written alarm monitoring agreement. This contract should be drafted by an attorney and specifically spell out the responsibilities of each party and limits of liability.
- Most commercial off-site alarm monitoring centers are Underwriters Laboratories (UL) Listed central stations. This UL listing is often required to meet building codes and insurance company requirements. While it is possible for a SOC at a gated community to become UL listed, this can be a difficult and expensive process. As a result, very few SOCs at gated communities have this listing. If your SOC is not UL listed, residents need to be made fully aware of this so that they don't unintentionally violate codes or invalidate their insurance coverage.
- Monitoring alarm systems requires that the SOC be staffed at all times – no exceptions. Leaving the SOC unmanned to use the restroom or to take a quick break is a bad practice in any case, but is an unforgiveable sin when resident alarm systems are being monitored.
- Larger communities that are monitoring many home alarms may wish to consider the use of central station automation software. This software speeds up the alarm dispatch process and provides accountability for the actions taken by the security officers when processing alarms.

---

[21] PSTN lines are also known as POTS (Plain Old Telephone Service) lines.

Security Staffing

The minimum staffing plan for security officers at a gated community should include:

- One security officer 24/7 at each attended gatehouse.
- One security officer 24/7 at the Security Operations Center (if provided)
- One security officer 24/7 to make roving patrols, respond to security calls, and relieve officers at gatehouse and SOC for breaks.
- One security supervisor. Works 40 hours per week during weekday hours. The security supervisor is used to manage the overall security operation and to serve as the security point of contact for residents and the property manager.

Please note that the above is a minimum staffing plan. Additional officers will likely be needed at sites that have larger areas to patrol, above average traffic volumes at gatehouses, more calls for security services, or require that special tasks be performed by officers. (See Chapter 26 for more on security officer staffing.)

Managing Resident Expectations

Once a security plan for the gated community is developed and implemented, it is important that residents have realistic expectations about what level of security is actually provided. For example, simply installing an automatic gate across the entrance to a property does not guarantee that unauthorized vehicles will not be able to drive on and does nothing to prevent an intruder from entering on foot. Residents need to clearly understand this.

Even at gated communities with a robust security program in place, it should be explained to residents that they are not in a protective bubble and still need to take steps to adequately secure their own individual home. Having a home within a gated community does not mean that they can leave the doors to their home or vehicle unlocked, or that they do not need to set their intrusion alarm when they are away.

Chapter 22: Securing Mixed-Use Properties

Definition of a Mixed-Use Property

A mixed-use property, sometimes called a mixed-use development, is a property where multiple uses are physically and functionally integrated into a single building or community. These functions can include owned residential units, leased residential units, hotels, co-ops, and commercial, retail, and entertainment uses.

One very popular type of mixed-use property involves combining residential and retail uses within the same multistory building. Typically, all or a portion of the ground floor of the building is used for retail purposes, while the upper floors of the building contain residential housing units.

In larger cities, buildings that contain owned condominium units, rental apartments, and hotel rooms all in a single structure have become popular. Complexes that combine affordable housing units and market-rate housing into the same development are also being built in many cities. Many higher-end gated communities may incorporate a golf course or country club within the boundaries of their properties.

Users of mixed-use properties often share many areas of the building and community, including parking facilities, entrances, stairways, elevators, mail rooms, trash rooms, and loading docks.

Challenges of Providing Security at Mixed-Use Properties

There can be many challenges in providing security at a mixed-use property. Some of these challenges include:

- Different uses within the same building may be owned and managed by different entities. For example, the residential units may be owned by a different owner than the retail units and may be managed by different property managers.
- Lack of communications between users. When different property owners and managers are involved, there can be a breakdown in communications. Often, one user will be experiencing significant security problems and other users will be totally unaware of it.
- Hours of operation may vary between uses. For example, the normal business hours of an apartment leasing office may be 8:00 AM to 5:00 PM Monday through Friday, while a restaurant located in the same building may open as early as 5:00 AM to receive deliveries and stay open as late as 2:00 AM to accommodate late night diners.
- Different degree of "security awareness" possessed by different users. For example, an owner of a residential condominium unit is much more invested in the building and would likely take more steps to protect the property than a part time employee of one of the retail businesses. Some users may care absolutely nothing about protecting the property and may actually engage in actions that compromise security.
- Certain uses may cause increased crime and security problems at the property. For example, a mixed-use residential property that had a 24-hour grocery store would likely have more security problems than a similar property that consisted only of residential apartments. Bars, restaurants, and nightclubs at the property can also increase the level of security risk.

- Lack of "ownership" of shared spaces. Often, an area such as a parking garage will be shared by two users, but each user assumes that the other has responsibility for the security of this space. The result: no one takes ownership of the space or takes steps to manage security in this portion of the property.
- Uneven allocation of security resources between users. For example, multiple users of a mixed-use building may evenly split the monthly cost of having a security officer, but one user consumes 90% of the security officer's time. This commonly occurs at combined residential and retail properties where most of the officer's time may be spent dealing with issues in the retail areas.

Key to a Successful Security Program at Mixed-Use Properties

The key to a successful security program at mixed-use properties is good communications and cooperation between all stakeholders. Users must not work in isolation but in collaboration with other users. The combined efforts of all parties will increase security for each individual user as well as improve the security of the property as a whole.

A joint security plan should be developed for each mixed-use property. The following steps are recommended:

1. Identify the person that will serve as representative for each user for the purposes of planning and operating the security program. This could be a property manager, store owner or manager, or representative of the homeowner's association.
2. Have an initial meeting with all user representatives to begin the security planning process. Each representative should describe how their portion of the property operates, explain their major security concerns, and discuss the security measures that they plan to use.
3. Working as a group, the user representatives should draft a written security plan for the property. At a minimum, this plan should address the following:
    a. Who has primary security responsibility for each physical space within the buildings and property?
    b. What security measures will be implemented and who will implement and maintain them?
    c. How will costs of security measures be shared between users?
    d. How will security incidents be reported and to whom?
    e. How will information concerning security incidents be shared between users?
    f. If the cost of security officers is shared, how will the officer's time be allocated between users?
    g. How will users communicate information about changes in their operations and special events with one another?
    h. How will problems and disputes between users be resolved?

At many mixed-use properties, getting started on developing the joint security plan is the hard part. Often it takes the dedicated efforts of one user to get the ball rolling, but once started, the plan can come together.

After the plan has been developed and implemented, members of the group should continue to meet periodically to review progress, identify problem areas that remain, and discuss any new security issues that have come up. These meetings should occur at least quarterly.

Managing Security in Mixed-Use Spaces

Mixed-use properties can offer many benefits to users. Residents who occupy buildings that also have retail stores and restaurants can enjoy the convenience of having these amenities only a few steps away. Shared plazas and courtyards foster interaction between community members and encourage people to mingle. Some mixed-use properties provide opportunities that allow people to live and work on the same property.

While mixed-use properties can provide many benefits, there is an inherent conflict between the openness required to allow the sharing of resources, while providing the physical separation required to provide good security. Achieving a reasonable balance between these two goals is necessary to provide adequate security while at the same time not reducing the benefits provided by the mixed-use property.

Parking Garages

Shared parking garages at mixed use properties have the potential to create security problems. Parking areas used by customers of retail businesses must usually be left open to the public, while from a security standpoint, access to residential parking areas should be restricted at all times.

The best solution is to provide a separate parking garage for residents and a separate parking garage for retail customers. Each garage should have its own separate entrance and exit.

The entrance at the residential garage should be equipped with an overhead door that is kept closed at all times. This overhead door should be equipped with an access control system that requires residents to use a wireless transmitter or RFID tag to enter. The entrance at the retail garage would be kept open during regular business hours, however an overhead door should be provided that allows this entrance to be secured after hours.

If providing separate parking garages is not practical, then the garage should be physically divided into two areas: one for retail parking, and the other for residential parking. In multilevel parking garages, it is common for one or more of the lower levels to be used for retail parking, with the upper levels used for residential parking.

An overhead door should be used at the separation point between the retail and residential parking areas. This door should be equipped with an access control system that requires the use of a wireless transmitter or RFID tag to enter the residential parking area. Fencing should be provided to fill in any openings beside or adjacent to the overhead door. The materials used to construct the door and fencing should be of a type that is difficult for an intruder to cut through. Ornamental iron fencing or manufactured metal fencing is preferred over chain-link fencing in this application.

Internal overhead doors within shared parking garages are often a weak point in security. Intruders will often enter the retail portion of the garage and linger near the door that controls access to the residential portion, waiting for an opportunity to sneak in.

This problem can be minimized by providing signs on both sides of the overhead door to remind residents to wait for the door to close before driving off. For best security, consider the use of a high-performance overhead door. (See page 75.)

Elevators

A mixed-use building should be designed so that separate elevators are provided for each class of user. For example, retail elevators should serve only the retail parking garage levels and retail floors, while the residential elevators should serve the residential parking garage levels and residential floors.

If providing separate elevators is not possible, then the elevators should be equipped with an access control system that allows access to individual floors to be controlled. In most cases, the system would be configured to allow free access between floors used by retail customers, but require the use of an access card to travel to any of the residential floors.

It should be kept in mind that access controlled elevators provide a relatively weak line of security defense, so providing separate elevators is always preferable to using shared elevators. (See page 141 for more on elevator control.)

Stairways

Stairways should be controlled so that each class of user has access only to the floors to which they are authorized.

Most stairways in retail spaces and retail parking areas are accessible to the public. The best solution is to keep these stairways completely separate from the stairways that serve the residential floors. If separate stairways cannot be provided, then steps should be taken to restrict access within the stairways themselves. (See page 218 for more on securing stairways.)

Building Entrances

If possible, separate building entrances should be provided for each class of user. For example, in a mixed-use retail/residential building, it is highly desirable to provide a separate entrance for retail customers and a separate entrance for residents and their visitors. Building entrances should be clearly marked to create a strong sense of identity for each user and so that those arriving at the property can easily locate the correct entrance.

If entrances must be shared, there should be physical separation between publicly accessible areas and the elevators and stairways that provide access to residential spaces. Relying only on a concierge to control access between a lobby and residential elevators is generally not effective as it is often easy to sneak past a concierge in a busy building.

Loading Docks

Loading docks can be a source of security problems at mixed-use buildings. Here are some suggestions for providing improved security at loading docks:

- If possible, loading docks used by retail tenants should not be used for residential purposes. It is preferable to have a separate loading area that is used for resident move-ins and move-outs and to receive residential deliveries. If loading docks must be shared, there needs to be careful coordination between all users to avoid conflicts.
- The entrance to the loading dock should be equipped with an overhead door that is kept closed except at times when deliveries are scheduled.
- A means for delivery drivers to contact someone in the building when they arrive at the loading dock should be provided. At attended buildings, this can be accomplished using a telephone or intercom system that communicates between the loading dock and the concierge desk. At

unattended buildings, this can be accomplished by using a telephone entry system that allows direct communications to retail tenants and residents.

- Any doors between loading dock areas and secured interior areas should be kept closed and locked except when attended by a responsible person. Many delivery drivers and movers will prop doors open for their convenience. Doors are often left propped open for long periods of time and don't get closed afterwards. If this is a problem, consider the use of a door-propped-open alarm. (See page 161 for more on door-propped-open alarms.)
- Service elevators that are directly accessible from the loading dock should be secured. If possible, a secured elevator lobby should be provided between the loading dock and the service elevator. The door to this lobby should be card reader controlled. The service elevator itself should also be card reader controlled.

Amenity Areas

Amenity areas that will be used exclusively by residents should not be directly accessible from non-residential areas. For example, resident storage rooms and resident bicycle rooms should not be located within the retail portion of shared parking garages, but rather within the secured residential parking area.

If amenity areas are shared by multiple users, then access between the amenity area and residential areas should be controlled. For example, if a fitness center is used by both residents and employees of retail tenants, the door between the fitness center and the residential hallway should be card reader controlled.

Shared Security Systems

There can be benefits when the same security systems are used by multiple users at the same mixed-use property. For example, a single access control system can be used to control all doors at a property, eliminating the need for individual users to purchase and install their own systems.

However, to do this successfully requires careful planning and a good understanding of each party's responsibilities. Too often, one user will install an access control system and then another tenant will ask if a door in their space can be added to it. Over time, doors for other tenants are gradually added, and the original user now has responsibility for managing access control for an entire building – something that he or she never originally intended and is not being compensated for.

If shared systems are used, it is best if they are managed by a property manager rather than a tenant. If there are multiple property managers, then the property manager responsible for the residential areas is generally best suited to manage the shared system.

When using shared systems, the following needs to be considered:

- Who will be responsible for the installation and maintenance of the system?
- How will installation and maintenance costs be shared?
- Who will be responsible for daily management of the system?
- Which specific individuals should be contacted with regards to the system? (both a primary and secondary contact person is recommended.)
- What type of response times can be expected to satisfy user requests? (addition or deletion of access cards, obtaining new or replacement cards, requests for activity reports, etc.)

Part IV – Security Operations

Chapter 23: Security Management and Operation

The Need to Manage Security

In order to provide effective security at a multifamily property, someone needs to manage it. This applies whether the property is a small rental apartment building or a gated community with thousands of homes. Regardless of the size of the property, there is always a need for someone to actively manage the security function. Thinking that security will manage itself or only thinking about security after a problem occurs is a big mistake.

While the need to manage security is universal, the way that security is managed will vary greatly depending on the size of the property and how it is owned and operated on a daily basis.

Security Management at Condominiums, Gated Communities, and Co-Ops

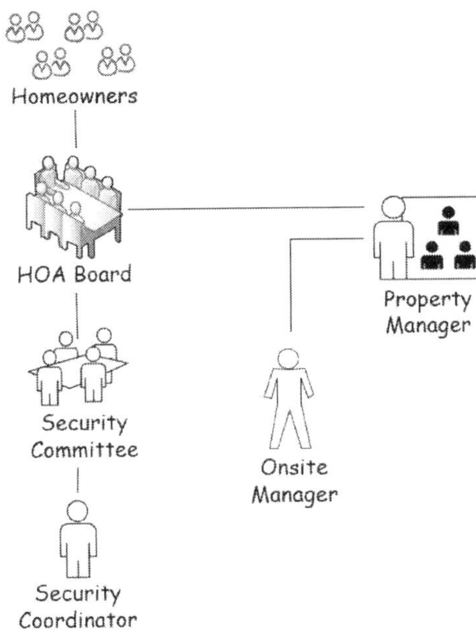

Figure 23-1 - Typical Security Stakeholders at Condominiums, Gated Communities, and Co-Ops

At condominiums, gated communities, and co-ops, the residential units or homes are owned by individual homeowners. These homeowners usually form a group, known as a Homeowners Association (HOA) to operate the overall property, and elect a leadership group, often called a Homeowners Association Board of Directors (HOA Board), to oversee the management of the property.

The HOA Board often hires a property management company to handle the day-to-day operations of the property. Depending on the size of the property, the property management company may provide an on-site property manager and other on-site staff. At these properties there can sometimes be confusion about who has responsibility for security – is this the HOA Board, or the management company? If it is the responsibility of the management company, which specific individuals will manage security?

A particular challenge can exist at smaller properties where there is no property management company, or where the services provided by the management company are limited. This often leaves the HOA Board saddled with the responsibility for managing security, whether they like it or not.

To effectively manage security at condominiums and gated communities, the following is recommended:

- The need to manage security and who will manage it should be formally addressed in the HOA's governing documents. These vary depending on the state in which the property is located and may be called bylaws, covenants, conditions, and restrictions (CC & Rs) or by another name.
- Written security policies and procedures should be developed for the property.
- The specific roles and responsibilities of each stakeholder as they relate to security should be identified and documented. This includes the HOA Board, property management company, on-site manager, and individual homeowners. Questions to be asked include:
    - Who has primary responsibility for actively managing security at the property?
    - Who should security incidents be reported to?
    - Who is responsible for the issuance of keys and access cards?
    - Who is responsible for coordination with security systems vendors and other security service providers?
    - Who will act as liaison to local law enforcement agencies and neighboring property owners for matters related to security?
    - Who will provide security awareness training to residents and staff?
    - Who will establish and enforce security policies and procedures?
- The topic of security should be a standing item on the agenda at HOA Board meetings.
- At larger properties, the HOA Board should form a Security Committee. This committee would be charged with identifying security risks, assessing the effectiveness of existing security measures, and developing and evaluating recommendations on ways that security at the property could be improved. This committee would serve in an advisory capacity and present its findings to the HOA Board, and when appropriate, to the Homeowners Association as a whole.
- It can be beneficial to appoint a Security Coordinator to serve as a single point of security contact for residents. (See Role of a Security Coordinator below.)

Security Management at Rental Properties

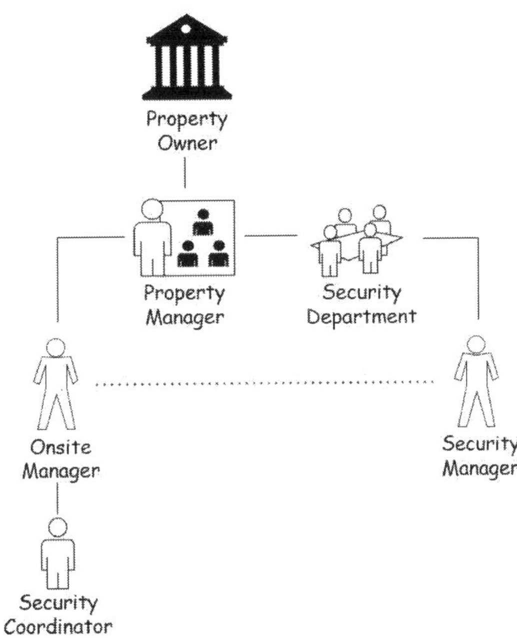

Figure 23-2 - Typical Security Stakeholders at Rental Properties

Rental properties may be owned by private investors or ownership groups such as real estate investment trusts (REITs). Rental properties that provide affordable housing may be owned by a local government agency or a non-profit organization.

Some property owners choose to manage their properties themselves, while others may hire a property management company. The entity managing the property generally has complete responsibility for managing security at the property.

At smaller properties that are managed by the owner, the owner would likely be the person who manages security on a daily basis. At properties that are managed by a larger owner or property management company, security would likely be managed by either the property manager or on-site manager. Very large owners and property management companies may have a dedicated Security Department that either manages security directly or acts in an advisory capacity to the on-site manager.

To effectively manage security at rental apartments, the following is recommended:

- Written security policies and procedures should be developed for the property. If an owner or property management company manages multiple properties, it can work well to develop standard policies and procedures that can be used across the portfolio, and then modify them as needed for each specific property.
- The specific security responsibilities of each team member within the organization should be clearly identified. Each team member should know what security functions that they and their fellow team members are responsible for.
- Security management works best when it occurs at the lowest levels in the organization. It is better to have security managed by someone who is at the property on a regular basis than it

is to have it managed by someone who is in a remote office and has rarely (if ever) seen the property.

- It can be beneficial to appoint a Security Coordinator to serve as a single point of security contact for residents. (See Role of a Security Coordinator below.)

Role of a Security Coordinator

At many multifamily properties, security responsibilities are often divided up between many different people. For example, a resident might be required to get their keys from a maintenance technician, their access card from the property manager, and their parking pass from the concierge. In some cases, residents are required to communicate directly with an outside vendor to get their security needs met.

When a security incident occurs, the resident may be unsure of what actions they should take or who they should report it to. All of this can be extremely frustrating for residents and may let many important things fall through the cracks.

To minimize these problems, a "Security Coordinator" should be appointed for each multifamily property. The Security Coordinator would provide a single point of contact for all security-related matters, allowing residents to call the same person for everything related to security. If the Security Coordinator couldn't handle the matter themselves, then he or she would get the correct people involved as required to meet the resident's needs.

At properties with paid property management staff, the role of Security Coordinator can be assigned to an employee. At small to medium sized properties, the time required to perform this role may allow it to be assigned to an existing employee. For example, a maintenance technician or leasing agent may be assigned the role of Security Coordinator in addition to his or her other duties. At larger properties, it may be necessary to assign a full-time employee to fulfill the role of Security Coordinator.

At smaller properties that do not use a property management company, a homeowner or resident volunteer may be capable of performing the duties of the Security Coordinator. In some cases, it may be appropriate to offer the person assuming this role a discount in their HOA dues or rent to compensate them for their time.

The responsibilities of the Security Coordinator can be adapted to meet the needs of each property and can include:

- Overall coordination of the security program, including security policies and procedures and physical and electronic security systems.
- Serving as primary point of contact for residents regarding matters related to physical security.
- Providing security awareness training to residents and employees.
- Administration and management of security systems such as the access control system, video surveillance system, and telephone entry systems.
- Initial point of contact for the reporting of thefts and security incidents.
- Initial point of contact for reporting problems with security systems.
- Issuance and replacement of keys and access cards.
- Coordination of the activities of on-site vendors and contractors as they relate to security.

- Oversight of the contract security company including daily review of security activity and incident reports. (If security officers are used.)
- Maintaining proactive relationships with neighboring properties and law enforcement agencies with regards to security related issues and other matters of mutual concern.

Will the Property be Attended or Unattended?

The decision of whether the multifamily property will be attended or unattended is a big one and greatly affects how security at the property will be managed.

An "attended" property is one that has staff continuously present to control access and to receive visitors. Examples of attended properties include apartments and condominiums that have a 24 hour concierge in the lobby, and gated communities that have a 24 hour security officer at a gatehouse. An "unattended" property is one that does not have a continuous staff presence. At unattended properties, access is controlled by security systems of various types and the residents themselves are responsible for receiving visitors.

When making a decision as to whether a property should be attended or unattended, the following factors should be considered:

- Size of property and number of residential units.
- Location of property.
- Level of security risk at the property.
- Desired level of service to be provided to residents and visitors.
- Operating budget.
- Competitive landscape (What are other similar properties doing?)

The decision to have an attended or unattended property has lasting consequences. If the property was designed with the understanding that there will always be staff on the premises, security can be negatively impacted if this staff is later removed.

For example, it is common for a developer to build a multifamily property with a concierge desk that is intended to be staffed at all times. The developer may hire a concierge to staff the desk when the building is initially occupied. However, when the HOA Board takes over the operation of the building, a decision is made to eliminate the concierge to reduce operating costs. This can create serious security vulnerabilities if the lobby was not designed to properly control access without the presence of a concierge.

A similar situation can exist at gated communities when a gatehouse is built as part of the original development, but a decision is later made to leave the gatehouse unattended. If the site entrances were not designed for unattended operation, this can create huge gaps in security. There can also be issues when security and surveillance systems intended to be monitored at the gatehouse must be diverted to other locations or go unmonitored.

Eliminating staffing from a lobby or gatehouse can also create resident dissatisfaction, particularly if an owner chose to purchase a home in the community specifically because it had a continuously staffed entrance. This owner could argue that the value of the home was greatly diminished because of the lack of a 24-hour staff presence.

Removing staffing should also be carefully considered from a liability perspective. As a general rule, previously established security measures should only be removed if there is a documented reduction in the security risks faced by the property, or if alternative security measures that provide equal or better protection are implemented.

Chapter 24: Security Policies and Procedures

The Need for Security Policies and Procedures

Security policies and procedures are written documents that provide an overall plan for operating the security program at a multifamily property. Every property, regardless of size, should create formal security policies and procedures in the form of a written *Security Manual*. While it usually works best to have the *Security Manual* as a standalone document, it can also be incorporated into another document that provides overall operating procedures for the property.

The *Security Manual* should describe all policies related to security at the property, as well as provide specific details on how these policies should be implemented.

Security policies and procedures, or the lack of them, can have important legal consequences. Properties who don't have adequate security policies and procedures in place, or who fail to follow security policies and procedures that have already been established, could find themselves in legal peril if they are ever the subject of a "negligent security" lawsuit.

This chapter provides recommended policies and procedures that may be included in the *Security Manual* for a multifamily property. These can be used as a starting point in developing your own *Security Manual*. Not all policies and procedures outlined in this chapter will apply to every property. The policies and procedures described here should be reviewed to determine if they are appropriate for your property, and then adapted to meet your specific needs. An outline of topics to be considered is provided in Appendix D.

Because some policies and procedures may have legal implications, the *Security Manual* should be reviewed by your attorney before it is finalized. Once put into place, the *Security Manual* should be reviewed and updated on at least an annual basis.

Responsibilities for Security

The *Security Manual* should clearly specify who has responsibility for managing security at the property as discussed in Chapter 23. If the property uses paid employees or resident volunteers, the roles played by each person as they relate to security should be completely described.

When assigning responsibilities to individuals within policies and procedures, it is best to refer to each person by job title ("Maintenance Supervisor") rather than by name ("John Smith"). This prevents the policies and procedures from becoming quickly obsolete when there are changes in staff.

Managing Access for Residents

The *Security Manual* should describe the procedures that will be used to manage resident access.

Properly managing access for residents is an important part of the security program at a multifamily property. The goal should be to provide quick, convenient access for residents, while at the same time restricting access by unauthorized people.

Depending on the systems used at a property, residents may be issued keys, access cards, wireless transmitters, Personal Identification Number (PIN) codes, and other devices to gain access.

Devices commonly issued to residents include:

Key to Individual Residential Unit

This key operates the doors of the residential unit. At rental properties, the keys to residential units are usually issued by the property manager. In condominiums or gated communities, locks and keys are usually the responsibility of the individual homeowner. At some properties, electronic locks may be used on the doors to residential units, allowing access using an access card or PIN code.

Key to Individual Mailbox

When indoor or outdoor mailbox clusters are used, this key opens the resident's individual mailbox.

Key to Storage Room

Where resident storage is provided, this key provides access to the storage room. In cases where a common storage room with individual storage lockers is provided, this key opens the common door to the storage room. The lock and key for the resident's individual locker is normally provided by the resident.

Common Area Key

This key, sometimes also known as an "amenity key", provides access to areas such as game rooms, fitness centers, swimming pools and other such amenity areas. This key may also provide access to storage rooms and allow entry through the exterior doors of the buildings.

Access Card

Access cards are issued to residents at properties that are equipped with access control systems. Access cards can be used to gain access through doors, gates, and elevators where card readers are installed.

PIN Code

PIN codes are issued to residents when keypad locks are used to control access through doors and gates. PIN codes may also be used to allow access using a telephone entry system.

Wireless Transmitter

Where wireless radio controls are used, wireless transmitters are used to gain access through overhead doors and gates.

RFID Tag

Where long-range RFID systems are used, RFID tags are issued to residents who require access through overhead doors and gates.

The following procedures are recommended for the effective management of resident access:

- Resident access should be limited to the specific areas where needed. For example, at an apartment complex that has ten separate buildings, residents should have access to only their own building, and not the other nine. Exceptions can be made for buildings where shared resident amenities are located. Similarly, in a high-rise building where access is controlled by floor, residents should only have access to the floor where their residential unit is located, the lobby, and any floors that contain shared amenities.

- If a door is controlled with a card reader, all residents should be required to use their access card to open it. Allowing residents to use both an access card and a key to unlock the door defeats the benefits provided by the access control system and is not recommended. (See page 88 for more on keying card reader doors.)
- All common area keys should be stamped with a sequential key number.
- All common area keys, access cards, and transmitters should be assigned by the property manager.
- All common area keys, access cards, and transmitters should be assigned to individual people, not to residential units. If a unit has multiple residents, each should be assigned a specific key, access card, and transmitter. Each person should be limited to receiving only one key, access card, or transmitter. Each person receiving a key, access card and transmitter should be required to individually sign for it. Records should be kept showing which key, access card, and transmitter was assigned to which person.
- When a homeowner rents out their unit, common area keys, access cards, and transmitters should be distributed to renters by the property manager, not by the homeowner. This allows management to keep better track of the specific individuals who have access to the property.
- Contractors, including those hired directly by the homeowner, should obtain common area keys, access cards, and transmitters only through the property manager.

Managing Access for Employees

Employees need access to the property to do their jobs. Property management, maintenance and other staff should be issued keys and access cards as needed to allow access. The access provided should be based strictly on job necessity and normal daily needs. Not every employee needs access to every area.

Keys may be issued permanently to employees for the duration of their employment, or employees can be required to sign their keys in and out at the beginning and end of each shift. Requiring employees to sign keys in and out daily is a minor inconvenience for employees, but reduces the chances that the keys will be lost, stolen, or misused.

Employees that are issued a permanent key or access card should be required to sign for it at the time that it is issued. Records should be kept showing which keys and access cards are assigned to each employee. Procedures should be put into place to immediately retrieve keys and cancel the access privileges of all employees at the end of their employment.

Employees should be issued photo identification badges that include employee name, employee photo, and the name of the company that they work for. Employees should be required to wear their badges in a visible location at all times while on the property.

Temporary Keys

Temporary keys are keys that are assigned on a temporary rather than permanent basis. For example, an employee may need to borrow a key to gain entry to an equipment room to which he or she does not normally have access. Another example would be a contractor who comes to the property to make repairs and needs keys to get to the areas where the work is being performed.

A good system should be put into place to allow the effective management of temporary keys. This begins by selecting a system that will be used to store the keys. These systems can include wall-mounted key cabinets, file cabinets with hanging key files, and drawers used to store keys that have been sealed in small envelopes.

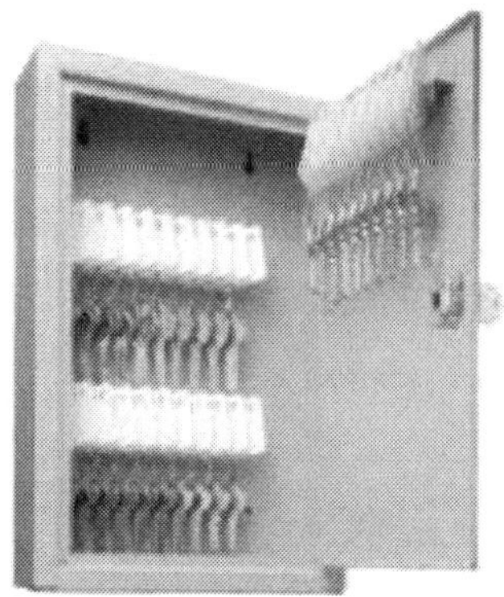

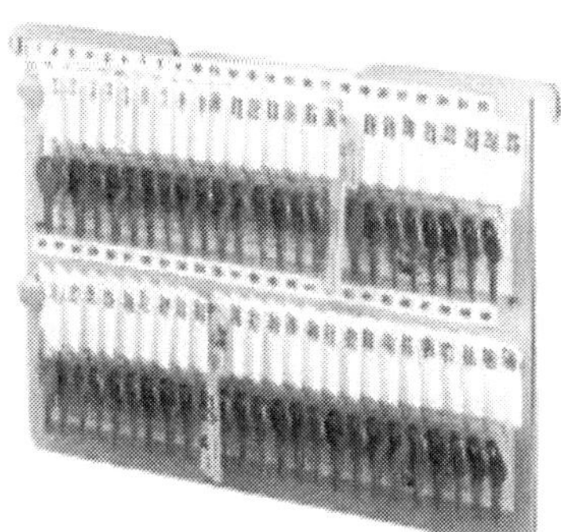

Hanging Key File

Figure 24-1 - Types of Key Storage Systems

At attended properties, the key storage system should be kept at the location where keys would be issued. At buildings with a concierge, this would normally be the concierge desk. At gated communities, this would normally be the gatehouse.

At unattended properties, key storage systems should be kept in a locked room that is only accessible to authorized people. This can be a building office, maintenance shop, or locked closet.

The key storage system should provide the ability to identify and locate each of the keys quickly, and to identify keys which are missing or have not been returned. A written key log should be kept. This log should track who each key has been issued to, who approved it, when the key was issued, when it is expected to be returned, and when it was actually returned.

A more sophisticated method of managing temporary keys is through the use of an automated key cabinet such as the one shown in Figure 24-2 below. These cabinets store and dispense keys and maintain an electronic record of which key has been issued to who and when. The cabinets also allow alerts to automatically be sent by email when a key isn't returned as expected.

Automated key cabinets typically require the use of a numeric PIN code in order to remove or return a key. Some cabinets are also capable of using the employee's access card or fingerprint to operate the cabinet and remove a key. Automatic key cabinets are expensive and not right for everyone, but can be a good choice for multifamily properties who sign in and out a large number of keys on a daily basis.

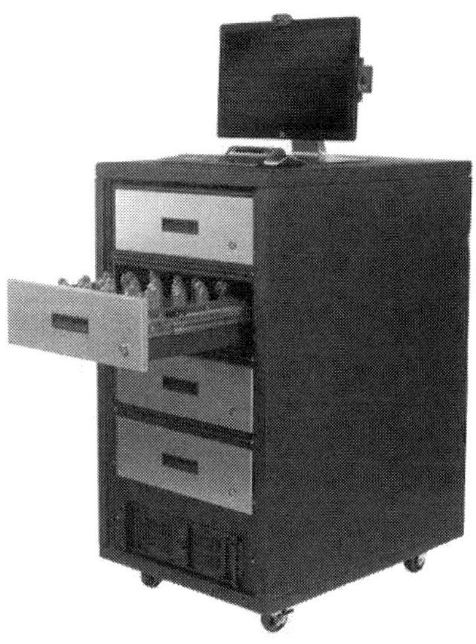

Figure 24-2 - Automated Key Cabinet

People who are issued a temporary key should be required to leave a driver's license or other form of photo identification when they are issued a key. This should be kept in a secure location near the key storage system and returned to the person when the key is returned.

Lost or Stolen Keys, Access Cards, or Transmitters

The *Security Manual* should address how lost or stolen keys, access cards, or transmitters will be managed.

Residents and employees should be encouraged to promptly report lost or stolen keys, access cards, and transmitters. There is sometimes hesitation for people to report a lost item, thinking that it has only been misplaced and it will be soon found. This can leave the property vulnerable during the time between when the item is lost and when it is reported.

When an access card or transmitter is lost or stolen, the access control system should be immediately reprogrammed so that the card or transmitter no longer allows access to the property. Procedures should be put into effect that allows this to occur not only during business hours, but at night and on weekends and holidays as well.

At attended properties, this can be accomplished by giving the concierge or security officer the ability to delete access cards and transmitters. At unattended properties, this can be accomplished by giving on-call maintenance staff the ability to remotely reprogram the access control system.

When a key is lost or stolen, the best practice is to rekey all locks that are operated by that key. When a key opens only a few doors, rekeying can be accomplished at a small cost and is usually done without hesitation. However, if a master key that opens hundreds of doors is lost, the cost of rekeying can be substantial. In many cases, the property manager or owner will not want to spend the money.

The loss of keys, particularly master keys, should be taken seriously. When a key is lost or stolen, an assessment of the risk it poses should be evaluated. Factors to be considered include:

- Was the key accidentally lost or deliberately stolen?
- Can the location where the key can be used be easily determined? (For example, it would be easy to determine this if the key was marked with the property name or was stolen from a leasing office or company truck.)
- Which rooms or areas does the key provide access to?

For example, if an employee accidentally dropped a set of unmarked keys into a lake while fishing, this would likely pose little security risk. On the other hand, if a set of keys were stolen from a marked maintenance truck, this would pose a much greater risk as the person stealing them knows where they work and likely has the intention to use them.

Locks should always be immediately rekeyed when a key is lost that would jeopardize the safety or security of residents and other people. Examples include:

- Keys that allow access to residential units.
- Keys that would allow tampering with critical systems such as elevators or fire protection systems.
- Keys that would allow the compromise of sensitive personal information concerning residents or employees.

Keys to Residential Units

The *Security Manual* should address how keys to residential units will be managed. Keys to residential units are obviously issued to the residents who will occupy these units. The number of other people who should have access to these units varies depending on property type.

At rental apartments, it is common for property management and maintenance staff to have the ability to enter the apartments when needed. The rules concerning when staff can enter the apartment and how the resident is to be notified are usually spelled out in the rental agreement or lease. The policies and procedures in the *Security Manual* should strictly align with the terms of the rental agreement or lease. Good records should be kept that documents the time when the apartment was entered and for what purpose. Employees should be instructed that entering a resident's home for any reason outside of that stated in the policies and procedures may be cause for immediate termination.

The master-keying of residential units is strongly discouraged due to the potential damage that can be caused if a master-key is lost, stolen, or misused. At rental apartments, duplicate keys to each apartment should be stored in a secure location and only issued to staff when entry is allowed by policy. The date and time that the key was removed and returned should be recorded, along with the reason that access was needed. Keys to apartments should be stored using the same systems as described for temporary keys above.

At most condominiums, co-ops, and gated communities, the locks and keys on the residential units are the responsibility of the homeowner. Unless required by local regulations or the property's bylaws, there is usually no requirement for owners to make their keys available to property management staff. However, some owners may choose to voluntarily do so to allow staff to enter in case of an emergency or to make repairs. This also provides a means of access in case that the owners themselves lose their keys.

Keys provided by owners should be stored with the greatest of care. Procedures should be put into place so that keys are stored securely until needed, and that a record is provided when a key is used. This provides better protection for all parties involved and helps to alleviate claims that a key may have been improperly used.

An excellent solution for managing keys provided by owners is to use an automated key cabinet as shown in Figure 24-2. However, due to their cost, these key cabinets may not be affordable at all properties. A less expensive solution is to use a sealed key envelope system. To implement this system requires the following:

1. All keys for occupied residential units should be stored in small key envelopes that have been sealed using security seals. Keys would be placed in the envelope, and then the envelope would be signed and sealed by two parties, such as the on-site manager and a HOA Board member, or two HOA Board members. These envelopes should be stored in a locked file cabinet or a small safe.
2. The envelopes should be marked with an identifying code number that does not match the unit number. The cross-reference between the code number and unit number should be stored in a separate location away from the key cabinet.
3. A written log should be kept that documents when keys are received and when they are removed for any purpose.
4. When a key is needed, the envelope would be opened, breaking the seal. A log entry should be made indicating the time that the key was issued, who it was issued to, and for what purpose.
5. When the key is returned, it should be placed in a new envelope and resealed. Two parties should verify that the use of the key was legitimate and properly documented in the log before signing and sealing the new envelope.
6. An email message should be sent to notify residents any time that a seal is broken and a key to their unit is issued. This should happen even if it was the resident themselves that requested the key.
7. The key cabinet and log should be periodically audited by an outside party who is not involved in the daily handling of the keys. Envelopes should be checked during each key audit to verify that no envelope is missing or has been tampered with.

Use of PIN Codes

The *Security Manual* should address how numeric PIN codes will be managed at the property. Using numeric PIN codes is convenient and avoids the expense of having to issue access cards. However, using PIN codes alone creates the following security vulnerabilities:

- PIN codes can be observed by people standing near the keypad when they are entered. Some criminals have been known to use binoculars to observe numeric codes being entered from a distance.
- Four-digit PIN codes can often be easily guessed, particularly when users are allowed to choose their own code. Sequentially entering the four digits of calendar years (such as 2001, 2002, 2003, etc.) results in gaining access a surprisingly large number of times, as users frequently choose the year of their birth, marriage, or graduation as their PIN code.

- PIN codes can be freely shared. Deliberately or accidently, residents and contractors can allow their code to become known by others. Once a code has been shared, there is no way to take it back.

Property managers should be aware of the limitations of numeric codes, and to the greatest extent possible, limit their use. The best practice for multifamily properties is to require all residents, delivery drivers, and contractors to use an access card rather than a PIN code to gain entry.

When absolutely necessary, PIN codes can be used on a limited basis by delivery drivers and by one-time vendors or contractors who don't need regular access to the property. Every user should always be assigned an individual, unique PIN code. The use of a common "vendor code" that is shared by multiple vendors is strongly discouraged.

Codes should only provide access to the specific areas needed, and only during specific times. The codes for one-time events should be immediately voided after the event has taken place. The codes used by delivery drivers should be routinely changed at least twice per year.

Visitor Management at Attended Buildings

The *Security Manual* should address how visitors at attended buildings will be managed. At attended buildings, all visitors should be required to check-in with the concierge upon their arrival. When the visitor arrives, they should be greeted by the concierge and asked their name and the name of the resident that is being visited. As an option, visitors can be required to provide a photo identification card (such as a driver's license) to verify their identity.

Residents should be encouraged to notify the concierge of all expected visitors in advance when possible. This allows visitors to be greeted warmly upon their arrival. ("Welcome, Mrs. Jones has been expecting you...."). If the concierge has not been previously notified of the visit, then a call should be made to the resident to confirm that the visitor is expected.

Prior to the visitor being admitted to the building, the visitor's information should be recorded in a visitor log. The log entry should include visitor name, name of resident being visited, and date and time. To assure accuracy and consistency, the concierge, not the visitor, should fill-out the visitor log. This also provides privacy by preventing the visitor from seeing the names of other previous visitors.

Residents can be asked to greet their visitor in the lobby, or the visitor can be allowed entry and directed to proceed to the resident's unit on their own. Depending on the layout of the property and types of security systems used, it may be necessary for the concierge to remotely unlock doors or activate elevators in order for the visitor to reach their destination.

Some properties may choose to issue visitor badges. Visitor badges provide a means to visually confirm that the visitor is authorized to be on the property. This can allow residents and staff to determine if an unknown person that they see walking around is an authorized visitor or an intruder.

Visitor badges can be reusable badges that are checked-out and returned at the concierge desk, or can be disposable badges that are thrown away at the conclusion of the visit. For additional security, "self-expiring" disposable badges can be used. These automatically display the word "VOID" on the badges after about 12 hours, preventing the badge from being used again on another day.

Electronic visitor management systems can be used to automate the visitor sign-in process. When using an electronic visitor management system, visitors are signed-in using a computer rather than on a paper sign-in sheet. Upon arrival, the visitor provides his or her name to the concierge. The concierge then enters the visitor's name and other information into the computer. If visitor badges are used, the system allows a disposable badge to be printed. When the visitor leaves, he or she checks out with the concierge, who then signs the visitor out on the computer.

Visitor management capabilities are included with many property management software platforms, allowing visitor management to be performed using the same software that is used for tracking packages, managing service orders, and other related functions. Standalone visitor management software can also be purchased.

Electronic visitor management systems can provide the following benefits:

- Visitor information can be recorded more accurately and more consistently.
- Visitor information can be retained in the system, allowing returning visitors to be quickly signed-in in the future.
- Visitors can be pre-registered in the system, speeding up the sign-in process when the visitor arrives.
- Visitor information is stored in a computer database, allowing reports of visitor activity to be quickly created. These reports can be used to tell how many times each visitor has signed-in and signed-out and when, and tell which visitors were in the facility during any given time period. This information can be useful when investigating security or safety incidents, and for auditing billings by vendors or contractors.

Visitor Management at Gated Communities

Visitor management procedures used at gated communities are similar to those used in attended buildings, except that most visitors will be arriving in a vehicle rather than on foot. When checking in vehicles, it is most common to gather information on the vehicle and its driver, but not gather information on other occupants of the vehicle. Where a higher degree of accountability is desired, information on everyone in the vehicle would be gathered.

The time available to process visitors at a gatehouse entrance is also a factor. Delays in reaching a resident to authorize a visitor can create significant traffic backups at the entrance. Residents should be strongly encouraged to notify the gatehouse in advance when they are expecting a visitor, food delivery, or taxi or rideshare. This can greatly speed up the sign-in process and improve traffic flow at the gatehouse.

Contractor Management

The *Security Manual* should address how contractor access to the property will be managed. Contractors can include housekeepers, maintenance people, gardeners, and a variety of other service employees. There are two types of contractors: short-term contractors, and long-term contractors.

Short-term contractors are usually hired to perform a specific project and are usually on site for a limited period of time. An example of a short-term contractor would be a repair person who was hired to repair an overhead door in the garage. This person would only be in the building for the time necessary to complete the repair.

Long-term contractors are those that may be on-site for a long period of time or indefinitely. An example of a long-term contractor would be a contract employee who was hired to work as a housekeeper at the property five days per week. This person would be on the property during the work week throughout the year.

For the purposes of security, short-term contractors should be treated similarly to regular visitors, and required to sign-in and sign-out at the beginning and end of their visit. Short-term contractors should be issued temporary identification badges that identifies them as contractors. This badge should be worn at all times when on the property.

For the purposes of security, long-term contractors should be treated similarly to employees. Each contractor employee should be issued a permanent contractor badge that includes employee name, employee photo, and the name of the company worked for. The employee should be required to visibly wear the badge at all times when on the premises.

It is common to allow long-term contractors to take their contractor badge home at night, however for increased control, contractors can be required to check their badge, access card and keys in and out at the beginning and end of their shifts.

Managing Special Events

The *Security Manual* should address how visitor access to special events held on the property will be managed. These events can include private parties, community meetings, classes and workshops and other functions that people outside of the community may attend.

For smaller events, visitor access can be managed using normal visitor management procedures. For larger events, special security procedures should be put into place specifically to manage the event.

The following is recommended:

- At least 30 days advance notice of the event should be given to the property manager and members of the security team.
- Every event should have a designated event coordinator that is appointed by the person or organization that is holding the event. The event coordinator should be available on site on the day of the event.
- A complete list of expected visitors and service workers (caterers, entertainers, etc.) should be provided at least 24 hours in advance. The list can be in printed or electronic form and should allow authorized visitors to be simply checked in rather than requiring them to go through a sign-in process.
- Additional staffing should be provided as needed to check-in visitors. This can be a person provided by the event, or additional concierge or security staff can be brought in.
- Provisions should be made to keep visitors from accessing secured areas of the property outside of where the event is being held. This may require that additional security staff be provided during the day of the event.
- All costs of providing additional staffing should be paid for by the person or organization holding the event.

Managing Construction Projects

Major remodeling and construction projects can bring large numbers of construction workers to the site. This may quickly overwhelm the capabilities of the concierge and security staff during the times that construction crews are coming and going. These projects may also require leaving parts of the site or buildings open, creating additional opportunities for intruders to enter.

To manage the increased security risks presented by construction projects, the following procedures are recommended:

- The property manager should be notified of all construction projects well in advance and participate in pre-construction planning meetings.
- All contractors should be made aware that security is taken very seriously at the property and that adequate site and building security must be maintained at all times throughout the construction process. Security requirements should be included as a written condition of all construction contracts.
- A specific security plan should be developed for each construction project and the contractor should agree to comply with this plan prior to the start of any construction activity.
- When possible, construction work areas should be physically cordoned off from other portions of the building. Contractor access points and storage areas should be located to minimize the need for contractor personnel to pass through secured portions of the building.
- Contractor personnel should stay within assigned work areas and not be allowed to wander throughout the building.
- Contractor personnel should park only in designated parking areas and use restrooms and other facilities that have been specifically assigned to them.
- Construction projects may require the bringing on of security officers during the construction period. The costs of providing additional officers should be included in the project budget.

Handling Mail and Deliveries

Multifamily properties can receive deliveries of all types, including mail, packages, food, flowers, and a variety of other items. In order to make their deliveries, delivery drivers require access to the site and buildings.

This can create security challenges in two ways. First, the people making the deliveries generally have no vested interest in the property and may do things to compromise security, such as letting unknown people into the building. Second, while the vast majority of delivery drivers are honest, a small percentage may choose to commit a crime after having gained access to the property. These are usually crimes of opportunity and occur when the driver comes across something desirable when making a delivery.

The items being delivered can also themselves pose a security risk. Often a driver will leave a valuable package in an unsecured area, such as in an unattended lobby or in the hallway outside of a residential unit. These packages are susceptible to theft by criminals who specifically target multifamily properties for this type of crime. Packages left in unsecured locations may also create an irresistible temptation to people who had no previous intention of committing a theft, but see a package and decide to take it.

Here are some tips for managing deliveries at multifamily properties:

- When possible, package deliveries should be received at a central location at the property rather than delivered to individual residences. At unattended properties, this should occur at a secured package room that is accessible only to delivery drivers and residents. At attended buildings, this should occur at the concierge desk or building office. Delivery drivers should not be allowed to proceed beyond the package receiving area.

- If packages are received by the concierge or property management staff, procedures should be put into place to document when packages are received and picked up by residents. A system should also be put into place to notify residents when a package has arrived. These capabilities are provided by many property management software platforms.
- At attended buildings, deliveries of items such as food or gift baskets should be left at the concierge desk rather than delivered to the resident's door. The resident should then be contacted to come to the desk to pick them up. If there are a large number of such deliveries each day, then a special area to store these items should be provided.
- The volume of packages received at multifamily properties has increased dramatically due to the popularity of on-line shopping. The time required to process packages can consume the majority of a concierge's time, causing other duties to be neglected. When needed, additional staffing should be brought on just to handle packages, or the use of an automated package locker system or automated parcel room should be considered. (See page 225 for more on these systems.)
- There is sometimes no secure way to receive packages at an unattended property. In these cases, the delivery of packages to an off-site mail center should be considered. Arrangements for this can be made by the individual resident, or the property can enter into an agreement with the mail center to receive packages for all residents.

There is always a trade-off between security and convenience. The tips above place an emphasis on security, and not all of these tips may be right for every property.

Vehicle Permits

The *Security Manual* should address how vehicles on the property will be managed from a security standpoint. As a general rule, it is advisable to provide a method to identify each and every vehicle on the property, whether it belongs to a resident, visitor, or contractor. While this is most often done for parking enforcement purposes, it also provides significant security benefits.

Here are some suggestions:

- Residents, employees, and long-term contractors should be issued a permanent vehicle permit. This permit can be in the form of a sticker or hang-tag pass that can be hung from a mirror [22]. The permits should have a distinct design that is unique to the property where it is used. Permits should be placed in a consistent location on each vehicle and be clearly identifiable from a distance.
- Each permit should include a registration number. The registration number should be kept in a database to allow property management and security staff to quickly determine which person owns each vehicle. Most property management and access control system software platforms provide databases that can be used for this purpose.
- RFID tags should not be considered a substitute for vehicle permits as they are not always recognizable or may be difficult to see from a distance. If RFID tags are used, they should be used in addition to, not in place, of the vehicle permit.

[22] The hanging of vehicle passes on a mirror may be prohibited in some jurisdictions because they have the potential to block the driver's view. Local laws should be checked before implementing hang-tag passes.

- Temporary vehicle permits should be issued to visitors and short-term contractors. These passes should include the date and time that the permit was issued and placed on the vehicle's dashboard. At attended buildings, temporary vehicle permits should be obtained from the concierge. At gated communities, permits should be obtained from the security officer at the gatehouse. At unattended buildings, temporary vehicle permits should be made available to residents so that they can provide them to their visitors.

Bicycle Permits

The *Security Manual* should address how bicycles on the property will be managed from a security standpoint.

A bicycle permit system should be implemented at each property that provides bicycle storage rooms or shared bicycle racks. All residents should be required to register their bicycle with the property manager and obtain a bicycle permit sticker. This sticker would be installed on the frame of each bicycle.

An audit of each bicycle room and shared bicycle rack should be conducted on at least an annual basis. This audit should confirm that all bicycles stored on the property have a valid permit and that the owner of the bicycle is still a current resident.

Procedures should be established for the disposal of bicycles that have been abandoned. These procedures should address how long the bicycle will be held before it is disposed of, how it will be disposed of (given to charity, sold, etc.) and what types of notifications will be made.

Move-In and Move-Out Procedures

The *Security Manual* should address the procedures that will be used when residents are moving in and out of the property. Moving activities can create opportunities for intruders to sneak into the building, especially when the building is located in a busy downtown area.

The following is recommended:

- Moves should be scheduled with the property manager well in advance. When a regular building entrance will be used for moving, the move should not be scheduled during hours of peak activity.
- If exterior doors must be propped open to allow loading or unloading, someone should be standing by the door to discourage unauthorized people from entering. A door should never be left propped open when it is unattended, even for a short time. At higher-risk properties and at properties where residents are less likely to follow security procedures, it may be necessary to provide a security officer to supervise the entrance while moving is taking place.
- Items should be moved directly from the truck to the residential unit or vice versa and not staged in the lobby or at other locations along the way. Items should never block emergency exits or interfere with other residents' ability to come and go.
- Moving trucks should not obstruct fire lanes or fire hydrants or interfere with other resident's ability to get their cars in and out of parking areas.

Short-Term Rentals

The *Security Manual* should address how the security issues related to short-term rentals will be handled.

Short-term rentals are usually defined as a type of lodging where a condominium or home (or a part of one) is rented for a fee for 30 consecutive nights or less. Short-term rentals are sometimes also called "vacation rentals". An online service is usually used to coordinate the transaction between the owner and the renter.

The issue of short-term rentals can be a highly-contentious topic at multifamily properties, with some owners being totally in support of it, some owners being totally against it, and some falling somewhere in between. Many HOA Boards are quickly rushing to modify their covenants, conditions, and restrictions (CC & Rs) in order to address the subject of short-term rentals one way or the other.

Some properties completely prohibit short-term rentals, while others may allow them with restrictions. When short-term rentals are allowed, owners may take advantage of this opportunity in different ways depending on their preferences and what is allowed by the HOA.

Owners who occupy their home most of the year may choose to rent out their unit only during the weeks while they are on vacation. Owners who have multiple homes may occupy their unit only part of the year, and choose to make it available for short-term rentals for the remainder of the year. Still other owners may not occupy their unit at all, but make it available for short-term rental year round.

Using a property for short-term rentals can affect the security of the building in many ways. Some factors to be considered include:

- Short-term renters have no vested interest in the property and may have little incentive to comply with good security practices.
- Short-term renters by definition will only be on the property for a short period of time. Properties with many short-term rental units can produce a large flow of people that are constantly coming and going. This can create an environment that is more like a hotel than a residential building and makes it nearly impossible for permanent residents to determine who legitimately belongs on the property and who does not.
- The methods used to provide access for short-term renters at unattended buildings usually involve the use of an exterior key box or the issuing of a PIN code. Both of these methods create security vulnerabilities. Keys can be lost or stolen, PIN codes can be shared with others or reused again on days after the rental is concluded. While these problems are solvable, it requires timely management by the property owner, something that may not always happen.
- When an attended building has many short-term rental units, and the concierge is used to check-in and check-out renters, this can greatly increase the concierge's workload and take away from the concierge's ability to perform other duties.

Properties that allow short-term rentals should fully understand the security risks involved and the impact on permanent residents. If short-term rentals are allowed, the following procedures should be considered:

- Owners should notify the property manager that the unit will be used for short-term rentals and give details on the expected weeks or months that the unit will be available to rent.

- It is preferable for the renter to check-in and obtain keys and access cards directly from the unit's owner, or from a responsible neighbor who lives in the building. At attended buildings, the concierge can be used to facilitate the check-in process and to issue keys and access cards.
- At unattended buildings where renters will check themselves in, the methods used to allow the renter to obtain keys and to gain access should be approved by the property manager. For example, an owner should not install a key box for renters or give renters a PIN code to the telephone entry system without prior approval from the property manager.
- The issuance of building entry keys and common area keys to renters should be avoided. It is preferable to issue an access card or PIN code whose access privileges can be quickly terminated when needed. If PIN codes are used, they should be changed at the conclusion of each rental. If access cards are not returned, their access privileges should be immediately cancelled.
- HOA Boards may wish to impose a service fee on owners who offer their units for short-term rentals. This fee would be to offset the additional staff time required to greet renters, issue keys and access cards, and make programing changes in the access control system. Owners should also be required to pay any direct costs associated with rekeying or card replacement as a result of a renter failing to return a key or access card.

Security Incident Reporting

The *Security Manual* should address how security incidents at the property are tracked and reported. Having a timely and accurate incident reporting system is essential to the success of any security program. You can't manage what you don't track.

A security incident report form should be created that allows the reporting of incidents. This can be a paper or electronic form. The report form should contain spaces to enter at least the following information:

- Date and time that event occurred.
- Type of event (burglary, trespasser, vandalism, etc.)
- Description of items taken, or damage caused, along with estimated value.
- Location of event (building, floor, unit number, area of property.)
- People involved in event (employee, contractor, resident, witnesses, etc.) along with contact information (phone number and email address).
- Physical description of criminal suspects (age, weight, height, clothing, distinguishing marks, etc.)
- Description of any vehicles involved (type, make, model, color, license plate number.)
- Police report number (if report filed.)

An incident report should be prepared for every event, no matter how insignificant it may seem. Reports of trespassers, thefts, vandalism, missing packages, and suspicious activity observed all warrant an incident report. Residents should be encouraged to promptly report security incidents of all types to the property manager. When in doubt, fill out a report.

A summary report of all security activity should be prepared on at least a quarterly basis and distributed to appropriate members of the property management team and property owners. The summary report should list security events by type and indicate the total number of incidents that occurred in each category during the period. Any significant changes in the number of incidents that have occurred compared to previous quarters should be highlighted to allow the team to spot possible problems that require immediate corrective action.

It is important to note that a summary report should be published even if there were no security incidents during the period. It can be useful to be able to document the absence of a history of crime if any type of litigation is encountered in the future.

If a security company is used to provide security officers at the property, the company probably has their own reporting system that they use to track officer activities and security incidents. While useful, these reports should not be considered as a substitute for the security incident reporting system that is described above.

Security Incident Follow-Up

The *Security Manual* should describe the procedures that will be used to follow-up on security incidents reported at the property.

All security incident reports should be reviewed by the property manager when they are received. Unless the report was taken personally by the property manager, the person reporting the incident should be contacted to acknowledge that the report was received and to obtain additional information if needed. The purpose of this is to send a message to the reporting party that the report is being taken seriously and will be investigated.

When reviewing security incident reports, the question should always be asked: "How could this incident have been prevented?". While security measures should never be implemented as a knee-jerk reaction to specific security incidents, evaluating specific incidents may be helpful in identifying vulnerabilities and improving your overall security plan.

Approximately thirty days after the incident report is filed, the property manager should contact the reporting party again to provide an update on what , if any, actions have been taken by the property in response to the security incident. If no corrective actions were possible, this should also be explained. Again, the intention is to communicate that the security incident was taken seriously and that filing the report was not just a formality.

Notification to Residents About Security Problems

The *Security Manual* should describe the procedures that will be used to notify residents of current security problems occurring at the property.

It is the duty of property managers to make residents aware of any security problems occurring at the property so that residents are aware of their risks and can take the appropriate steps to protect themselves. Some property management staff are hesitant to share information with residents and say things such as "*we don't want to scare residents*" or "*we don't want residents to think that this property is unsafe*". This approach to keep residents in the dark about security problems is unfair to residents and could create legal liability.

When security problems occur, all residents should be notified in a timely manner. The problem should be described, along with the things, if any, that property management is doing to keep the problem from happening again. Residents should also be reminded of any established procedures that should be followed to minimize the chances that this type of problem will occur in the future. An example of such a notification would be:

> *"There has been a recent string of car break-ins in the South Parking Garage. In response to this problem, we have increased the frequency of security patrols in the garage. Residents are reminded to always wait for the overhead door to fully close before driving off. This discourages intruders from sneaking into the garage as a vehicle enters or exits. This simple step takes less than a minute and greatly improves the security of our property".*

Responding to Resident Complaints About Security

The *Security Manual* should describe the procedures that will be used to respond to resident complaints about security. These may include complaints about security equipment that is not working, complaints about security officers that are acting inappropriately, or general concerns about crime at the property that don't involve a specific incident. (Complaints about specific incidents should be made using the security incident reporting procedures described earlier).

All complaints from residents regarding security should be taken seriously. All complaints should be acknowledged by the property manager in a timely manner, even if the issue cannot be resolved immediately. Complaints should never be ignored.

If the complaint concerns defective equipment (for example, a door that doesn't close properly), corrective action should be taken immediately. If the complaint involves inappropriate behavior on the part of a security officer, employee, or other resident, the situation should be investigated so that appropriate action can be taken. All complaints and any actions taken should be documented in writing.

Multiple complaints from different residents concerning the same security issue can suggest areas where there may be weaknesses in the existing security program. If the issue is serious, corrective measures may need to be implemented immediately. If less serious, the issue can be addressed during the property's next update of its security plan.

Relationships With Law Enforcement

The *Security Manual* should describe the procedures that will be used to interact with the police or other local law enforcement agencies.

Good relationships with local law enforcement agencies are an essential part of a successful security program. While law enforcement agencies are available to respond on a reactive basis by calling 911, there can be considerable benefit in establishing a proactive relationship with law enforcement as well.

Here are some tips:

- Get to know the person in charge of the law enforcement precinct in which your property is located. The title of this individual may be precinct commander, commanding officer, station commander, or something else depending on how the agency is structured. The property manager should reach out to this person and introduce himself or herself and ask about ways in which a mutually beneficial relationship can be established.
- In some larger cities, the precinct commander may refer you to a neighborhood coordination officer that has been assigned to your area. These officers spend all their working hours within the confines of their assigned areas, actively engaging with local community members and residents. These officers get to know the neighborhood, its people, and its problems extremely well.
- Learn what specialized departments may exist within the law enforcement agency that can be of help. This could include a crime prevention unit that may be able to help you to conduct a security survey or provide training, a traffic unit that may be able to help you with speeding

vehicles in the neighborhood, or a gang unit that may be able to help you with gang-related crime problems.

- Invite the local officers who patrol your neighborhood to tour the inside and outside of your property. Consider scheduling specific events for this purpose where tours can be conducted, and possibly refreshments served.
- Consider making facilities within the property available to local officers while they are on duty. These facilities could include restrooms, breakrooms, or other places where officers could take breaks and complete paperwork somewhere off of the street.

Crime Free Housing Program

Many cities across the United States have implemented Crime Free Housing Programs. These programs are public safety partnerships that assists residents, owners, and managers of multifamily rental properties in keeping drugs and other illegal activity off their property.

The Crime Free Housing Program began in 1992 and is currently in use in approximately 1,700 American and Canadian cities. The Crime Free Housing Program is administered by a law enforcement agency or other government entity. One key component of the program is the Crime Free Lease Addendum, which stipulates that the resident and affiliated parties (family members, visitors, etc.) will not engage in criminal activity on the property. This addendum is signed by the resident prior to occupancy and is attached to the lease agreement. Violation of this addendum can be cause for eviction from the property

The Crime Free Housing Program typically involves the following five steps:

1. The property manager and other staff at the property are given training. This training includes creating and enforcing rental agreements, identifying illegal activity, and working with police, human services, fire, code enforcement and other city staff. Special emphasis is given to training owners and managers on applicant screening and the eviction process.
2. An on-site physical security survey is conducted at the property. This survey includes examination of lighting, landscaping, locks, and other aspects of physical security both inside and outside of the buildings.
3. An on-site review of leasing records and policies is conducted. The purpose of this review is to verify that the Crime Free Lease Addendum is being used, and that policies for the screening and eviction of residents is being followed.
4. Resident crime prevention meetings are conducted. These meetings allow residents to meet with one another and learn how to make their community safer and more secure
5. After completing all requirements, the property is awarded full certification in the Crime Free Program and is authorized to display Crime Free signs and logos on the property.

Participation in the Crime Free Housing Program is voluntary in some jurisdictions and mandatory in others. In some cases, the use of a Crime Free Lease Addendum is mandatory, but other aspects of the program are voluntary. Property managers should check with local authorities to see what may be required in their jurisdiction.

It should be noted that some security professionals, while valuing the benefits of this program, object to the term "Crime Free", as it implies a complete absence of all crime at the property. This goal is nearly impossible to attain, especially given the limited security resources available at most multifamily properties.

Residential Unit Inspection at Rental Properties

The *Security Manual* should describe the procedures that will be used to inspect the security and safety devices used at the individual residential units at rental properties.

The security and safety devices used at residential units should be inspected just before new residents move in. This inspection should examine the locks on the doors and windows, smoke and CO2 detectors, and any other security and safety devices provided. The resident should be present during this inspection and required to sign a form that confirms that everything was inspected and was working satisfactorily at the time of move-in.

Follow-up inspections of security and safety devices should be conducted at least annually, unless mandated more frequently by local laws.

Security System Inspection and Maintenance

The *Security Manual* should describe the procedures that will be used to inspect and maintain the property's physical and electronic security systems.

All security systems should be inspected on a scheduled basis. These inspections should take a look at each of the various physical security systems used in common areas of the property, such as fencing, gates, lighting, doors, lock hardware, access control systems, video surveillance systems and other such systems. Landscaping should also be inspected to confirm that it permits natural surveillance and does not obstruct lighting or video surveillance cameras.

The property manager should assign responsibility for conducting the inspections and specify how often they will be conducted. Inspections should be conducted monthly for larger properties, and at least quarterly for other properties. The results of all inspections should be documented in writing.

Certain parts of the inspection, such as inspection of the lighting, will need to be conducted at night. It is common to find outdoor light fixtures that have been defective for many months or even years without being reported. This is because the lights are not scheduled to come on until after the property management and maintenance staff has left for the day.

Maintenance problems that are discovered during inspections or reported by residents should be promptly corrected. This should normally take place within hours or days, not weeks or months. Leaving security systems inoperable for long periods of time can be considered negligence and could be used as a contributory factor in a negligent security lawsuit against the property.

When a failure occurs that creates a major security vulnerability, and that failure cannot be immediately corrected, then temporary measures should be put into place to provide an equivalent level of security until the problem is corrected. For example, if an exterior entrance door cannot be locked, it may be necessary to temporarily post a security officer at the door until the problem can be fixed. Simply leaving the door unlocked and hoping for the best places residents at risk and is unacceptable.

Video Surveillance System Policies

The *Security Manual* should establish policies for the use of video surveillance systems at the property. The installation of a video surveillance system at the property can provide benefits, but can also be the source of numerous problems that you might not have thought of when you first installed the system.

Many property managers are blindsided when a resident asks to see a video from a parking lot camera to determine who may have backed into her car, or when a resident requests video to see when his son came home from a party on the previous night. Requests for recorded video are also often made by neighbors and members of the public. How should the property manager handle these requests?

Residents can also have unrealistic expectations of what the video surveillance system can do, often thinking that the single camera that views the parking lot will provide a close-up view of a person breaking into their car, even though it is located 200' away. If cameras are monitored, residents may think that the concierge or security officer watching the cameras should have seen the crime happening and done something to stop it.

To effectively manage these issues, every property that uses a video surveillance system should establish written policies regarding its purpose and use. These policies should be known by everyone at the property so that expectations are realistic and so that there are no surprises after an incident has occurred.

These written policies should provide guidelines to the property manager telling exactly how each specific type of situation should be handled. At a minimum, the video surveillance policy should address the following topics:

- The purpose of the video surveillance system.
- Locations on the property where cameras are used and not used.
- Locations, if any, where the cameras can be monitored on a real-time basis.
- Ability, if any, for the people monitoring cameras to detect inappropriate activity and take action.
- Duration of time that video recordings are kept.
- Parties who are allowed access to video recordings and for what purposes.
- Procedures for requesting video recordings.
- Limitations of video surveillance system: what it can and cannot do.

Resident Alarm System Policies

The *Security Manual* should establish policies for the use of alarm systems by residents.

In condominiums and gated communities, the installation of alarm systems is usually done by the individual homeowner. At rental properties, the property owner may provide an alarm system in rental units as an amenity, or renters may be allowed to install their own systems provided that they meet certain requirements.

Written policies that address the following issues should be developed:

- Types of alarm systems that can be used and how they are to be installed.
- Types of visual and audible notification devices (bells, sirens, etc.) that can be used.

- Maximum time that audible notification devices can sound before they automatically shut-off (Five minutes maximum is recommended.)
- Who will respond to alarms when they are activated? (police, on-site security officers, etc.)
- Who will let police into locked residential units when they respond to investigate alarms?
- How will property management and maintenance staff gain access to residential units with alarm systems at times when needed?

The initial response to panic alarms and intrusion alarms should always be made by the police or a well-trained and capable security officer. Non-security personnel, such as concierges or maintenance staff, should never be the first person to respond to alarms as it can place them at great risk if an actual crime is in progress.

Resident Screening Process

The *Security Manual* should explain the processes used to screen prospective residents and how these impact the security program.

Most rental properties use some type of screening process to evaluate a potential resident's creditworthiness, past rental history, and criminal background. The goal of the criminal background portion of this screening process is to identify people who would create an unacceptable security risk and possibly endanger other residents at the property.

While once widely used, there is now increased scrutiny surrounding the use of background checks for prospective renters and many practices used in the past are now either restricted or prohibited entirely. All practices related to security background checks should be reviewed and approved by an attorney familiar with the applicable state and local laws.

Security Background Checks for Employees

The *Security Manual* should explain the processes used to conduct security background checks on employees and contractors.

People with a past history of violent crime or sexual offences who are given access to a property may pose a risk to residents and can create a liability for property owners and managers. This is particularly true when some or all of the population at the property is considered to be especially vulnerable (the young, the elderly, people who are disabled, etc.).

Security background checks are a way of preventing dangerous people from being hired and showing due diligence as an employer. Security background checks can be conducted on employees employed directly by the property, as well as on contract employees that work for outside service providers such as janitorial or landscape maintenance companies.

Conducting preemployment security background checks on employees is often permissible provided that the criteria used to disqualify applicants is specifically related to job requirements and is consistently applied. All practices related to security background checks for employees should be reviewed by an attorney before they are implemented.

Vendor Credentialing Services

The *Security Manual* should explain whether or not vendor credentialing services will be used at the property, and if so, how the information provided by these services will be used as a part of the security program.

The use of vendor credentialing services has become popular at multifamily properties. The use of these services requires that all vendors and contractors register with the service to establish an account. The service then requests a variety of information from the vendor or contractor, including insurance information, licensing information, safety information, and other data. The service may also review the criminal history of all employees who will be assigned to work at the property.

The service then reviews all the information that was submitted to determine that it satisfies all requirements established by the property. If so, the vendor or contractor is certified as "approved" and allowed to work on the property.

The use of the vendor credentialing service eliminates much of the work necessary to bring on a new vendor or contractor, removing this burden from the property manager.

The security policies and procedures used to manage contractors should be closely coordinated with the information provided by the vendor credentialing service. Keys and access cards should only be issued after the vendor has been officially approved and not before. If security background checks are conducted by the vendor credentialing service, each individual contractor employee sent to the property should be specifically approved.

The vendor credentialing service will notify the property anytime that the vendor or contractor falls out of compliance. It is important that the person receiving the notice communicates this information to the person that manages the security program so that the appropriate actions (such as cancelling access privileges) can be taken.

A common mistake is to have notifications sent to an administrative person who simply files the information away and fails to notify the person in charge of security. This can allow a terminated vendor to have access to the property for an extended period of time before it is noticed.

Lost and Found Items

The *Security Manual* should provide procedures for the handling of lost and found items at the property. These procedures should include:

- Information as to whom lost and found items should be reported to.
- Location where found items will be stored and what methods will be used to store them.
- What efforts, if any, will be made to locate the owner of the found item.
- How long unclaimed items will be stored before they are disposed of.
- How unclaimed items will be disposed of (donated to charity, sold, made available to residents., etc.)

Domestic Situations

The *Security Manual* should provide guidance on how domestic situations that occur at a multifamily property will be handled.

It is an unfortunate reality that domestic disputes are likely to occur at multifamily properties. The larger the property, the more likely it is these incidents will occur. These disputes can occur between domestic partners, between parents and children, and between roommates. Domestic disputes can sometimes escalate into situations that involve domestic abuse or violence.

Domestic disputes can create security problems that can include noise complaints, property damage, and physical assaults. There can also be issues when property management or security staff are asked to take sides with one party involved in the dispute, or to provide access to residential units to allow the retrieval of property. When a restraining order has been issued, the concierge and security officers may be asked to keep the abuser out of the building and to notify the police when he or she shows up.

The specific ways in which these situations should be handled can vary from state to state. Your attorney should be asked to help with the drafting of a policy on how each of the issues involving domestic situations should be managed from a security perspective. These policies should be well understood by property management and security staff .

Overselling Security

The *Security Manual* should explain the precautions that should be taken to prevent the level of security provided at the property from being misrepresented.

Security at a multifamily property can often be "oversold" when a home or residential unit is being promoted for sale or rent. This can be done unintentionally by an overzealous leasing agent or real estate broker, or by the owners themselves.

Examples of such statements that could be found in promotional materials or advertisements include:

- *"Relax in complete comfort and security knowing that you and your belongings are protected..."*
- *"Secure indoor parking garage...."*
- *"The property is under constant 24-hour video surveillance...."*
- *"State-of-the-art security systems to keep you safe..."*
- *"Complete protection provided by our in-house security team..."*

Such statements overrepresent the level of security provided at the property and can create unrealistic expectations on the part of residents and their visitors. No property is ever 100% safe, and no property manager can guarantee that their property is crime free, regardless of how many security measures are put into place.

Property managers should review the promotional materials and advertisements used to promote their properties and have them modified if needed. Homeowners should be cautioned about overselling security in their listings. Property managers should periodically check listings of units up for sale to see if security features of a property are being exaggerated. If so, the seller should be asked to correct any inaccuracies.

Chapter 25: Security Awareness Training

The Need for Security Awareness Training

The majority of people are honest and want to do the right thing. Sometimes, people unintentionally violate security policies simply because they don't know what the policies are. In other cases, people unknowingly do things that can place the property at risk and jeopardize their own safety.

One important part of an effective security program at a multifamily property is "security awareness training". This is a structured program intended to educate residents and employees on proper security procedures and the ways that they can better protect themselves and the property.

Having residents and employees become part of the solution rather than part of the problem greatly leverages the effectiveness of your security program and is one of the very best things that you can do to improve security at a property.

Security Awareness Training for Residents

Resident security awareness is crucial for success in providing security at a multifamily property. Residents can either be your biggest strength or biggest weakness when it comes to managing security. Alert and well-trained residents can detect suspicious activity far better than any security system can, while careless or uneducated residents can render even the best of security measures useless.

The key to success is for residents to become educated on good security practices and procedures . This won't happen on its own – a structured training program to increase resident security awareness must be developed and implemented. This training program should be tailored to meet the specific needs of the property where it will be implemented.

Topics that should be considered for incorporation into the training program include:

- The need for security at the property.
- Types of security measures used at the property.
- Each resident's role in security and safety.
- Security policies and procedures.
- Securing your residential unit and storage locker.
- Securing your automobile and bicycle.
- Receiving packages and deliveries
- What is suspicious activity and how to report it.
- Confronting unknown or unauthorized people on the property.
- Managing visitors and contractors.
- Reporting thefts and other security incidents.
- Reporting lost or stolen access cards and keys.
- The problem of "tailgating" at building entrances: keeping unknown people from getting in the building as you leave or enter.

- Personal safety and security: the simple steps that each resident can take to protect personal assets and to be safer while on the property.
- Security resources available to residents.
- Limitations of security program.

The security training program can include written training materials, in-person training sessions, or self-paced learning through a web-based E-learning platform.

A good place to start is to develop a *Resident's Security Guide* in booklet form. This manual should provide a concise summary of security awareness topics written in a manner that is easily understandable. An example of a Resident Security Guide is provided in Appendix D.

The *Resident's Security Guide* should be distributed to all existing residents, as well as given to all new residents at the time that they move in. For new residents, the manual can be included in the "welcome packet" often given to residents when they first arrive at the property. It can also be helpful for the property manager or leasing agent to verbally discuss some of the more important security topics in the manual with the new resident as a part of their new resident orientation.

Security Awareness Training for Employees

Employees also play a crucial role in the success of the security program at a multifamily property. This includes employees that work directly for the property, and employees of contractors who work at the site on a regular basis.

Employees such as housekeepers, maintenance technicians, and landscapers are constantly moving throughout the property and are in an excellent position to spot suspicious people and activity. However, unless they are trained on what to look for, they may be oblivious to what is normal and abnormal.

Employees who do see something suspicious may choose to act in a way that endangers them or creates liability for the property. For example, a maintenance employee may see someone breaking into a car and attempt to physically restrain that person. This can result in serious injury to the employee, particularly if the person being confronted is armed. On the flip side, if the employee uses excessive force in restraining the person, the employee could be criminally charged for assault, and the property sued for liability.

A special security awareness training program should be developed for employees. This program should include most topics in the resident training program, but also specifically address the security issues faced by employees.

Some areas to be covered should include:

Observing Suspicious Activity

Employees should be observant of people that they see while working on the property, and watch for people who appear to be:

- Nervous and glancing to see if being watched.
- Changing behavior when seen.
- Repeatedly entering and exiting the building or garage.
- Lingering near locked doors and gates.

- Going from door to door and trying to open them.
- Carrying items that are unusual for the setting.
- Mumbling to self or making irrational gestures with hands.
- Sitting in a parked car for extended periods of time.
- Looking inside of parked cars or trying doors of the cars in parking areas.
- Driving slowly and aimlessly around the property.
- Carrying a dangerous object or weapon.

Unwittingly Helping a Criminal

It is common for criminals to attempt to use an employee to unwittingly help them commit a criminal act. This can include asking the employee to unlock a door for them, give them a PIN code to a keypad lock or telephone entry system, or to provide personal information about a resident.

Criminals using these techniques can be surprisingly deceptive and always have a convincing story about why they need help. They may claim to be a relative of a resident, a contractor or utility worker, or a government official. These criminals often are aggressive and apply pressure on the employee, making them feel guilty if they are not cooperative.

Designated employees, such as the on-site manager or concierge, should have the authority to provide access to locked areas according to established policies and procedures. All other employees should understand that they are never to provide access to a locked area to an unknown person, regardless of the reason.

Employees should also be instructed to never give out personal information about a resident. This includes information about where they live, where they park, what kind of car they drive, what hours they work, or even acknowledging that they are associated with the property.

Employees who receive such requests should politely decline them and refer the person making the inquiry to the concierge desk, building office, or property manager. Owners and property managers should always fully support employees who follow the proper procedures, even if it offends or inconveniences someone who may be legitimate.

Maintaining Security While Working

Employees often inadvertently compromise security by leaving doors propped open or unlocked while they are working. Employees should be reminded to only leave doors open when they are actually working in the area and in sight of the door. If they step away, even for a short period, the door should be closed and locked.

When working in residential units alone, employees sometimes unlock the entry door and then leave it propped open while they are inside working. This can allow someone to enter the unit unnoticed. For example, a plumber could be working in a bathroom, and someone could walk into the living room and steal something without the plumber being aware of it.

Employees working alone in residential units should be advised to keep the entry door closed and locked. To avoid surprising residents who come home while the employee is present, it can be helpful to hang a sign ("*Maintenance Working Inside*") on the door to alert the resident to the employee's presence.

Securing Tools and Equipment

Employees should be instructed to keep their tools and equipment secure at all times, both to protect them from theft, and to prevent them from being used to commit a crime. For example, a crowbar or axe left in an unsecured maintenance shed could be used by a burglar to force open a door. A ladder left unsecured could be used to gain access to a residential unit through an open window on an upper floor.

Confronting Suspicious People

Employees should be trained on the correct procedures to be followed when confronting people on the property who are unknown and appear to be acting suspicious. When it appears safe, the employee may approach the unknown person and simply ask "may I help you?".

If not satisfied with the answer, the employee can direct the person to the concierge desk or building office to sign-in, or ask the person to leave the property. If the person refuses to cooperate, the employee should back off and call for help.

Employees should never make direct contact with a person who appears to be actively committing a crime, but instead call the police to report it. The employee should make no attempt to pursue or capture the criminal suspect. If it can be done safely from a distance, the suspect should be observed to obtain a description, identify any vehicles used, and determine direction of travel when leaving.

Security Training for Front-Line Employees

Front-line employees are those who serve in public-facing positions and regularly interact with people as a part of their jobs. Examples of front-line employees at multifamily properties include the on-site property management staff, leasing agents, concierges, and receptionists.

Due to their positions, front-line employees may encounter people that are hostile or confrontational and may choose to act out in violence. This could be a disgruntled resident or ex-resident, a visitor, a neighbor, or a person from the surrounding community who somehow has a problem with the property. To allow them to deal with these situations, front-line employees should receive additional training on how to identify the signs of potential violence. Some clues are provided in Figure 25-1 below.

CLUES THAT A PERSON MAY BECOME VIOLENT

- Posing in stance with chest out
- Tightened jaws
- Clinched fists
- Pacing or squirming
- Yelling threats
- Bullying behavior
- Invading your personal space

Figure 25-1 - Signs of Potential Violence

Once it is determined that a situation has the potential to get out of control, the employee should take active steps to de-escalate it. Some recommended guidelines are provided in Figure 25-2 below.

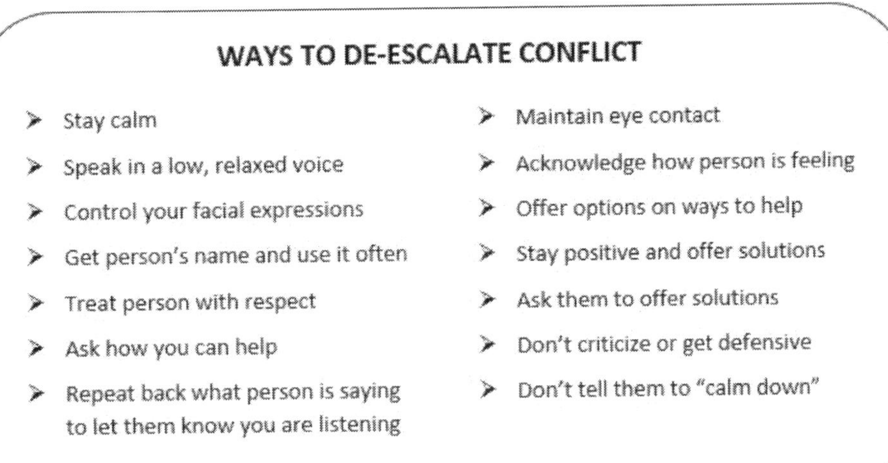

Figure 25-2 - Techniques for Conflict De-Escalation

When possible, an employee should never confront a potentially violent person alone, however care should be taken so that the person does not feel that they are being "ganged-up on". One employee should take the lead role in the conversation, with the other participating only when asked.

Employees should maintain as much distance as possible between themselves and the person while still remaining close enough to communicate. There should be a plan in place to safely escape if the situation begins to go the wrong way.

Employees Working Alone

Employees who work alone on the property can face increased security risks. Examples of such employees include:

- Leasing agents who show apartments to prospective tenants.
- Housekeeping and maintenance employees who work in individual residential units.
- Off-site property management staff who make periodic visits to an unattended property.
- On-site managers who work alone.

Employees who work alone should receive additional training on the ways that they can better protect themselves. Here are some suggestions:

- Employees should always let someone else know where on the property that they will be working and the time that they are expected to return.
- Except in emergencies, visits to residential units should be made only during daytime hours when it is light.
- Employees should wear comfortable clothing and shoes that would allow them to run if needed.
- Employees should always carry a fully-charged cell phone.
- Employees should be aware of their surroundings as they walk the property and avoid walking in dark or concealed places.

- Before entering an occupied residential unit, the employee should make an assessment of conditions inside. If conditions appear unsafe, do not enter the home, and reschedule your visit. Some warning signs include:
    - Larger than expected number of people in the home.
    - "Party atmosphere".
    - People who appear to be under the influence of drugs or alcohol.
    - Strong or unusual odors.
    - Aggressive animals.
    - People jeering or making rude or inappropriate comments.
    - People arguing or fighting.

Leasing agents or managers showing vacant units should observe the following precautions:

- Request photo identification from prospective tenants and make a copy that is stored in the office until the showing is complete. Be sure to let fellow employees know where this information is kept.
- When walking to the unit, don't get in front of the prospective tenant, have them walk ahead of you or beside you instead.
- Once inside the unit, avoid getting into locations like bathrooms where you could get easily trapped. If possible, stay in the entryway and let the prospective tenant explore the unit on their own.

Higher-risk properties should consider establishing a "two-person rule" where employees always work in pairs when out on the property.

The use of portable panic alarm devices should also be considered. These devices can be carried by employees and can be used to summon help in the event of an emergency either on or off property. (See page 159 for more on portable panic alarm devices.)

Crime Prevention Workshops

Crime prevention workshops [23] provide a means to educate residents on the steps that they can take to better protect themselves and their property. These workshops also allow residents to discuss security problems of mutual concern and brainstorm about creative ways in which security at their homes could be improved.

The crime prevention workshops should be facilitated by the property manager. Outside speakers should be invited to participate in these workshops when appropriate. These speakers could include police crime prevention officers, security consultants, locksmiths, and security system providers.

In some jurisdictions, crime prevention workshops are required by law at multifamily properties, sometimes as often as quarterly. When so required, records of attendance must be kept and be available for inspection by regulatory authorities. Where not mandated otherwise by law, crime prevention workshops should be conducted at least annually.

---

[23] Crime prevention workshops are sometimes known by other names such as neighborhood safety meetings, neighborhood watch meetings or block watch meetings.

Chapter 26: Security Staffing

The Need for Security Staffing

The security at many multifamily properties can be managed entirely by residents and property management staff. This is particularly true at smaller properties, whose security needs can be met without the need to hire any type of security staff.

However, at larger or higher-risk properties, the duties that must be performed to provide effective security exceed the capabilities of residents and on-site property management employees. While security technology can help, there are many duties that can only be accomplished by a human, and someone needs to be there to perform them. In these cases, it becomes necessary to bring on staff specifically to perform security-related duties.

Determining whether or not to have on-site security officers is a big decision. The ongoing costs of having security officers is substantial and can become one of the larger line items in a property's operating budget. Having on-site security officers also places additional administrative responsibilities on property management staff and can change the way that the property operates.

The decision to have an on-site security staff should be made as part of the overall security planning process and based on a comprehensive security risk assessment. Due to the ongoing costs involved, it can be a wise decision to have an independent security consultant validate the assumptions used to justify the decision one way or the other.

Roles of Security Staff

Security officers can perform many functions at a multifamily property. These functions can include making patrols, responding to resident complaints, monitoring security systems, signing in visitors, providing escorts, enforcing parking regulations, and many others.

Security officers are often assigned to stay at a fixed location, such as a desk in a lobby, throughout their shift. In the security industry, fixed locations where officers are assigned are known as "posts". For example, the desk in the lobby might be called the "lobby post". Security officers may also be assigned to make roving patrols of the property. These are often called "roving posts" and the officers who perform the patrols are often known as "rovers".

The following are some security officer posts that are commonly used at multifamily properties:

Fixed-Post Officers

Fixed-post officers are assigned to work at stationary locations such as security desks and gatehouses. The responsibilities of fixed-post officers typically include:

- Greeting and signing-in visitors and contractors.
- Issuing temporary keys and access cards.
- Receiving packages and deliveries.
- Monitoring security and surveillance systems.
- Receiving calls for service and dispatching roving security officers.

It is most common for a multifamily property to have only one fixed post; however large properties may have more. For example, a large condominium with multiple residential towers might have one fixed-post at a gatehouse entrance and separate fixed-posts in the lobbies in each of the towers.

Roving-Post Officers

Roving-post officers are assigned to proactively patrol the property. The responsibilities of roving-post officers typically include:

- Making random patrols of the site and buildings.
- Responding to security incidents and service requests from residents.
- Scheduled locking and unlocking of doors.
- Enforcing parking regulations.
- Escorting residents to and from their cars.
- Relieving fixed-post officers for breaks.

The number of roving-post officers needed depends on the size of the property and the duties that the officers are expected to perform. When multiple roving post officers are used, it is common to assign them responsibility for a specific geographical area. For example, if two roving officers were used to patrol a twelve building apartment complex, one officer would be assigned responsibility for Building 1 through 6, while the other officer would be assigned Building 7 through 12.

Security Operations Center (SOC) Officers

At properties that are large enough to have a Security Operations Center (SOC), security officers are needed to operate it. Duties of the SOC officers would typically include:

- Monitoring security and surveillance systems.
- Monitoring building management and fire alarm systems.
- Receiving calls for service and dispatching roving security officers.
- Providing remote access for visitors and contractors arriving at unattended entrances.

Typical staffing for a SOC would be one security officer. At larger or busier SOCs, two or more officers may be needed.

Special Posts

Security officers may be needed to fill special posts at the property from time to time. Examples of where special officers may be needed include:

- Special events such as weddings or parties.
- Construction projects.
- Times of increased security risks, such as when protest activities are occurring in the community.
- To provide security at times when a security system is defective, such as when a gate at a parking garage entrance is stuck in the open position.

Security Site Supervisor

When multiple security officers are assigned to a site, it becomes necessary for someone to supervise them. This is typically done by a security site supervisor, whose duties include:

- Supervising and training on-site security officers.
- Scheduling of officers to cover shifts.
- Processing time sheets and payroll information.
- Reviewing security incident and activity reports.
- Handling disciplinary problems related to officers.
- Acting as a liaison between the security officers and the property management team.

Security supervisors normally work during weekday business hours so that they are available to interact with the property management team. In most cases, the security supervisor role would be a full-time job, however at smaller properties, the security supervisor may perform this role while filling another security post.

Determining The Number of Officers Required

One of the more challenging aspects of managing on-site security officers is determining how many officers are needed and when. Having too many officers on duty wastes money, while having too few officers on duty can reduce the effectiveness of the security program and place residents at risk.

The number of officers needed is typically specified in Full-Time Equivalents (FTEs) One FTE equates to one full-time officer working a forty-hour week.

It is relatively easy to determine the number of officers required to fill a fixed security officer post. Each continuously staffed (24 hours per day, seven day per week) post requires 4.2 FTEs. This is based on the total number of hours required to cover the post (24 hours x 7 days = 168) divided by the hours in a typical workweek (40 hours).

Calculating FTEs for roving posts can be much more difficult. The number of officers needed depends on the size of the areas that they are expected to patrol, the time it takes to complete each patrol, the number of patrols that they are expected to make each shift, the average number of calls for service that they are expected to receive, and the average time that it takes them to complete each call.

One approach is to arbitrarily pick the number of roving officers that will be used and then calculate the number of FTEs required. For example, a HOA Board may come to the conclusion that they need three roving officers 24/7. This would require 12.6 FTEs.

Using this approach, the three officers would make patrols and handle calls for service to the best of their abilities during their shifts. If the size of the property were too large for three officers to effectively patrol, or if the numbers of calls for service exceeded the officer's capacity to respond, things would likely begin to fall through the cracks. On the other hand, if three officers were too many for the property, the officers may be challenged to find enough productive activity to keep them busy.

A far better approach is to calculate FTEs based on hard data. The first step is to calculate the number of FTEs that would be needed to make patrols. This is calculated by multiplying the time it takes to make each patrol by the number of patrols that are expected to be made each week. This number would be divided by 40 to determine the number of FTEs required to perform the patrol function.

The time that it takes to make each patrol should be determined by making an actual study of the time that it takes the officer to cover the patrol route and perform the desired activities. Be sure to factor in any additional activities that the officer is expected to perform, such as the locking and unlocking of doors, providing escorts to residents, etc. The number of patrols required per week should be determined based on the level of risk at the property and the objectives of the security program.

	Time to make each patrol	x	Number of patrols per week	÷	40 hour shifts	=	FTEs required for patrols
Example:	1 hour	x	84	÷	40	=	2.1

FTEs Required to Perform Patrol Function

The second step is to calculate the number of FTEs that would be needed to respond to calls for service. This is calculated by multiplying the average time it takes to complete a call for service by the average number of calls for service that are expected to be received each week. This number would be divided by 40 to determine the number of FTEs required to respond to calls for service.

Information about the average numbers of calls for service is best obtained by reviewing the past history of security incidents, based on incident reports and other data. For new properties without an established incident history, it may be possible to obtain data by contacting other properties of a similar type and size.

	Average time to complete call for service	x	Average Number of calls for service per week	÷	40 hour shifts	=	FTEs required to handle calls for service
Example:	1 hour	x	105	÷	40	=	2.6

FTEs Required to Respond to Calls for Service

The third step is to add the number of FTEs required to perform patrols to the total number of FTEs required to respond to calls for service. This would give you the total FTEs required for roving posts at your property.

	FTEs required for patrols	+	FTEs required to handle calls for service	=	Total FTEs required for roving posts
Example:	2.1		2.6		4.7

Total FTEs Required for Roving Posts

The total number of FTEs for fixed-posts and roving-posts should be added together to determine the minimum number of security FTEs required for your property. Other factors to be considered when calculating FTEs include:

- It is common to round FTE numbers up by 5% to 10% to provide an allowance for sick days and vacations.
- Officers will typically be assigned a shift that consists of an even number of hours (4 hours, 8 hours, or 12 hours). It may be necessary to round the total FTE number up so that it matches actual shifts.
- Additional FTEs should be added as needed to accommodate special posts and any dedicated site supervisors.
- Depending on the activity patterns at the property, the actual numbers of officers needed per shift will likely vary throughout the week and month. For example, more officers may be needed on weekends than during weekdays. There may also be seasonal variations that impact the number of officers needed. For example, additional officers may be needed to observe the swimming pool area during the peak summer season.

Security Officer Post Orders

Security Post Orders are written operating procedures used by security officers working at the property. At a minimum, *Security Post Orders* should contain the following:

- Overview of the property's overall security program and the role that the security officers play in it.
- Description of each fixed, roving, and special security post established for the property.
- Description of duties and responsibilities of the officer assigned to each post, including detailed instructions on how specific tasks and duties are to be performed.
- Requirements for the reporting of daily activities and security incidents.
- Rules of conduct for security officers.
- Officer uniform and equipment requirements.
- Contact information for property management, maintenance, and security personnel.

The *Security Post Orders* should be carefully coordinated with the policies and procedures outlined in the property's *Security Manual* so that there are no inconsistencies. When a contract security company is used, the *Security Post Orders* would normally be written by the security company, and then approved by the property manager. When proprietary officers are used, the *Security Post Orders* would normally be written by the person that supervises the in-house security operation.

All officers should be required to read and understand the *Security Post Orders* and the duties and responsibilities associated with each post to which they are assigned.

Security Post Orders should be reviewed and updated on at least an annual basis and when any significant changes in security operating procedures are made.

Security Officer Qualifications

Security officers should have the skills and capabilities necessary to effectively carry out their jobs. Determining the minimum qualifications required of officers is crucial to the success of the security operation.

When establishing qualifications, the following should be considered:

- Minimum level of education required.
- Previous law enforcement, military, or security experience required.
- Ability to perform physical requirements of job.
- Written and verbal communications skills.
- Skills in using computers and other technology.
- Fluency in the primary languages used at the property.
- Ability to meet licensing and certification requirements.

Officer qualifications should be based on the minimum skills and capabilities necessary to carry out the job and may differ from post to post. For example, officers assigned to work at a Security Operations Center (SOC) would need to have a higher level of technical and communications skills than a patrol officer. On the other hand, an officer who was qualified to work at the SOC may not necessarily need to have the same physical capabilities as an officer assigned to a post that required a lot of walking.

Within the security industry, there is a wide spectrum of different types of security officers, each with different sets of capabilities. At the lower end of the spectrum are what are known as "observe and report" officers. These officers typically have minimum training and usually lack the skills, equipment, and physical ability to do anything other than call the police when they see a crime. These officers are typically paid only a modest salary, which keeps the total security costs paid by the property to a minimum.

At the upper end of the spectrum are security officers that are well-trained and well-equipped and have the physical ability to engage with a criminal suspect when the need arises. In many ways, the skills and capabilities of these officers closely matches that of a police officer. These officers are typically well paid, which results in much higher security costs being paid by the property.

It is important to match officer qualifications with the security needs of the property and the available budget. Property owners, managers, and residents should understand the relationship between qualifications and cost, and not have unrealistically high expectations when officers are being paid a wage at the lower end of the spectrum.

Security Officer Licensing and Training

Security officers should be licensed as required in the state and local jurisdiction where they will be working. In many states, licensing is required for officers who work for contract security companies, but is not required for officers who work as proprietary (in-house) security officers.

Licensing laws usually specify mandatory training requirements for officers. It should be kept in mind that these requirements are minimums, and that for officers to be effective, additional training is almost always required.

The training curriculum for security officers at multifamily properties should include:

- Basic duties of a private security officer.
- Limitations of legal authority of the security officer.
- Policies on detaining subjects and the use of force.
- Taking notes and writing reports.
- Effective patrol procedures.
- Spotting and mitigating safety hazards.
- Responding to emergencies.
- Protecting crime scenes and preserving evidence.
- First Aid, CPR and AED training.
- Conflict resolution training.

In addition to the general training above, each officer should receive specific training on the posts to which they will be assigned. This training should include a minimum of eight hours of working with another officer who has experience in working the post.

Contract Security Officers Versus Proprietary Security Officers

There are two primary types of security officers: contract security officers, and proprietary security officers.

Contract security officers are provided by a contract security company, who employs the officers and then sells their services on a contract basis to the property. The officers are recruited, hired, trained, and supervised by the contract security company, not the property.

Contract security officers are the preferred choice of most multifamily properties as they are generally the least expensive alternative and offer a turnkey solution to providing security services at a facility. The property simply pays a monthly fee, and the security company takes care of everything else.

Proprietary security officers, sometimes called "in-house" security officers, work as direct employees of the property. They are recruited, hired, trained, and supervised by the property. The property must actively manage the security operation and provide all tools, uniforms and equipment needed by the officers.

The decision as to whether to use contract security officers or proprietary security officers can be a difficult one to make, and one in which there is no general consensus, even among security experts.

In general, contract security officers are most commonly used at facilities with relatively simple security needs. Officers working at these facilities can become effective with only a minimal amount of training and require little understanding of the property's business operations.

Proprietary security officers are most commonly used at facilities that have more sophisticated security needs and where greater technical skills are required. Officers here require more extensive training and a much greater understanding of the property's business. Proprietary security officers are often used at high-end gated communities and luxury properties where it is desired for security officers to project a highly-professional image to the public.

The tables below outline some of the advantages and disadvantages of using each type of security officer:

CONTRACT SECURITY OFFICERS	
Advantages	**Disadvantages**
▪ Contract company responsible for recruiting, hiring, and training of officers. ▪ Contract company provides uniforms and equipment. ▪ Contract company responsible for payroll, benefits, insurance, and taxes. ▪ Contract company responsible for employee supervision and discipline. ▪ Contract company responsible for resolving schedule conflicts (sick days, vacations, etc.) ▪ Contract company can quickly respond to requests for additional officers to handle special events [24]. ▪ Specific officers can be removed from property at request of property manager with or without cause. ▪ Contract company assumes legal liability for actions or inactions of officers. [25] ▪ Usually lower cost.	▪ Inconsistency in officer abilities and skill levels – some officers may have difficulty learning technical skills required at the property. ▪ High turnover rate of officers. ▪ Loyalty is to contract security company - not to the property. ▪ Officers may be transferred to other customer's sites with little notice. ▪ "Rent-a-Cops" are often perceived poorly by residents, visitors, and members of the public. ▪ Officers may be treated as outsiders rather than members of the property management team.

PROPRIETARY SECURITY OFFICERS	
Advantages	**Disadvantages**
▪ Better ability to recruit and train qualified officers. ▪ Better rate of retention and lower officer turnover. ▪ Better perception of officers by residents, visitors, and the general public. ▪ Officers are an integral part of property management team and feel loyalty to the community.	▪ Property responsible for recruiting, hiring, and training. ▪ Property responsible for payroll, benefits, insurance, and taxes. ▪ Property must provide uniforms and equipment. ▪ Property responsible for employee supervision and discipline. ▪ Normal HR policies concerning disciplinary actions and employee terminations must be followed. ▪ Property responsible for resolving schedule conflicts (sick days, vacations, etc.) ▪ Property may have difficulty in coming up with additional officers to handle special events. ▪ Property assumes legal liability for actions or inactions of officers. ▪ Usually higher cost.

[24] Contract companies sometimes have difficulties in filling positions so extra officers may not always be available.

[25] Security company liability may be limited due to provision in contracts and/or prevailing laws – an attorney should be consulted to determine specifics.

It is possible to use a combination of contract security officers and proprietary security officers at the same property. A popular approach is to use contract officers to fill the majority of the security posts, while using proprietary officers at certain more critical posts such as the Security Operations Center (SOC) or main gatehouse.

Historically, it has almost always been less expensive to use the services of contract security officers rather than to use proprietary security officers. Customers who did choose to use proprietary security officers usually did so to obtain better quality security officers, not to achieve cost savings.

This situation has changed in some metropolitan areas in the United States in recent years. A combination of a higher mandated minimum wage, the unionization of officers at the larger contract security companies, and the shortage of people seeking security positions have all increased the hourly cost of contract officers. In some cases, the cost difference between contract officers and proprietary officers is now minimal.

The decision as to whether to use contract or proprietary officers should only be made after a careful analysis of costs and the advantages and disadvantages of each option.

Should Security Officers be Armed?

The majority of private security officers are unarmed. When a crime is observed, their role is to observe it and report it, not directly intervene. These officers lack the ability to confront an armed criminal and would in fact likely flee themselves if someone with a weapon were encountered on the property.

At some properties, the level of security risk may be so great that property owners feel that armed security officers are needed. The thinking is that armed officers would serve as a greater deterrent to crime, and that if a violent criminal is encountered, these officers would have a better ability to protect residents and themselves.

When contemplating the use of armed security officers, the following should be considered:

- Cost: The cost of armed security officers can be 50% or more greater than the cost of unarmed security officers.
- Liability: The property may have greater legal liability when armed security officers are used.
- Increased Risk: The risks at the property may actually increase because security officers are carrying a lethal weapon. Every encounter has the potential to become an armed encounter because the security officer is bringing the weapon.
- Perception: The presence of armed officers may be perceived negatively by some residents and visitors, detracting from the desired image of the property.

When considering the use of armed security officers, some security professionals suggest that property owners ask themselves the following question: "*Who do I want them to shoot, and when do I want them to shoot them*?" While this question may be considered insensitive, it touches on an important point.

The decision to use armed officers should only be made after a careful analysis of all factors and in consultation with your attorney and insurance company.

If armed officers are used, written policies concerning the use of the weapon should be established and thoroughly understood by all officers. These policies should be reviewed by an attorney before they are implemented. All officers should be licensed as required by local law and receive both initial and ongoing training on the use of firearms.

Training should highlight the "use of force continuum" which emphasizes that a lethal weapon should only be used when all other options have been exhausted. All training should be conducted by a certified firearms instructor.

Officers should be required to qualify with their primary duty firearm at a shooting range, and requalify again on at least an annual basis as a condition of their employment.

Using Off-Duty Police Officers

Many law enforcement agencies allow their officers to work off-duty for private employers. In some cases, the officers are prohibited from working for certain types of businesses such as bars and nightclubs, but working for a multifamily property is usually completely acceptable.

Depending on local laws and customs, off-duty officers may be hired directly from the law enforcement agency, through a labor organization such as a union, or from a private security company that acts as a broker. In some locations, the officer is allowed to personally contract with the property that is hiring them.

In some cases, a multifamily property may consider using off-duty police officers instead of a contract security company to provide security services. In other cases, contract or proprietary security officers may be used as the primary security force, but off-duty police officers are hired to supplement them.

Some properties may not hire off-duty police officers directly, but instead offer rental units to officers at a discount to encourage a police presence at the property. In these cases, the officer may agree to make themselves available to handle security issues when they are at home, and/or to make periodic security walk-throughs of the property.

When unarmed security officers are used at a property, there may be times when a specific threat is received that warrants the temporary use of an armed officer. For example, a resident may have received a credible death threat and it is determined that an armed officer in the lobby is required until the matter is resolved. Using an off-duty police officer is often the quickest and best way to handle this type of situation.

The table below outlines some of the advantages and disadvantages of using off-duty police officers:

OFF-DUTY POLICE OFFICERS	
Advantages	**Disadvantages**
▪ Highly qualified and well-trained. ▪ Officer is armed and proficient in use of weapons. ▪ Have ability to make arrests and use force if needed.[26] ▪ Much greater deterrent to criminals than private security officers. ▪ May be allowed to use uniform, radio, vehicle, and other equipment provided by agency. ▪ May receive greater cooperation and faster response from fellow law enforcement officers and agencies	▪ Much higher cost (hourly cost can be 2 or 3 times that of contract security). ▪ May not have adequate licensing or insurance. ▪ May create legal liabilities for property. ▪ Officers who are moonlighting may be fatigued and not always at their best. ▪ Officer's duty to enforce laws may not always be in property's best interests. ▪ Presence of armed police officers may not be perceived well by all members of the community. ▪ Officer is subject to being recalled by their agency during times of emergency (protests, natural disasters, etc.)

[26] Typically, sworn law enforcement officers retain most of their powers while off-duty. This may not be the case in all jurisdictions.

Because of the potential legal and liability issues involved, properties contemplating the use of off-duty police officers in any capacity should review the matter with their attorney and insurance broker before a decision is made. If off-duty police officers are used, a written agreement and the proper insurance policies should be put into place to protect the property.

Security Officer Equipment

The types of equipment used by security officers should be mandated by the property and not left to the discretion of the individual officer. Equipment requirements should be clearly outlined in the *Security Post Orders*. Officers should not be allowed to carry any equipment unless it has been specifically authorized.

Security officer equipment can include:

Uniforms

Security officer uniforms come in two types: "hard uniforms" and "soft uniforms".

"Hard" uniforms are the traditional police-style uniform that consists of a dress shirt, slacks, and a tie. The shirt usually contains a shoulder patch that contains the name of the property or security company, and a badge or badge patch is worn on the front of the shirt.

When jackets are worn with the hard uniform, the jacket usually also contains a shoulder patch and badge or badge patch. The jacket may also have a large patch on the back of it that says "Security". A peaked uniform cap or campaign style hat may also be worn with the hard uniform.

A modified style of the hard uniform has become popular in recent years. This style of uniform is more casual and uses a polo style shirt rather than dress shirt, khaki pants rather than slacks, and a ballcap style hat rather than a peaked uniform or campaign hat.

"Soft" uniforms are a business-style uniform that usually consists of a dress shirt, dress slacks, tie, and blazer. The blazer usually has a patch on the front of it that contains the name of the property or security company. The blazer may also contain an engraved nameplate that has the officer's name.

As a general rule, the use of a hard uniform is recommended for officers who are assigned roving posts. These uniforms allow officers to be clearly identified from a distance and signal that the property has an active security presence.

Soft uniforms are generally best suited for use at fixed-posts where visitors and other members of the public are received. These uniforms present a less harsh image and can be used to place an emphasis on the officer's customer service role. Soft uniforms are recommended for officers who work posts at concierge desks and gatehouses.

All officers who work outdoors should be issued the appropriate foul weather gear, including overcoats, gloves, and hats. Officers who patrol roadways and parking areas should be issued reflective safety vests. Overcoats and reflective vests should have the word "Security" embossed on them so that the officer can be identified from a distance.

Body Armor

At certain high-risk properties, it may be appropriate to issue body armor to security officers. The most common type of body armor comes in the form of a protective vest, sometimes incorrectly referred to as a "bulletproof" vest. It should be understood that no vest is truly "bulletproof", but that each type is designed to protect only against a certain type and caliber of weapon.

Protective vests come in versions that can be worn inside or outside of the uniform and come in a variety of protection levels, each designed to resist a certain caliber of bullet. Protective vests are also available that provide protection against edged weapons such as knifes or spiked objects such as needles.

Body armor that is capable of resisting larger caliber bullets is usually heavy and not comfortable or practical to wear all day. It is often necessary to find an acceptable compromise between the level of protection that a vest provides and its wearability.

If it is decided to issue body armor to security officers, the type chosen should correspond to the expected level of risk. Body armor should be purchased from a reputable dealer who can provide assistance in the selection of an appropriate product.

Disposable Gloves

All security officers should be issued disposable gloves that can be used when handling suspicious objects or when it is necessary to make physical contact with a person. Roving-post officers should be issued a disposable glove pouch that can be worn on a belt.

Flashlight

Roving-post officers should be issued a flashlight and a belt-worn flashlight holder. This flashlight should be carried at all times, even during the day. The use of a high-intensity LED type flashlight is recommended as they are capable of providing an extremely bright light using a relatively small flashlight.

Officers should be prohibited from carrying large multi-cell flashlights that could be used as a weapon.

Notebook and Pen

All officers should be issued and required to carry a pocket notebook and pen.

Less-Lethal Weapons

Most unarmed security officers working in an "observe and report" capacity at a multifamily property do not require weapons of any type.

However, at certain properties, the level of risk may not be great enough to justify the use of armed officers, but management may feel that the unarmed officers need additional tools to protect themselves. One such tool is "less-lethal" weapons, which may include pepper spray, electroshock weapons [27], clubs, batons, and other similar devices.

The term "less-lethal" rather than "non-lethal" or "less-than-lethal" is used because there is always the chance that the use of a weapon of any type could result in an unintentional death.

---

[27] Electroshock weapons are also be called "tasers", the brand name of one popular manufacturer of such products, TASER© Self-Defense.

Although rare, a person with an underlying medical condition can have an adverse reaction to being sprayed with pepper spray or being shocked with an electroshock weapon. Blows from a club or baton can be fatal if applied to the wrong place.

Pepper spray and electroshock devices are often the less-lethal weapon of choice for security officers, as they are thought to be the types least likely to inflict permanent harm.

If the use of less-lethal weapons is allowed, strict policies regarding their use should be established. These policies should be reviewed by an attorney before they are implemented. All officers issued less-lethal weapons should be thoroughly trained on their use by a qualified defensive-tactics instructor.

Handcuffs and Restraints

Like with weapons, most unarmed security officers working in an "observe and report" capacity at a multifamily property do not require handcuffs or other types of restraint devices.

However, at some properties, management may feel that security officers need to have the ability to detain a person until the police arrive, both for their own safety, and to prevent the person from fleeing. To provide this ability, officers may be issued handcuffs or disposable restraints.

Detaining a person for any reason can have serious legal consequences. If someone needs to be detained, it is usually best to call the police and have the restraint done by a police officer. If the use of restraint devices is allowed, strict policies regarding their use should be established. These policies should be reviewed by an attorney before they are implemented. All officers issued restraint devices should be thoroughly trained and certified on their use by a qualified instructor.

Body Worn Cameras

Body worn cameras are now being issued to police officers in cities across the United States. These cameras are capable of being worn on the front of the officer's uniform and record activity that occurs during the officer's shift. These video recordings can be used to establish accountability for the officer's conduct and used to prove or disprove claims that an officer acted improperly.

Some private security officers also use cameras of this type for the same purpose. This can raise privacy concerns when used in a residential setting. The local laws in your jurisdiction should be reviewed to determine any restrictions concerning body worn cameras. Even if legal, many residents may find the use of these cameras objectionable and inappropriate for use at a multifamily property. Officers may come across situations that could be embarrassing to a resident and the last thing that the resident would want is for the event to be captured on video.

The pros and cons of using body worn cameras should be carefully considered before making a decision to implement them.

Security Officer Communications

Security officers need a method to communicate between each other when working at a multifamily property. Residents and property management staff also need a means to communicate with the security officers when needed.

At smaller properties that have only a single security officer on duty, a cell phone can be used for communications. Residents and property management staff can use this cell phone to reach this officer, and the officer can use this phone to call for help when necessary.

At larger properties that have multiple security officers on duty, a two-way radio system rather than cell phones should be used for communications. These systems allow "one-to-many" communications, where all officers can hear all communications. This can be very beneficial when multiple officers are responding to the same security incident, and also provides officers with an awareness of what other officers on the property are doing.

Two-way radio systems are also capable of working during times of crisis (such as an earthquake or tornado) when the cell phone network may be overloaded or inoperable.

Here are some tips for the use of cell phones and two-way radios for security:

- The cell phones used by security officers should be provided by the property, not the officer.
- In general, security officers should carry only a single type of communications device while on duty. If officers are issued two-way radios, the carrying of cell phones (including personal cell phones) by officers should not be allowed. An exception can be made for supervisory officers who may occasionally have a legitimate need to use a cell phone. A formal policy concerning the use of cell phones while on duty should be written and enforced.
- When a continuously staffed location (such as a gatehouse or Security Operations Center) has been established, all communications to and from security officers in the field should be routed through this location.
- The two-way radios should be a professional-grade type that operate on a licensed commercial business frequency. Inexpensive consumer-grade radios that operate on Family Radio Service (FRS) or General Mobile Radio Service (GMRS) frequencies should not be used.
- The two-way radio system should provide complete coverage of the property and the immediately surrounding neighborhood. Reliable coverage within all floors of all buildings, including the parking garages, should be provided. This may require the use of a radio repeater and/or a distributed antenna system within the buildings. A qualified two-way radio system provider should be consulted to determine the proper types of equipment needed.
- Portable two-way radios should be provided for each security officer. These radios should include a carrying case that can be worn on a belt and a remote speaker/microphone that can be worn on the officer's lapel.
- A base station two-way radio with an external antenna should be provided at fixed-posts such as concierge desks, gatehouses, and the Security Operations Center (SOC).
- There can be benefits in sharing the two-way radio system used by the security officers with other workers, such as maintenance technicians and housekeepers. This provides these workers with a quick way to report suspicious activity and is valuable when all team members are needed to respond to an emergency situation. When a shared system is used, the radios

should have two channels: one that can be used by everyone, and one that is exclusively for security use.

Security Vehicles

Security vehicles are used at multifamily properties that are too large for security officer patrols to be made exclusively on foot. Security vehicles are used by officers to make patrols and respond to security incidents. Security vehicles may also be used to transport equipment and people.

There are different types of security vehicles that can be used at a multifamily property. These include cars, trucks, sport utility vehicles (SUVs), golf carts, bicycles, and personal transportation devices such as the Segway.

When choosing the types of vehicles to be used, the following should be considered:

- Roads and pathways that the vehicle must travel on.
- Climate and weather conditions.
- Equipment that must be transported.
- The size of the property and required response times.
- Availability of parking.
- The need to transport residents, employees, or visitors.
- Initial purchase price and ongoing operating costs.
- Skills and physical capabilities of officers who will be operating the vehicle.

Cars, SUVs, and trucks are good choices when protection from the weather is required or when the vehicle must be used to transport people or equipment. Golf cart style patrol vehicles are a popular choice when the vehicle must be driven on trails and pathways in addition to roads. Personal transportation devices and bicycles can be used both inside and outside of buildings and can offer the advantage of stealth when officers are making patrols.

There is an increased trend towards using electric rather than gas or diesel-powered security vehicles. When electric vehicles are used in a 24 hour security operation, careful consideration must be given to the operating time provided by each charge and the time needed to recharge batteries. It may be necessary to provide additional vehicles so that some vehicles can be charging while others are in use.

Here are some suggestions for the use of security vehicles:

- All security vehicles should be clearly marked as such. Vehicle markings should include the name of the property or contract security company, and the words "Security" on all sides of the vehicle. The color scheme and signage used on the vehicle should make it easily identifiable as a security vehicle from a distance.
- All security vehicles should be provided by either the property itself or the contract security company. The use of the officer's own personal vehicle for security patrols is not recommended. The type and condition of personally-owned vehicles varies greatly, and unmarked patrol vehicles do not provide a consistent or professional appearance.
- Security vehicles can be equipped with spotlights that can be helpful when officers are making patrols at night. Vehicles can also be equipped with lightbars that contain flashing lights, which

can enhance safety when the vehicle must be parked in a hazardous location. The presence of a visible lightbar can also reinforce the image that the vehicle is a security vehicle. The permissibility of using lightbars and the specific colors that can be used should be verified with local authorities before lightbars are installed.

- It can be beneficial to install a permanently mounted mobile two-way radio with an external antenna in patrol vehicles. These are higher-powered than portable two-way radios and can provide an increased communications range.

Guard Tour Systems

Guard tour systems are used to establish accountability for security officer patrol activity. The use of this type of system encourages proper behavior and allows discrepancies in patrol procedures to be quickly identified. The audit trail provided by the guard tour system can also be used for incident investigation, and as proof of patrol activities should the officer's performance ever be called into question by an outside party.

Most guard tour systems include the use of "checkpoint stations" that can be installed at various locations throughout the property. These checkpoint stations can consist of a barcode sticker that can be scanned, or a memory button that can be read with a contact reader. Security officers are issued a portable device, sometimes called a "wand", that allows them to scan the checkpoint stations. Some systems allow the use of a mobile device such as a cell phone to scan the checkpoints instead of a wand.

When on patrol, the security officer stops at each checkpoint station along the patrol route and scans it with the wand or mobile device. The location of the checkpoint station and the date and time that it was scanned is recorded. When wands are used, this information is downloaded to the guard tour system when the officer plugs the wand into a docking station at end of shift. If mobile devices are used, this information is usually uploaded immediately at the time that the scan is made.

Once the information is gathered, it can be used in a variety of ways. Reports can be created that show the activities of individual officers and any patrols that were missed or not performed in the proper sequence or at the scheduled time.

When mobile devices are used, many systems allow an immediate notification to be made when the officer fails to scan a checkpoint station at the designated time. For example, if an officer were expected to scan a checkpoint station at a gate every hour, and failed to do so, the security supervisor could be immediately notified.

Many guard tour systems also have GPS capabilities that allow the officer's activity to be tracked on a real-time basis as well as recorded. Some guard tour systems also incorporate features that allow officers to submit daily activity reports and incident reports using the mobile device.

Here are some tips for using guard tour systems:

- Provide an adequate number of checkpoint stations. Stations should be placed at locations within the buildings and on the property that are important for the security officer to check.
- When officers are expected to check something within a room, it is best to place the station near the item that is to be checked rather than on the entrance to the room. For example, if you have a fire sprinkler system that must be checked, it is best to place the station near the sprinkler riser rather than at the entrance door to the sprinkler room.

- Don't forget to provide stations at the perimeter of the site (along fence lines and at gates) as well as at critical equipment (generators, pump stations, etc.) located on the exterior of the property.
- Make certain that security officers are trained to remain observant while on patrol and don't just travel from station to station. With a guard tour system, there can be a tendency for officers to be so focused on "hitting the stations" that they become oblivious to their surroundings.
- The best guard tour system is worthless if the information that it produces is not regularly monitored. Guard tour information should be reviewed on a daily basis by the security supervisor. The property manager should also periodically review guard tour reports. If a contract security company is used, the property manager should have direct access to guard tour reports without having to request them from the security company.

Differences Between Concierges and Security Officers

Many multifamily properties employ both concierges and security officers. There can be an overlap in the duties performed by the two and there can be confusion when a concierge is expected to act as a security officer or vice versa.

Concierges are used to provide a wide range of services to residents and their visitors. These duties vary from property to property but may include:

- Answering telephone and routing calls to appropriate team members
- Greeting and signing-in visitors and contractors.
- Greeting prospective residents and directing them to a leasing agent or sales representative.
- Issuing temporary keys and access cards.
- Issuing parking permits and passes.
- Receiving packages and deliveries.
- Arranging pick-up and delivery of laundry.
- Managing the use of the loading dock and the elevators for move-ins and move-outs.
- Scheduling the use of amenity rooms.
- Arranging transportation needs of residents and visitors (taxis, rideshare, etc.)
- Being knowledgeable of and establishing relationships with local restaurants, entertainment venues, and retail shops to allow referrals to be made to residents and visitors.
- Providing refreshments to residents and visitors.

A concierge must have excellent people skills and organizational abilities in order to successfully perform the job. A good concierge has the ability to effectively interact with a diverse group of people, stay calm under pressure, and maintain a cheerful disposition at all times.

The primary role of a security officer should be to provide security. While security officers must certainly have a degree of people skills and organizational abilities, the typical security officer is generally not ideally suited to work as a concierge. On the other hand, the typical concierge may lack the skills necessary to be a good security officer and may be uncomfortable when having to perform security duties.

The distinction between the roles of the concierge and the security officer should be clearly understood and the two should not be considered to be interchangeable. That is not to say that a single person can't competently do both jobs, but only that this is uncommon and requires that a special type of person be chosen to fill the position.

It is generally recommended that a concierge rather than a security officer be used to staff the primary concierge desk in a building lobby. At very busy buildings where there is lots of activity, it often works well to staff the desk with both a concierge and a security officer. The concierge can greet visitors and perform customer service activities, while the security officer can concentrate on security activities.

It is also possible to staff the concierge desk with a concierge during some hours and use a security officer to staff it at other hours. If this is done, the hours that the concierge is used should directly correspond to the hours when there is most resident and visitor activity.

If security officers are used to act as concierges, they should be specifically recruited and trained for this role and possess the necessary people skills and organizational abilities. Simply pulling a security officer off of patrol and asking him or her to staff the concierge desk will almost never yield acceptable results.

Using Security Officers To Perform Non-Security Duties

Some property owners and managers fail to appreciate the importance of the security officer's role and may assign them tasks and responsibilities not related to security. The thinking is "*Since they are standing around doing nothing anyway, we might as well give them something to do......*".

This wrong-headed thinking can result in numerous non-security duties being assigned to officers that can include doing general office work, performing housekeeping chores, setting up chairs and tables for events, washing cars, and other things bordering on the absurd. Performing these duties detract from the officer's ability to focus on security matters and can degrade their image in the eyes of residents and the general public. Performing non-security duties can also affect the officer's sense of self-esteem and make them question their own worth.

While security officers can be asked to perform some minor tasks unrelated to security, these should never take more than a small percentage of the officer's time and should never take precedence over the officer performing his or her regular security duties.

"Courtesy Patrol" Versus "Security"

Some property owners and managers use the term "Courtesy Patrol" rather than "Security" when describing the people that are used to patrol their properties. The theory is that by using this term, residents will have less of an expectation of security and that the property's legal liabilities will be reduced.

While the validity of this theory is best debated by attorneys, many security professionals feel that this theory is false and does little to shield a property from liability. Their argument is based on the often quoted statement "If it looks like a duck, swims like a duck, and quacks like a duck, then it probably is a duck". Their argument is further bolstered by the fact that most properties hire contract security companies to provide their "courtesy patrol" services. The people sent to the site are usually licensed as security officers, wear security uniforms, and drive security patrol vehicles. It is doubtful that the average resident has any question that these are security officers, regardless of what management may choose to call them.

Using Security Officers Only Part of the Time

Some multifamily properties may choose to use security officers on the premises only part of the time, such as only at night, or only on the weekends. Some properties use only a single security officer that staffs a security desk part of the time, but leaves the desk periodically to make roving patrols of the building. Both of these things are usually done for budgetary reasons – the property owners feel that they can't afford to have 24/7 security or have a dedicated officer to staff the security desk at all times.

The decision to use security officers only part of the time should be supported by risk-assessment data and not be made arbitrarily. The property manager should be able to provide reasonable answers to questions such as "Why is a security officer needed on weekends but not Monday through Friday?" or "Why is the security desk staffed during the day but not at night?".

Once a schedule for security officer staffing has been established, it should be clearly communicated to residents and employees. Otherwise, a resident may incorrectly assume that an officer is on the premises at all times. It is important for residents and employees to understand the hours that security officers are on the property and the reasoning behind why these hours were chosen.

Security Patrol Services

Security patrol services provide security officers who make roving patrols of multiple unrelated properties within a city or town. Unlike on-site security officers who have responsibility for only a single property, these officers drive from property to property throughout their shift. Depending on the arrangements made, the security patrol officer may make one, two, or more visits to each property per shift. Security patrol officers may just drive through the property and make a visual check, or may stop and get out to check doors and interior areas.

Security patrol services are also available to respond to calls from residents when they see something that is suspicious but don't feel that it warrants the calling of the police. The response time to these calls can vary depending on where the security officer is located when the call is received and how busy that the officer is.

Security patrol services charge a monthly fee based on days and times that coverage will be provided and the number of visits that will be made to the property each shift. There is an additional charge for each call made to respond to security incidents or alarms, although a fixed number of these calls may be included in the monthly fee.

Security patrol services are often used as a stopgap measure at properties that don't have on-site security officers but feel that some type of a security presence is required. Security patrol services can provide some benefits, but their limitations should be clearly understood.

Security patrol services are good for detecting abnormal conditions such as a gate that is stuck open, a light that is burnt out, or a broken window. Security patrol services are generally not effective in detecting crimes in progress as the chances of the officer arriving at the time that the act is being committed is very small. An officer driving through the property only a couple of times a night leaves the property unpatrolled most of the time. Criminals aware of the patrol service may simply wait until the officer leaves and then commit their crime.

There can be benefits in having a security patrol service available for a resident to call when they see something suspicious. However, this benefit can be diminished if it takes an excessive amount of time for the security officer to respond. Also, if a large number of calls from residents are received each month, the "per call" charge imposed by the security patrol service may become a major expense. To curb this, some property managers may limit the ability of residents to call the patrol service directly, largely defeating the benefits that the patrol service provides.

Security Services Offered to Residents

When security officers are used at a multifamily property, residents should be made aware of the services that they provide. For example, if security officers are authorized to escort residents to and from their cars at night, the availability of this service along with details (what hours available, expected wait times, etc.) should be clearly explained in resident security awareness training materials.

It is just as important to let residents know what security officers will not do. For example, if it is against policy for security officers to jump-start a vehicle or change a flat tire on a resident's car, this should be explained, and an alternative solution offered (such as the use of a local 24-hour towing service).

Resident Patrols

Residents at multifamily properties can gather together to reduce crime in their community by forming what is known as a "Resident Patrol" [28]. A Resident Patrol consists of a group of residents who volunteer to patrol their community on a regular basis. These patrols are made by two or more members working together, usually working in two to four hour shifts scheduled throughout the week. By making these patrols, members of the Resident's Patrol become more familiar with their community and are better able to recognize suspicious activity and notify the proper authorities.

Some local law enforcement agencies will provide assistance in creating a Resident Patrol and in giving training to its members. In some cases, members may be required to undergo a background check and commit to serving a minimum number of hours each month.

Resident Patrols can act as the "eyes and ears" of the community and may be able to spot things that would otherwise go unreported. The members of the Resident Patrol should act strictly in an "observe and report" capacity and never attempt to directly confront or detain a person committing a crime. Members of the Resident Patrol should not carry weapons and should never forget that they are ordinary citizens, not police officers.

Resident Patrols are intended to supplement, not replace, other types of security measures employed at the property. Resident Patrols work best when they coordinate their efforts with the HOA Board and on-site property management team. Policies and procedures for Resident Patrols should be outlined in the property's *Security Manual.*

---

[28] Resident Patrols are sometimes known by other names such as "Citizen's Patrols" or "Block Patrols".

Chapter 27: Reducing Security Officer Turnover

Learning to effectively control the rate of officer turnover can be crucial to the success of security programs that use an on-site security staff. While turnover is a particular problem when contract security officers are used, it can also be a factor at some properties where proprietary (in-house) officers are used.

The Problem

The rate of turnover in the contract security industry is legendary, with annual turnover rates averaging 200% or more at many client sites. High turnover results in increased costs for recruitment and training on an ongoing basis, and increases administrative expenses for both the client and the contract security company.

More importantly, high rates of turnover decrease the overall effectiveness of the contract security force. It can take six months or more for security officers to become fully proficient at their duties, and having constant officer turnover means that there is a good chance that some or all officers on site during any given shift may be new and inexperienced. Inexperienced officers have less ability to detect unusual activity because of their unfamiliarity with the site, and are less able to make good decisions about what to do or not do.

Constantly having new and inexperienced security officers on site also reinforces the negative perception that many people have of security officers and can prevent residents and employees from taking them seriously.

Isn't This The Security Company's Problem?

Many clients feel that reducing security officer turnover is entirely the responsibility of the contract security company. While the contract security company certainly has an important role to play, they cannot do it alone. In fact, many of the steps necessary to improve security officer retention can only be done by the multifamily property. Only by working together can the property and the contract security company get a handle on the turnover problem.

It's The Low Pay, Right?

The rate of pay that security officers receive in some parts of the country is ridiculously low, with some officers being paid at the minimum wage or just slightly above. In many areas, security officers are paid less than any other class of worker, including food service and janitorial employees.

While improving the rate of officer pay is one important factor in reducing turnover, it is by no means the only factor. Security officers who are dissatisfied with their jobs often say that other issues are as important to them, or even more important to them, than the rate of pay that they receive. When examining these issues, most revolve around the conditions under which the security officer must work.

Some of the issues of importance to security officers include:

- Being treated with respect by the residents and employees at the site where they are assigned to work.
- Receiving clear direction about what they are supposed to be doing.

- Having a professional work environment and properly functioning equipment.
- Being supported by management when they enforce an established policy or procedure.
- Doing work that they feel is important and valued.
- Receiving acknowledgment when they are doing a good job.
- Having a realistic schedule that allows them to get enough rest between shifts and gives them enough hours of pay to live on.
- Having medical and retirement benefits.
- Feeling that they are being listened to.

As you can see, many things of importance to the security officer revolve around the way that they are treated rather than what they are paid. Many of the changes that can greatly improve working conditions for security officers center around improving the way that they are managed, and can be implemented at little or no additional cost.

Things That Can Improve Working Conditions for Security Officers

The following are some ways in which security officer working conditions can be improved at your property:

Treat Security Officers with Respect

Security officers are treated as second-class citizens at many sites, and often are insulted or ignored by both residents and employees. The property management team and HOA Board members should set the tone for treating security officers with respect and make it clear that abuse of security officers will not be tolerated.

Get To Know Your Officers

The property manager and HOA Board members should make a point to introduce themselves to the security officers and if possible, try and remember their names. Something as simple as saying "hello" to a person by name can go a long way in improving working conditions for a security officer.

When a new officer is brought on at a property, it can be helpful to send a notice to all residents. This notice should include the officer's name and photo and a little information on the officer's background. This allows residents to know a little more about the people who are providing security at the property that they call their home.

Provide Security Officers with Clear Direction

Security officers should be provided with clear written instructions that describe their job responsibilities and the policies and procedures that they must follow. Adequate training should be provided to officers and this training should be consistent with the written instructions.

All verbal directions given to officers should be consistent with the written instructions. Security officers should never be asked by the property management team or HOA Board members to deviate from written procedures without the request going through the proper channels.

Having written instructions that are constantly being overridden by a set of "unwritten rules" is a surefire way to frustrate even the best security officer and should be avoided at all costs. If there is a legitimate reason to have an exception to a rule, it should be clearly documented in the security officer's written instructions.

Stand Behind Security Officers When They Do the Right Thing

Security officers should receive the full backing of the property manager and HOA Board when the officer follows established procedures, even if this offends a resident or visitor. For example, if procedures prohibit the parking of vehicles in a fire lane, the officer should not be reprimanded when he or she issues a citation to the HOA President's wife for violating this rule.

Acknowledge Excellent Performance

Security officers who do an excellent job should be immediately acknowledged. For example, if an officer sees a water leak in a parking garage and reports it before it can cause damage, he or she should receive an acknowledgment of this from the property manager and/or the HOA Board. A simple written note costs little to send, yet can mean a great deal to the individual security officer receiving it.

The property should also consider adopting a "Security Officer of the Month" program where officers who perform above and beyond the call of duty can be officially recognized. Officers who win this award should be given a certificate and some type of small gift (such as a gift card for a local restaurant.)

Provide a Professional Working Environment

Many security offices and gatehouses are cramped, cluttered places that don't appear to have been cleaned in years. Patrol vehicles issued to officers are often beaten up wrecks that don't run dependably. Flashlights, two-way radios, and other equipment issued to security officers is often in poor condition and is unreliable.

Security officers perform best when they are given a professional working environment that includes professional-grade tools and equipment. In order to get an officer to act as a professional, you must first treat him or her as one.

While security offices and gatehouses don't have to be built like the Taj Mahal, they should be clean, adequately-sized, and provide a professional working environment for your security officers. Security workspaces should be serviced by your housekeeping staff and cleaned regularly just like any other workspace at the property.

The tools and equipment used by your security officers should be up-to-date and in good working condition. The costs of routinely repairing and replacing equipment should be included in your annual security budget.

Encourage Open Lines of Communication With Security Officers

The security officers at each site should meet as a group at least twice per year. Officers should be paid to attend these meetings to encourage full participation. The primary purpose of these meetings is to provide updates to officers on security procedures for the site and to give officers an opportunity to air their grievances and express their ideas and opinions.

The property manager should regularly attend security officer meetings so that he or she can directly hear security officer opinions without them being filtered through the contract security company's site supervisor or branch manager.

Create Realistic Schedules

Creating a schedule that meets the security needs of a multifamily property at a reasonable cost can be challenging, but responsibility for solving scheduling problems should not be placed on the backs of individual security officers. Asking a security officer to drive all the way across town to cover a two-hour shift, or asking an officer that got off duty at 2:00 AM to report back at 8:00 AM the same day, is unrealistic and inconsiderate to the needs of the security officer.

Officers should not work more than 12 consecutive hours in any 24 hour period, and for not more than 60 hours in any seven-day period. Off-duty periods should be scheduled to provide for an uninterrupted eight-hour sleep cycle.

Officers should receive a minimum of four hours of pay anytime that they are called in. Schedules should be balanced so that all officers receive an adequate number of hours to live on. Attempts should be made to accommodate any special scheduling requests of individual officers when it can be done so without impacting the operation of the property.

Security Officer Pay

Quality contract security officers prefer to work at the sites that offer the best pay and the best working conditions. Once assigned to such a site, officers want to stay there, and generally perform at a high level so that they can maintain their position. The result: much lower officer turnover and better quality officers.

Trying to cut corners on officer pay can be false economy. Paying the absolute lowest rate may appear to reduce costs, but in actuality costs more because of increased administrative and training expenses.

Often paying only one or two dollars per hour above the median market rates can attract the best quality officers and greatly reduce officer turnover. Increasing the rate of officer pay by a dollar or two usually only increases the total annual cost of providing security services by 10% to 20%. Most security professionals feel that this is a small price to pay for improved security officer performance.

Property managers should conduct a survey of the rates that security officers are being paid in their city or town. Information on pay rates can be obtained by talking with your peers at other properties, and by looking at recruiting listings posted to online job boards.

Once rates of pay in your city or town have been established, create a chart that allows you to see how the rates that your property is paying compares to that being paid at other sites. If the rate that you are paying is significantly below that being paid at other sites, this is something that should be further evaluated.

The value of any benefits provided should be included in your pay rate evaluation. Many people working as security officers greatly value things such as medical benefits, and may be happy working for a lower rate of pay at a site that provides such benefits.

Chapter 28: Buying Security Products and Services

Buying Security Products and Services

Multifamily properties use a variety of security products and services. The property manager is usually responsible for procuring these products and services and making sure that they are correctly implemented at the property. While most property managers have experience in purchasing a wide range of products and services, they may be unfamiliar with those related to security.

The word "security" itself can have many meanings, and companies calling themselves "security companies" may be selling everything from guard services to fencing. Knowing which company offers which product or service can be confusing even to a seasoned security professional. The matter is compounded by the fact that some companies don't like to turn away business and may say that they can provide something even though it is outside of their area of expertise.

Types of Security Product and Service Providers

The first thing to understand is that there are many different providers of security products and services. Each of these providers usually specializes in one specific product or service, but may also offer related products and services that they can provide but are not specialists in.

Here are some security service products and services providers commonly used at multifamily properties:

Alarm Companies

Alarm companies provide fire alarm systems, intrusion alarm systems and panic alarm systems. Most alarm companies also provide monitoring services, either directly, or through a contract alarm monitoring company.

Alarm companies may also offer intercom systems, access control systems, and video surveillance systems. While many can do a good job with these systems at smaller facilities, alarm companies are not always the best choice for larger and more complicated access control and video surveillance systems.

Automated Gate Companies

Automated gate companies provide gates, gate operators, and gate accessories such as exit motion detectors, safety beams and loops, and other such devices. Most automated gate companies are also capable of providing telephone entry systems and simple access control systems, such as standalone keypads and card readers.

Contract Security Companies

Contract security companies, also known as guard companies, provide on-site security officers at multifamily properties. Many contract security companies also provide security patrol services. Some contract security companies also offer ancillary services such as providing security consulting or conducting investigations.

Electrical Contractors

Electrical contractors are used to install interior and exterior light fixtures and to provide electrical power to overhead doors, gate operators and other security equipment. Many electrical contractors are also capable of installing simple alarm, access control, and video surveillance systems. Other security systems providers may also hire an electrical contractor to install the conduits and cable for the systems that they are installing.

Elevator Contractors

Elevator contractors are involved in anything related to security that involves the elevators, including card readers, key-operated switches, and video surveillance cameras in the elevator cars. Elevator contractors are usually capable of providing simple access control devices, such as an electronic keypad in the elevator, on their own.

For larger access control systems and video surveillance systems, the elevator contractor usually works in conjunction with a security systems integrator. The security systems integrator provides the security devices and takes responsibility for the overall system. The elevator contractor installs the devices in the elevator car and provides connections between the devices and a location outside of the elevator equipment room.

Fencing Companies

Fencing companies install exterior fencing of various types and vehicle and pedestrian gates made of fencing materials. Fencing companies may also install fencing within the interior of the building to create storage rooms, bicycle cages, or to separate different areas of a parking garage. Some fencing companies may also install automatic gate operators and gate accessories.

General Contractors

General contractors are used to perform general construction work such as the building of walls, sidewalks, and roadways. General contractors can also do work necessary for the installation of other types of security measures, such as the pouring of a foundation for a gate operator, or the trenching and patching necessary for the installation of conduit to a video surveillance camera. General contractors can also be hired to repair or replace doors and windows.

General contractors can also act as overseers of large or complicated security improvement projects. For example, if a new unattended vehicle entrance was being added, the property owner could hire a general contractor to perform the overall project. The general contractor might then hire a fencing company, automated gate company, electrical contractor, and security systems integrator as sub-contractors. The general contractor would coordinate the work of all sub-contractors to deliver a complete project to the owner.

Locksmiths

Locksmiths install and maintain locks, produce keys, and install door hardware and accessories. Many locksmiths can also install and maintain electric locking hardware, exit alarms, and ADA door openers. Some locksmiths are also capable of providing telephone entry systems and simple access control systems, such as standalone keypads and card readers.

Locksmiths are generally not the best choice to install larger or more complicated access control systems that involve controlling elevators, overhead doors, or automatic gates.

Monitoring Services

Monitoring services, also known as central stations, operate facilities that are used to monitor fire, intrusion, and panic alarm systems. Monitoring stations may also be used to receive calls from emergency phones and call boxes. Monitoring services are staffed 24 hours per day and notify the appropriate authorities when an alarm or emergency call is received.

Monitoring services are usually procured through an alarm company or security systems integrator who installs the necessary equipment at the property and programs it to call the monitoring service.

Ornamental Iron Fabricators

Ornamental iron fabricators design and custom-manufacture ornamental iron fences and gates. These fabricators can also produce ornamental iron window bars and panels used to fill-in gaps and openings.

Overhead Door Companies

Overhead door companies install and maintain overhead doors, door operators and related accessories. Most overhead door companies are also capable of providing simple access control systems, such as wireless radio controls and standalone keypads.

Security Systems Integrators

Security systems integrators design, install, and service complex security systems. These systems typically include access control systems, security intercom systems, and video surveillance systems. They have special expertise in tying multiple systems together and in integrating security systems with elevators, overhead doors, and automatic gates.

While alarm companies and locksmiths can be used to install smaller systems, security systems integrators are generally the best choice to install larger and more complicated systems.

Security Window Film Installers

Window film companies install security window film, anti-graffiti window film, solar window film and decorative window film.

Other providers of security-related products and services may include automated package locker companies, background screening companies, cloud-based software providers, sign companies, and others.

As a general rule, companies who specialize in a narrow range of products and services do a better job than companies who try to be everything to everybody. There are exceptions to this rule, but most multifamily properties are best served by finding proven specialists in each area rather than trying to find a single company that can do it all.

Some companies may attempt to broaden their product offerings by partnering with other companies. For example, an alarm company may partner with a locksmith to install an access control system for a multifamily property. The alarm company installs the access control system equipment and cabling, while the locksmith installs the electric lock hardware. Another example would be a contract security company who partnered with a security systems integrator to provide both on-site security officers and the video surveillance system for the property.

The Ways That Security Products Are Distributed

There are different ways that security products are sold to multifamily properties. Some products, such as a padlock, can be purchased directly from a local retail outlet or ordered online. However, many types of security products are only available through a local specialty dealer.

For example, an intrusion alarm system would normally be purchased from an alarm company who would both sell and install the system. Along the same lines, a gate operator would normally be purchased from an automated gate company who would both sell and install the gate operator. While some versions of some products may be available for purchase directly by the property, most professional-grade products can only be purchased through a local dealer.

There are two common models used to sell security products to multifamily properties: the distributor model, and the authorized dealer model.

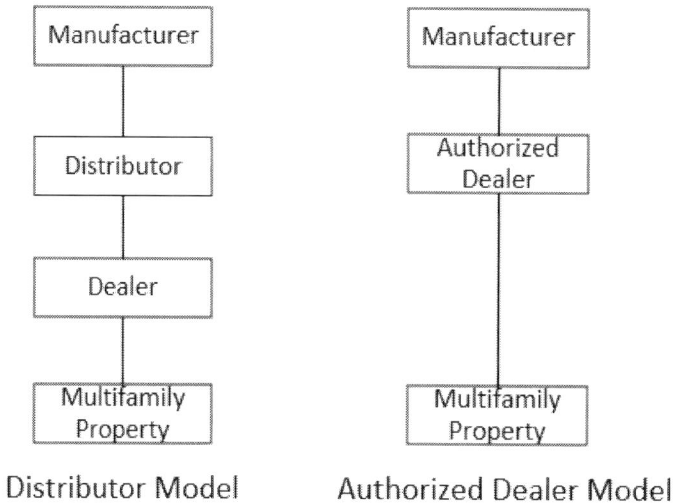

Figure 28-1 - Ways That Security Products are Distributed

<u>Distributor Model</u>

Products sold using the distributor model begins with the manufacturer selling the product to a distributor, who in turn sells it to a dealer. This dealer then sells the product to the multifamily property. This dealer is usually also responsible for installing the product and servicing it in the future. Products sold through the distributor model are usually sold to any dealer, making them widely available.

<u>Authorized Dealer Model</u>

When using the authorized dealer model, the manufacturer sells the product directly to the dealer, who in turn sells it to the multifamily property. This dealer is usually also responsible for installing the product and servicing it in the future.

Products sold using the authorized dealer model are more controlled, and usually require that the dealer go through a prequalification process in order to purchase the product. This prequalification process can include making a commitment to sell a specified amount of product each year and completing the manufacturer's training program. Proof of experience and financial stability may also be required. Once a dealer has completed this prequalification process, they become a "authorized dealer [29]" for this manufacturer.

Manufacturers who use the distributor model will sometimes allow the distributor to sell the product directly to a multifamily property or a general or electrical contractor. This is because they consider these customers to be "commercial users" and so have no problem in selling directly to them.

Manufacturers who use the authorized dealer model will almost never sell directly to a multifamily property or contractor, but require them to buy from a local authorized dealer instead. Manufacturers typically limit the number of authorized dealers that they have in any geographical area. This means that there may be only one or two dealers in your city or town that can provide that manufacturer's product. This can restrict the ability to obtain competitive bids and limits options for obtaining service on the product in the future.

The authorized dealer model can sometimes pose a dilemma for property managers who wish to pick the best product in each class but want to work with only a single dealer. For example, the company who is an authorized dealer for the desired access control system may not be an authorized dealer for the desired video surveillance system. This requires that two separate dealers be used (one for each system), or that the use of different brands of equipment be allowed so that a single dealer can provide all products.

Property owners and managers who operate different properties across a large geographical region and wish to standardize on systems across the portfolio can face additional challenges. It may be difficult to find authorized dealers for certain manufacturers in some cities, particularly in more rural areas. This requires either compromising on the brand of product used, or using an out-of-town dealer that is located a considerable distance from the property.

The Components that Make Up a Security "System"

The term "system" is used to describe many types of security products because the product is not a single item, but rather a collection of components that are connected together to provide the desired function. For example, the components used in a wired intrusion alarm system may include a control panel, keypad arming station, siren, a motion detector, and a magnetic contact switch. Each of these components are connected together to create the intrusion alarm system.

Security system components can be generic or proprietary. Generic components are ones that are compatible with any type of system and are not unique to any specific manufacturer. Items such as sirens, motion detectors, and magnetic contact switches in a wired intrusion alarm system are examples of generic components that can typically be used interchangeably between all types of systems.

Proprietary components are those that only work with a specific manufacturer's system. An example of a proprietary product would be a keypad arming station that is capable of only being used with that manufacturer's own brand of control panel. The keypad arming station produced by one manufacturer would not be compatible with the control panel of another manufacturer, so the keypad would be considered to be a proprietary rather than generic component.

It is most common for security systems to be made up of components produced by multiple different equipment manufacturers. For example, a wired intrusion alarm system could use motion detectors made by one manufacturer, magnetic contact switches made by another, and a siren made by yet

---

[29] Authorized dealers may also be called "Partners", "Value-Added Resellers" or other names.

another. Because these components are generic, they can be used with any manufacturer's brand of control panel. However, the keypad arming station used with this system would have to be the same brand as the control panel because the keypad arming station is a proprietary component.

Some manufacturers do in fact make all components of a system. Systems where all components are made by a single manufacturer are often called "end-to-end solutions". End-to-end solutions usually involve the use of proprietary rather than generic components.

Some manufacturers and dealers may create the illusion of offering an end-to-end solution by simply placing their label on generic components. These components are known as "private-labeled" products. For example, a manufacturer might place its company's name on a generic motion detector so that it appeared as if the manufacturer produced the product. Some alarm companies and security systems integrators also private-label the generic products that they install to promote their company and perhaps imply that they are the only ones who can service them.

When purchasing security systems of any type, it is usually best to stick with generic rather than proprietary or private-labeled components. Generic components offer the most flexibility and prevent you from being "locked-in" to any specific equipment manufacturer in the future.

Process Used to Procure Security Products and Services

The process used to procure security products and services will vary depending on what is being purchased. Many simple purchases, such as the buying of a padlock or a key cabinet, can be made online or at a local retailer. This type of purchase usually requires little thought.

In many cases, a property manager may have a trusted company that has been used in the past and this company can be called again to provide the needed product or service. For example, if a locksmith has a history of providing good service to the property, this locksmith could be called again when new security astragals were needed on the exterior doors. Along the same lines, if a property manager has had good experience in using a certain type of automated package locker system at other properties, this same provider could be called to provide lockers at this property.

When a more complicated or expensive purchase must be made, and there is no existing relationship with a trusted service provider, then the property manager must go on a hunt to find a company who can fulfill the requirement. A common approach is to simply call a few companies in the area who appear to provide the desired product or service and ask them to submit bids or proposals. While this sometimes works, it can yield inconsistent results. Often, each vendor will propose a different type of solution using different types of products, making it almost impossible to compare proposals "apples-to-apples".

To minimize this difficulty, a more structured process should be used to solicit proposals and select a service provider. This process is known as a Request-for-Proposal (RFP) process and involves multiple steps.

Using the RFP Process

To provide an example of the RFP process we will assume that the property manager at a small condominium building wishes to purchase an access control system to control access through the front and back doors of the building. To procure this system, the property manager would take the following steps:

Step #1 - Prepare Preliminary Requirements Statement

The first step is to clearly define the requirements of the project in a simple written statement. In this example, the requirements statement might include the following:

Requirements Statement for Access Control System at Acme Apartments

- *System shall allow entry through the front and back doors using an access card that can be issued to residents and contractors.*
- *System shall allow the access privileges of each card to be programmed from a computer in the building office.*
- *The days and times that each access card can be used shall be individually programmable, allowing the times that each user can enter the building to be controlled. (For example, residents can enter 24/7, but contractors can enter only between 8:00 AM and 5:00 PM on weekdays.).*
- *System shall track activity and allow reports to be created showing which access card was used and when.*
- *System shall allow access cards that have been lost or stolen to be quickly deleted.*

Step #2 - Research Options

The second step is to conduct research to determine the options available to meet the requirements stated in Step #1. In our example, the property manager could use the following methods to conduct research on possible access control systems that could be used at the building:

- Read articles in online and print publications to get an overview of the various types of access control systems available. (For example, an overview of access control systems is provided in Chapter 11 of this book.)
- Meet with access control system vendors to have them explain their system offerings and to provide product demonstrations. Be honest about your intentions; explain that you are doing preliminary research and that at this stage you are only seeking to educate yourself on what's available. (Don't waste the vendor's time by asking them to prepare a formal proposal if you are only doing research.)
- Talk with your peers at other properties to see what types of systems that they are using and how well they have worked. Ask specifically about things that aren't working as expected and what they would do differently if they had to do it again.
- Attend any local seminars or security trade shows that may be put on by local vendors or association management groups.

Step #3 - Prepare Final Requirements Statement

The third step is to refine the preliminary requirements statement created during Step #1 based on what was learned in Step #2.

For example, while watching an equipment demonstration, you may have learned that many access control systems are capable of being programed remotely using a smartphone. You decide that this is a feature that you want and so add it to the requirements statement.

When discussing access control systems with your peers at other properties, one may have stated that they were surprised at just how often they had to change batteries on their electronic keypad locks, and that if they had to do it again, they would install a centrally-powered system instead. Another peer may have stated that they were unhappy with the sloppy way that their contractor had installed cabling to each of their doors.

Based on these comments, you modify the requirements statement to specify that the access control system must be centrally-powered and must not use batteries as its primary power source. You also specify that all cabling to doors must be either completely hidden in the walls, or installed in a surface metal raceway.

Step #4 - Prepare Request-For-Proposal (RFP)

The fourth step is to prepare a Request-For-Proposal (RFP). The RFP should include the final requirements statement created in Step #3, plus any administrative requirements that may apply at your property. Example of administrative requirements include:

- Working hours.
- Security and safety requirements.
- Availability of parking.
- Loading/unloading procedures.
- Availability of storage for tools and equipment on-site.
- Insurance and bonding requirements.
- Training requirements.
- Warranty requirements.

To avoid problems, you must clearly define working conditions in advance. These can have an impact on costs and must be understood by the contractor before he or she prepares the proposal. It is unfair to ask a contractor to comply with working conditions that were not properly explained when the RFP was issued. For example, if a contractor's workers can't park at the building but must park in a lot two blocks away, this is not something that he or she should learn only after the project has started.

Before incorporating standard terms or conditions into your RFP, carefully review them to determine if they make sense for your specific project. In particular, look at things such as insurance requirements to make sure that they are reasonable and appropriate considering the size of your project. Asking a contractor to have $5,000,000 in liability insurance for a $10,000 access control system project probably doesn't make sense and can drive away all but the very largest of contractors. This can limit competition and increase costs.

Step #5 - Identify Bidders and Issue RFP

The fifth step is to identify companies who are qualified to submit proposals on your project and issue them the RFP. Companies asked to bid should be regularly engaged in providing the type of product or service that you are seeking. If you happened to have found a particular brand of product that you prefer during your research (Step #2), identify the authorized dealers that represent that product. Also ask your peers for recommendations and don't forget to include the companies that were helpful to you when you were doing your research if they are qualified.

When issuing an RFP, always establish a final date by which proposals must be submitted. Be sure that you give bidders ample time to prepare their proposals. Keep in mind that bidders may have to obtain pricing information from suppliers and subcontractors, and this can take time. A minimum of two weeks should be allowed for small to medium sized projects, with as much as a month allowed for very large projects.

If the project involves work at an existing property, it is helpful to conduct a pre-bid walkthrough so that bidders can see actual conditions at the site. It is best to conduct a single walkthrough with all bidders present rather than doing individual walkthroughs with each bidder separately. This allows all bidders to see the same things and hear the answers to the same questions.

Any questions asked at the pre-bid walkthrough that change or clarify the requirements in the RFP should be answered in writing and distributed to all bidders. Any questions asked during the time between the pre-bid walkthrough and the date that the RFP is due should be answered and distributed in the same way. Again, this assures that all bidders are receiving the same information and basing their bids on the same set of facts.

Step #6 - Evaluating Proposals and Awarding Contract

When proposals are received, they should be evaluated. Factors to be considered when evaluating proposals should include:

- Proposer's ability to meet requirements stated in RFP.
- Are the products proposed generic products or proprietary products?
- Are there other companies in the area that can service the product should the proposer perform unsatisfactorily or go out of business?
- Proposer's track record with projects of a similar type and size.
- Proposer's experience in working with multifamily properties.
- Results of checks with proposer's references.
- Training and after-the-sale support provided.
- Warranty and service response times.
- Initial price and ongoing support costs.

A common mistake is to ask for references in the RFP and then fail to check them. Always call all references before awarding a contract to a company. Also check with any of your peers that may have used the company before, even if the proposer has not specifically listed them as a reference.

Be cautious when any bid received is priced substantially lower than the others. While there can be a legitimate reason for the lower price, a low bid usually indicates that the proposer doesn't fully understand the scope of work, or that a mistake has been made in preparing the bid. The best way to clarify this is to ask for an itemized line-by-line breakdown of the bid to make sure that all requested items are included in the bid.

If this doesn't reveal anything, arrange a face-to-face meeting with the owner or general manager (not just the salesperson) of the company submitting the low bid. Be frank; explain that his or her company has submitted a bid that is substantially lower than the other bidders and that you would like an explanation of how this is possible.

Step #7 - Awarding The Contract

Once a satisfactory proposal has been identified, a written agreement should be prepared using a standard contract form that is used by the property, or one can be drafted specifically for the project by your attorney. The contract should incorporate by reference the scope of work outlined in the RFP including all terms and conditions. The contract should include the expected start date and completion date of the project.

If the proposer's contract is used, it should be carefully reviewed by your attorney before it is signed. Many proposer contracts are heavily slanted towards the proposer at the expense of the customer. If a proposer's contract is used, it should reference the scope of work in the RFP, not just the proposer's sales order. It is common for proposers to want to throw out any specific requirements of an RFP and get the customer to agree to just what is in their sales order instead. For example, a certain type of accessory may have been specified in the RFP, but if the sales order omits this accessory, the contractor may not agree to provide it without being paid an extra charge.

The procurement process described above can be used for the purchase of any type of security system or physical security product. A modified version of this process can be used to procure services, such as the solicitation of bids for contract security officer services.

Seeking Outside Help with Procurements

There are certain cases when the property manager may wish to seek the help of an outside professional to assist with the procurement of security products and services. This can be appropriate when the project is large and highly technical and involves a significant investment. A procurement may also require more time and expertise than the property manager or HOA Board has available.

The type of professional that should be chosen depends on the nature of the project. Here are some examples of some professionals who may be capable of providing assistance at a multifamily property:

Architects and Engineers

Architects and engineers (A/Es) are licensed design professionals who are well-suited to provide assistance with projects involving fencing, automatic gates, gatehouses, or other types of general construction work. In some cases, the plans for a project must be prepared and submitted by a licensed A/E in order to get a building permit. While A/Es may be able to design and specify simple security systems, most lack the technical expertise necessary to design larger and more complicated systems.

Project Managers

Project Managers are professionals who assist with the organization and management of construction projects. Project managers are capable of managing a project on a daily basis and coordinating the efforts of A/Es, consultants, and contractors. A project manager can serve as owner's representative and make day-to-day decisions with the owner's best interests in mind. While it is common for the project manager to start after a contractor has been selected, project managers can also get involved in the early stages of the project and assist with the preparation of the RFP and the solicitation of bids.

Security Management Consultants

Security management consultants are independent consultants who specialize in the operational and management aspects of security. Security management consultants can conduct assessments of the overall security program, develop security policies and procedures, prepare RFPs for contract security services, evaluate proposals, and negotiate contracts with contract security companies. With some exceptions, security management consultants don't have technical expertise and are not well suited to design and specify security systems.

Technical Security Consultants

Technical security consultants are independent consultants who specialize in the design and planning of electronic security systems such as access control, video surveillance, intercom, and intrusion detection systems. Technical security consultants can help to prepare the RFP, evaluate vendor proposals, oversee the construction process, and inspect the completed installation.

(See Chapter 29 for more on working with security management consultants and technical security consultants.)

Do-It-Yourself Products

There are many do-it-yourself (DIY)) security products available for sale both online and at retail stores. These products include video doorbells, video surveillance systems, intrusion alarm systems, electronic keypad locks, and a multitude of different types of security hardware products.

Most DIY products are intended for use at individual homes and usually cost significantly less than commercial products of the same type. For example, a complete DIY video surveillance camera kit with eight cameras can often be purchased for less than the price of a single commercial grade video surveillance camera.

Some multifamily properties may choose to purchase DIY security products as a less expensive alternative to professionally-installed security systems. These products would be purchased online or from a retail store, and then installed by an in-house maintenance technician or a homeowner volunteer.

Before making a decision to use DIY products, the following should be considered:

- DIY security products typically lack the features and capabilities found in commercial security products of the same type.
- DIY products intended for residential use are usually not rugged enough to withstand the amount of use (and abuse) typically found at a multifamily property.
- It may be difficult to obtain parts to service or expand the DIY system in the future.
- The in-house staff or volunteers who originally installed the system may not be available when it comes time to service the system or expand it in the future. Finding a contractor who is willing to work on a system that uses DIY equipment may prove to be impossible.

As a general rule, most multifamily properties are best served by buying commercial grade security products and having them professionally installed. When DIY products are used, their limitations should be clearly understood.

Buying Security Products Online

Almost every type of security product can be purchased online. Online purchasing is a good way to procure many types of security supplies and simple security equipment. Examples of things that can be effectively purchased online include security signs, identification badges, parking and bicycle permits, and key storage cabinets.

Things like access cards, access fobs, and wireless transmitters can also be purchased online, but great care must be taken to assure compatibility with existing systems. Some access cards and access fobs come in formats that are available only through authorized dealers.

When security systems are supported by an in-house maintenance team, many security products are available for purchase online, including lock hardware and generic equipment such as motion detectors, magnetic contact switches, and batteries. However, care should be taken before purchasing any type of equipment that is proprietary or only intended for sale through authorized dealers.

Most security manufacturers who distribute their products using authorized dealers strictly prohibit online sales, as it weakens the integrity of their distribution network and diminishes the value of an authorized dealership. Authorized dealers who sell their products online are in violation of their dealer agreement.

Products sold outside of the manufacturer-approved distribution chain are known as "gray-market products". Gray market security products usually come from two sources; authorized dealers who choose to sell online in violation of their dealer agreement, and liquidators who purchase excess inventory from authorized dealers and offer them for sale online. In some cases, a gray-market product may have been intended for sale in another country.

While the sale of gray-market products is usually not illegal, it does come with some risks for the purchaser. These risks include:

- Manufacturer may not choose to honor warranty on product.
- Manufacturer may not provide technical support on product.
- Product may be out of date or not have the latest features supported by current software.
- Product instructions and configuration menus may be in a foreign language.
- Attaching gray-market products to existing systems may void warranty or service agreement.

When it is necessary to purchase or expand a security system, many property managers do a search online and find commercial grade products listed at prices significantly less than those being quoted by their local provider. These are very likely gray-market products and should only be purchased with a full understanding of the risks involved.

Security Systems Maintenance

Like other building systems, security systems must be regularly maintained. However, in some cases, a property will budget for the initial purchase of a security system, but fail to budget for ongoing maintenance.

A good rule of thumb is to budget 10% to 15% of the initial purchase price as a maintenance budget. For example, if an access control system cost $25,000 to install, $2,500 to $3,750 should be budgeted for annual maintenance.

Many security systems providers offer service agreements on security systems. These can provide a predictable cost for maintenance each year, but care should be taken to understand exactly what the agreement does and does not include. Some questions to be asked include:

- What types of service and repair does the agreement include? All materials and labor? Materials only? Labor only?
- What types of repairs does the agreement exclude? Many agreements exclude repairs caused by vandalism or "acts of god" (such as damage caused by lightning). Some agreements also exclude items caused by normal "wear and tear" or items that must be replaced on a regular basis, such as batteries.
- During what hours will the service be provided? Many standard agreements provide service only during normal working hours (typically 8:00 AM to 5:00 PM Monday through Friday). Service calls provided after hours or on weekends cost extra.
- How quickly will service be provided? Does the service agreement guarantee a response within a certain number of hours after you place your call?
- Does the service agreement include preventive maintenance (such as the cleaning of exterior camera housings or the lubrication and adjusting of mechanical equipment)?
- Does the service agreement include periodic tests or inspections of the system?
- Does the service agreement provide loaner equipment while yours is in the shop? Many types of security equipment cannot be repaired on-site and must be sent into the factory for service.

Software Support Agreements

Server-based access control systems and video management systems use sophisticated software that is constantly being improved. Most manufacturers issue updated versions of their software at least annually. There is usually a cost associated with each upgrade.

Most manufacturers offer what is known as a "Software Support Agreement" (SSA) which is sold on an annual subscription basis. The SSA includes software upgrades as well as "bug-fixes" that are issued to fix problems in previously released versions of the software. Some bug-fixes correct serious problems such as vulnerabilities that would allow hackers to gain access to the system.

It is recommended that multifamily properties purchase SSAs to keep their systems current and to guarantee technical support from the manufacturer. Some manufacturers will not offer technical support to users that don't have the current version of their software.

SSAs must usually be purchased through an authorized dealer of the manufacturer. When a service agreement is purchased from a dealer, the cost of the SSA is usually in addition to the cost of the service agreement.

Chapter 29: Using an Independent Security Consultant

What Is an Independent Security Consultant?

The dictionary defines a consultant as a "person who provides expert advice professionally", "one who consults another", and "one who gives professional advice or services". It would be natural to assume then that a "security consultant" is a person that provides expert security advice professionally.

Unfortunately, within the security industry, the term "security consultant" has been hijacked. The majority of the people who use this title are in fact sellers of security products and services, and while these people probably do "consult" on a limited basis, their primary goal is to sell the particular product or service that they represent.

To make a distinction between salespeople and actual security consultants, the term "independent security consultant" was coined. This term is used to describe professionals who provide expert security advice but who are unaffiliated with any other security product or service. Like an accountant, doctor, or attorney, the independent security consultant charges a fee for his or her services, and derives no revenue from the sale of products that he or she recommends.

Types of Independent Security Consultants

There are two primary types of independent security consultants used at multifamily properties:

<u>Security Management Consultants</u>

Security management consultants are the "general practitioners" of the security consulting profession. Security management consultants provide generalized advice on managing a client's overall security and loss prevention program. Security management consultants typically conduct security assessments, write security policies and procedures, provide security training, and provide assistance in the procurement of contract security services.

<u>Technical Security Consultants</u>

Technical security consultants, sometimes called "security engineers", provide advice related to physical and electronic security systems. Technical security consultants design security systems for new and existing buildings, develop specifications for security equipment, assist with the procurement of security systems, and provide oversight of the security system installation process.

There is a third type of security consultant that may be needed at a multifamily property on rare occasions. This type of security consultant is known as a forensic security consultant and provides advice and testimony related to litigation and legal matters. Hopefully, you will not need the services of this type of consultant, but if you do, he or she would likely be retained directly by your attorney.

Benefits of Using an Independent Security Consultant

There can be many benefits in using an independent security consultant. Some of these benefits include:

- The consultant has experience with similar security problems and conditions at many other multifamily properties. Most problems are not unique, and others have figured out answers to them before. A good consultant is familiar with solutions that have worked at other properties and can immediately transfer this knowledge to you.

- The consultant has the ability to provide a fresh, unbiased opinion. Sometimes the property manager and owners can be too close to a situation to see it clearly.
- The consultant has up-to-date knowledge of security best practices and the latest security technology.
- The consultant has no need to temper his or her opinions for political reasons— he or she can "tell it like it is" without fear of retribution. Many property managers are afraid to bring up important issues within their organization or with homeowners because they are afraid of stepping on toes or making enemies.
- An outside consultant can often have more credibility and sell ideas that the property manager alone cannot. Rightly or wrongly, a consultant and property manager can present the same idea, but owners will accept it when presented by the consultant - while they would reject it if it was presented by the property manager.
- A consultant can often save the property time and money by doing things more efficiently, avoiding costly mistakes, and preventing the purchase of unnecessary equipment or services. Often the money saved greatly outweighs the costs of hiring the consultant.

What Do Independent Security Consultants Charge?

The fee that independent security consultants charge varies depending on the types of services being provided and the consultant's qualifications and experience. Expect to pay an hourly rate similar to that paid to an experienced attorney or other similarly qualified professional.

Most independent security consultants work on an hourly basis where the client is charged for every hour that the consultant works. In most cases, it is possible for the consultant to provide an approximate estimate of the hours that will be required to complete the requested task in advance.

Sometimes, the consultant will only be able to provide an estimate for the complete project after a preliminary investigation has been conducted. In these cases, it is common to authorize the consultant to perform a certain number of hours of work to conduct the initial investigation and determine the scope of the project. Once the scope has been determined, the consultant can then provide an estimate of what it would take to complete the overall project.

Many consultants are willing to work for a fixed-fee amount rather than charge by the hour if the scope of work can be precisely determined in advance. This arrangement is often preferred by both the client and the consultant because the total fee is known in advance and there are no surprises.

It is customary for the consultant to get reimbursed for expenses in addition to the agreed upon hourly or fixed-fee. When the consultant must travel to the project from out of town, reimbursable expenses may include the cost of airfare, lodging, rental car fees, and meals. Other reimbursable expenses may include the cost of printing drawings and reports, using paid services to provide crime forecast data, and hiring specialists to perform certain tasks related to the project, such as conducting a lighting study.

Most independent consultants require an advance retainer payment (deposit) before starting work on a project. This payment is normally one-third to one-half of the total anticipated fee amount and expenses.

A written agreement should be drafted between the property and the consultant that documents all details concerning the agreed upon scope of work, consulting fees, reimbursable expenses, and project completion dates. This agreement should be signed by both parties before any work starts.

What Qualifications Should an Independent Security Consultant Have?

Most states do not have professional licensing requirements for independent security consultants. A person can simply claim to be a consultant and start offering his or her services to the public. This makes it especially important for the client to thoroughly vet the qualifications of any consultant that they are considering hiring.

Security management consultants should have a thorough knowledge of security management principles and practices and actual experience in the private security industry. Security management consultants should have security industry credentials such as the Certified Protection Professional (CPP) issued by ASIS International or the Certified Security Consultant (CSC) issued by the International Association of Professional Security Consultants (IAPSC).

Technical security consultants should have a knowledge of engineering principles and specific expertise in access control systems, alarm monitoring systems, video surveillance systems, and other electronic security systems. Technical security consultants should understand the architectural design and construction process and be able to manage complex projects through all phases of planning, design, and execution. Technical security consultants should have credentials such as the Physical Security Professional (PSP) or Registered Communications Distribution Designer (RCDD).

A property hiring a security management consultant is generally best served when the consultant has prior experience working with multifamily properties. Knowing how a multifamily property operates is necessary for the consultant to effectively assess risks and to develop an overall security plan for the property.

When hiring a technical security consultant, previous multifamily experience is helpful, but not mandatory. With a few exceptions, most security system technology is applied in the same way at facilities of all types, so having specific experience with multifamily properties is not essential.

Be sure that any independent security consultant that you are considering is truly independent. Some people that claim to be independent consultants either work for or have referral arrangements with other providers of security products or services. This can prevent the consultant from acting in the client's best interests.

Some people who have recently retired from law enforcement agencies often claim to be security consultants. Prior experience in law enforcement can be helpful, but this experience alone does not make one qualified to act as a security consultant. Law enforcement and private security are two entirely different things, and retired law enforcement officers usually need to acquire a substantial number of additional skills before they can competently practice as security consultants.

Are Larger Consulting Firms Better Qualified Than Smaller Firms?

Contrary to what people might think, the quality of service provided by a large national or international consulting firm is usually no better than that provided by a smaller independent firm, and in many cases, may actually be worse.

Consulting projects are performed by people, not companies. If the large consulting firm assigns competent people to your project, you will probably get excellent results. However, it is very common for large consulting firms to win a contract using the resumes of their most senior people during the proposal process. Once the project is won, the vast majority of the actual work may be assigned to junior people who are considerably less qualified.

The managers of some large consulting firms are usually under constant pressure to generate lots of "billable hours" and to maximize revenue. Sometimes, the need to meet revenue targets get in the way of doing what's right for the client or project. It's hard to think long-term when you are trying to meet this month's quotas.

With a small independent consulting firm, it is very likely that the owners of the firm will be personally involved in every project, including yours. You will generally get a higher level of personal service from the smaller firm, and your project will be treated with greater importance. While the smaller firm needs to generate profits to stay in business, there is less emphasis on short term results and a greater emphasis on developing a long-term and mutually beneficial relationship with the client.

Where larger firms do have an advantage is when dealing with large scale projects that must be completed within a short time frame. Large firms can assemble a large team of people that can quickly begin working on your project almost immediately. A larger firm will probably also have offices in multiple cities. This can be an advantage when a project is spread across multiple states. For example, a property manager may have a portfolio of properties scattered across the country and wants to have a single consulting firm conduct security assessments at all of them. The larger firm can assign consultants from local offices, reducing costs of travel.

To offset these advantages, many smaller consulting firms often collaborate with other similarly-sized firms when working on large projects, or when working on projects that have multiple locations. For example, consultants who are members of the International Association of Professional Security Consultants (IAPSC) frequently collaborate on projects where representation in various geographical regions is required.

How Do I Find an Independent Security Consultant?

Security consulting is a specialized profession and there are surprisingly few truly independent security consulting firms when compared to the security industry as a whole.

The exact number of independent security consultants in the United States is unknown, but the leading organization representing independent consultants, the International Association of Professional Security Consultants (IAPSC), currently has under 150 members at the time of this writing. Even if the total number of practicing consultants is three or four times this figure, the total number of consultants is very small when compared to other professions. The field of independent consultants that have actual experience with multifamily properties is even smaller.

Due to the specialized nature of their work, most independent security consultants work nationally or internationally. While you may be lucky enough to find a consultant located in your city, it is most common to have to look out-of-town for a qualified consultant who has multifamily project experience. While using an out-of-town consultant can increase costs somewhat, it is better to pay a little more to get someone who is truly qualified than it is to use a local consultant who lacks the appropriate experience.

Finding the right independent security consultant can be a challenge. Here are some tips for locating possible consultants:

- Check with your peers at other properties and property management companies. A referral to a consultant by someone who has previously used their services and was satisfied with them is one of the best ways to locate a qualified consultant.

- Use the "Find a Consultant" locator service provided on the International Association of Professional Security Consultants (IAPSC) website (www.iapsc.org).
- Look for consultants who have written articles on multifamily property security in books, publications, and online blogs. If you like the information provided and the style of writing used by a specific author, this consultant may be a good candidate to consider.
- Do a web search for security consultants who claim to have expertise with multifamily housing projects. Be cautious when a consultant lists multifamily properties along with dozens of other types of facilities that he or she claims to have expertise in. If a consultant appears promising, call to get details on the specific multifamily projects that the firm has completed in the past.

Keys for Success When Working With an Independent Security Consultant

Here are some keys to success when working with an independent security consultant:

- Be clear about your expectations: carefully define a scope of work in writing that fully describes what services and deliverables are expected and the desired outcome.
- Establish a realistic schedule. Keep in mind that most qualified consultants are very busy and may not be able to immediately start work on your project. Don't expect results overnight. Allow adequate time for the consultant to evaluate the situation, conduct research, and complete the work. Set deadlines for the completion of the project and hold the consultant accountable for meeting them.
- Designate a specific individual at the property for the consultant to work with. This person should be responsible for providing access, coordinating meetings with other team members, and providing documentation and other materials requested by the consultant.
- Provide all documentation and materials requested by the consultant in a timely manner.
- Let the consultant know who all the players at the property are, including management staff, on-site workers, and representatives of the HOA Board and committees.
- Make all players available to be interviewed in a timely manner.
- Expect the security consultant to be independent and to tell the truth, no matter how unpopular the facts may be. Don't ask the consultant to "rubberstamp" recommendations made by the property manager or HOA Board members, or to delete findings from a report just because they may not go over well with managers or owners.
- Consider the security consultant to be a long-term resource. Feel free to call with questions about previously completed consulting projects and security matters in general, even if unrelated to a previous project. Most consultants are happy to answer a quick question by phone or email at no charge. If they won't, you probably have the wrong consultant.

Chapter 30: Solving Specific Types of Security Problems

This chapter talks about some common security problems faced at multifamily properties and offers some solutions that may be used to solve them. More detailed information on how to implement most solutions can be found in other chapters of this book. The list of problems and solutions offered here is by no means complete, and not every solution will be appropriate for every property or circumstance.

Trespassers On the Site

- Remove or modify items that may attract trespassers to the site:
  - Outdoor electrical outlets that can be used to charge phones and other mobile devices.
  - Outdoor water faucets that can be used to fill water bottles or to bathe.
  - Items that can be easily stolen (outdoor artwork, unsecured equipment, unsecured packages, etc.).
  - Trash and recycle containers that may contain things of perceived value. (Recyclable metals, information that could be used to commit identity theft, etc.).
  - Benches and tables that offer places to lie down or sleep.
- Minimize places that can be used as spots to set-up camp or to consume alcohol or illegal drugs. Consider using fencing or other barriers to enclose pockets on the exterior the building that create places to hide.
- Provide good lighting of the site and exterior areas. (10 to 20 Lux minimum is recommended).
- Use CPTED principals to define site boundaries, establish ownership, and allow effective natural surveillance.
- Provide "No Trespassing" signs at site perimeter and at site entrances.
- Use fencing and landscaping to limit points of access to the site. Consider using automatic vehicle gates and pedestrian gates to restrict access to only authorized people.
- If on-site security officers are used, provide frequent patrols of outdoor areas.

Trespassers In the Building

- Harden exterior doors using guidelines in Appendix A.
- Provide good lighting at building entrances. (30 to 50 Lux minimum is recommended).
- Use CPTED principals at building entrances to allow natural surveillance and eliminate hiding places.
- Educate residents on the proper procedures to prevent tailgating through exterior pedestrian doors.
- Minimize the time that doors are held open by ADA door openers.
- Ask residents to wait for overhead garage doors to fully close before driving off to prevent tailgating.
- Consider use of high-performance overhead doors at garage entrances.

- Provide "No Trespassing" signs at exterior entrances.
- Take steps to eliminate vulnerabilities associated with telephone entry systems (ability to tamper with postal lock switch to gain entry, default programming codes).
- Minimize the use of key boxes on the exterior of the building.
- Consider enclosing open parking garages and courtyards.

Bicycle Theft

- Take steps to reduce ability of trespassers to gain access to the building (see above).
- Harden doors to bicycle rooms using guidelines in Appendix A.
- Remove signs that identify locations of bicycle rooms.
- Obscure windows that allow looking into bicycle rooms.
- Use bicycle racks that have security features and are difficult to compromise.
- Use tamper-resistant fasteners to assemble and mount bicycle racks or tack weld fasteners to prevent their removal.
- Encourage residents to use high-quality bicycle locks.

Burglary of Residential Units

- Take steps to reduce ability of trespassers to gain access to the site and building (see above).
- Use high-quality (ANSI Grade 2 or better) lock hardware on entry doors.
- Provide reinforcement of wood doors and door frames on entry doors.
- Use supplemental locks on windows and sliding patio doors.
- Keep doors and windows locked.
- Don't "hide" keys outside of the unit and avoid using exterior key boxes.
- Provide good exterior lighting at ground floor units. (10 to 20 Lux minimum is recommended).
- Use CPTED landscaping principals to allow good visibility at ground floor units.
- Use timers to activate indoor lights when away.
- Consider use of security window film or security window screens or bars on ground floor units.
- Consider use of intrusion alarm system.

Gang Problems

- Work with your attorney to develop effective legal solutions for:
    - Background screening of prospective new residents.
    - Background screening for the extended stay of visitors of residents.
    - Lease agreement that includes provisions for the removal of residents who violate the law. (such as in Crime Free Lease Addendum).

   - Eviction procedures for residents who must be removed.

- Establish relationship with local law enforcement agencies. Communicate regularly with patrol officers and gang specialists. Promptly report signs of gang activity.
- Establish parking control procedures that allow unauthorized vehicles on the property to be promptly identified and removed.
- Provide security awareness training for residents and encourage them to reports signs of improper activity.

Vehicle Theft

- Educate residents to:
   - Keep vehicle doors and windows locked.
   - Don't leave keys inside of vehicle.
   - Don't' keep spare keys "hidden" outside of vehicle.
   - Don't leave car running when unattended, even for a minute.

Outdoor Graffiti

- Provide good exterior lighting in graffiti-prone areas. (10 to 20 Lux minimum is recommended).
- Use CPTED principals to allow good visibility of exterior areas.
- Control access to exterior stairways and roofs.
- Promptly remove graffiti to minimize the time that it is exhibited.
- Consider use of anti-graffiti wall coatings to allow quick removal of graffiti.
- Consider the use of anti-graffiti film to protect windows.
- Consider painting murals on walls to discourage graffiti artists who respect the work of other artists.
- Consider blocking wall surfaces with thorny bushes or other landscaping
- Consider replacing solid fences with picket or chain-link fences to minimize the surface area where graffiti can be applied.

Package Thefts

- Take steps to reduce ability of trespassers to gain access to the building (see above).
- Don't allow packages to be placed in unsecured areas such as in unattended lobbies or on top of mailboxes. Require that all packages be delivered to a secured package room that is centrally located.
- If providing a package room is not possible, consider providing either a manual package locker or automated package locker system.
- Restrict access to package rooms and mail rooms to allow access only by authorized people.
- Locate mailbox clusters in visible locations rather than in hidden away spots.

- Harden doors to package rooms and mail rooms using guidelines in Appendix A.
- If packages cannot be received securely at the property, consider the use of an off-site mail center.

Theft of Items from Motor Vehicles

- Take steps to reduce ability of trespassers to gain access to the site and building (see above).
- Provide good lighting of both exterior and interior parking areas. (10 to 40 Lux minimum is recommended for outdoor parking lots, 20 to 70 Lux minimum for indoor parking areas.)
- If on-site security officers are used, provide frequent patrols of the parking areas.
- Encourage residents to take steps to better protect the items kept in their vehicle:
    - Keep vehicle doors and windows locked.
    - Don't leave items displayed in vehicle that would tempt a thief.

Thefts from Resident Storage Rooms

- Take steps to reduce ability of trespassers to gain access to the building (see above).
- Harden doors to resident storage rooms using guidelines in Appendix A.
- Remove signs that identify locations of resident storage rooms.
- Consider upgrading lockers to a type that provides greater security.
- Encourage residents to use high-quality locks on their lockers.
- When it is possible to visually see into lockers, encourage residents to hide desirable items that could tempt a thief.
- Consider use of intrusion alarm system on resident storage room.

Vandalism

- Take steps to reduce ability of trespassers to gain access to the site and building (see above).
- Provide good exterior lighting in vandalism-prone areas. (10 to 20 Lux minimum is recommended).
- Remove items in and around the property that could be used to commit acts of vandalism.

Part V - Appendices

Appendix A: Best Practices for Securing Doors

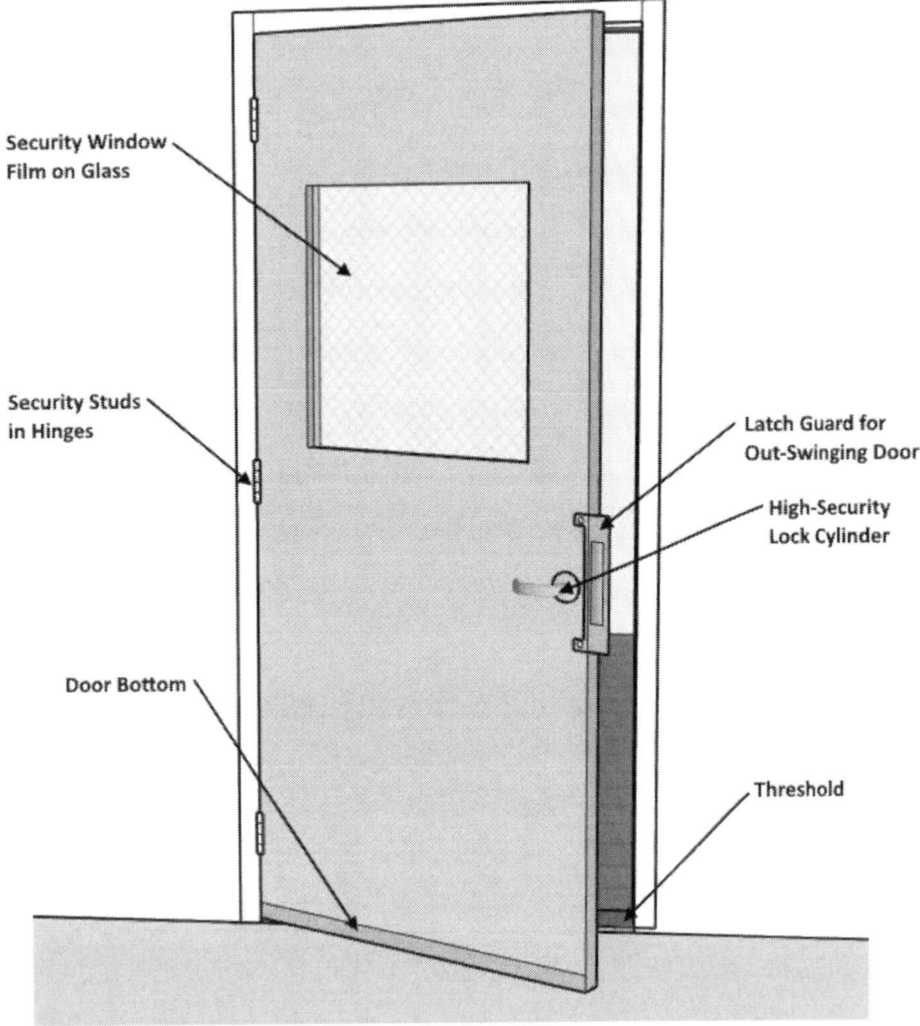

Figure A-1 - Out-Swinging Hollow-Metal Door

All hardware used should be ANSI Grade 2 or better.

For even more security:

- Use full-length astragal instead of latch guard.
- Use lever guard to protect cylindrical lock <u>or</u> replace cylindrical lock with mortise lockset or rim exit device.
- Instead of security window film, use polycarbonate glazing to replace existing glass.

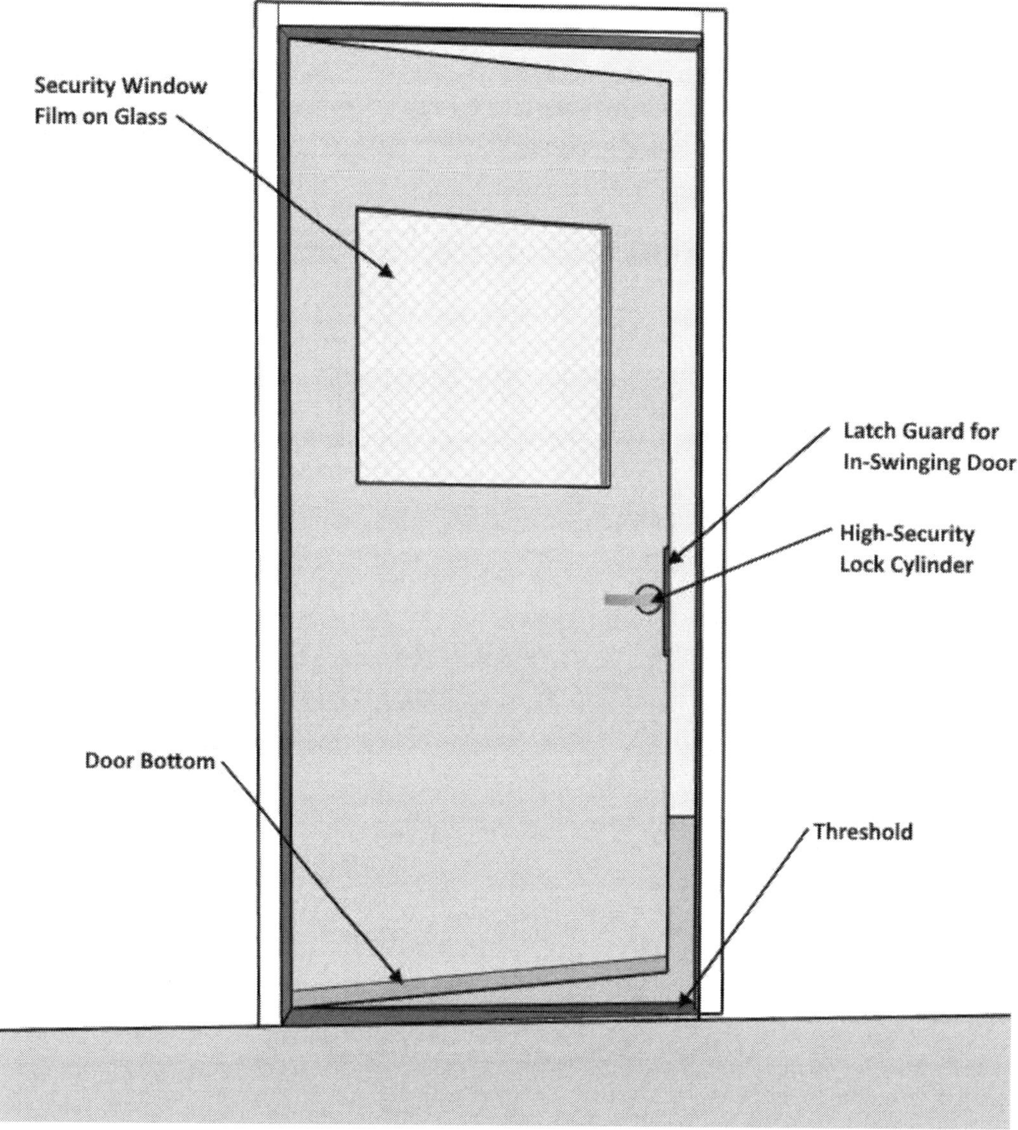

Figure A-2 - In-Swinging Hollow-Metal Door

All hardware used should be ANSI Grade 2 or better.

For even more security:

- Use full-length astragal instead of latch guard.
- Use lever guard to protect cylindrical lock <u>or</u> replace cylindrical lockset with mortise lockset.
- Instead of security window film, use polycarbonate glazing to replace existing glass.

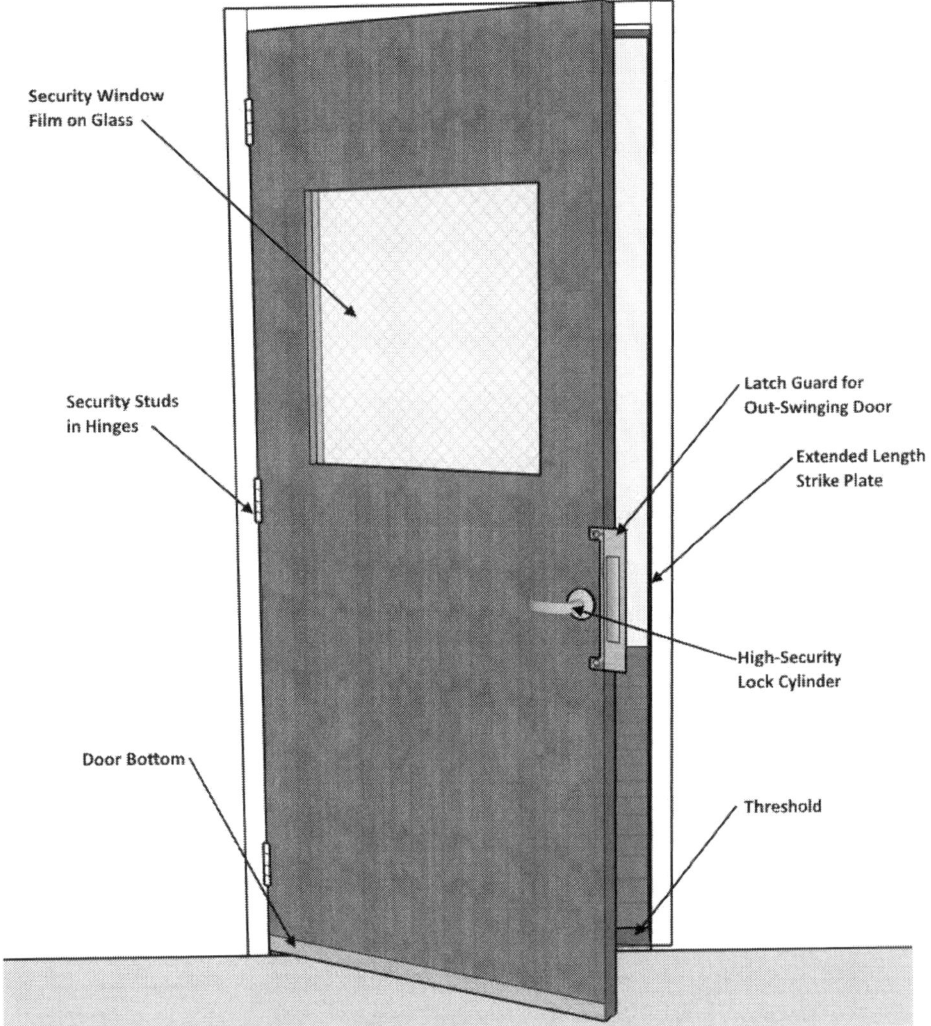

Figure A-3 - Out-Swinging Wood Door

All hardware used should be ANSI Grade 2 or better.

For even more security:

- Use full-length astragal instead of latch guard.
- Install door and frame reinforcement kit.
- Use lever guard to protect cylindrical lock <u>or</u> replace cylindrical lock with mortise lockset or rim exit device.
- Use hollow-metal door and frame instead of wood door and frame.
- Instead of security window film, use polycarbonate glazing to replace existing glass.

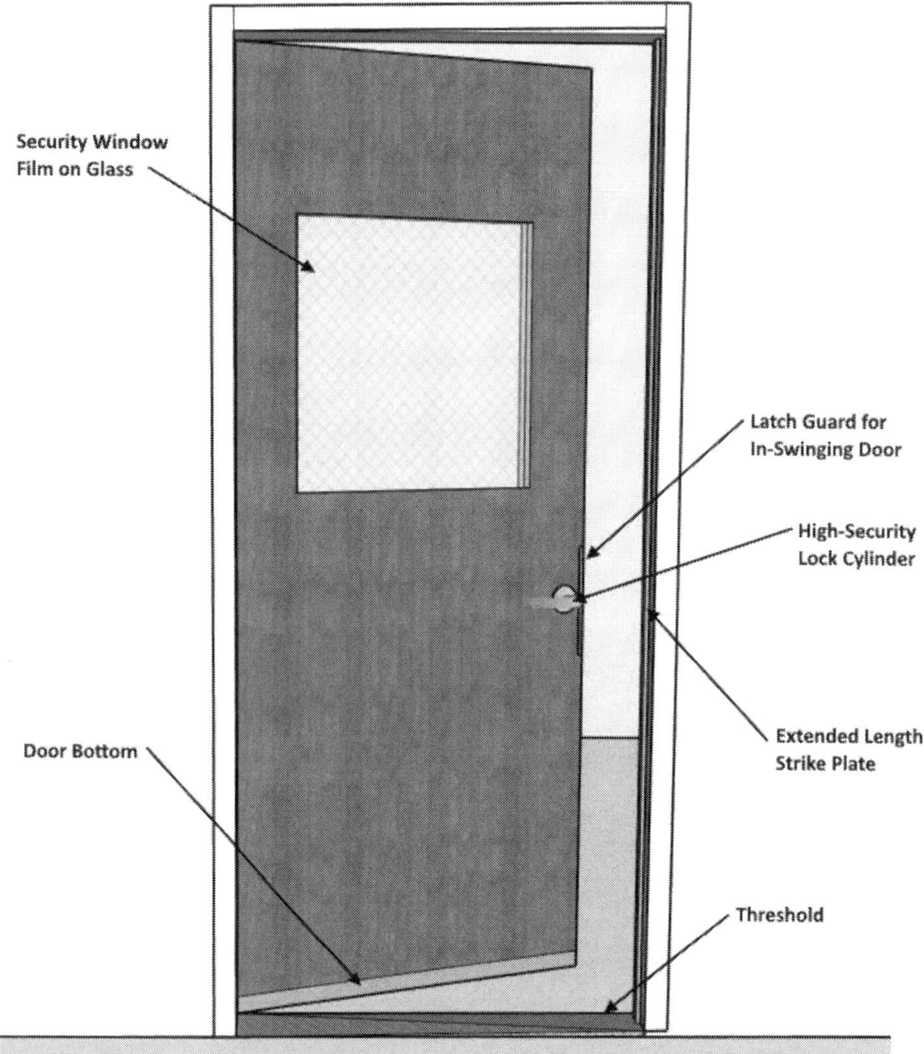

Figure A-4 - In-Swinging Wood Door

All hardware used should be ANSI Grade 2 or better.

For even more security:

- Use full-length astragal instead of latch guard.
- Install door and frame reinforcement kit.
- Use lever guard to protect cylindrical lock <u>or</u> replace cylindrical lock with mortise lockset.
- Use hollow-metal door and frame instead of wood door and frame.
- Instead of security window film, use polycarbonate glazing to replace existing glass.

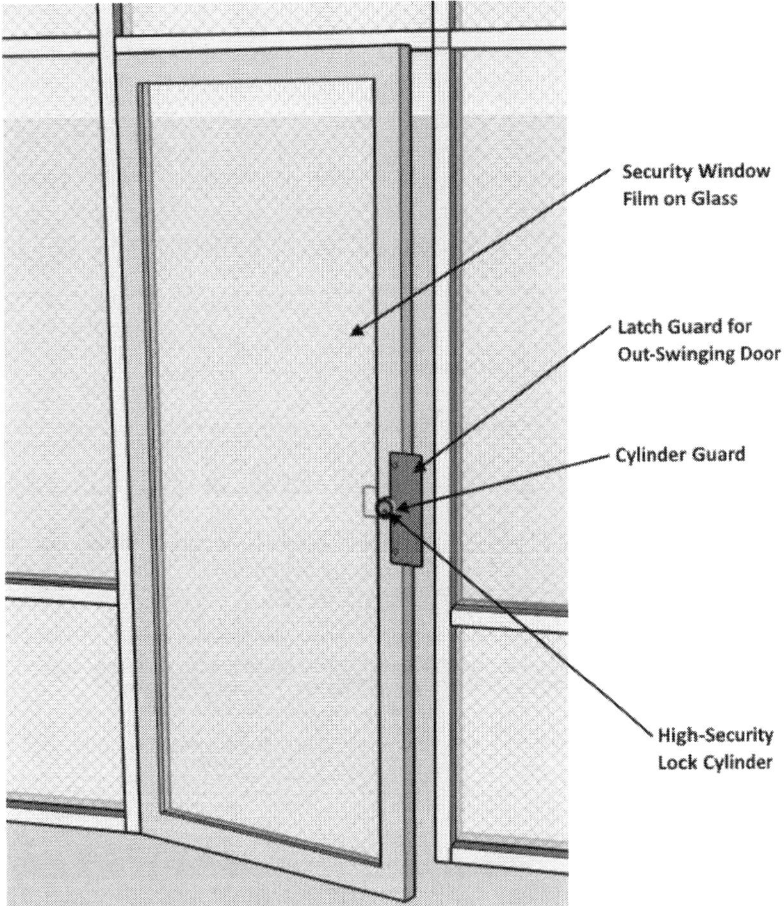

Figure A-5 - Aluminum Storefront Door

All hardware used should be ANSI Grade 2 or better.

For even more security:

- Use full-length astragal instead of latch guard.
- Provide security window film on windows surrounding door.
- Instead of security window film, use polycarbonate glazing to replace existing glass.

Appendix B: Security Survey Checklist

Property Name: ________________________________

Date of Survey: ________________________________

Page 1 of 10

Site Perimeter	Satisfactory	Needs Work	Unsatisfactory	Not Applicable
Boundaries of the site are well-defined by fencing, barriers, landscaping, or other features	☐	☐	☐	☐
Number of entry points to site is kept to a minimum	☐	☐	☐	☐
Fencing and other barriers are in good condition with no gaps or breaks	☐	☐	☐	☐
Design of fencing and barriers does not provide "ladder" to permit climbing over	☐	☐	☐	☐
Objects that would allow climb-over not stored next to fence or barrier	☐	☐	☐	☐
Automatic vehicle gates programmed to close quickly after vehicle passes	☐	☐	☐	☐
"*Wait for Gate to Close*" signs provided at automatic vehicle gates	☐	☐	☐	☐
Purpose of all exterior key boxes is known and the need to have them is confirmed	☐	☐	☐	☐
Key switches that operate gates are tamper-resistant	☐	☐	☐	☐
Telephone entry system is tamper-resistant	☐	☐	☐	☐
Pedestrian gates are in good condition and designed to prevent forced entry	☐	☐	☐	☐
Landscaping trimmed around site entrances to eliminate hiding places	☐	☐	☐	☐
Minimum light level of 30 Lux provided at site entrances	☐	☐	☐	☐
Address sign clearly visible from street	☐	☐	☐	☐
"*No Trespassing*" signs provided at site entrances and at 100' intervals around site	☐	☐	☐	☐

Parking Lots	Satisfactory	Needs Work	Unsatisfactory	Not Applicable
Boundaries of the parking lot are defined by fencing, barriers, or other features	☐	☐	☐	☐
Number of entry points to the parking lot is kept to a minimum	☐	☐	☐	☐
Minimum light level of 10 Lux is provided in parking lot	☐	☐	☐	☐
Landscaping in parking lot maintained in accordance with CPTED guidelines	☐	☐	☐	☐
"*No Trespassing*" signs provided at parking lot entrances and at 50' intervals within the parking lot itself	☐	☐	☐	☐
Parking stalls are not identified by resident name or unit number	☐	☐	☐	☐
Parking lot is well-maintained and free of debris	☐	☐	☐	☐
No junk or abandoned vehicles in parking lot	☐	☐	☐	☐
Storage of other than vehicles not allowed in parking lot	☐	☐	☐	☐

Property Name: ____________________
Date of Survey: ____________________
Page 2 of 10

	Satisfactory	Needs Work	Unsatisfactory	Not Applicable
Walkways				
Walkways visible from nearby residential units or street	☐	☐	☐	☐
Landscaping maintained in accordance with CPTED guidelines to allow natural visibility and to eliminate hiding places	☐	☐	☐	☐
Minimum light level of 10 Lux is provided along walkways	☐	☐	☐	☐
Directional signage is provided along walkways to direct people to building entrances	☐	☐	☐	☐
Walkways clear of tripping hazards	☐	☐	☐	☐
Exterior Mailboxes				
Mailboxes located in a visible place and not tucked away in a hidden location	☐	☐	☐	☐
Mailbox shelter is open on all sides and does not create a place for criminals to hide or to work without being seen.	☐	☐	☐	☐
Landscaping is maintained in accordance with CPTED guidelines to allow natural visibility of mailbox area	☐	☐	☐	☐
Minimum light level of 50 Lux is provided at mailboxes	☐	☐	☐	☐
Exterior Trash and Recycle Areas				
Trash and recycle areas located away from buildings and carports	☐	☐	☐	☐
Enclosures built around trash and recycling areas allow visibility from outside	☐	☐	☐	☐
Minimum light level of 10 Lux is provided at trash and recycle areas	☐	☐	☐	☐
Trash and recycle areas and containers are kept locked	☐	☐	☐	☐
Signs provided that state that unauthorized dumping is prohibited	☐	☐	☐	☐
Outdoor Bicycle Racks				
Bicycle racks located in visible place and not tucked away in a hidden location	☐	☐	☐	☐
Bicycle racks constructed of heavy-gauge metal (10 gauge or thicker)	☐	☐	☐	☐
Bicycle racks imbedded in concrete base or installed using tamper-resistant fasteners	☐	☐	☐	☐
Fasteners used to assemble racks are tamper-resistant or have been tack-welded	☐	☐	☐	☐

Property Name: ______________________________
Date of Survey: ______________________________
Page 3 of 10

	Satisfactory	Needs Work	Unsatisfactory	Not Applicable
Outdoor Storage				
Tools and equipment that could be used to commit burglaries is not stored in unsecured outdoor areas	☐	☐	☐	☐
Ladders are not stored outdoors or are securely locked with chain and padlock	☐	☐	☐	☐
Residents are not allowed to store items outdoors in common areas	☐	☐	☐	☐
Outdoor Swimming Pools				
Separate fencing provided to secure swimming pool area (6' high minimum)	☐	☐	☐	☐
All gates and doors to swimming pool are kept locked	☐	☐	☐	☐
Access to pool is restricted to residents and their accompanied guests	☐	☐	☐	☐
Gates to pool are in good condition and are designed to prevent forced entry	☐	☐	☐	☐
Gates close and lock reliably on their own without being pulled shut	☐	☐	☐	☐
Auto-dialing emergency telephone is provided and is in good working order	☐	☐	☐	☐
Pool safety signage is provided	☐	☐	☐	☐
Pool cover is provided to cover pool when not in use	☐	☐	☐	☐
State and local requirements for pool safety are being complied with	☐	☐	☐	☐
General Outdoor Areas				
Skate deterrent devices are provided on edges of retaining walls, planters, and railings	☐	☐	☐	☐
Outdoor benches, tables, and art objects are securely fastened to ground	☐	☐	☐	☐
Benches equipped with armrest dividers to prevent them from being used to lie down	☐	☐	☐	☐
Hidden areas that could be used as places to linger or camp are enclosed	☐	☐	☐	☐
Landscaping trimmed to allow natural surveillance using CPTED principles	☐	☐	☐	☐
Outdoor electrical outlets equipped with locking covers to prevent unauthorized use	☐	☐	☐	☐
Outdoor faucets equipped with locking devices to prevent unauthorized use	☐	☐	☐	☐

Property Name: ______________________________
Date of Survey: ______________________________
Page 4 of 10

Building Entrances	Satisfactory	Needs Work	Unsatisfactory	Not Applicable
Number of building entrances kept to a minimum	☐	☐	☐	☐
Good quality lock hardware is used on doors and it is functioning properly	☐	☐	☐	☐
Doors close and lock reliably without being pulled shut	☐	☐	☐	☐
Latch guard or astragal used to protect edge of door and latch	☐	☐	☐	☐
Threshold and door bottom is used to prevent use of under-door tool	☐	☐	☐	☐
Wood doors and frames reinforced to prevent forced entry	☐	☐	☐	☐
Motion detectors used with electromagnetic locks cannot be activated from outside of door using object inserted through door or by compressed air or smoke	☐	☐	☐	☐
Gaps between double-doors equipped with astragals to prevent use of double-door tool to activate push bar	☐	☐	☐	☐
Access control system door unlock time is not excessive	☐	☐	☐	☐
ADA door openers do not hold doors open for excessive time	☐	☐	☐	☐
Purpose of all exterior key boxes is known and the need to have them is confirmed	☐	☐	☐	☐
Telephone entry system is tamper-resistant	☐	☐	☐	☐
"*No Trespassing*" signs provided at entrances	☐	☐	☐	☐
Minimum light level of 30 Lux is provided at entrances	☐	☐	☐	☐
Landscaping trimmed around site entrances to eliminate hiding places	☐	☐	☐	☐
Windows in and around doors equipped with security window film	☐	☐	☐	☐

Exterior Windows in Common Areas				
Number of operable windows kept to a minimum	☐	☐	☐	☐
Stops installed on operable windows to limit distance that they can be opened	☐	☐	☐	☐
Supplemental locking devices added to windows that have inadequate factory locks	☐	☐	☐	☐
Windows equipped with security window film	☐	☐	☐	☐

Property Name: ____________________
Date of Survey: ____________________
Page 5 of 10

	Satisfactory	Needs Work	Unsatisfactory	Not Applicable
Ventilation Grilles				
Ventilation grilles secured with tamper-resistant fasteners or welded in place	☐	☐	☐	☐
Ventilation grilles on doors secured using carriage bolts through door	☐	☐	☐	☐
Roof Doors and Hatches				
Roof doors and hatches equipped with locks to prevent unauthorized access to roof	☐	☐	☐	☐
Mail and Drop Slots				
Need to have through-wall drop slot instead of exterior drop box is confirmed	☐	☐	☐	☐
Enclosure to fully contain area inside of drop slot is provided	☐	☐	☐	☐
Unattended Building Lobbies				
Location of lobby entrance is clearly identifiable from outside	☐	☐	☐	☐
Minimum light level of 10 Lux is provided in lobby	☐	☐	☐	☐
Only necessary furnishings and equipment kept in lobby	☐	☐	☐	☐
Higher-value items in lobby fastened to wall or floor	☐	☐	☐	☐
Lobby kept free of clutter and debris	☐	☐	☐	☐
Mail, packages, and other deliveries not allowed to be left in unsecured areas in lobby	☐	☐	☐	☐
Attended Building Lobbies				
Concierge desk is positioned so that it provides clear view of entrance and lobby	☐	☐	☐	☐
Access between lobby and secured portion of building is controlled by door or gate	☐	☐	☐	☐
Concierge desk is fully enclosed from lobby side	☐	☐	☐	☐
Panic button is provided at concierge desk and is operational	☐	☐	☐	☐
Exterior lobby doors capable of being kept locked	☐	☐	☐	☐
Concierge desk has drawers that can be locked when concierges are away	☐	☐	☐	☐

Property Name: ______________________________

Date of Survey: ______________________________

Hallways	Satisfactory	Needs Work	Unsatisfactory	Not Applicable
Minimum light level of 10 Lux distributed evenly along length of hallways	☐	☐	☐	☐
Hallways kept free of clutter and debris	☐	☐	☐	☐
Residents not allowed to place unauthorized items in hallways	☐	☐	☐	☐
Hallways free of trip hazards	☐	☐	☐	☐

Stairways	Satisfactory	Needs Work	Unsatisfactory	Not Applicable
Physical separation provided between mixed-use floors and residential floors in stairways	☐	☐	☐	☐
Physical separation provided between parking garage floors and residential floors in stairways	☐	☐	☐	☐
Minimum light level of 30 Lux is provided in stairways	☐	☐	☐	☐
Stairways well-maintained and kept free of clutter and debris	☐	☐	☐	☐
Stairways not used for storage	☐	☐	☐	☐
Stairway doors close and lock reliably without being pulled shut	☐	☐	☐	☐

Resident Storage Rooms	Satisfactory	Needs Work	Unsatisfactory	Not Applicable
Good quality lock hardware is used on doors and it is functioning properly	☐	☐	☐	☐
Doors close and lock reliably without being pulled shut	☐	☐	☐	☐
Latch guard or astragal used to protect edge of door and latch	☐	☐	☐	☐
Threshold and door bottom used to prevent use of under-door tool	☐	☐	☐	☐
Wood doors and frames reinforced to prevent forced entry	☐	☐	☐	☐
Gaps between double-doors equipped with astragals to prevent use of double-door tool to activate push bar	☐	☐	☐	☐
Signs that identify locations of storage rooms have been removed	☐	☐	☐	☐
Residents educated on the best types of locks to be used to secure lockers	☐	☐	☐	☐
Residents not allowed to store items outside of their lockers	☐	☐	☐	☐

Property Name: ______________________________
Date of Survey: ______________________________
Page 7 of 10

	Satisfactory	Needs Work	Unsatisfactory	Not Applicable
Bicycle Rooms				
Good quality lock hardware is used on doors and it is functioning properly	☐	☐	☐	☐
Doors close and lock reliably without being pulled shut	☐	☐	☐	☐
Latch guard or astragal used to protect edge of door and latch	☐	☐	☐	☐
Threshold and door bottom used to prevent use of under-door tool	☐	☐	☐	☐
Wood doors and frames reinforced to prevent forced entry	☐	☐	☐	☐
Gaps between double-doors equipped with astragals to prevent use of double-door tool to activate push bar	☐	☐	☐	☐
Signs that identify locations of bicycle rooms have been removed	☐	☐	☐	☐
Bicycle racks specifically designed to provide security are used	☐	☐	☐	☐
Bicycle racks securely fastened to wall or floor using tamper-resistant fasteners	☐	☐	☐	☐
Fasteners used to assemble racks are tamper-resistant or have been tack-welded	☐	☐	☐	☐
Residents educated on the best types of locks to be used to secure bicycles	☐	☐	☐	☐
Amenity Rooms				
Good quality lock hardware is used on doors and it is functioning properly	☐	☐	☐	☐
Doors close and lock reliably without being pulled shut	☐	☐	☐	☐
Doors kept locked to limit access to residents and their accompanied guests	☐	☐	☐	☐
Building Office				
Good quality lock hardware is used on doors and it is functioning properly	☐	☐	☐	☐
Latch guard or astragal used to protect edge of door and latch	☐	☐	☐	☐
Threshold and door bottom used to prevent use of under-door tool	☐	☐	☐	☐
Wood doors and frames reinforced to prevent forced entry	☐	☐	☐	☐
Locked room provided inside office for storage of files, keys, and access cards	☐	☐	☐	☐
Locking file cabinet used to store confidential files	☐	☐	☐	☐
Locked cabinet or safe used to store keys	☐	☐	☐	☐
Office equipped with intrusion alarm system and it is operational	☐	☐	☐	☐
Panic buttons provided for office staff and are operational	☐	☐	☐	☐
Security window film provided on office windows	☐	☐	☐	☐

Property Name: ____
Date of Survey: ____
Page 8 of 10

	Satisfactory	Needs Work	Unsatisfactory	Not Applicable
Mailboxes				
Mailboxes located in visible place and not tucked away in a hidden location	☐	☐	☐	☐
Mailboxes located in locked mail room	☐	☐	☐	☐
Mail, packages, and other deliveries not allowed to be left in unsecured areas	☐	☐	☐	☐
Package Rooms				
Good quality lock hardware is used on doors and it is functioning properly	☐	☐	☐	☐
Latch guard or astragal used to protect edge of door and latch	☐	☐	☐	☐
Threshold and door bottom used to prevent use of under-door tool	☐	☐	☐	☐
Wood doors and frames reinforced to prevent forced entry	☐	☐	☐	☐
Locking cabinets used to store packages	☐	☐	☐	☐
Automated package locker system or automated parcel room used	☐	☐	☐	☐
Parking Garages				
High-quality overhead doors used at parking garage entrances	☐	☐	☐	☐
Rolling code type wireless controls used to operate overhead doors	☐	☐	☐	☐
Proximity card readers or RFID readers used to operate overhead doors	☐	☐	☐	☐
Door operators do not hold doors open for excessive time	☐	☐	☐	☐
"Wait for Door to Close" signs provided on both sides of overhead doors	☐	☐	☐	☐
Landscaping trimmed around garage entrances to eliminate hiding places	☐	☐	☐	☐
High-quality lock hardware used on exterior pedestrian doors to garage	☐	☐	☐	☐
Latch guard or astragal used to protect edge of door and latch on pedestrian doors	☐	☐	☐	☐
Inside button stations that operate overhead doors cannot be activated from outside	☐	☐	☐	☐
Emergency release mechanisms on overhead doors cannot be activated from outside	☐	☐	☐	☐
Minimum light level of 30 Lux is provided at garage entrances	☐	☐	☐	☐
Minimum light level of 20 Lux is provided in interior areas of garage	☐	☐	☐	☐
Parking stalls are not identified by resident name or unit number	☐	☐	☐	☐
Parking garage is well-maintained and free of debris	☐	☐	☐	☐
Residents not allowed to store items openly in unsecured areas of garage	☐	☐	☐	☐

Property Name: ____________________
Date of Survey: ____________________
Page 9 of 10

	Satisfactory	Needs Work	Unsatisfactory	Not Applicable
Residential Units				
Good quality lock hardware is used on doors and it is functioning properly	☐	☐	☐	☐
Latch guard or astragal used to protect edge of door and latch	☐	☐	☐	☐
Wood doors and frames reinforced to prevent forced entry	☐	☐	☐	☐
Peephole viewer or video doorbell provided on entry door	☐	☐	☐	☐
Address or unit number clearly visible from outside of unit	☐	☐	☐	☐
Stops installed on operable windows to limit distance that they can be opened	☐	☐	☐	☐
Supplemental locking devices added to windows that have inadequate factory locks	☐	☐	☐	☐
Landscaping outside of ground floor units is maintained to allow visibility	☐	☐	☐	☐
Spare keys not stored in unsecured area outside of unit	☐	☐	☐	☐
Valuable items not stored on exterior decks and patios	☐	☐	☐	☐
Inventory of home assets has been prepared	☐	☐	☐	☐
Family emergency plan has been developed and practiced by family members	☐	☐	☐	☐
Security Policies and Procedures				
Written *Security Manual* with updated policies and procedures has been developed	☐	☐	☐	☐
Written *Resident's Security Guide* has been created and issued to all residents.	☐	☐	☐	☐
Residents have received security awareness training	☐	☐	☐	☐
Employees have received security awareness training	☐	☐	☐	☐
Crime prevention workshops are held on a periodic basis	☐	☐	☐	☐
Video Surveillance Systems				
Cameras provide satisfactory images during day	☐	☐	☐	☐
Cameras provide satisfactory images at night	☐	☐	☐	☐
Cameras point in intended direction	☐	☐	☐	☐
Camera views not obstructed by landscaping	☐	☐	☐	☐
Camera domes and lenses are clean and don't obscure views	☐	☐	☐	☐
Cameras are accurately named in NVR or VMS software	☐	☐	☐	☐
Video monitors are in good condition	☐	☐	☐	☐
Remote video viewing features work correctly	☐	☐	☐	☐
Video recording and retrieval functions tested and are working satisfactorily	☐	☐	☐	☐

Property Name: ____________________
Date of Survey: ____________________
Page 10 of 10

	Satisfactory	Needs Work	Unsatisfactory	Not Applicable
Access Control Systems				
Card reader or keypad is in satisfactory condition and works properly	☐	☐	☐	☐
Electric lock hardware is in satisfactory condition and works properly	☐	☐	☐	☐
Door monitoring features (door-forced and door-propped alarms) working correctly	☐	☐	☐	☐
Access controlled doors close and lock reliably on their own	☐	☐	☐	☐
Doors are accurately named in access control software	☐	☐	☐	☐
Access control reporting feature works correctly	☐	☐	☐	☐
Access control alarm notification feature works correctly	☐	☐	☐	☐
Intrusion Alarm Systems				
All alarm devices physically inspected and appear to be in good condition	☐	☐	☐	☐
All alarm detection devices tested and report correctly to alarm monitoring center	☐	☐	☐	☐
Motion detectors are not blocked	☐	☐	☐	☐
Audible and visual alarm notification devices tested and are working correctly	☐	☐	☐	☐
All authorized users have code to system and have been instructed on its use	☐	☐	☐	☐
Codes for users who no longer require access have been deleted	☐	☐	☐	☐
Codes not visibly posted near keypad arming station	☐	☐	☐	☐
Telephone Entry Systems				
Standard factory lock on panel replaced with high-security lock	☐	☐	☐	☐
Supplemental locking devices provided to better secure panel	☐	☐	☐	☐
Default programming codes not used	☐	☐	☐	☐
Use of PIN codes to allow entry is prohibited or strictly limited	☐	☐	☐	☐
Unneeded PIN codes have been deleted from system	☐	☐	☐	☐

Appendix C: Security Manual Outline

The following is an outline of the recommended contents of a Security Manual for a typical multifamily property. Not all contents will be applicable to all properties.

This outline can be used as a starting point in developing a Security Manual for your multifamily property. Information and suggestions for developing content for each topic can be found in the relevant chapters within the main body of this book.

SECURITY MANUAL FOR
ACME CONDOMINIUM

1. Goals of Security Program.
2. Responsibility for Security.
3. Day-to-Day Security Operations.
4. Resident Access.
5. Visitor Access.
6. Contactor and Vendor Access.
7. Issuance of Temporary Keys.
8. Lost or Stolen Keys or Access Cards.
9. Keys to Residential Units.
10. Construction Projects.
11. Mail and Deliveries.
12. Vehicle Permits.
13. Bicycle Permits.
14. Move-ins and Move-Outs.
15. Short-Term Rentals.
16. Security Incident Reporting.
17. Security Incident Follow-Up.
18. Notification to Residents About Security.
19. Responding to Resident Complaints About Security.
20. Relationships with Law Enforcement.
21. Crime-Free Housing Program.
22. Security Inspections of Residential Units.
23. Security System Inspection and Maintenance.
24. Video Surveillance System Policies.
25. Resident Alarm System Policies.
26. Resident Screening Process.

27. Background Checks for Employees.
28. Vendor Credentialling Service.
29. Lost and Found Items.
30. Procedures to Avoid Overselling of Security.
31. Policies for Handling Domestic Situations.
32. Security Awareness Training for Residents.
33. Security Awareness Training for Employees.
34. Use of Security Officers.

Appendix D: Example of Resident's Security Guide

The following is an example of a *Resident's Security Guide* for a typical multifamily property.

This example can be used as a starting point in developing a *Resident's Security Guide* for your property.

ACME CONDOMINIUM
RESIDENT'S SECURITY GUIDE

Section 1: Introduction

Purpose of This Guide

This Guide provides important information to residents about the security policies and procedures that are in use at the Acme Condominium. This guide is intended to provide guidance to residents on how security issues are to be handled on a daily basis at the Condominium.

This guide contains our current security policies and procedures and supersedes all verbal or written security directives that you may have received in the past.

Section 2: Responsibilities for Security

General

Providing effective security at the Condominium requires cooperation on the part of everyone, including homeowners, renters, employees of the property management company, and contractors. Even the best security systems cannot provide effective security of the building without the active participation and support of the people who live and work in the building on a daily basis.

Homeowner's Association

The Acme Condominium is governed by an association of homeowners known as the "Acme Homeowners Association". The elected members of this association make executive level decisions concerning operation of the Condominium.

Security responsibilities of the Homeowner's Association include:

- Establishing security policies and procedures.
- Allocating resources for security improvements and ongoing maintenance of the security program.
- Providing oversight of the property management company.

Property Management Company

Daily management of the condominium is performed by XYZ Associates, a professional property management company. XYZ employs a full-time Property Manager who is assigned to this condominium. The Property Manager coordinates with the Homeowner's Association and is responsible for the management of all on-site services, including security.

Security responsibilities of the Property Manager include:

- Daily management of the security program at the Condominium.
- Enforcing security policies and procedures.
- Programming and management of the building security systems including security intercom, access control system and video surveillance system.
- Issuing common area building keys and garage door transmitters.
- Maintaining the building and arranging for repairs of defective equipment.

Resident's Responsibilities

Residents of the Acme Condominium, including both homeowner's and renters, play a vital role in protecting the building and its occupants. Security responsibilities of residents include:

- Complying with established security policies and procedures.
- Promptly reporting crimes, suspicious activity, and security violations.
- Taking precautions to not let unauthorized people into the building.
- Promptly notifying the Property Manager of any changes in the occupancy status of their residential unit (move-in, move-out, new renter, etc.).

The security responsibilities of residents are explained in greater detail within this Guide.

Section 3: Limitations of Security Program

While many steps have been taken to reduce the risk of criminal activity occurring at the Acme Condominium, nothing can guarantee personal safety and security and no type of security program can provide protection against all crime.

Residents of the Acme Condominium face security risks that are the same as residents that live in other properties in the surrounding community. Neither the Acme Homeowner's Association or the property management company make representations that this is a "secure" or "crime free" building and are not responsible for criminal acts occurring on the property.

Homeowners who are renting their units should be careful not to oversell the level of security provided at the building when marketing their unit.

Section 4: Reporting Crimes and Security Incidents

Reporting Crimes and Suspicious Activity

Crimes in progress and suspicious people or activity should be immediately reported to the Acme Police by calling 911. In general, if there is any doubt about whether a situation should be reported, the police would prefer that you report it rather than to not report it.

If you should arrive home and there are signs that your unit has been broken into, do not enter, but instead move to a safe place and call the police. There is always a chance that the burglar may still be on the premises.

All burglaries, thefts and vandalism should always be reported to the police. After notifying the police, please notify the Property Manager of the incident by either telephone or email. To effectively manage the security program, it is important that the Property Manager be aware of all criminal activity occurring at the building.

Reporting Security Violations

Examples of security violations include people propping open exterior doors, letting unknown people into the building, driving out of the parking garage without waiting for the door to close, or the loaning out of keys or garage door transmitters to other parties.

All security violations observed by residents should be promptly reported to the Property Manager. If you see something that compromises building security, report it. Your name will be kept confidential.

Reporting Defective Equipment or Property Damage

Residents should promptly report any defective equipment or signs of damage to the building to the Property Manager. This can include burned-out lights in common areas, exterior doors that don't close or latch properly, or signs of graffiti or vandalism.

Section 5: Keys and Garage Door Transmitters

Keys to Residential Units

The locks and keys used on the doors of residential units are the responsibility of the individual homeowner. For best results, it is recommended that "building standard" Sargent locksets be used on all doors, however homeowners are free to use whatever type of lock that they feel best meets their needs.

Homeowners are asked (but are not required) to provide one copy of their exterior door key to the Property Manager. This key will be stored in a secure lockbox and only used in an emergency or at the request of the homeowner.

Common Area Keys

All exterior building doors and doors that lead to common areas (storage rooms, recreational room, pool area, trash room, etc.) are keyed using a high-security Medeco lock system. This lock system is managed by the Property Manager who is responsible for issuing keys to all residents.

The following procedures shall apply:

- All common area keys are assigned to individual people, not to residential units. If a unit has multiple residents, each will be assigned a specific key.
- The cost of each key is $100. Each person is limited to receiving only one key. There will be no provisions made to provide "spare" keys to residents.

- Each person receiving a key is required to individually sign for it. Records will be kept showing which key was assigned to which person.
- Common area keys will be issued to renters by the Property Manager, not by the individual homeowner.
- Contractors who require common area keys, including those hired directly by the homeowner, will obtain them only through the Property Manager.
- Common area keys should not be issued to real estate agents or placed in real estate lockboxes. (Please make arrangements for real estate agent access with the Property Manager.)
- Keys should never be loaned out to others. If you have a guest who will be staying with you for an extended visit, a temporary key assigned to them may be obtained from the Property Manager.

Residents should treat their keys as they would any other piece of valuable property such as jewelry or cash. A lost or stolen key may require the rekeying of the locks and the reissuance of new keys to all residents. This can cost more than $1,500.

The Homeowner's Association reserves the right to charge individual homeowners for the costs of rekeying in cases of negligence or carelessness.

Garage Door Transmitters

The overhead doors to the parking garage are controlled using garage door transmitters. These transmitters will be issued by the Property Manager to those residents who have assigned parking spaces within the garage. The cost of each transmitter is $150.

Reporting Lost or Stolen Keys or Garage Door Transmitters

Lost or stolen keys or garage door transmitters should be immediately reported to the Property Manager. At night or on weekends, please use the 24-hour emergency contact number listed on the inside front cover of this Guide.

Section 6: Telephone Entry System

The building is equipped with a telephone entry intercom system located at the main lobby entrance. This system allows visitors to contact residents when they arrive at the building. The system will dial a telephone number designated by the resident. Upon receiving the call, the resident may unlock the door for the visitor by pressing the number "9" on the telephone.

The following procedures shall apply:

- Provide the telephone number that you wish to use to the Property Manager so that he may program it into the system. If you change your number, be sure to notify the Property Manager.
- Don't unlock the door unless you have positively confirmed the identity of the visitor. When in doubt, go to the lobby to visually verify who is at the door.
- Don't unlock the door for people who claim to be visiting or making deliveries to other residents - only let in people who you personally know.

Section 7: Visitors and Contractors

Residents are responsible for their visitors, guests, and any contractors that they have allowed into the building. The following procedures shall apply:

- Visitors or contractors who are not well-known to you should be escorted in and out of the building.
- Visitors are only welcome to use the recreational and pool areas while a resident is present.
- Visitors and contractors must park on the street outside of the building and are not allowed to park in the parking garage.
- Contractors and delivery drivers should never be allowed to prop open building doors while loading or unloading.

Section 8: Mail Room

The building contains a mailroom which is located next to the main lobby entrance. The mailroom contains locked individual mailboxes for each residential unit. The mailroom also contains a box for outgoing mail.

Many of the delivery services such as the US Postal Service, UPS and FedEx have recently adopted the practice of leaving packages for residents in the mail room next to the mailboxes. Residents are advised that this practice is not encouraged by the Homeowner's Association or the Property Manager. The mailroom is not secure and not a safe place to leave packages unattended.

Residents who are not at home when packages are delivered should make other arrangements to assure that their packages are safe. This may include having packages delivered to a neighbor who is at home, receiving packages at work, or using some type of private mailbox service

Section 9: Move-In and Move-Out Procedures

Residents who are moving in or out of the building should observe the following procedures:

- Provide not less than seven days advance notice to the Property Manager prior to moving in or out of the building.
- Don't allow movers to prop open exterior doors when loading or unloading unless someone is standing constant watch over the doors.
- Use protective pads as needed to protect walls, stairways, and the elevator.
- Be respectful of other residents; don't obstruct entrances or hallways. Don't tie up the elevator for extended periods - take a break to let others use it.
- Return common area keys and garage door transmitters to the Property Manager after you have vacated your unit.

Section 10: Resident Security Awareness

The actions of residents can make a big difference in just how secure the building will be.

Buildings where the residents are careless about security often are plagued by crime problems, even in low-crime neighborhoods. Conversely, buildings where residents take simple precautions to protect themselves and their property often experience far lower rates of crime than similar properties, even in high-crime areas.

The following are some steps that you can take to provide an improved level of security:

Security of Your Residential Unit

- Always lock the entrance door to your unit. If the door is equipped with a deadbolt lock, use it.
- Don't hide a spare key outside of your unit. No matter how clever you think your hiding place is, it can be obvious to an experienced burglar.
- Don't leave patio doors or windows unlocked when you leave, even if your unit is on an upper floor.
- Don't store valuable items such as bicycles on your patio where they can be seen from the street or alley.

Security of Your Automobile

- Always keep your car locked with the windows fully rolled up.
- Don't leave valuables displayed visibly in your car. Many car prowlers will break into a car for something as small as a handful of coins.

Security When Entering and Exiting the Building on Foot

- Before entering or exiting, look for people standing outside the door. If someone is standing outside the door and you don't feel comfortable, call a friend or neighbor in the building, and ask him or her to accompany you in or out.
- Don't let unknown people slip into the building as you leave or enter, no matter how friendly they may seem or what story they may tell.
- Be sure doors and gates close and latch behind you as you leave.
- Don't prop exterior doors open for any reason.

Security When Entering and Exiting the Garage by Car

- A rule for good overhead door safety and security is: "If you can't see it, don't open it." Residents should only start opening the overhead door when their car is close enough to the door so that they can see it and anyone who is standing around it.
- When using the automatic garage doors, pause to allow doors to close before driving off both when entering and exiting. Our doors take about 20 seconds to fully close - waiting this short period of time is a small price to pay for improved building security.
- Be on the lookout for people who appear to be standing outside of the overhead door waiting for it to open.

Section 11: Peddlers and Solicitors

Peddlers, door-to-door salespeople, and solicitors of any type are not permitted in the building at any time.

Section 12: Video Surveillance System

Purpose

The Acme Condominium has installed a video surveillance system at the building. The video surveillance system is used to record access at the building entrances and in the parking garage.

The purpose of the video surveillance system is to allow the after-the-fact investigation of crimes committed on the property. The video surveillance system is not monitored on a real-time basis (no one is watching the cameras) and is not intended to detect or prevent crimes as they are occurring.

Video Surveillance Recording

All video surveillance cameras are capable of being recorded continuously by a digital video recording system. Recorded video is used exclusively for the investigation of crimes and not for other purposes. The Property Manager is responsible for the management of the video surveillance system and has exclusive control of the release of video recordings produced by this system.

Recorded video is not made directly available to residents or homeowners. In the event that a crime occurs, residents should report the incident to the police. If the police believe that recorded video from the building's cameras would assist in the investigation of the crime, a permanent video clip of the incident will be produced and made available to the police officer who is investigating the case.

Recorded video is stored for a period of thirty days.

Section 13: Securing Your Bicycle

Bicycle theft is a significant problem at multifamily properties in urban areas. Many bicycles have a high resale value and can be readily turned into cash by thieves. Many bicycle thieves are semi-professional and use advanced tools and techniques to allow them to steal bicycles quickly and efficiently.

The following are some suggestions for the securing of bicycles:

- All bicycles should always be kept locked to a bike rack or other fixed anchor point.
- The bicycle lock should be placed to protect the most valuable portions of the bicycle first. In most cases, this will be the bicycle frame and back wheel. This is where the primary lock should be placed. If desired, a secondary locking device can be placed to protect the front wheel.
- Not all bicycle locks are the same. Some locks cost as little as $3, while some cost $200 or more. It is suggested that a heavy-duty "U-Lock" type of lock be used as the primary bicycle lock. For best security, the size of the locking shackle should be at least 16mm thick. As a general rule, the heavier and thicker the shackle, the better protection it provides.
- A secondary locking device can be used to secure the front wheel. One popular method is to use a double looped armored cable that is looped through the front wheel and then attached to the U-Lock that is used to secure the frame and back wheel. (See Figure D-1 below). Another method is to use a second U-Lock that is attached between the frame and front wheel.
- Most inexpensive bicycle locks that use cables or chains can be easily defeated. Locks that use a combination dial rather than a key are especially vulnerable and can be quickly compromised by even an inexperienced thief.
- It should be understood that no lock is impenetrable if the thief has the skills, the right tools, and enough time. The goal is to provide protection against the common thief, and to make your bicycle look so secure that the bad guy chooses to move along to an easier target.

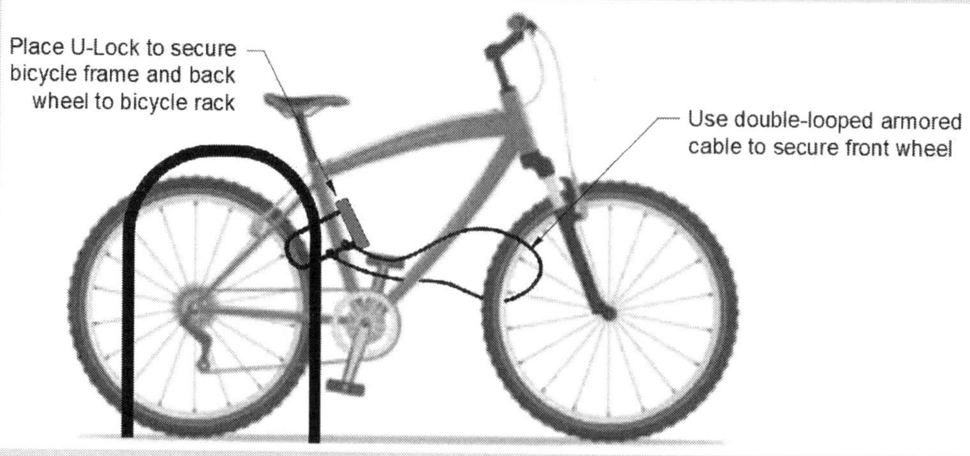

Figure D-1 - Locking Your Bicycle

Section 14: Personal Safety and Security

General Principals

- Trust your instincts and intuition – if it doesn't feel right, it probably isn't.
- Make good choices, error on the side of caution.
- Don't take unnecessary risks just to save a little time or money or to maintain your pride.
- Don't think that you are already too "street savvy" to have a need to take reasonable precautions.

Avoid Becoming a Victim

- Most predatory acts are opportunistic. How you look and carry yourself can determine whether or not a predator views you as a good target.
- Things that make you more likely to be a target:
  - Displaying high-value items such as cash, jewelry, camera, or laptop computer bag.
  - Driving a new or expensive car.
  - Being inappropriately dressed (overdressed) for surroundings.
  - Appearing lost, distracted, or unaware of surroundings.
  - Appearing vulnerable (elderly, frail, sick, intoxicated)
  - Being alone.
  - Being in a dark or isolated place.

Before You Leave Home

- Plan your trip and take only those items that you feel are absolutely necessary to have with you. Avoid carrying items that will attract attention or increase risks.
- Carry only a minimum number of credit cards and a limited amount of cash.
- Keep some emergency money and your keys in a location separate from your wallet or purse.
- At home, keep a current list of all of your credit card numbers, along with the telephone numbers needed to quickly cancel them.
- Dress appropriately for your surroundings; it's better to be underdressed than overdressed.
- Wear shoes that will allow you to run if necessary.
- Not carrying a purse greatly reduces your risk of robbery. Consider carrying your items in a fanny pack, or a wallet that can be placed in your pocket.

When Walking

- One of the best deterrents against street crime is the "buddy system". Lone people are the preferred targets of criminals. Walk in pairs or with a group whenever possible.
- Be alert and aware of people around you.

- Walk deliberately and confidently. Keep your head up.
- Avoid distractions such as talking on a cell phone or listening to loud music.
- Stay on busy, well-lighted streets whenever possible. Avoid short-cuts through unsafe areas – it's better to walk a longer distance on a safer route.
- Walk down the middle of the sidewalk, facing oncoming traffic if possible.
- Clutch your purse close to you. Avoid hanging your purse on your shoulder where it is a tempting target. Avoid having purse straps wrapped around your neck or wrist to prevent being injured when someone grabs your purse.
- If a person or car seems to be following you, stay on the sidewalk and continue walking. If you feel threatened, head toward a busy street, a business that is open, or a well-lit area with other people.

When Driving

- Keep your car windows rolled up and doors locked when in urban areas.
- Don't stop or roll down your windows to engage in conversations with strangers.
- Don't get involved in "road rage" situations; back-off and get away from an aggressive vehicle even though you may feel that you have the right of way.
- Scan your surroundings before you drive into a parking area. Observe people who seem to be lingering around or appear suspicious. Drive on if you don't feel comfortable.
- Park in well-lit, visible areas with lots of traffic when possible. Avoid remote, dark, or isolated parking areas. Its sometime better to park a little farther away in a safe parking area than it is to park in an unsafe parking area that is close by.
- When getting out of a car, stay observant, especially when removing items from your seats or trunk. Don't get so caught up in what you are doing that you become oblivious to what's going on around you.
- If your car has an alarm system that can be activated by your key fob, carry it in your hand when you are walking to and from your car. Hover your finger over the activate button so that it can be quickly pressed.
- When leaving, quickly get in your car and drive away. Don't linger in parking areas.

When Taking the Bus

- Plan your trip so that you spend only a minimum amount of time at the bus stop. Wait in a nearby store or coffee shop if necessary.
- Choose bus stops and transfer points in well-lit, well-trafficked areas when possible.
- Walk to the next bus stop if the closest one doesn't feel safe.
- Sit close to the front of the bus near the driver when possible.
- If someone sitting next to you is making you feel uncomfortable, get up and move.
- Alert the bus driver and other passengers if you are being harassed or threatened. Don't be afraid to be loud or to make a scene.

- If a stranger who seems to have an interest in you appears to be getting off at the same stop as you, stay on the bus and ride to the next stop. Alert the driver if necessary.

Signs That a Person May Be Potential Trouble

- People who are hanging around or lingering on the street for no apparent reason.
- People who start to move towards you once they see you or change direction to follow you.
- People who display aggressive behavior; won't respect your space, won't take no for an answer.
- People who use ploys to get closer to you, such as asking for change, time, or directions.
- People who appear to be drunk, high, or mentally-ill.

When Encountered by a Potential Predator

- Avoid encountering and keep your distance from a potential predator if possible. Try to get away if you can.
- Predators take advantage of people not wanting to seem rude. If uncomfortable, disengage with the predator and make it clear that you don't want further contact: ("I've got to go"; "get away", "stop", etc.).
- Don't be afraid to ask people around you for help.
- Immediately comply with demands of a predator who displays a weapon. Give up valuables if asked. No possession is worth your life. Avoid making sudden movements and don't push or strike a predator that is armed.

If You are Physically Attacked

- Think about what you would do if attacked in advance. Mentally rehearse scenarios based on your physical condition and level of capability.
- Yell, scream, and make a lot of noise to attract attention.
- Some self-defense experts consider an attacker's nose and throat to be the most vulnerable spots on the body. Quick jabs to either area may render an attacker disabled long enough to get away. Despite popular opinion, it is difficult to effectively render an attack to a man's groin.
- Do whatever possible to keep from being taken away from the scene by a predator. Chances of survival go way down when you are moved to a second location.

Defensive Weapons

- Your best defensive weapon is your brain.
- The use of other defensive weapons is a personal choice.
- Only carry weapons that you have been trained on and are prepared to use.
- Personal alarms make a loud noise when activated and may alert passersby and disorient your attacker. They are non-lethal and the best choice for people who are not prepared to carry another type of weapon.

- Pepper spray (sometimes called "mace" or "tear gas") is used by many people as a defensive weapon. If you choose to carry pepper spray, keep the following in mind:
    - Be sure that pepper spray is legal in the jurisdiction in which you intend to carry it.
    - Pepper spray works best when carried in your hand and "at the ready". It is useless if just carried in a purse or glove box of a car because you won't have time to use it when you need it.
    - Pepper spray requires practice in order to be effectively used. Some manufacturers offer inert (non-functioning) sprays for practice purposes.
    - Pepper spray is not effective on every person – some people (especially if drunk or high) can continue to function even after being sprayed.
    - Using pepper spray may enrage your attacker, making him or her even more dangerous.
    - Pepper spray can be blown back at you by the wind, making you even more vulnerable to your attacker.
    - Pepper spray should never be used against someone armed with a weapon such as a gun or knife.
    - A good quality, professional grade pepper spray should be used. Pepper sprays have a limited life and should be periodically replaced prior to the expiration date shown on the can.

Other Tips

- If you normally walk or take a bus home, consider getting a ride from a friend or calling a cab or rideshare when working extra late or when the environment doesn't feel safe. Paying for a ride can be cheap insurance.
- Let other people know where you are going, how you are going to get there, and when you expect to arrive. Consider developing a system to check in with a friend or coworker by phone when you arrive and depart your destination.
- If you have a cell phone with a headset, consider placing a call to a friend or coworker who can stay on the line while you are walking to or from your car or bus stop. (But don't get so engaged in conversation that you become unaware of your surroundings.)
- Consider having a friend or coworker meet you when you arrive at your destination.
- Carry your car and house keys in a convenient location and have them out and ready long before you reach the door. Fumbling for keys at the last minute can make you vulnerable.
- Consider the use of smartphone apps that can automatically send an emergency call for help as well as your last known location when a button on your screen is pressed. Many of these apps are available for a low cost or for free.
- Criminals who choose to specifically attack people for their political or professional activities almost always conduct advance surveillance on their intended victim days or even weeks in advance of their attack. Pay close attention to people who appear to be following you or watching you or taking pictures of your home or automobile. Be observant of unknown vehicles parked outside of your home. Talk to your neighbors and family and ask them to let you know immediately when a suspicious person seems to be lingering around your home.

Index

3

3 Ds of Security ... 18

A

Access control systems ... 127–43
- access cards ... 133
- biometric ... 136
- card readers ... 133
- cloud-based ... 131
- control panels ... 129
- electronic keypad locks ... 128
- elevator control ... 141
- hybrid ... 132
- keypads ... 135
- license plate recognition (LPR) ... 143
- mechanical pushbutton locks ... 127
- mobile devices as access credentials ... 135
- RFID readers ... 137
- server computer ... 130
- server-based ... 129
- wireless radio controls ... 138

ADA door openers ... 93
Alarm companies ... 319
Alarm systems ... 153–63
- door-propped-open alarms ... 161
- exit alarms ... 160
- high or low temperature ... 160
- intrusion alarm ... 153
- notification options ... 161
- object protection ... 157
- outdoor protection ... 157
- panic alarms ... 158
- water leak detection ... 160

Amazon Key ... 143
Amenity buildings ... 204
Amenity rooms ... 223
ANSI grades of hardware ... 84
Astragals ... 95
Automated gate companies ... 319

B

Badges
- employee ... 267
- visitor ... 272

Balanced Approach to Security ... 18
Barbed wire ... *See* Fencing
Barrier arm gates ... 45
Basic Crime Theory ... 17
Benches and tables ... 202
Best practices for securing doors ... 345
Bicycle cages ... 223
Bicycle racks
- indoor ... 222
- outdoor ... 203

Bicycle rooms ... 223
Bicycle storage ... 222
Bicycle theft ... 340
Bolts ... 90
Building entrances ... 207
Building lobbies
- attended ... 216
- unattended ... 215

Building office ... 223
Building security, common points of weakness in ... 211
Burglary of residential units ... 340
Buying security products and services ... 319
- authorized dealer model ... 322
- buying online ... 330
- components that make up a security system ... 323
- distributor model ... 322
- do-it-yourself products ... 329
- gray-market products ... 330
- request-for-proposal (RFP) process ... 324

C

Carports ... 197
Concentric Circles of Protection ... 19
Contract security companies ... 319
Courtesy patrol versus security ... 312
Courtyards ... 199
CPTED *See* Crime Prevention Through Environmental Design
Crime data
- from neighboring properties ... 8
- from police ... 9

Crime forecast reports ... 11
Crime Free Housing Program ... 282
Crime Prevention Through Environmental Design ... 20
- maintenance ... 25
- natural access control ... 22
- natural surveillance ... 21
- territorial reinforcement ... 23

Custom crime analyses ... 12
Cybersecurity
- of video surveillance systems ... 185

Cylinder guard ... 96

D

Default codes 193
Delayed-egress locking systems 105
Door and frame reinforcement 100
Door and lock hardware 77–111
Door bottoms 97
Door closers 92
Door thresholds 97
Door viewers 107
Doors 65–75
  automatic sliding 70
  best practices for securing 345
  fire-rated 69
  high-performance overhead 75
  overhead 72
  patio 115
  pedestrian 65
    all glass 68
    aluminum storefront 67
    hollow-metal 66
    wood 65
  revolving 71
  sliding 115
Double-door tool 95
Drop slots 210

E

Electric locking hardware 102–5
  electric locks 103
  electric strikes 102
  electromagnetic locks 104
  exit devices with electrified trim 103
  exit devices with latch retraction 103
  fail-safe vs fail-secure 105
Electrical contractors 320
Electrical receptacles, outdoor 205
Elevator contractors 320
Elevators 220
  access control of 141
  fire service mode 143
  key switches 110
Exit alarms 160
Exterior Walls 40

F

Fencing
  anti-climb strips 36
  barbed wire 35
  chain-link 33
  height 41
  manufactured metal 38
  ornamental iron 37
  wood 39
Fencing companies 320

G

Gang problems 340
Gated communities
  attended vehicle entrances 243
  definition of 241
  developing a security plan for 241
  gatehouses 245
  managing resident expectations 250
  pedestrian entrances 245
  perimeter detection systems 248
  providing alarm monitoring services 249
  security operations center 247
  security staffing 250
  service entrances 245
  turnarounds and holding areas 246
  unattended vehicle entrances 242
  video surveillance systems 247
  visitor management systems 247
Gates .... *See* Pedestrian Gates and Vehicle Gates
General contractors 320
Graffiti 341
Guard companies .... *See* contract security companies
Guard tour systems 310

H

Hallways 218
High-performance overhead doors 75
High-security locks 85
Hinge protection 99
Hinges 92
HomeLink systems 140

I

IAPSC 335, 336
Independent security consultants
  benefits of using 333
  cost of using 334
  definition of 333
  how to locate 336
  keys for success when working with 337
  large versus small firms 335
  qualifications 335
  security management consultants 333
  technical security consultants 333
Interchangeable core lock cylinders 88
Intercom systems .... *See* Security intercom systems
International Association of Professional Security Consultants .... *See* IAPSC
Intrusion alarm systems 153

K

Key boxes 107
- fire department 108
- real estate 108
- utility company 108

Key-operated switches 110

L

Landscaping 48
- hedges 48
- site features 49

Latch guards 94
Lock cylinder protection 96
Lock hardware 77–111
Locks
- aluminium storefront doors 81
- cabinet 90
- cylindrical 77
- deadbolt 78
- exit devices 79
- grades of 84
- high-security 85
- interchangeable core 88
- keying of 86
- lock cylinders 85
- lock functions 83
- mechanical pushbutton 127
- mortise 77
- padlocks 89
- quick-change 89

Locksmiths 320

M

Mag locks .... *See* Electric locking hardware
Mailboxes
- exterior 198
- indoor 225

Maintenance XE "Service contracts" service agreements330
Minimum illumination levels 57
Mixed-use properties
- amenity areas 255
- building entrances 254
- definition of 251
- elevators 254
- keys to successful security at 252
- loading docks 254
- parking garages 253
- security challenges faced by 251
- shared security systems 255
- stairways 254

Monitoring Services 321

O

Ornamental iron fabricators 321
Outdoor hiding places, minimizing 201
Outdoor storage 204
Overhead door companies 321
Overselling security 287

P

Package lockers, automated 225
Package thefts 341
Panic buttons 158
Parcel rooms, automated 227
Parking garages
- emergency callboxes 233
- garage door controls 231
- importance of securing 229
- lighting 232
- overhead doors 230
- parking stalls 232
- pedestrian doors 232
- video surveillance cameras 233

Parking lots 195
Pedestrian gates 41
PIN codes, vulnerabilities of 271
Playgrounds and sport courts 200
Police
- calls for service reports 10
- relationships with 281

Portable panic buttons 159
POTS line 146

R

Remote access for delivery drivers 143
Resident patrols 314
Resident storage 220
Residential units
- exterior doors 236
- family emergency plan 240
- home inventory 239
- intrusion alarm systems 237, 239
- responsibility for securing 235
- storage on decks and patios 237
- storing a key outside of 237
- windows and sliding doors 236

Resident's security guide 363
Risk assessment .... *See* Security risk assessment
Roof access 210

S

Safes 224, 238
Security awareness training
- cime prevention workshops 294

for employees 290
for employees working alone 293
for front-line employees 292
for residents 289
Security coordinator 262
Security guards .... *See* Security officers
Security incident reports 7, 279
Security intercom systems 145–51
auto-dialing telephones 149
hardwired entry systems 147
point-to-point 148
telephone entry systems 145
video doorbells 150
Security lighting 51–63
amount needed 57
color of 52
conducting a lighting survey 61
importance of 51
in parking garages 232
intensity of 52
lighting controls 58
motion activated 59
types of light sources 53
types of luminares 55
uniformity of 52
Security management
at condominiums, gated communities & co-ops 259
at rental properties 261
Security Manual .... *See* Security policies and procedures
Security manual outline 361
Security officers
arming of 303
communications 308
contract versus proprietary (in-house) 301
determing what to pay 318
determining number required 297
equipment 305
guard tour systems used by 310
licensing and training 300
post orders 299
posts 295
qualifications 300
reducing turnover of 315
roles of 295
uniforms 305
used as concierge 311
used to perform non-security duties 312
using off-duty police officers as 304
using part time 313
vehicles 309
Security patrol services 313
Security Plan
creating 27
keeping current 30
Security planning 27–30
Security policies and procedures 265
bicycle permits 277
contractor management 273
crime free housing program 282
handling mail and deliveries 275
keys to residential units 270
lost and found items 286, 287
lost or stolen keys or access cards 269
managing access for employees 267
managing access for residents 265
managing construction projects 274
managing special events 274
move-in and move-out procedures 277
notification to residents 280
overselling security 287
relationships with law enforcement 281
resident screening 285
residential unit inspection 283
responding to resident complaints 281
responsibilities for security 265
security background checks for employees 285
security incident follow-up 280
security incident reporting 279
security system inspection 283
short-term rentals 278
temporary keys 267
use of PIN codes 271
vehicle permits 276
vendor credentialing services 286
video surveillance systems policies 284
visitor management 272
Security risk assessment, conducting a 13
Security signage 123–25
directional 124
no trespassing signs 123
security awareness 125
Security survey checklist 351
Security system maintenance 330
Security systems integrators 321
Security window film 117
Security window film installers 321
Security window screens 120
Service contracts 330
Site security 189–92
common points of weakness in 191
developing a plan for 189
Skate deterrents 203
Software support agreements 331
Stairways 218
Swimming pools 199

T

Tailgating 191, 211
Theft from motor vehicles 342
Thefts from resident storage rooms 342
Trash and recycle areas 198

Trespassers 339

U

Under-door tool 98
Utility buildings 204

V

Vandalism 342
Vehicle gates 43
  accessories 46
  barrier arm 45
  cantilever 44
  considerations when choosing 47
  emergency access devices 46
  sliding 43
  swinging 45
Vehicle theft 341
Ventilation grilles 208
Video doorbells 150
Video surveillance cameras 166–78
  box cameras 168
  bullet cameras 167
  camera lens 171
  camera technology *166*
  determining what a camera will see 174
  dome cameras 167
  fisheye cameras 169
  frame rate 173
  light processing capabilities 172
  multi-sensor cameras 168
  pan-tilt-zoom (PTZ) cameras 169
  pinhole cameras 169
  resolution of 170
  sensitivity of 171
  where to place 177
Video surveillance systems 165–86
  cybersecurity of 185
  limitations of 186
  policies related to using 284
  purposes of *165*
  used in gated communities 247
  video analytics 184
  video management systems 181
  video recording 178
  video system communications 184
  video system monitoring 182
  wireless communications 185

W

Walkways 197
Water faucets, outdoor 206
Window bars 121
Window film .... *See* Security window film
Windows 113–21
  awning 114
  bars on 121
  casement 115
  double-hung 115
  fixed 114
  hopper 114
  locking hardware 116
  screens on 120
  securing in common areas 208
  sliding 115
  types of glass 113

Made in the USA
Las Vegas, NV
08 February 2022